Edward Alfred Pollard

The First Year of the War

Edward Alfred Pollard

The First Year of the War

ISBN/EAN: 9783337009465

Printed in Europe, USA, Canada, Australia, Japan

Cover: Foto ©ninafisch / pixelio.de

More available books at **www.hansebooks.com**

THE

FIRST YEAR OF THE WAR.

BY

EDWARD A. POLLARD,

AUTHOR OF "BLACK DIAMONDS," ETC.

CORRECTED AND IMPROVED EDITION.

RICHMOND:
WEST & JOHNSTON, 145 MAIN STREET.
1862.

CHAS. H. WYNNE, PRINTER.

PREFACE.

It is scarcely necessary to state that the following pages have been written without any thing like literary ambition. They have been composed by the author, with but little aid, within the short period of three months, and in the midst of exacting occupations in the editorial department of a daily newspaper.

These explanations are not made to disarm criticism. Their purpose is only to define the claim which the author's work makes at the bar of public criticism. He does not pretend to have written a brilliant or elaborate book; but he does claim to have composed, without seeking after literary ornaments, or taxing his style with intellectual refinements, a compact, faithful, and independent popular narrative of the events of the first year of the existing war.

The author acknowledges some assistance from Mr. B. M. DeWitt, in the collection of materials. He has but little other of obligation to express, except to his publishers, Messrs. West & Johnston, of Richmond, to whom he would make a public acknowledgment for their generous encouragement, liberality, and enterprising endeavors, which have enabled him, under many inauspicious circumstances, to complete his work.

Richmond, Virginia, July, 1862.

PREFACE TO SECOND EDITION.

The author, in presenting to the public a second edition of his work, has taken occasion to correct some errors, to make material annotations, and to add a supplementary chapter, tracing the progress and developments of the war from the concluding point of the first year of its history to the period of publication.

He desires to make his grateful acknowledgments for the favor with which his work has already been received by the public; for numerous kind notices of the newspaper press, and for words of encouragement spoken by many whom he is proud to call his friends. The success with which his work has so far met, being unprecedented, he believes, in the literary enterprises of the South, has surprised and gratified the author. He protests, however, that, under any circumstances, he has but little literary vanity to be inflated; that he composed his work in haste, with neither time nor purpose to polish his style, or to captivate the taste of readers, and that he is content to ascribe the success of his book to the fact that, though rudely written and imperfect in many particulars, it is, as he believes, honest, fair, independent, and outspoken.

While such has been the general character of the reception given his book by the public, the author is sensible that some attacks have been made upon it from malicious and disappointed sources, and that the honest record which he has attempted of the truth of history, has been encountered by many unjust, ignorant, and contemptible criticisms, emanating mainly from favorites of the government and literary slatterns in the Departments. The author has made no attempt to conciliate either these creatures or their masters; he is not in the habit of toadying to great men, and courting such public whores as "official" newspapers; he is under no obligations to any man living to flatter him, to tell lies, or to abate any thing from the honest convictions of his mind. He proposed to write an independent history of some of the events of the existing war. He is willing for his work to be judged by the strictest rule of truth; he asks no favors for it, in point of accuracy; he only protests against a rule of criticism, which exalts paid panegyric above honest truth, and reduces the level of the historian to that of the scrubs and scribblers who write poetry and puffs in newspaper corners.

The flatterer's idea of the history of the present war would no doubt be to plaster the government with praises; to hide all the faults of the people of the South while gilding their virtues; to make, for a consideration, "especial mention" of all the small trash in the army; to coat his puffs thickly with fine writing and tremendous adjectives; and to place over the whole painted and gilded mass of falsehood, the figure of Mr. Jefferson Davis, as the second Daniel come to judgment. The author has no ambition to gratify in these literary elegances.

In the eyes of the historian the person of Mr. Jefferson Davis is no more sacred than that of the meanest agent in human affairs. The author has not been disposed to insult the dignity of office by coarse speeches; he recognizes a certain propriety of style even in attacking the grossest public abuses; but, while he has avoided indecency and heat of language, and has, on the other hand, not attempted the elegance and elevation of the literary artist, he trusts that he has given his opinions of the government and public persons with the decent but fearless and uncompromising freedom of the conscientious historian. He is certain that he has given these opinions without prejudice against the Administration in this war. The danger is, in such a contest as we are waging, that we will be too favorably and generously disposed towards the government, rather than prejudiced against it—that we will be blind to its faults, rather than eager and exacting in their exposure.

The author is aware that the views expressed in this work of the autocracy of President Davis, and the extraordinary absorption in himself of all the offices of the government, have been resented with much temper by critics in some of the newspapers. He would ask these persons who are so anxious to vindicate the character of Mr. Davis in this respect, for a single instance in the history of the war, where the Cabinet has interposed any views of its own, addressed any counsel to the government, or been any thing more than a collection of dummies. In all our experience hitherto of republican government, we hear of views of the Cabinet and the counsel of this or that member. In this war these common observations are lacking; the Cabinet is dumb or absolutely servile; we have never heard a syllable from it on a single question of national importance, and the voice of the President alone decides the conduct of the war, distributes the patronage of the government, and forces into practice the constitutional fiction of himself being the commander-in-chief of our armies. These facts are notorious in the streets of Richmond.

The Cabinet of President Davis has really no constitutional existence The Cabinet has many objects to serve in our system of government. It was designed as a check to Executive power; it was intended to cull and collect the wisdom of the country in the management of public af fairs; it shares the qualities of a popular system of representation with the conservatism and virtues of aristocracy; it constitutes the highest and gravest council in our form of government. Certainly not one of these constitutional offices has been fulfilled by the Cabinet of President Davis, and history is forced to confess that the harmony of our government has been deranged by striking from it an important, valuable, and essential part.

The author is sensible that another ignorant rule of criticism besides that of the professional political flatterer, has been unjustly applied to his work. He is informed that there are persons so childish and contemptibly ignorant as to have decried his work on the ground that it has exposed abuses in our administration, and faults in our people, which will be a gratification and comfort to the enemy. The objection is simply absurd and contemptible. Throwing out of consideration the interest of truth, it is surely much better, even on the narrow ground of expediency, to expose abuses, and to let the enemy have what pleasure and comfort he can from them, than to permit them, unnoticed and uncorrected, to sap the strength of our country, and publish their conclusion to the world in the ultimate ruin of our cause. There are ignoramuses in the Southern Confederacy who think it necessary in this war that all the books and newspapers in the country should publish every thing in the South in *couleur de rose;* drunken patriots, cowards in epaulets, crippled toadies, and men living on the charity of Jefferson Davis, trained to damn all newspapers and publications in the South for pointing out abuses in places of authority, for the sage reason that knowledge of these abuses will comfort the enemy and tickle the ears of the Yankees. These creatures would have a history written which would conceal all the shortcomings of our administration, and represent that our army was perfect in discipline, and immaculate in morals; that our people were feeding on milk and honey; that our generalship was without fault, and that Jefferson Davis was the most perfect and admirable man since the days of Moses—all for the purpose of wearing a false mask to the enemy. They would betray our cause while hoodwinking the enemy; they would make a virtue of falsehood; they would destroy the independence of all published thought in the country. The author spits upon the criticisms of such creatures.

So much the author has thought it necessary to say with reference to two classes of critics, who have attacked not only his book, but every form of free and independent thought in the country. With reference to the public, confident as the author is of the rectitude of their decision, he is content to submit his work to their judgment, without importuning their favor.

Finally, the author begs to make, without temper and in the fewest words, a plain and summary vindication of the character and objects of his work.

Every candid mind must be sensible of the futility of attempting high order of historical composition in the treatment of recent and incomplete events; but it does not follow that the contemporary annal, the popular narrative, and other inferior degrees of history, can have no value and interest, because they cannot compete in accuracy with the future retrospect of events. The vulgar notion of history is, that it is a record intended for posterity. The author contends that history has an office to perform in the present, and that one of the greatest values of contemporary annals is to vindicate in good time to the world the fame and reputation of nations.

With this object constantly in view, the author has composed this work. He will accomplish his object and be rewarded with a complete satisfaction, if his unpretending book shall have the effect of promoting more extensive inquiries; enlightening the present; vindicating the principles of a great contest to the contemporary world; and putting before the living generation, in a convenient form of literature, and at an early and opportune time, the name and deeds of our people.

Richmond, September, 1860.

CONTENTS.

CHAPTER I.

Delusive Ideas of the Union.—Administration of John Adams.—The "Strict Constructionists."—The "State Rights" Men in the North.—The Missouri Restriction.—General Jackson and the Nullification Question.—The Compromise Measures of 1850.—History of the Anti-Slavery Party.—The "Pinckney Resolutions."—The Twenty-first Rule.—The Abolitionists in the Presidential Canvass of 1852.—The Kansas-Nebraska Bill.—The Rise and Growth of the Republican Party.—The Election of President Buchanan.—The Kansas Controversy.—"Lecompton" and "Anti-Lecompton."—Results of the Kansas Controversy.—The John Brown Raid.—"Helper's Book."—Demoralization of the Northern Democratic Party.—The Faction of Stephen A. Douglas.—The Alabama Resolutions.—The Political Platforms of 1860.—Election of Abraham Lincoln, President of the United States.—Analysis of the Vote.—Political Condition of the North.—Secession of South Carolina.—Events in Charleston Harbor.—Disagreements in Mr. Buchanan's Cabinet.—The Secession Movement in Progress.—Peace Measures in Congress.—The Crittenden Resolutions.—The Peace Congress.—Policy of the Border Slave States.—Organization of the Confederate States Government.—President Buchanan.—Incoming of the Administration of Abraham Lincoln.—Strength of the Revolution...PAGE 11

CHAPTER II.

Mr. Lincoln's Journey to Washington.—Ceremonies of the Inauguration.—The Inaugural Speech of President Lincoln.—The Spirit of the New Administration.—Its Financial Condition.—Embassy from the Southern Confederacy.—Perfidious Treatment of the Southern Commissioners.—Preparations for War.—The Military Bills of the Confederate Congress.—General Beauregard.—Fortifications of Charleston Harbor.—Naval Preparations of the Federal Government.—Attempted Reinforcement of Fort Sumter.—Perfidy of the Federal Government.—Excitement in Charleston.—Reduction of Fort Sumter by the Confederate Forces.—How the News was received in Washington.—Lincoln's Calculation.—His Proclamation of WAR.—The "Reaction" in the North.—Displays of Rancor towards the South.—Northern Democrats.—Replies of Southern Governors to Lincoln's Requisition for Troops.—Spirit of the South.—Secession of Virginia.—Maryland.—The Baltimore Riot.—Patriotic Example of Missouri.—Lincoln's Proclamation blockading the Southern Ports.—General Lee.—The Federals evacuate Harper's Ferry.—Burning of the Navy Yard at Norfolk.—The Second Secessionary Movement.—Spirit of Patriotic Devotion in the South.—Supply of Arms in the South.—The Federal Government and the State of Maryland.—The Prospect...PAGE 41

tenden.—Death of General Zollicoffer.—Sufferings of Crittenden's Army on the Retreat.—Comparative Unimportance of the Disaster.—The BATTLE OF ROANOKE ISLAND.—Importance of the Island to the South.—Death of Captain Wise.—Causes of the Disaster to the South.—Investigation in Congress.—Censure of the Government.— Interviews of General Wise with Mr. Benjamin, the Secretary of War.—Mr. Benjamin censured by Congress, but retained in the Cabinet.—His Promotion by President Davis.—Condition of the Popular Sentiment..PAGE 220

CHAPTER X.

The Situation in Tennessee and Kentucky.—The affair at Woodsonville.—Death of Colonel Terry.—The Strength and Material of the Federal Force in Kentucky.—Condition of the Defences on the Tennessee and Cumberland Rivers.—The Confederate Congress and the Secretary of the Navy.—The Fall of Fort Henry.—Fort Donelson threatened.—The Army of General A. S. Johnston.—His Interview with General Beauregard.—Insensibility of the Confederate Government to the Exigency.—General Johnston's Plan of Action.—BATTLE OF FORT DONELSON.—Carnage and Scenery of the Battle-field.—The Council of the Southern Commanders.—Agreement to surrender. —Escape of Generals Floyd and Pillow.—The Fall of Fort Donelson develops the Crisis in the West.—The Evacuation of Nashville.—The Panic.—Extraordinary Scenes.—Experience of the Enemy in Nashville.—The Adventures of Captain John Morgan.—General Johnston at Murfreesboro.—Organization of a New Line of Defence South of Nashville.—The Defence of Memphis and the Mississippi.—Island No. 10.— Serious Character of the Disaster at Donelson.—Generals Floyd and Pillow "relieved from Command."—General Johnston's Testimony in favor of these Officers.— President Davis's Punctilio.—A sharp Contrast.—Negotiation for the Exchange of Prisoners.—A Lesson of Yankee Perfidy.—Mr. Benjamin's Release of Yankee Hostages..PAGE 235

CHAPTER XI.

Organization of the permanent Government of the South.—The Policy of England. —Declaration of Earl Russell.—Onset of the Northern Forces.—President Davis's Message to Congress.—The Addition of New States and Territories to the Southern Confederacy.—Our Indian Allies.—The Financial Condition, North and South.—Deceitful Prospects of Peace.—Effect of the Disasters to the South.—Action of Congress. —The Conscript Bill.—Provisions vs. Cotton.—Barbarous Warfare of the North.—The Anti-slavery Sentiment.—How it was unmasked in the War.—Emancipation Measures in the Federal Congress.—Spirit of the Southern People.—The Administration of Jefferson Davis.—His Cabinet.—The Defensive Policy.—The NAVAL ENGAGEMENT IN HAMPTON ROADS.—Iron-clad Vessels.—What the Southern Government might have done.—The Narrative of General Price's Campaign resumed.—His Retreat into Arkansas.—The BATTLE OF ELK HORN.—Criticism of the Result.—Death of General McCulloch.—The BATTLE OF VALVERDE.—The Foothold of the Confederates in New Mexico.—Change of the Plan of Campaign in Virginia.—Abandonment of the Potomac Line by the Confederates.—The BATTLE OF KERNSTOWN.—Colonel Turner Ashby.— Appearance of McClellan's Army on the Peninsula.—Firmness of General Magruder. —The New Situation of the War in Virginia.—Recurrence of Disasters to the South on the Water.—The Capture of Newbern.—Fall of Fort Pulaski and Fort Macon.— Common Sense vs. "West Point.".......................................PAGE 259

CHAPTER XII.

The Campaign in the Mississippi Valley.—Bombardment of Island No. 10.—The Scenes, Incidents, and Results.—Fruits of the Northern Victory.—Movements of the Federals on the Tennessee River.—The BATTLE OF SHILOH.—A "Lost Opportunity." —Death of General Albert Sidney Johnston.—Comparison between the Battles of Shiloh and Manassas.—The Federal Expeditions into North Alabama.—Withdrawal of the Confederate Forces from the Trans-Mississippi District.—General Price and his Command.—The FALL OF NEW ORLEANS.—The Flag Imbroglio.—Major-general Butler.—Causes of the Disaster.—Its Results and Consequences.—The Fate of the Valley of the Mississippi..PAGE 291

CHAPTER XIII.

CONCLUSION.

Prospects of the War.—The Extremity of the South.—Lights and Shadows of the Campaign in Virginia.—Jackson's Campaign in the Valley.—The Policy of Concentration.—Sketch of the Battles around Richmond.—Effect of McClellan's Defeat upon the North.—President Davis's congratulatory Order.—The War as a great Money Job.—*Note:* Gen. Washington's Opinion of the Northern People.—Statement of the Northern Finances.—Yankee Venom.—Gen. Pope's Military Orders.—Summary of the War Legislation of the Northern Congress.—Retaliation on the part of the Confederacy.—The Cartel.—Prospects of European Interference.—English Statesmanship. —Progress of the War in the West.—The Defence of Vicksburg.—Morgan's great Raid.—The Tennessee-Virginia Frontier.—A Glance at the Confederate Congress.— Mr. Foote and the Cabinet.—The Campaign in Virginia again.—Rapid Movements and famous March of the Southern Troops.—*The signal Victory of the Thirtieth of August on the Plains of Manassas.*—Reflections on the War.—Some of its Characteristics.—A Review of its Military Results.—Three Moral Benefits of the War.—Prospects and Promises of the Future..PAGE 322

THE FIRST YEAR OF THE WAR.

CHAPTER I.

Delusive Ideas of the Union.—Administration of John Adams.—The "Strict Constructionists."—The "State Rights" Men in the North.—The Missouri Restriction.—General Jackson and the Nullification Question.—The Compromise Measures of 1850.—History of the Anti-Slavery Party.—The "Pinckney Resolutions."—The Twenty-first Rule.—The Abolitionists in the Presidential Canvass of 1852.—The Kansas-Nebraska Bill.—The Rise and Growth of the Republican Party.—The Election of President Buchanan.—The Kansas Controversy.—"Lecómpton" and "Anti-Lecompton."—Results of the Kansas Controversy.—The John Brown Raid.—"Helper's Book."—Demoralization of the Northern Democratic Party.—The Faction of Stephen A. Douglas.—The Alabama Resolutions.—The Political Platforms of 1860.—Election of Abraham Lincoln, President of the United States.—Analysis of the Vote.—Political Condition of the North.—Secession of South Carolina —Events in Charleston Harbor.—Disagreements in Mr. Buchanan's Cabinet.—The Secession Movement in Progress.—Peace Measures in Congress.—The Crittenden Resolutions.—The Peace Congress.—Policy of the Border Slave States.—Organization of the Confederate States Government.—President Buchanan.—Incoming of the Administration of Abraham Lincoln.—Strength of the Revolution.

The American people of the present generation were born in the belief that the Union of the States was destined to be perpetual. A few minds rose superior to this natal delusion; the early history of the Union itself was not without premonitions of decay and weakness; and yet it may be said that the belief in its permanency was, in the early part of the present generation, a popular and obstinate delusion, that embraced the masses of the country.

The foundations of this delusion had been deeply laid in the early history of the country, and had been sustained by a false, but ingenious prejudice. It was busily represented, especially by demagogues in the North, that the Union was the fruit of the Revolution of 1776, and had been purchased by the blood of our forefathers. No fallacy could have been more erroneous in fact, more insidious in its display, or more effective in addressing the passions of the multitude. The Revolution achieved our national independence, and the Union had no connection with it other than consequence in point of time. It was founded, as any other civil institution, in the exigencies and necessities of a certain condition of society, and had no other claim to popular reverence and attachment than what might be found in its own virtues.

But it was not only the captivating fallacy that the Union was hallowed by the blood of a revolution, and this false inspiration of reverence for it, that gave the popular idea of its power and permanency. Its political character was misunderstood by a large portion of the American people. The idea predominated in the North, and found toleration in the South, that the Revolution of '76, instead of securing the independence of thirteen States, had resulted in the establishment of a grand consolidated government to be under the absolute control of a numerical majority. The doctrine was successfully inculcated; it had some plausibility, and brought to its support an array of revolutionary names; but it was, nevertheless, in direct opposition to the terms of the Constitution—the bond of the Union—which defined the rights of the States and the limited powers of the General Government.

The first President from the North, John Adams, asserted and essayed to put in practice the supremacy of the "National" power over the States and the citizens thereof. He was sustained in his attempted usurpations by all the New England States and by a powerful public sentiment in each of the Middle States. The "strict constructionists" of the Constitution were not slow in raising the standard of opposition against a pernicious error. With numbers and the most conspicuous talents in the country they soon effected the organization of a party; and, under the leadership of Jefferson and Madison, they rallied their forces and succeeded in overthrowing the Yankee Administration, but only after a tremendous struggle.

From the inauguration of Mr. Jefferson, in 1801, the Federal Government continued uninterruptedly in Southern hands for the space of twenty-four years. A large proportion of the active politicians of the North pretended to give in their adhesion to the State Rights school of politics; but, like all the alliances of Northern politicians with the South—selfish, cunning, extravagant of professions, carefully avoiding trials of its fidelity unhealthy, founded on a sentiment of treachery to its own section, and educated in perfidy—it was a deceitful union, and could not withstand the test of a practical question.

While acting with the South on empty or accidental issues, the "State Rights" men of the North were, for all practical purposes, the faithful allies of the open and avowed consolidationists on the question that most seriously divided the country—that of negro slavery. Their course on the admission of Missouri afforded early and conclusive evidence of the secret disposition of all parties in the North. With very few exceptions, in and out of Congress, the North united in the original demand of the prohibition of slavery in the new State as the indispensable condition of the admission of Missouri into the Union; although the people of Missouri, previous to their application to Congress, had decided to admit within its jurisdiction the domestic institution of the South. The result of the contest was equally unfavorable to the rights of the South and to the doctrine of the constitutional equality of the States in the Union. The only approach that the North was willing to make to this fundamental doctrine was to support a "compromise," by which slavery was to be tolerated in one part of the Missouri Territory and to be forever excluded from the remaining portion. The issue of the controversy was not only important to the slave interest, but afforded a new development of the Northern political ideas of consolidation and the absolutism of numerical majorities. The North had acted on the Missouri matter as though the South had no rights guaranteed in the bond of the Union, and as though the question at issue was one merely of numerical strength, where the defeated party had no alternative but submission. "The majority must govern" was the *decantatum* on the lips of every demagogue, and passed into a favorite phrase of Northern politics.

The results of the acquiescence of the South in the wrong of the Missouri Restriction could not fail to strengthen the idea in the North of the security of the Union, and to embolden its people to the essay of new aggressions. Many of their politicians did not hesitate to believe that the South was prepared to pledge herself to the perpetuity of the Union upon Northern terms. The fact was, that she had made a clear concession of principle for the sake of the Union; and the inference was plain and logical, that her devotion to it exceeded almost every other political trust, and that she would be likely to prefer any sacrifice rather than the irreverent one of the Union of the States.

The events of succeeding years confirmed the Northern opinion that the Union was to be perpetuated as a consolidated government. It is not to be denied that the consolidationists derived much comfort from the course of President Jackson, in the controversy between the General Government and the State of South Carolina, that ensued during the second term of his administration. But they were hasty and unfair in the interpretation of the speeches of a choleric and immoderate politician. They seized upon a sentiment offered by the President at the Jefferson anniversary dinner, in the second year of his first term—"*The Federal Union—it must be preserved*"—to represent him as a "*coercionist*" in principle; and, indeed, they found reason to contend that their construction of these words was fully sustained in General Jackson's famous proclamation and official course against Nullification.

General Jackson subsequently explained away, in a great measure, the objectionable doctrines of his proclamation; and his emphatic declaration that the Union could *not* be preserved by force was one of the practical testimonies of his wisdom that he left to posterity. But the immediate moral and political effects of his policy in relation to South Carolina were, upon the whole, decidedly unfavorable to the State Rights cause. His approval of the Force Bill gave to the consolidationists the benefit of his great name and influence at a most important juncture. The names of "Jackson and the Union" became inseparable in the public estimation; and the idea was strongly and vividly impressed upon the public mind, that the great Democrat was "a Union man" at all hazards and to the last extremity.

The result of the contest between South Carolina and the General Government is well known. The Palmetto State came out of it with an enviable reputation for spirit and chivalry; but the settlement of the question contributed to the previous popular impressions of the power and permanency of the Union. The idea of the Union became what it continued to be for a quarter of a century thereafter—extravagant and sentimental. The people were unwilling to stop to analyze an idea after it had once become the subject of enthusiasm; and the mere name of the "Union," illustrating, as it did, the power of words over the passions of the multitude, remained for years a signal of the country's glory and of course the motto of ambitious politicians and the favorite theme of demagogues. This unnatural tumor was not peculiar to any party or any portion of the country. It was deeply planted in the Northern mind, but prevailed also, to a considerable extent, in the South. Many of the Southern politicians came to the conclusion that they could best succeed in their designs as advocates and eulogists of what was paraphrased as "the glorious Union;" and for a long time the popular voice of the South seemed to justify their conclusion.

The settlement of the sectional difficulties of 1850, which grew out of the admission of the territory acquired by the Mexican War, was but a repetition of the "Compromise" of 1820, so far as it implied a surrender of the rights of the South and of the principle of constitutional equality. The appeals urged in behalf of the Union had the usual effect of reconciling the South to the sacrifice required of her, and embarrassed any thing like resistance on the part of her representatives in Congress to the "compromise measures" of 1850. South Carolina was the only one of the Southern States ready at this time to take the bold and adventurous initiative of Southern independence. In justice, however, to the other States of the South, it must be stated, that in agreeing to what was called, in severe irony or in wretched ignorance, the "Compromise" of 1850, they declared that it was the last concession they would make to the North; that they took it as a "finality," and that they would resist any further aggression on their rights, even to the extremity of the rupture of the Union.

This declaration of spirit was derided by the North. The anti-slavery sentiment became bolder with success. Stimulated by secret jealousies and qualified for success by the low and narrow cunning of fanaticism, it had grown up by indirection, and aspired to the complete overthrow of the peculiar institution that had distinguished the people of the South from those of the North, by a larger happiness, greater ease of life, and a superior tone of character. Hypocrisy, secretiveness, a rapid and unhealthy growth, and at last the unmasked spirit of defiance, were the incidents of the history of the anti-slavery sentiment in the North, from the beginning of its organization to the last and fatal strain of its insolence and power.

Until a comparatively recent period, the Northern majority disavowed all purpose of abolishing or interfering in any way with the institution of slavery in any State, Territory, or District where it existed. On the contrary, they declared their readiness to give their "Southern brethren" the most satisfactory guaranties for the security of their slave property. They cloaked their designs under the disguise of the Right of Petition and other concealments equally demagogical. From the organization of the government, petitions for the abolition of slavery, signed in every instance by but a few persons, and most of them women, had, at intervals, been sent into Congress; but they were of such apparent insignificance that they failed to excite any serious apprehensions on the part of the South. In the year 1836, these petitions were multiplied, and many were sent into both Houses of Congress from all parts of the North. An excitement began. On motion of Mr. H. L. Pinckney, of South Carolina, a resolution was adopted by the House of Representatives, to refer to a select committee all anti-slavery memorials then before that body, or that might thereafter be sent in, with instructions to report against the prayers of the petitioners and the reasons for such conclusion.

On the 18th of May, 1836, the committee made a unanimous report, through Mr. Pinckney, its chairman, concluding with a series of resolutions, the last of which was as follows:

"*Resolved*, That all petitions, memorials, resolutions, propositions, or papers relating, in any way, or to any extent whatever, to the subject of slavery, or the abolition of slavery, shall, without being either printed or referred, be laid upon the table, and that no further action whatever shall be had thereon."

The resolutions were carried by a vote of 117 yeas to 68 nays. A majority of the Northern members voted against the resolution, although there was then scarcely an avowed Abolitionist among them. They professed to be in favor of protecting the slaveholder in his right of property, and yet declared by their votes, as well as by their speeches, that the right of petition to rob him of his property was too sacred to be called in question.

The passage of the "Pinckney resolutions," as they were called, did not silence the anti-slavery agitation in the House. In the month of December, 1837, a remarkable scene was enacted in that body, during the proceedings on a motion of Mr. Slade, of Vermont, to refer two memorials praying the abolition of slavery in the District of Columbia to a select committee. Mr. Slade, in urging his motion, was violent in his denunciations of slavery, and he spoke for a considerable time amid constant interruptions and calls to order. At length, Mr. Rhett, of South Carolina, called upon the entire delegation from all the slaveholding States to retire from the hall, and to meet in the room of the Committee on the District of Columbia. A large number of them did meet for consultation in the room designated. The meeting, however, resulted in nothing but an agreement upon the following resolution to be presented to the House:

"*Resolved*, That all petitions, memorials, and papers touching the abolition of slavery, or the buying, selling, or transferring of slaves in any State, District, or Territory of the United States, be laid on the table without being debated, printed, read, or referred, and that no further action whatever shall be had thereon."

This resolution was presented to the House by Mr. Patton, of Virginia, and was adopted by a vote of 122 to 74.

In the month of January, 1840, the House of Representatives, on motion of Mr. W. Cost Johnson, of Maryland, adopted what was known as the "Twenty-first Rule," which prohibited the reception of all Abolition petitions, memorials, and resolutions.

The Twenty-first Rule was rescinded in December, 1844, on motion of John Quincy Adams, by a vote of 108 to 80. Several efforts were afterwards made to restore it, but without success. The Northern people would not relinquish what they termed a "sacred right"—that of petitioning the government, through their representatives in Congress, to deprive the Southern people of their property.

During the agitation in Congress upon the right of petition, there was, as before stated, but very few open and avowed Abolitionists in either House, and the declaration was repeatedly made by members that the party was contemptibly small in every free State in the Union. Mr. Pierce, of New Hampshire (afterwards President of the United States), declared, in 1837, in his place in Congress, that there were not two hundred Abolitionists in his State; and Mr. Webster, about the same time, represented their numbers in Massachusetts as quite insignificant. Mr. Calhoun, of South Carolina, with characteristic sagacity, replied to these representations, and predicted that "Mr. Webster and all Northern statesmen would, in a few years, yield to the storm of Abolition fanaticism and be overwhelmed by it." The prophecy was not more remarkable than the searching analysis of Northern "conservatism" with which the great South Carolinian accompanied his prediction. He argued that such a consequence was inevitable from the way in which the professed "conservatives" of the North had invited the aggressions of the Abolitionists, by courteously granting them the right of petition, which was indeed all they asked; that the fanaticism of the North was a disease which required a *remedy*, and that palliatives would not answer, as Mr. Webster and men like him would find to their cost.

In the Thirtieth Congress, that assembled in December, 1849, the professed Abolitionists numbered about a dozen members. They held the balance of power between the Democratic and Whig parties in the House, and delayed its organization for about a month. Both the Whig and Democratic parties then claimed to be conservative, and, of course, the opponents of the anti-slavery agitation.

In the Presidential canvass of 1852, both Pierce and Scott were brought out by professed national parties, and were supported in each section of the Union. John P. Hale, who ran upon what was called the "straight-out" Abolition ticket, did not receive the vote of a single State, and but 175,296 of the popular vote of the Union. The triumphant election of Pierce, who was a favorite of the State Rights Democracy of the South, was hailed by the sanguine friends of the Union as a fair indication of the purpose of the North to abide, in good faith, by the Compromise of 1850. But in this they were deceived, as the sequel demonstrated.

During the first session of the first Congress under Mr. Pierce's administration, the bill introduced to establish a territorial government for Nebraska, led to an agitation in Congress and the country, the consequences of which extended to the last period of the existence of the Union. The Committee on Territories in the Senate, of which Mr. Douglas, of Illinois, was chairman, reported the bill, which made two territories—Nebraska and Kansas—instead of one, and which declared that the Missouri Compromise act was superseded by the Compromise measures of 1850, and had thus become inoperative. The phraseology of the clause repealing the Missouri Compromise was drawn up by Mr. Douglas, and was not supposed at the time to be liable to misconstruction. It held, that the Missouri Compromise act, "being inconsistent with the principles of non-intervention by Congress with slavery in the States and Territories, as recognized by the legislation of 1850, commonly called the Compromise Measures, is hereby declared inoperative and void; it being the true intent and meaning of this act not to legislate slavery into any Territory or State, nor to exclude it therefrom, but to leave the people thereof perfectly free to form and regulate their domestic institutions in their own way, subject only to the Constitution of the United States." The clause here quoted, as drawn up by Mr. Douglas, was incorporated into the Kansas-Nebraska bill in the Senate on the 15th of February, 1854. The bill passed the House at the same session.

The repeal of the Missouri Compromise caused the deepest excitement throughout the North. The Abolitionists were wild with fury. Douglas was hung in effigy at different places, and was threatened with personal violence in case of his persistence in his non-intervention policy. The rapid development of a fanatical feeling in every free State startled many who had but recently indulged dreams of the perpetuity of the Constitutional Union. Abolitionism, in the guise of "*Republicanism*," swept almost every thing before it in the North and Northwest in the elections of 1854 and 1855. But few professed conservatives were returned to the Thirty-first Congress;

not enough to prevent the election of Nathaniel Banks, an objectionable Abolitionist of the Massachusetts school, to the Speakership of the House.

The South had supported the repeal of the Missouri Compromise because it restored her to her rightful position of equality in the Union. It is true, that her representatives in Congress were well aware that, under the operations of the new act, their constituents could expect to obtain but little if any new accessions of slave territory, while the North would necessarily, from the force of circumstances, secure a number of new States in the Northwest, then the present direction of our new settlements. But viewed as an act of proscription against her, the Missouri Compromise was justly offensive to the South; and its abrogation, in this respect, strongly recommended itself to her support.

The ruling party of the North, calling themselves "Republicans," had violently opposed the repeal of the act of 1820, in the same sentiment with which it was fiercely encountered by the Abolitionists. The two parties were practically identical; both shared the same sentiment of hostility to slavery; and they differed only as to the degree of indirection by which their purposes might best be accomplished.

The election of Mr. Buchanan to the Presidency, in 1856, raised, for a time, the spirits of many of the true friends of the Constitutional Union. But there was very little in an analysis of the vote to give hope or encouragement to the patriot. Fremont, who ran as the anti-slavery candidate, received 1,341,812 votes of the people, and it is believed would have been elected by the electoral college, if the anti-Buchanan party in Pennsylvania had united upon him.

The connection of events which we have sought to trace, brings us to the celebrated Kansas controversy, and at once to the threshold of the dissensions which demoralized the only conservative party in the country, and in less than four years culminated in the rupture of the Federal Union. A severe summary of the facts of this controversy introduces us to the contest of 1860, in which the Republican party, swollen with its triumphs in Kansas, and infecting the Democratic leaders in the North with the disposition to pander to the lusts of a growing power, obtained the control of the government, and seized the sceptre of absolute authority.

When Mr. Buchanan came into office, in March, 1857, he flattered himself with the hope that his administration would settle the disputes that had so long agitated and distracted the country; trusting that such a result might be accomplished by the speedy admission of Kansas into the Union, upon the principles which had governed in his election. Such, at least, were his declarations to his friends. But before the meeting of Congress, in December, he had abundant evidence that his favorite measure would be opposed by a number of Senators and Representatives who had actively supported him in his canvass; among them the distinguished author of the Kansas-Nebraska bill, Mr. Douglas.

In the month of July, 1855, the Legislature of the Territory of Kansas had passed an act to take the sense of the people on the subject of forming a State government, preparatory to admission into the Union. The election took place, and a large majority of the people voted in favor of holding a convention for the purpose of adopting a Constitution. In pursuance of this vote, the Territorial Legislature, on the 19th of February, 1857, passed a law to take a census of the people, for the purpose of making a registry of the voters, and to elect delegates to the Convention. Mr. Geary, then Governor of Kansas, vetoed the bill for calling the Convention, for the reason that it did not require the Constitution, when framed, to be submitted to a vote of the people for adoption or rejection. The bill, however, was reconsidered in each House, and passed by a two-thirds' vote, and thus became a binding law in the Territory, despite the veto of the Governor.

On the 20th of May, 1857, Mr. F. P. Stanton, Secretary and acting Governor of Kansas Territory, published his proclamation, commanding the proper officers to hold an election on the third Monday of June, 1857, as directed by the act referred to.

The election was held on the day appointed, and the Convention assembled, according to law, on the first Monday of September, 1857. They proceeded to form a Constitution, and, having finished their work, adjourned on the 7th November

The entire Constitution was not submitted to the popular vote; but the Convention took care to submit to the vote of the people, for ratification or rejection, the clause respecting slavery. The official vote resulted: For the Constitution, with Slavery, 6,226; for the Constitution, without Slavery, 509.

The Abolitionists, or "Free State" men, as they called themselves, did not generally vote in this or any other election held under the regular government of the Territory. They defied the authority of this government and that of the United States, and acted under the direction of Emigrant Aid Societies, organized by the fanatical Abolitionists of the North, to colonize the new territory with voters. The proceedings of this evil and bastard population occasioned the greatest excitement, and speedily inaugurated an era of disorder and rebellion in this distant portion of the Federal territory.

The Free State party assembled at Topeka, in September, 1855, and adopted what they called a "Constitution" for Kansas. This so-called Constitution was submitted to the people, and was ratified, of course, by a large majority of those who voted; scarcely any but Abolitionists going to the polls. Under their Topeka Constitution, the Free State party elected a Governor and Legislature, and organized for the purpose of petitioning Congress for the admission of Kansas into the Union. The memorial of the Topeka insurgents was presented to the Thirty-fourth Congress. It met with a favorable response in the House of Representatives, a majority of that body being anti-slavery men of the New England school; but found but a poor reception in the Senate, where there was still a majority of conservative and law-abiding men.

On the 2d of February, 1858, Mr. Buchanan, at the request of the President of the Lecompton Convention, transmitted to Congress an authentic copy of the Constitution framed by that body, with a view to the admission of Kansas into the Union. The message of the President took strong and urgent position for the admission of Kansas under this Constitution; he defended the action of the Convention in not submitting the entire result of their labors to a vote of the people; he explained that, when he instructed Governor Walker, in general terms, in favor of submitting the Constitution to the people, he had no other object in view beyond the all-absorbing topic of slavery; he considered that, under the organic act, the Convention was bound to submit the all-important question of slavery to the people; he added, that it was never his opinion, however, that, independently of this act, the Convention would be bound to submit any portion of the Constitution to a popular vote, in order to give it validity; and he argued the fallacy and unreasonableness of such an opinion, by insisting that it was in opposition to the principle which pervaded our institutions, and which was every day carried into practice, to the effect that the people had the right to delegate to representatives, chosen by themselves, sovereign power to frame Constitutions, enact laws, and perform many other important acts, without the necessity of testing the validity of their work by popular approbation. The Topeka Constitution Mr. Buchanan denounced as the work of treason and insurrection.

It is certain that Mr. Buchanan would have succeeded in effecting the admission of Kansas under the Lecompton Constitution, if he could have secured to the measure the support of all the Northern Democrats who had contributed to his election. These, however, had become disaffected; they opposed and assailed the measure of the Administration, acting under the lead of Mr. Douglas; and the long-continued and bitter discussion which ensued, perfectly accomplished the division of the Democratic party into two great factions, mustered under the names of " Lecompton" and " Anti-Lecompton."

The latter faction founded their opposition to the Administration on the grounds, that the Lecompton Constitution was not the act of the people of Kansas, and did not express their will; that only half of the counties of the Territory were represented in the Convention that framed it, the other half being disfranchised, for no fault of their own, but from failure of the officers to register the voters, and entitle them to vote for delegates; and that the mode of submitting the Constitution to the people for "ratification or rejection" was unfair, embarrassing, and proscriptive.

In reply, the friends of the Administration urged that twenty-one out of the thirty-four organized counties of Kansas were embraced in the apportionment of representation; that, of the thirteen counties not embraced, nine had but a small population, as shown by the fact that, in a succeeding election, to which the Anti-Lecomptonites had referred as an indication of public sentiment in Kansas, they polled but ninety votes in the aggregate; that, in the remaining four counties, the failure to register the voters, and the consequent loss of their representation, were due to the Abolitionists themselves, who refused to recognize all legal authority in the Territory; and that the submission of the Constitution, as provided by the Lecompton Convention, afforded a complete expression of the popular will, as the slavery question was the only one about which there was any controversy in Kansas.

The bill for the admission of Kansas under the Lecompton Constitution, was passed by the Senate. In the House, an amendment, offered by Mr. Montgomery, of Pennsylvania, was adopted, to the effect that, as it was a disputed point whether the Constitution framed at Lecompton was fairly made, or expressed the will of the people of Kansas, her admission into the Union as a State was declared to be upon the fundamental condition precedent, that the said constitutional instrument should first be submitted to a vote of the people of Kansas, and assented to by them, or by a majority of the voters, at an election to be held for the purpose of determining the question of the ratification or rejection of the instrument.

The Senate insisted upon its bill; the House adhered to its amendment; and a committee of conference was appointed. The result of the conference was the report of a bill for the admission of Kansas, which became a law in June, 1858, and substantially secured nearly all that the North had claimed in the controversy.

The bill, as passed, rejected the Land Ordinance contained in the Lecompton Constitution, and proposed a substitute. Kansas was to be admitted into the Union on an equal footing, in all respects, with the original States, but upon the fundamental condition precedent, that the question of admission, along with that of the Land substitute, be submitted to a vote of the people; that, if a majority of the vote should be against the proposition tendered by Congress, it should be concluded that Kansas did not desire admission under the Lecompton Constitution, with the condition attached to it; and that, in such event, the people were authorized to form for themselves a Constitution and State government, and might elect delegates for that purpose, after a census taken to demonstrate the fact, that the population of the Territory equalled or exceeded the ratio of representation for a member of the House of Representatives.

Thus ended the six months' discussion of the Kansas question in Congress in 1858. The substitute to the Land Ordinance was rejected by the voters of the Territory; and Kansas did not come into the Union until nearly three years afterwards—just as the Southern States were going out of it. She came in under an anti-slavery constitution, and Mr. Buchanan signed the bill of admission.

The discussions of the Kansas question, as summed in the preceding pages, had materially weakened the Union. The spirit of those discussions, and the result itself of the controversy, fairly indicated that the South could hardly expect, under any circumstances, the addition of another Slave State to the Union. The Southern mind was awakened; the sentimental reverences of more than half a century were decried; and men began to calculate the precise value of a Union which, by its mere name and the paraphrases of demagogues, had long governed their affections.

Some of these calculations, as they appeared in the newspaper presses of the times, were curious, and soon commenced to interest the Southern people. It was demonstrated to them that their section had been used to contribute the bulk of the revenues of the Government; that the North derived forty to fifty millions of annual revenue from the South, through the operations of the tariff; and that the aggregate of the trade of the South in Northern markets was four hundred millions of dollars a year. It was calculated by a Northern writer, that the harvest of gain reaped by the North from the Union, from unequal taxations and the courses of trade as between the two sections, exceeded two hundred millions of dollars per year.

These calculations of the commercial cost of the "glorious Union" to the South, only presented the question in a single aspect, however striking that was. There were other aspects no less important and no less painful, in which it was to be regarded. The swollen and insolent power of Abolitionism threatened to carry every thing before it; it had already bro ken the vital principle of the Constitution—that of the equality of its parts; and to injuries already accomplished, it added the bitterest threats and the most insufferable insolence.

While the anti-slavery power threatened never to relax its fforts until, in the language of Mr. Seward, a senator from New York, the "irrepressible conflict" between slavery and freedom was accomplished, and the soil of the Carolinas dedicated to the institutions of New England, it affected the insolent impertinence of regarding the Union as a concession on the part of the North, and of taunting the South with the disgrace which her association in the Union inflicted upon the superior and more virtuous people of the Northern States. The excesses of this conceit are ridiculous, seen in the light of subsequent events. It was said that the South was an inferior part of the country; that she was a spotted and degraded section; that the national fame abroad was compromised by the association of the South in the Union; and that a New England traveller in Europe blushed to confess himself an American, because half of the nation of that name were slaveholders. Many of the Abolitionists made a pretence of praying that the Union might be dissolved, that they might be cleared, by the separation of North and South, of any implication in the crime of slavery. Even that portion of the party calling themselves "Republicans" affected that the Union stood in the way of the North. Mr. Banks, of Massachusetts, who had been elected Speaker of the House in the Thirty-first Congress, had declared that the designs of his party were not to be baffled, and was the author of the coarse jeer—"*Let the Union slide.*" The New York *Tribune* had complained that the South "could not be *kicked* out of the Union." Mr. Seward, the great Republican leader, had spread the evangely of a natural, essential, and irrepressible hostility between the two sections; and the North prepared to act on a suggestion, the only practical result of which could be to cleave the Union apart, and to inaugurate the horrors of civil war.

The raid into Virginia of John Brown, a notorious Abolitionist, whose occupations in Kansas had been those of a horse thief and assassin, and his murder of peaceful and unsuspecting citizens at Harper's Ferry in the month of October, 1859, was a practical illustration of the lessons of the Northern Re publicans, and of their inevitable and, in fact, logical conclusion in civil war. Professed conservatives in the North predicted that this outrage would be productive of real good in their section, in opening the eyes of the people to what were well characterized as "*Black* Republican" doctrines. This prediction was not verified by succeeding events. The Northern elections of the next month showed no diminution in the Black Republican vote. The manifestations of sympathy for John Brown, who had expiated his crime on a gallows in Virginia, were unequivocal in all parts of the North, though comparatively few openly justified the outrage. Bells were tolled in various towns of New England on the day of his execution, with the knowledge of the local authorities, and in some instances, through their co-operation; and not a few preachers from the pulpit alloted him an apotheosis, and consigned his example to emulation, as one not only of public virtue, but of particular service to God.

The attachment of the South to the Union was steadily weakening in the historical succession of events. The nomination in December, 1859, to the Speakership of the House of Representatives of Mr. Sherman, of Ohio, who had made himself especially odious to the South by publicly recommending, in connection with sixty-eight other Republican members, a fanatical document popularly known as "*Helper's Book*,"*

---

* The tone of this book was violent in the extreme. We add a few extracts, which will enable the reader to form a correct opinion of the character and object of the work—

"Slavery is a great moral, social, civil, and political evil, to be got rid of at the earliest practical period."—(*Page* 168.)

"Three-quarters of a century hence, if the South retains slavery, which God forbid! she will be to the North what Poland is to Russia, Cuba to Spain, and Ireland to England."—(*P.* 163.)

"Our own banner is inscribed—No co-operation with slaveholders in politics; no fellowship with them in religion; no affiliation with them in society; no recognition of pro-slavery men, except as ruffians, outlaws, and criminals."—(*P.* 156.)

"We believe it is as it ought to be, the desire, the determination, and the destiny of the Republican party to give the death-blow to slavery."—(P. 234.)

"In any event, come what will, transpire what may, the institution of slavery must be abolished."—(P. 180.)

"We are determined to abolish slavery at all hazards—in defiance of all the opposition, of whatever nature, it is possible for the slaveocrats to bring

from the name of the author, and which openly defended and sought itself to excite servile insurrections in the South, produced a marked effect in Congress, and was encountered by the Southern members with a determined spirit of opposition. The entire Southern delegation gave warning that they would regard the election of Mr. Sherman, or of any man with his record, as an open declaration of war upon the institutions of the South; as much so, some of the members declared, as if the Brown raid were openly approved by a majority of the House of Representatives. The Black Republican party defiantly nominated Sherman, and continued to vote for him for near two months, giving him within four votes of a majority upon every trial of his strength. Although he was finally withdrawn, and one of his party, not a subscriber to the *Helper Book*, was elected, yet the fact that more than three-fourths of the entire Northern delegation had adhered to Mr. Sherman for nearly two months in a factious and fanatical spirit, produced a deep impression on the minds of Southern members and of their constituents. The early dissolution of the Union had come to be a subject freely canvassed among members of Congress.

With the unveiling of the depth of the designs of the Black Republican party, another danger was becoming manifest to the South. It was the demoralization of the Northern Democratic party on the slavery question. This whole party had been an unhealthy product; its very foundation was a principle of untruth, and false to its own section, it could not be expected to adhere to friends whom it had made from interest and who had fallen into adverse circumstances. It had united with the South for political power. In the depression of that power, and the rapid growth of the anti-slavery party in the

---

against us. Of this they may take due notice, and govern themselves accordingly."—(*P*. 149.)

"It is our honest conviction that all the pro-slavery slavcholders deserve at once to be reduced to a parallel with the basest criminals that lie fettered within the cells of our public prisons."—(*P*. 158.)

"Shall we pat the bloodhounds of slavery? Shall we fee the curs of slavery? Shall we pay the whelps of slavery? No, never."—(*P*. 329.)

"Our purpose is as firmly fixed as the eternal pillars of heaven; we have determined to abolish slavery, and, so help us God! abolish it we will."—*P*. 187.)

North, it had no hesitation in courting and conciliating the ruling element. This disposition was happily accommodated by the controversy which had taken place between Mr. Douglas and the administration of Mr. Buchanan. The anti-slavery sentiment in the North was conciliated by the partisans of the Illinois demagogue, in adopting a new principle for the government of the Territories, which was to allow the people to determine the question of slavery in their territorial capacity, without awaiting their organization as a State, and thus to risk the decision of the rights of the South on the verdict of a few settlers on the public domain. This pander to the anti-slavery sentiment of the North was concealed under the demagogical name of "popular sovereignty," and was imposed upon the minds of not a few of the Southern people by the artfulness of its appeals to the name of a principle, which had none of the substance of justice or equality. The concealment, however, was but imperfectly availing. The doctrine of Mr. Douglas was early denounced by one of the most vigilant statesmen of the South as "a short cut to all the ends of Black Republicanism;" and later in time, while the "Helper Book" controversy was agitating the country, and other questions developing the union of all the anti-slavery elements for war upon the South, a senator from Georgia was found bold enough to denounce, in his place in Congress, the entire Democratic party of the North as unreliable and "*rotten.*"

The State Rights party of the South had co-operated with the Democracy of the North in the Presidential canvass of 1856, upon the principles of the platform adopted by the National Democratic Convention, assembled in Cincinnati, in June of that year. They expressed a willingness to continue this co-operation in the election of 1860, upon the principles of the Cincinnati platform; but demanded, as a condition precedent to this, that the question of the *construction* of this platform should be satisfactorily settled. To this end, the State Rights Democratic party in several of the Southern States defined the conditions upon which their delegates should hold seats in the National Convention, appointed to meet at Charleston on the 23d of April, 1860. The Democracy in Alabama moved first On the 11th of January, 1860, they met in convention at Montgomery, and adopted a series of resolu tions, from which the following are extracted, as presenting a summary declaration of the rights of the South, a recapitulation of the territorial question, and a definition of those issues on which the contest of 1860 was to be conducted:

Resolved, by the Democracy of the State of Alabama in Convention assembled, That holding all issues and principles upon which they have heretofore affiliated and acted with the National Democratic party to be inferior in dignity and importance to the great question of slavery, they content themselves with a general reaffirmance of the Cincinnati platform as to such issues, and also indorse said platform as to slavery, together with the following resolutions:

* * * * * * * * *

Resolved, That the Constitution of the United States, is a compact between sovereign and co-equal States, united upon the basis of perfect equality of rights and privileges.

Resolved, further, That the Territories of the United States are common property, in which the States have equal rights, and to which the citizens of any State may rightfully emigrate, with their slaves or other property recognized as such in any of the States of the Union, or by the Constitution of the United States.

Resolved, further, That the Congress of the United States has no power to abolish slavery in the Territories, or to prohibit its introduction into any of them.

Resolved, further, That the Territorial Legislatures, created by the legislation of Congress, have no power to abolish slavery, or to prohibit the introduction of the same, or to impair by unfriendly legislation the security and full enjoyment of the same within the Territories; and such constitutional power certainly does not belong to the people of the Territories in any capacity, before, in the exercise of a lawful authority, they form a Constitution, preparatory to admission as a State into the Union; and their action in the exercise of such lawful authority certainly cannot operate or take effect before their actual admission as a State into the Union.

Resolved, further, That the principles enunciated by Chief Justice Taney, in his opinion in the Dred Scott case, deny to the Territorial Legislature the power to destroy or impair, by any legislation whatever, the right of property in slaves, and maintain it to be the duty of the Federal Government, in *all* of its departments, to protect the rights of the owner of such property in the Territories; and the principles so declared are hereby asserted to be the rights of the South, and the South should maintain them.

Resolved, further, That we hold all of the foregoing propositions to contain "cardinal principles"—true in themselves—and just and proper and necessary for the safety of all that is dear to us; and we do hereby instruct our delegates to the Charleston Convention to present them for the calm consideration and approval of that body—from whose justice and patriotism we anticipate their adoption.

Resolved, further, That our delegates to the Charleston Convention are hereby expressly instructed to insist that said Convention shall adopt a plat form of principles, recognizing distinctly the rights of the South as asserted in the foregoing resolutions; and if the said National Convention shall refuse to adopt, in substance, the propositions embraced in the preceding resolutions, prior to nominating candidates, our delegates to said Convention are hereby positively instructed to withdraw therefrom.

Under these resolutions the delegates from Alabama received their appointment to the Charleston Convention. The delegates from some of the other Cotton States were appointed under instructions equally binding. Anxious as were the Southern delegates to continue their connection with the Convention, and thus to maintain the nationality of the Democratic party, they agreed to accept, as the substance of the Alabama platform, either of the two following reports which had been submitted to the Charleston Convention by the majority of the Committee on Resolutions—this majority not only representing that of the States of the Union, but the only States at all likely to be carried by the Democratic party in the Presidential election:

I.

Resolved, That the platform at Cincinnati be reaffirmed with the following resolutions:

Resolved, That the Democracy of the United States hold these cardinal principles on the subject of slavery in the Territories: First, that Congress has no power to abolish slavery in the Territories. Second, that the Territorial Legislature has no power to abolish slavery in any Territory, nor to prohibit the introduction of slaves therein, nor any power to exclude slavery therefrom, nor any power to destroy and impair the right of property in slaves by any legislation whatever.

* * * * * * * * *

II.

Resolved, That the platform adopted by the Democratic party at Cincinnati be affirmed, with the following explanatory resolutions:

First. That the government of a Territory, organized by an act of Congress, is provisional and temporary; and, during its existence, all citizens of the United States have an equal right to settle with their property in the Territory, without their rights, either of person or property, being destroyed or impaired by congressional or territorial legislation.

Second. That it is the duty of the Federal Government, in all its departments, to protect, when necessary, the rights of persons and property in the Territories and wherever else its constitutional authority extends.

Third. That when the settlers in a Territory having an adequate population form a State Constitution, the right of sovereignty commences, and being consummated by admission into the Union, they stand on an equal footing with the people of other States; and the State thus organized, ought to be admitted into the Federal Union, whether its Constitution prohibits or recognizes the institution of slavery.

The Convention refused to accept either of the foregoing resolutions, and adopted, by a vote of 165 to 138, the following as its platform on the slavery question:

1. *Resolved*, That we, the Democracy of the Union, in Convention assembled, hereby declare our affirmance of the resolutions unanimously adopted and declared as a platform of principles by the Democratic Convention at Cincinnati, in the year 1856, believing that Democratic principles are unchangeable in their nature, when applied to the same subject-matters; and we recommend as the only further resolutions the following:

Inasmuch as differences of opinion exist in the Democratic party as to the nature and extent of the powers of a Territorial Legislature, and as to the powers and duties of Congress under the Constitution of the United States, over the institution of slavery within the Territories:

2. *Resolved*, That the Democratic party will abide by the decisions of the Supreme Court of the United States on the questions of constitutional law.

The substitution of these resolutions for those which were satisfactory to the South, occasioned the disruption of the Convention, after a session of more than three weeks, and its adjournment to Baltimore, on the 18th of June. The Cotton States, all, withdrew from the Convention; but the Border Slave States remained in it, with the hope of effecting some ultimate settlement of the difficulty. The breach, however, widened. The reassembling of the Convention at Baltimore resulted in a final and embittered separation of the opposing delegations. The majority exhibited a more uncompromising spirit than ever; and Virginia and all the Border Slave States, with the exception of Missouri, withdrew from the Convention, and united with the representatives of the Cotton States, then assembled in Baltimore, in the nomination of candidates representing the views of the South. Their nominees were John C. Breckinridge of Kentucky for President, and Joseph Lane of Oregon for Vice-President.

The old Convention, or what remained of it, nominated Stephen A. Douglas of Illinois for President, and Benjamin Fitzpatrick of Alabama for Vice-President. The latter declining, Herschel V. Johnson of Georgia was substituted on the ticket.

The Southern Democracy and the Southern people of all parties, with but few exceptions, sustained the platform demanded by the Southern delegates in the Convention, and justified the course they had pursued. They recognized in the platform a legimate and fair assertion of Southern rights. In view, however, of the conservative professions and glozed speeches of a portion of the Northern Democracy, a respectable number of Southern Democrats were induced to support their ticket. Mr. Douglas proclaimed his views to be in favor of non-intervention; he avowed his continued and unalterable opposition to Black Republicanism; his principles were professed to be "held subject to the decisions of the Supreme Court"—the distinction between judicial questions and political questions being purposely clouded; and his friends, with an ingenious sophistry that had imposed upon the South for thirty years with success, insisted that the support of Stephen A. Douglas was a support of the party in the North which had stood by the South amid persecution and defamation. In consequence of these and other protestations, tickets were got up for Mr. Douglas in most of the Southern States. The great majority, however, of the Democracy of the slave-holding States, except Missouri, supported Breckinridge.

A Convention of what is called the "Constitutional Union" party met in Baltimore on the 9th of May, 1860, and nominated for President and Vice-President, John Bell of Tennessee and Edward Everett of Massachusetts. Their platform consisted of a vague and undefined enumeration of their political principles; as, "The Constitution of the Country, the Union of the States, and Enforcement of the Laws."

The National Convention of the Black Republican party was held at Chicago, in the month of June. It adopted a platform declaring freedom to be the "normal condition" of the Territories; but ingeniously complicating its position on the slavery question by a number of vague but plausible articles, such as the maintenance of the principles of the Constitution, and especial attachment to the Union of the States.

The Presidential ticket nominated by the Convention was Abraham Lincoln of Illinois for President, and Hannibal

Hamlin of Maine for Vice-President. Governed by the narrow considerations of party expediency, the Convention had adopted as their candidate for President a man of scanty political record—a Western lawyer, with the characteristics of that profession—acuteness, slang, and a large stock of jokes—and who had peculiar claims to vulgar and demagogical popularity, in the circumstances that he was once a captain of volunteers in one of the Indian wars, and, at some anterior period of his life, had been employed, as report differently said, in splitting rails, or in rowing a flat-boat.

The great majority of the Southern Democracy supported the Breckinridge ticket; it was the leading ticket in all the Slave States, except Missouri; but in the North but a small and feeble minority of the Democratic party gave it their support. In several States, the friends of Douglas, of Breckinridge, and of Bell coalesced, to a certain extent, with a view to the defeat of Lincoln, but without success, except in New Jersey, where they partially succeeded.

The result of the contest was, that Abraham Lincoln received the entire electoral vote of every free State, except New Jersey, and was, of course, elected President of the United States, according to the forms of the Constitution.

The entire popular vote for Lincoln was 1,858,200; that for Douglas, giving him his share of the fusion vote, 1,276,780; that for Breckinridge, giving him his share of the fusion vote, 812,500; and that for Bell, including his proportion of the fusion vote, 735,504. The whole vote against Lincoln was thus 2,824,874, showing a clear aggregate majority against him of nearly a million of votes.

During the canvass, the North had been distinctly warned by the conservative parties of the country, that the election of Lincoln by a strictly sectional vote would be taken as a declaration of war against the South. This position was assumed on the part of the South, not so much on account of the declaration of the anti-slavery principles in the Chicago platform, as from the notorious *animus* of the party supporting Lincoln. The Chicago Convention had attempted to conceal the worst designs of Abolitionism under professions of advancing the cause of freedom in strict accordance with the Constitution and the laws. The South, however, could not be igno rant of the fact, or wanting in appreciation of it, that Lincoln had been supported by the sympathizers of John Brown, the indorsers of the "Helper Book," the founders of the Kansas Emigrant Aid Societies, and their desperate abetters and agents, "Jim" Lane and others, and by the opponents of the Fugitive Slave law. It was known, in a word, that Lincoln owed his election to the worst enemies of the South, and that he would naturally and necessarily select his counsellors from among them, and consult their views in his administration of the government.

Threats of resistance were proclaimed in the South. It is true that a few sanguine persons in that section, indulging narrow and temporizing views of the crisis, derived no little comfort and confidence from the large preponderance of the popular vote in the Presidential contest in favor of the conservative candidates; and viewed it as an augury of the speedy overthrow of the first sectional administration. But those whose observations were larger and comprehended the progress of events, took quite a different view of the matter. They could find no consolation or encouragement from the face of the record. The anti-slavery party had organized in 1840, with about seven thousand voters; and in 1860 had succeeded in electing the President of the United States. The conservative party in the North had been thoroughly corrupted. They were beaten in every Northern State in 1860, with a single exception, by the avowed enemies of the South, who, but a few years ago had been powerless in their midst. The leaders of the Northern Democratic party had in 1856 and in 1860, openly taken the position that freedom would be more certainly secured in the Territories by the rule of non-intervention than by any other policy or expedient. This interpretation of their policy alone saved the Democratic party from entire annihilation. The overwhelming pressure of the anti-slavery sentiment had prevented their acceding to the Southern platform in the Presidential canvass. Nothing in the present or in the future could be looked for from the so-called conservatives of the North; and the South prepared to go out of a Union, which no longer afforded any guaranty for her rights or any permanent sense of security, and which had brought her under the domination of a growing fanaticism in the North, the sentiments of which, if carried into legislation, would destroy her institutions, confiscate the property of her people, and even involve their lives.

The State of South Carolina acted promptly and vigorously, with no delay for argument, and but little for preparation. Considering the argument as fully exhausted, she determined, by the exercise of her rights as a sovereign State, to separate herself from the Union. Her Legislature called a Convention immediately after the result of the Presidential election had been ascertained. The Convention met a few weeks thereafter, and on the 20th day of December, 1860, formally dissolved the connection of South Carolina with the Union, by an ordinance of Secession, which was passed by a unanimous vote.

On the same day Major Anderson, who was in command of the Federal forces in Charleston harbor, evacuated Fort Moultrie, spiking the guns and burning the gun carriages, and occupied Fort Sumter, with a view of strengthening his position. On the 30th of December, John B. Floyd, Secretary of War, resigned his office, because President Buchanan refused to order Major Anderson back to Fort Moultrie—Mr. Floyd alleging that he and the President had pledged the authorities of South Carolina that the existing military *status* of the United States in that State should not be changed during the expiring term of the Democratic administration.

The withdrawal of South Carolina from the Union produced some sensation in the North, but the dominant party treated it lightly. Many of these jeered at it; their leaders derided the "right of secession;" and their newspapers prophesied that the "rebellion" in South Carolina would be reduced to the most ignominious extremity the moment the "paternal government" of the United States should resolve to have recourse from peaceful persuasions to the chastisement of "a spoilt child." The events, however, which rapidly succeeded the withdrawal of South Carolina, produced a deep impression upon all reflecting minds, and startled, to some extent, the masses of the North, who would have been much more alarmed but for their vain and long-continued assurance that the South had no means or resources for making a serious resistance to the Federal authority; and that a rebellion which could at any time be crushed on short notice, might be pleasantly humored or wisely tolerated to any extent short of the actual commencement of hostilities.

On the 9th day of January, 1861, the State of Mississippi seceded from the Union. Alabama and Florida followed on the 11th day of the same month; Georgia on the 20th; Louisiana on the 26th; and Texas on the 1st of February. Thus, in less than three months after the announcement of Lincoln's election, all the Cotton States, with the exception of Alabama, had seceded from the Union, and had, besides, secured every Federal fort within their limits, except the forts in Charleston harbor, and Fort Pickens, below Pensacola, which were retained by United States troops.

The United States Congress had, at the beginning of its session in December, 1860, appointed committees in both houses to consider the state of the Union. Neither committee was able to agree upon any mode of settlement of the pending issue between the North and the South. The Republican members in both committees rejected propositions acknowledging the right of property in slaves, or recommending the division of the territories between the slaveholding and non-slaveholding States by a geographical line. In the Senate, the propositions, commonly known as Mr. Crittenden's, were voted against by *every Republican senator;* and the House, on a vote of yeas and nays, refused to consider certain propositions, moved by Mr. Etheridge, which were even less favorable to the South than Mr. Crittenden's.

A resolution, giving a pledge to sustain the President in the use of force against seceding States, was adopted in the House of Representatives by a large majority; and, in the Senate, every Republican voted to substitute for Mr. Crittenden's propositions, resolutions offered by Mr. Clarke, of New Hampshire, declaring that no new concessions, guaranties, or amendments to the Constitution were necessary; that the demands of the South were unreasonable, and that the remedy for the present dangers was simply to enforce the laws—in other words—*coercion and war.*

On the 19th day of January, the Legislature of the State of Virginia had passed resolutions having in view a peaceful settlement of the questions which threatened the Union, and suggesting that a National Peace Conference should be held in Washington on the 4th of February. This suggestion met with a favorable response from the Border Slave States and from professed conservatives in the North. The Conference met on the day designated, and Ex-President Tyler, of Virginia, was called to preside over its deliberations. It remained in session several days, and adjourned without agreeing upon any satisfactory plan of adjustment.

Most of the delegates from the Border Slave States indicated a willingness to accept the few and feeble guaranties contained in the resolutions offered, a short time before, in the Senate by Mr. Crittenden. These guaranties, paltry and ineffectual as they were, would not be conceded by the representatives of the Northern States. The Peace Conference finally adopted what was called the Franklin Substitute in lieu of the propositions offered by Mr. Guthrie, of Kentucky—a settlement less favorable to the South than that proposed by Mr. Crittenden. It is useless to recount the details of these measures. Neither the Crittenden propositions, the Franklin Substitute, nor any plan that pretended to look for the guaranty of Southern rights, received a respectful notice from the Republican majority in Congress.

Shortly after its assemblage in January, the Virginia Legislature had called a Convention of the people to decide upon the course proper to be pursued by the State, with reference to her present relations to the Union and the future exigencies of her situation. The election was held on the 4th of February, and resulted in the choice of a majority of members opposed to unconditional secession. Subsequently, Tennessee and North Carolina decided against calling a Convention—the former by a large, the latter by a very small majority. These events greatly encouraged the enemies of the South, but without cause, as they really indicated nothing more than the purpose of the Border Slave States to await the results of the peace propositions, to which they had committed themselves.

In the mean time, the seceding States were erecting the structure of a government on the foundation of a new Confederation of States. A convention of delegates from the six seceding States assembled in Congress at Montgomery, Alabama, on the 4th of February, 1861, for the purpose of organizing a provisional government. This body adopted a Constitution for the Confederate States on the 8th of February. On the 9th of February, Congress proceeded to the election of a President and Vice-President, and unanimously agreed upon Jefferson Davis, of Mississippi, for President, and Alexander H. Stephens, of Georgia, for Vice-President. Mr. Davis was inaugurated Provisional President on the 18th of February, and delivered an address, explaining the revolution as a change of the constituent parts, but not the system, of the government, and referring to the not unreasonable expectation that, with a Constitution differing only from that of their fathers, in so far as it was explanatory of their well-known intent, freed from sectional conflicts, the States from which they had recently parted might seek to unite their fortunes to those of the new Confederacy.

President Buchanan had, in his message to Congress, denounced Secession as revolutionary, but had hesitated at the logical conclusion of the right of "coercion," on the part of the Federal Government, as not warranted by the text of the Constitution. Timid, secretive, cold, and with no other policy than that of selfish expediency, the remnant of his administration was marked by embarrassment, double-dealing, and weak and contemptible querulousness. He had not hesitated, under the pressure of Northern clamor, to refuse to order Major Anderson back to Fort Moultrie, thus violating the pledge that he had given to the South Carolina authorities, that the military status of the United States in Charleston harbor should not be disturbed during his administration. He added to the infamy of this perfidy by a covert attempt to reinforce Fort Sumter, under the specious plea of provisioning a "starving garrison;" and when the Federal steamship, the Star of the West, which was sent on this mission, was, on the 9th of January, driven off Charleston harbor by the South Carolina batteries on Morris Island, he had the hardihood to affect surprise and indignation at the reception given the Federal reinforcements, and to insist that the expedition had been ordered with the concurrence of his Cabinet, including Mr. Thompson, of Mississippi, then Secretary of the Interior, who repelled the slander, denounced the movement as underhanded, and as a breach not only of good faith towards South Carolina, but of personal confidence between the President and his advisers, and left the Cabinet in disgust.

On the incoming of the administration of Abraham Lincoln, on the 4th of March, the rival government of the South had perfected its organization; the separation had been widened and envenomed by the ambidexterity and perfidy of President Buchanan; the Southern people, however, still hoped for a peaceful accomplishment of their independence, and deplored war between the two sections, as "a policy detrimental to the civilized world." The revolution in the mean time had rapidly gathered, not only in moral power, but in the means of war and the muniments of defence. Fort Moultrie and Castle Pinckney had been captured by the South Carolina troops; Fort Pulaski, the defence of the Savannah, had been taken; the arsenal at Mount Vernon, Alabama, with 20,000 stand of arms, had been seized by the Alabama troops; Fort Morgan, in Mobile Bay, had been taken; Forts Jackson, St. Philip, and Pike, near New Orleans, had been captured by the Louisiana troops; the Pensacola Navy-Yard and Forts Barrancas and McRae had been taken, and the siege of Fort Pickens commenced; the Baton Rouge Arsenal had been surrendered to the Louisiana troops; the New Orleans Mint and Custom-House had been taken; the Little Rock Arsenal had been seized by the Arkansas troops; and, on the 16th of February, General Twiggs had transferred the public property in Texas to the State authorities. All of these events had been accomplished without bloodshed. Abolitionism and Fanaticism had not yet lapped blood. But reflecting men saw that the peace was deceitful and temporizing; that the temper of the North was impatient and dark; and that, if all history was not a lie, the first incident of bloodshed would be the prelude to a war of monstrous proportions.

CHAPTER II.

Mr. Lincoln's Journey to Washington.—Ceremonies of the Inauguration.—The Inaugural Speech of President Lincoln.—The Spirit of the New Administration.—Its Financial Condition.—Embassy from the Southern Confederacy.—Perfidious Treatment of the Southern Commissioners.—Preparations for War.—The Military Bills of the Confederate Congress.—General Beauregard.—Fortifications of Charleston Harbor.—Naval Preparations of the Federal Government.—Attempted Reinforcement of Fort Sumter.—Perfidy of the Federal Government.—Excitement in Charleston.—Reduction of Fort Sumter by the Confederate Forces.—How the News was received in Washington.—Lincoln's Calculation.—His Proclamation of War.—The " Reaction" in the North.—Displays of Rancor towards the South.—Northern Democrats.—Replies of Southern Governors to Lincoln's Requisition for Troops.—Spirit of the South.—Secession of Virginia.—Maryland.—The Baltimore Riot.—Patriotic Example of Missouri.—Lincoln's Proclamation blockading the Southern Ports.—General Lee.—The Federals evacuate Harper's Ferry.—Burning of the Navy Yard at Norfolk.—The Second Secessionary Movement.—Spirit of Patriotic Devotion in the South.—Supply of Arms in the South.—The Federal Government and the State of Maryland.—The Prospect.

THE circumstances of the advent of Mr. Lincoln to Washington were not calculated to inspire confidence in his courage or wisdom, or in the results of his administration. His party had busily prophesied, and sought to innoculate the North with the conviction, that his assumption of the Presidential office would be the signal of the restoration of peace; that by some mysterious ingenuity he would resolve the existing political complication, restore the Union, and inaugurate a season of unexampled peace, harmony, and prosperity. These weak and fulsome prophecies had a certain effect. In the midst of anxiety and embarrassment, in which no relief had yet been suggested, the inauguration of a new administration of the government was looked to by many persons in the North, outside the Republican party, with a vague sense of hope, which was animated by reports, quite as uncertain, of the vigor, decision, and individuality of the new President. For months since the announcement of his election, Mr. Lincoln's lips had been closed. He had been studiously silent; expectations were raised by what was thought to be an indication of a mysterious wisdom; and the North impatiently waited for the hour when the oracle's lips were to be opened.

These vague expectations were almost ludicrously disappointed. On leaving his home, in Springfield, Illinois, for

Washington. Mr. Lincoln had at last opened his lips. In the speeches with which he entertained the crowd that at different points of the railroad watched his progress to the capital, he amused the whole country, even in the midst of a great public anxiety, with his ignorance, his vulgarity, his flippant conceit, and his Western phraseology. The North discovered that the new President, instead of having nursed a masterly wisdom in the retirement of his home at Springfield, and approaching the capital with dignity, had nothing better to offer to an agonized country than the ignorant conceits of a low Western politician, and the flimsy jests of a harlequin. His railroad speeches were characterized by a Southern paper as illustrating "the delightful combination of a Western county lawyer with a Yankee bar-keeper." In his harangues to the crowds which intercepted him in his journey, at a time when the country was in revolutionary chaos, when commerce and trade were prostrated, and when starving women and idle men were among the very audiences that listened to him, he declared to them in his peculiar phraseology that "*nobody was hurt*," that "*all would come out right*," and that there was "*nothing going wrong*." Nor was the rhetoric of the new President his only entertainment of the crowds that assembled to honor the progress of his journey to Washington. He amused them by the spectacle of kissing, on a public platform, a lady-admirer, who had suggested to him the cultivation of his whiskers; he measured heights with every tall man he encountered in one of his public receptions, and declared that he was not to be "overtopped;" and he made public exhibitions of his wife—"the little woman," he called her—whose chubby figure, motherly face, and fondness for finery and colors recommended her to a very limited and very vulgar portion of the society of her sex.

These jests and indecencies of the demagogue who was to take control of what remained of the Government of the United States, belong to history. Whatever their disgrace, it was surpassed, however, by another display of character on the part of the coming statesman. While at Harrisburg, Pennsylvania, and intending to proceed from there to Baltimore, Mr. Lincoln was alarmed by a report, which was either silly or jocose, that a band of assassins were awaiting him in the latter city. Frightened beyond all considerations of dignity and decency, the new President of the United States left Harrisburg at night, on a different route than that through Baltimore; and in a motley disguise, composed of a Scotch cap and military cloak, stole to the capital of his government. The distinguished fugitive had left his wife and family to pursue the route on which it was threatened that the cars were to be thrown down a precipice by Secessionists, or, if that expedient failed, the work of assassination was to be accomplished in the streets of Baltimore. The city of Washington was taken by surprise by the irregular flight of the President to its shelter and protection. The representatives of his own party there received him with evident signs of disgust at the cowardice which had hurried his arrival in Washington; but as an example of the early prostitution of the press of that parasitical city to the incoming administration that was to feed its venal lusts, the escapade of Mr. Lincoln was, with a shamelessness almost incredible, exploited as an ingenious and brilliant feat, and entitled, in the newspaper extras that announced his arrival, as "*another Fort Moultrie coup de main*"—referring to the fraud by which the government had stolen a march by midnight to the supposed impregnable defences of Fort Sumter.

But Mr. Lincoln's fears for his personal safety evidently did not subside with his attainment of the refuges of Washington. A story was published seriously in a New York paper, that at the moment of his inauguration he was to be shot on the Capitol steps, by an air-gun, in the hands of a Secessionist selected for this desperate and romantic task of assassination. The President, with nerves already shattered by his flight from Harrisburg, was easily put in a new condition of alarm. An armed guard was posted around Willard's hotel, where he had taken temporary quarters. Preparations were busily made to organize a military protection for the ceremony of the inauguration. The city of Washington had already been invested with large military forces, under the immediate command of General Scott, whose vanity and weak love of public sensations had easily induced him to pretend alarm, and to make a military display, more on his own account than for the ridiculous and absurd object of Mr. Lincoln's personal security. For weeks the usually quiet city had been filled with Federal bayonets; the bugle's reveille, the roll of drums, and the tramp of armed guards startled, in every direction, the civilian of Washington, who had been accustomed to nothing more warlike than parades at the Navy Yard and rows in Congress: companies of flying artillery daily paraded the streets and thundered over its pavements; and no form of ostentation was omitted by the senile and conceited general in command, to give the Federal metropolis the appearance of a conquered city.

The hour of the inauguration—the morning of the fourth of March—at length arrived. Mr. Lincoln was dressed in a suit of black for the occasion, and, at the instance of his friends, had submitted to the offices of a hair-dresser. He entered the barouche that was to convey him to the Capitol, with a nervous agitation and an awkwardness, that were plainly evident to the crowd. His person attracted the curiosity of the mob. Of unusual height, the effect of his figure was almost ludicrous, from a swinging gait and the stoop of his shoulders; a cadaverous face, whose expression was that of a sort of funereal humor; long, swinging arms, with the general hirsute appearance of the Western countryman, made up the principal features of the new President.

The inauguration ceremony was attended by a most extraordinary military display, under the immediate direction of General Scott; who, to give it an appearance of propriety, and to increase its importance, affected the most uneasy alarms. Previous to inauguration day, the vaults of the Capitol were explored for evidences of a gunpowder plot to hurry Mr. Lincoln and his satellites into eternity. In the procession along Pennsylvania Avenue, the President was hid from public view in a hollow square of cavalry, three or four deep. The tops of the houses along the route were occupied by soldiery watching for signs of tumult or assassination. Artillery and infantry companies were posted in different parts of the city; officers were continually passing to and fro; and as the procession approached the Capitol, Gen. Scott, who was in constant communication with all quarters of the city, was heard to exclaim, in a tone of relief, "every thing is going on peaceably; thank God Almighty for it." The expression of relief was simply ridiculous. The ceremony was disturbed by but a single incident: as the procession neared the portico of the Capitol, a drunken man, who had climbed up one of the trees on the avenue, amused himself by striking with a staff the boughs of the tree and shouting to the crowd. The thought flashed upon the minds of the special police, that he might be the identical assassin with the air-gun; he was instantly seized by a dozen of them, and hurried from the scene of the ceremony with a rapidity and decision that for a moment alarmed, and then amused, the crowd. Mr. Lincoln delivered his inaugural from the East portico of the Capitol, to an audience huddled within the lines of the District militia, and with a row of bayonets glittering at his feet.

The inaugural was intended to be ambiguous; it proposed to cozen the South by a cheap sentimentalism, and, at the same time, to gratify the party that had elevated Mr. Lincoln, by a sufficient expression of the designs of the new administration. These designs were sufficiently apparent. Mr. Lincoln protested that he should take care that the laws of the United States were faithfully executed in all the States; he declared that in doing this, there was no necessity for bloodshed or violence, "*unless* it was forced upon the national authority." He promised that the power confided to him would be used to hold, occupy, and possess the forts and places belonging to the government, "but," continued the ambidexterous speaker, "*beyond what may be necessary* for these objects, there will be no invasion, no using of force against or among any people anywhere."

In the South, the inaugural was generally taken as a premonition of war. There were other manifestations of the spirit of the new administration. Violent Abolitionists and men whose hatred of the South was notorious and unrelenting, were placed in every department of the public service. William H. Seward was made Secretary of State; Salmon P. Chase, Secretary of the Treasury; and Montgomery Blair, Postmaster-general. Anson Burlingame was sent as representative to Austria; Cassius M. Clay, to Russia; Carl Shurz, to Spain; James E. Harvey, to Portugal; Charles F. Adams, to England; and Joshua R. Giddings, to Canada. In the Senate, which was convened in an extra session to confirm executive appointments and to transact other public business, Charles Sumner was appointed Chairman of Foreign Relations; Wil liam P. Fessenden, of Finance; and Henry Wilson, of Military Affairs. A portion of the time of this extra session was consumed in discussing the policy of the administration. Mr. Douglas, who had represented the Northern Democracy in the Presidential contest, and still claimed to represent it, and who had already courted the new administration of his rival—had held Mr. Lincoln's hat at the inauguration ceremony, and enacted the part of Mrs. Lincoln's cavalier at the inauguration ball—essayed to give to the President's inaugural a peace interpretation, and to soften what had been foreshadowed of his policy. The efforts of the demagogue were ill-timed and paltry. Senators from Delaware, Maryland, Virginia, Kentucky, Arkansas, Missouri, and North Carolina, who still continued in the councils of the government, remained long enough to witness the subversion of all the principles that had before contributed to the prosperity and stability of the American Government; to learn, as far as possible, the course the government would pursue towards the Confederate States; and to return home to prepare their people for the policy of discord, conflict, and civil war which had been inaugurated.

The financial condition of the government at the time of Mr. Lincoln's accession was by no means desperate. There was a balance in the Treasury of six millions, applicable to current expenses; the receipts from customs were estimated at eighty thousand dollars per day; and it was thought that a loan would not be called for for some time, should there be a happy continuation of peace.

The Confederate States government at Montgomery had shown nothing of a desperate or tumultuous spirit; it had not watched events with recklessness as to their conclusion; it was anxious for peace; and it gave a rare evidence of the virtue and conservatism of a new government, which was historically the fruit of a revolution, by the most sedulous efforts to avoid all temptations to violence, and to resist the consequence of war. Soon after the inauguration of Mr. Lincoln, it had deputed an embassy of commissioners to Washington, authorized to negotiate for the removal of the Federal garrisons from Forts Pickens and Sumter, and to provide for the settlement of all claims of public property arising out of the separation of the States from the Union. Two of the commissioners, Martin

Crawford, of Georgia, and John Forsythe, of Alabama, attended in Washington, and addressed a communication to Mr. Seward, which explained the functions of the embassy and its purposes.

Mr. Seward declined for the present to return an official answer to the commissioners, or to recognize in an official light their humane and amicable mission. His government had resolved on a policy of perfidy. The commissioners were amused from week to week with verbal assurances that the government was disposed to recognize them; that to treat with them at the particular juncture might seriously embarrass the administration of Mr. Lincoln; that they should be patient and confident; and that in the mean time the military status of the United States in the South would not be disturbed. Judge Campbell, of the Supreme Court, had consented to be the intermediary of these verbal conferences. When the sequel of the perfidy of the administration was demonstrated, he wrote two notes to Mr. Seward, distinctly charging him with overreaching and equivocation, to which Mr. Seward never attempted a defence or a reply.

The dalliance with the commissioners was not the only deceitful indication of peace. It was given out and confidently reported in the newspapers, that Fort Sumter was to be evacuated by the Federal forces. The delusion was continued for weeks. The Black Republican party, of course, resented this reported policy of the government; but a number of their newspapers endeavored to compose the resentment by the arguments that the evacuation would be ordered solely on the ground of military necessity, as it would be impossible to reinforce the garrison without a very extensive demonstration of force, which the government was not then prepared to make; that the purposes of the administration had not relaxed, and that the evacuation of Sumter was, as one of the organs of the administration expressed it, but "the crouch of the tiger before he leaped."

It was true that the condition of the garrison of Fort Sumter had been a subject of Cabinet consultation; but it was afterwards discovered that all that had been decided by the advisers of the President, among whom General Scott had been admitted, was that military reinforcement of the fort was, under the circumstances, impracticable. There never was an intention to evacuate it. The embarrassment of the government was, to avoid the difficulty of military reinforcements by some artifice that would equally well answer its purposes. That artifice continued for a considerable time to be the subject of secret and sedulous consultation.

While a portion of the public were entertained in watching the surface of events, and were imposed upon by deceitful signs of peace, discerning men saw the inevitable consequence in the significant preparations made on both sides for war. These preparations had gone on unremittingly since the inauguration of the Lincoln government. The troops of the United States were called from the frontiers to the military centres; the Mediterranean squadron and other naval forces were ordered home; and the city of Washington itself was converted into a school where there were daily and ostentatious instructions of the soldier. On the other hand, the government at Montgomery was not idle. Three military bills had been passed by the Confederate Congress. The first authorized the raising of one hundred thousand volunteers when deemed necessary by the President; the second provided for the Provisional Army of the Confederate States, which was to be formed from the regular and volunteer forces of the different States; and the third provided for the organization of a Regular Army, which was to be a permanent establishment. But among the strongest indications of the probability of war, in the estimation of men calculated to judge of the matter, and among the most striking proofs, too, of devotion to the cause of the South, was the number of resignations from the Federal army and navy on the part of officers of Southern birth or association, and their prompt identification with the Confederate service. These resignations had commenced during the close of Mr. Buchanan's administration. On the accession of Mr. Lincoln, Adjutant-general Cooper had immediately resigned; and the distinguished example was followed by an array of names, which had been not a little illustrious in the annals of the Federal service.

While the South was entreating peace, and pursuing its accomplishment by an amicable mission to Washington, a strong outside pressure was being exerted upon the administration of Mr. Lincoln to hurry it to the conclusion of war.

He had been visited by a number of governors of the Northern States. They offered him money and men; but it was understood that nothing would be done in the way of calling out the State militia and opening special credits, until the Southern revolutionists should be actually in aggression to the authority of the Federal government. Another appeal was still more effectively urged. It was the argument of the partisan. The report of the intended evacuation of Fort Sumter, and the apparent vacillation of the administration, were producing disaffection in the Black Republican party. This party had shown a considerable loss of strength in the municipal elections in St. Louis, Cincinnati, and other parts of the West; they had lost two congressmen in Connecticut and two in Rhode Island. The low tariff, too, of the Southern Confederacy, brought into competition with the high protective tariff which the Black Republican majority in Congress had adopted, and which was popularly known as "the Morrill Tariff," was threatening serious disaster to the interests of New England and Pennsylvania, and was indicating the necessity of the repeal of a law which was considered as an indispensable party measure by the most of Mr. Lincoln's constituents.

For weeks the Cabinet of Mr. Lincoln had been taxed to devise some artifice for the relief of Fort Sumter, short of open military reinforcements (decided to be impracticable), and which would have the effect of inaugurating the war by a safe indirection and under a plausible and convenient pretence. The device was at length hit upon. It was accomplished by the most flagrant perfidy. Mr. Seward had already given assurances to the Southern commissioners, through the intermediation of Judge Campbell, that the Federal troops would be removed from Fort Sumter. Referring to the draft of a letter which Judge Campbell had in his hand, and proposed to address to President Davis, at Montgomery, he said, "before that letter reaches its destination, Fort Sumter will have been evacuated." Some time elapsed, and there was reason to distrust the promise. Colonel Lamon, an agent of the Washington government, was sent to Charleston, and was reported to be authorized to make arrangements with Governor Pickens, of South Carolina, for the withdrawal of the Federal troops from Fort Sumter. He returned without any accomplishment of his reported mission. Another confidential agent of Mr. Lincoln, a Mr. Fox, was permitted to visit Fort Sumter, and was discovered to have acted the part of a spy in carrying concealed dispatches to Major Anderson, and collecting information with reference to a plan for the forcible reinforcement of the fort. On the 7th of April, Judge Campbell, uneasy as to the good faith of Mr. Seward's promise of the evacuation of Sumter, addressed him another note on the subject. To this the emphatic and laconic reply was: "*Faith as to Sumter fully kept—wait and see.*" Six days thereafter a hostile fleet was menacing Charleston, the Lincoln government threw down the gauntlet of war, and the battle of Sumter was fought.

On the day succeeding the inauguration of Abraham Lincoln, General P. G. Toutant Beauregard* was put in command of the Confederate troops besieging Fort Sumter. His military record was slight, but gave evidence of genius. He was the son of a wealthy and influential Louisiana planter. He had graduated at the military academy at West Point, taking the second honors in his class, and had served in the Mexican war with distinction, being twice brevetted for gallant and meritorious conduct in the field—the first time as captain for the battles of Contreras and Cherubusco, and again as major for the battle of Chapultepec. He was subsequently placed by the Federal government in charge of the construction of the mint and custom-house at New Orleans. He had been ordered by Mr. Buchanan to West Point as superintendent of the military academy. The appointment was revoked within forty-eight hours for a spiteful reason—the family connection of the nominee with Mr. Slidell, of Louisiana; and Major Beauregard, resigning his commission at once, received higher rank in the army of the Southern Confederacy.

---

* Beauregard is forty years of age. He is small, brown, thin, extremely vigorous, although his features wear a dead expression, and his hair has whitened prematurely. Face, physiognomy, tongue, accent—everything about him is French. He is quick, a little abrupt, but well educated and distinguished in his manners. He does not care to express the manifestation of an ardent personality which knows its worth. He is extremely impassioned in he defence of the cause which he serves. At least he takes less pains to conceal his passion under a calm and cold exterior than do most of his comrades in the army. The South found in him a man of an uncommon ardor, a ceaseless activity, and an indomitable power of will.

On taking command of the Confederate forces at Charleston, General Beauregard at once gave the benefit of his eminent skill as a military engineer, which merit had been recognized in him before, and had procured his elevation to the important and critical command in front of Fort Sumter, to the construction of works for the reduction of the fort, and the defence of the entrances to the harbor. At the time of Major Anderson's removal to Sumter, the approaches to the harbor were only defended by the uninjured guns at Fort Moultrie, and three 24-pounder guns mounted *en barbette* on a hastily constructed and imperfect earthwork on Morris' Island. The injured guns were replaced, and all, amounting to thirty-eight in number, of various calibres, were protected by well-constructed merlons; lines of batteries were constructed on the east and west on Sullivan's Island; at Cummings' Point on Morris' Island, the nearest land to Fort Sumter, batteries of mortars and columbiads were erected, protected by an iron fortification of novel and formidable construction; and another novelty in iron fortifications was perfected by the skilful and practical genius of the commander in a floating battery, constructed of the peculiarly fibrous palmetto timber, sheathed with plate iron, and embrasured for and mounting four guns of heavy calibre.

Notwithstanding the extent and skill of the besiegers' works, Fort Sumter was declared, by a number of military critics, to be impregnable. It certainly had that appearance to the unscientific eye. The fortification, a modern truncated pentagonal fort, rose abruptly out of the water at the mouth of Charleston harbor, three and a half miles from the city. It was built on an artificial island, having for its base a sand and mud bank, which had been made secure by long and weary labors in firmly imbedding in it refuse blocks and chips from the granite quarries of the Northern States. The foundation alone had cost the government half a million of dollars, and had occupied ten years in its construction. At the time of Major Anderson's occupation of the fortification, it was so nearly completed as to admit the introduction of its armament. The walls were of solid brick and concrete masonry, sixty feet high and from eight to twelve feet in thickness, and pierced for three tiers of guns on the northern, eastern, and western exterior sides. They were built close to the edge of the water and without a berme.

The advantages of delay which the Lincoln government had obtained by the pretence of the evacuation of Sumter, and the adroitness of Mr. Seward with the commissioners, had been profitably employed by it in naval and other preparations for its meditated blow on the Southern coasts. Unusual activity was perceptible in all the dock-yards, armories, and military depots throughout the North. The arsenals of Troy and Watertown were constantly occupied, and the creaking of blocks, the clang of hammers, and the hum of midnight labor resounded through every manufactory of arms. Numerous large transports were employed by the government for the conveyance of soldiers and war material, and the signs of the times betokened that the administration was preparing for a long and bloody struggle. Within ten days from the first of April, over eleven thousand men were sent from Fort Hamilton and Governor's Island. The recruiting offices in New York were daily engaged in enrolling men for the Federal service. On the 6th of April, the frigate Powhatan was ready for sea, and, with her armament of ten heavy guns and four hundred men, prepared as convoy to the transports Atlantic, Baltic, and Illinois. On the 8th, the Atlantic sailed with Barry's battery (four guns and ninety-one men), four hundred soldiers and a large store of supplies. The same morning the steam-cutter Harriet Lane, Captain J. Faunce, eight guns and one hundred men, sailed for Charleston harbor. Late at night, the transport Baltic, with twenty surf-boats, stores, and two hundred recruits from Governor's Island, and the transport Illinois, with five hundred cases of muskets, stores, three hundred soldiers, and the steam-tug Freeborn, sailed from New York harbor. On the whole, besides the Powhatan, eleven vessels were ordered to be got in readiness, with an aggregate force of 285 guns and 2400 men. There was now not the slightest doubt that the first blow of the rival forces would be struck at Sumter. The fleet dispatched to Charleston harbor consisted of the sloop-of-war Pawnee, the sloop-of-war Powhatan, and the cutter Harriet Lane, with three steam transports.

No sooner was the hostile fleet of the Federal government safely on its way to the Southern coasts, than the perfidy of

Abraham Lincoln and his advisers was openly and shamelessly consummated. The mask was dropped. The Southern commissioners who had been so long cozened, were distinctly rebuffed; and simultaneously with the appearance of the Federal fleet in the offing of the Charleston harbor, an official message, on the 8th day of April, was conveyed to Governor Pickens, of South Carolina, by Lieutenant Talbot, an authorized agent of the Lincoln government, announcing the determination of that government to send provisions to Fort Sumter, "peaceably if they can, forcibly if they must." The message was telegraphed by General Beauregard to Montgomery, and the instructions of his government asked. He was answered by a telegram from Mr. Walker, the Secretary of War, instructing him to demand the evacuation of the fort, and, if that was refused, to proceed to reduce it. The demand was made; it was refused. Major Anderson replied that he regretted that his sense of honor and of his obligations to his government prevented his compliance with the demand. Nothing was left but to accept the distinct challenge of the Lincoln government to arms.

The most intense excitement prevailed in Charleston. No sooner had the official message of Mr. Lincoln been received, than orders were issued to the entire military force of the city to proceed to their stations. Four regiments of one thousand men each, were telegraphed for from the country. Ambulances for the wounded were prepared; surgeons were ordered to their posts, and every preparation made for a regular battle. Among the portentous signs, the community was thrown into a fever of excitement by the discharge of seven guns from the Capitol Square, the signal for the assembling of all the reserves ten minutes afterwards. Hundreds of men left their beds, hurrying to and fro towards their respective locations. In the absence of sufficient armories, the corners of the streets, the public squares, and other convenient points formed places of meeting. All night long the roll of the drum and the steady tramp of the military and the gallop of the cavalry, resounding through the city, betokened the progress of preparation for the long-expected hostilities. The Home Guard corps of old gentlemen, who occupied the position of military exempts, rode through the city, arousing the soldiers and doing other duty required at the moment. Hundreds of the citizens were up all night. A terrible thunder-storm prevailed until a late hour, but in nowise interfered with the ardor of the soldiers.

On the 12th day of April, at half-past four o'clock in the morning, fire was opened upon Fort Sumter. The firing was deliberate, and was continued, without interruption, for twelve hours. The iron battery at Cumming's Point did the most effective service, perceptibly injuring the walls of the fortification, while the floating battery dismounted two of the parapet guns. The shell batteries were served with skill and effect, shells being thrown into the fort every twenty minutes. The fort had replied steadily during the day. About dark, its fire fell off, while ours was continued at intervals during the night. The contest had been watched during the day by excited and anxious citizens from every available point of observation in Charleston—the battery, the shipping in the harbor, and the steeples of churches—and, as night closed, the illuminations of the shells, as they coursed the air, added a strange sublimity to the scene to men who had never before witnessed the fiery splendors of a bombardment. The next morning, at seven o'clock, the fort resumed its fire, doing no damage of consequence. A short while thereafter, the fort was discovered to be on fire, and through the smoke and glare, its flag was discovered at half mast, as a signal of distress. The Federal fleet, which was off the bar, contrary to all expectations, remained quietly where it was; they did not remove from their anchorage or fire a gun. In the mean time, the conflagration, which had seized upon the officers' quarters and barracks at the fort, continued; it no longer responded to our fire, which was kept up with an anxious look-out for tokens of surrender; its garrison, black and begrimed with smoke, were employed in efforts to extinguish the conflagration, and in some instances had to keep themselves lying upon their faces to avoid death from suffocation. During the height of the conflagration, a boat was dispatched by General Beauregard to Major Anderson, with offers of assistance in extinguishing the fire. Before it could reach the fort, the long-expected flag of truce had been hoisted; and the welcome event was instantly announced in every part of the city by the ringing of bells, the pealing of cannon, the shouts of couriers dashing through the streets, and by every indication of general rejoicing. Major Anderson agreed to an unconditional surrender, as demanded of him; he received of his enemy in return, the most distinguished marks of lenity and consideration: his sword was returned to him by General Beauregard; himself and garrison allowed to take passage, at their convenience, for New York; and, on leaving the fort, he was permitted to salute his flag with fifty guns, the performance of which was attended with the melancholy occurrence of mortal injuries to four of his men by the bursting of two cannon. There was no other life lost in the whole affair.

Thus ended the bombardment of Sumter. It had continued during two days; it was estimated that two thousand shots had been fired in all; a frowning fortification had been reduced to a blackened mass of ruins; and yet not a life had been lost, or a limb injured in the engagement.

The news of the fall of Fort Sumter, when it was received in Washington, did not disturb President Lincoln. He received it with remarkable calmness. The usual drawing-room entertainment at the White House was not intermitted on the evening of the day of the commencement of civil war. The same evening the President turned to a Western Senator and asked, "Will your State sustain me with military power?" He made no other comment on the news, which was agitating every part of the country to its foundation.

The fact was that the President had long ago calculated the result and the effect, on the country, of the hostile movements which he had directed against the sovereignty of South Carolina. He had procured the battle of Sumter; he had no desire or hope to retain the fort: the circumstances of the battle and the non-participation of his fleet in it, were sufficient evidences, to every honest and reflecting mind, that it was not a contest for victory, and that "the sending provisions to a starving garrison" was an ingenious artifice to commence the war that the Federal Government had fully resolved upon, under the specious but shallow appearance of that government being involved by the force of circumstances, rather than by its own volition, in the terrible consequence of civil war.

On the 14th day of April, Mr. Lincoln published his proc

lamation of war. He acted to the last in a sinister spirit. He had just assured the commissioners from Virginia, who had been deputed to ascertain the purposes of his government, that he would modify his inaugural only so far as to "perhaps cause the United States mails to be withdrawn" from the seceded States. The following proclamation was the "modification" of the inaugural:

"Whereas the laws of the United States have been for some time past, and now are, opposed, and the execution thereof obstructed in the States of South Carolina, Georgia, Alabama, Florida, Mississippi, Louisiana, and Texas, by combinations too powerful to be suppressed by the ordinary course of judicial proceeding, or by the powers vested in the Marshals by law—

"Now, therefore, I, Abraham Lincoln, President of the United States, in virtue of the power in me vested by the Constitution and the laws, have thought fit to call forth, and hereby do call forth the militia of the several States of the Union, to the aggregate number of seventy-five thousand, in order to suppress said combinations, and to cause the laws to be duly executed. The details for this object will be immediately communicated to the State authorities through the War Department.

"I appeal to all loyal citizens to favor, facilitate, and aid this effort to maintain the honor, the integrity, and the existence of our National Union, and the perpetuity of popular government, and to redress wrongs already long enough endured.

"I deem it proper to say that the first service assigned to the forces hereby called forth, will probably be to repossess the forts, places, and property which have been seized from the Union; and in every event the utmost care will be observed, consistently with the objects aforesaid, to avoid any devastation and destruction of, or interference with property, or any disturbance of peaceful citizens in any part of the country. And I hereby command the persons composing the combinations aforesaid, to disperse and retire peaceably to their respective abodes within twenty days from this date.
* * * * * * * *
"ABRAHAM LINCOLN."

The trick of the government, to which we have referred, in its procurement of the battle of Sumter, is too dishonest and shallow to account for the immense reaction of sentiment in the North that ensued. That reaction is certainly to be attributed to causes more intelligent and permanent than the weak fallacy that the Lincoln government was not responsible for the hostilities in Charleston harbor, and that the South itself had dragged the government and people of Abraham Lincoln unwillingly into the inauguration of war. The problem of this reaction may be more justly solved. In fact, it involved no new fact or principle. The Northern people, including all parties, secretly appreciated the value of the Union to themselves; they knew that they would be ruined by a permanent secession of the Southern States; many of them had sought to bring the dissatisfied States back into the Union by the old resource of artful speeches and fine promises; and finding, at last, that the South was in earnest, and was no longer to be seduced by cheap professions, they quickly and sharply determined to coerce what they could not cozen. This is the whole explanation of the wonderful reaction. The North discovered, by the fiery *dénouement* in Charleston harbor, that the South was in earnest, and itself became as instantly in earnest. The sudden display of Northern rancor was no reaction; it was no new fact; it revealed what was already historical, and had been concealed only for purposes of policy—the distinct and sharp antipathy between the two sections, of which war or separation, at some time, was bound to be the logical conclusion.

The crusade against the South involved all parties, and united every interest in the North by the common bond of attachment to the Union. That attachment had its own reasons. The idea of the restoration of the Union was conceived in no historical enthusiasm for restoring past glories; it was animated by no patriotic desires contemplating the good of the whole country; the South was to be "whipped back into the Union," to gratify either the selfishness of the North, or its worse lusts of revenge and fanaticism. The holiness of the crusade against the South was preached alike from the hustings and the pulpit. The Northern Democratic party, which had so long professed regard for the rights of the Southern States, and even sympathy with the first movements of their secession, rivalled the Abolitionists in their expressions of fury and revenge; their leaders followed the tide of public opinion: Mr. Edward Everett, of Massachusetts, who some months before had declared in a public speech that if the seceded States were "determined to separate, we had better part in peace," became a rhetorical advocate of the war; Daniel S. Dickinson, of New York, rivalled the Abolition leaders in his State in inflaming the public mind; and in the city of New York, where but a few months before it had been said that the Southern

Confederacy would be able to recruit several regiments for its military service, demagogues in the ranks of the "National Democracy," such as John Cochrane, harangued the multitude, advising them to "crush the rebellion," and, if need be, to drown the whole South in one indiscriminate sea of blood. Old contentions and present animosities were forgotten; Democrats associated with recreants and fanatics in one grand league for one grand purpose; foreigners from Europe were induced into the belief that they were called upon to fight for the "liberty" for which they had crossed the ocean, or for the "free homesteads" which were to be the rewards of the war; and all conceivable and reckless artifices were resorted to to swell the tide of numbers against the South. New England, which had been too conscientious to defend the national honor in the war with Great Britain, poured out almost her whole population to aid in the extermination of a people who had given to the nation all the military glory it had achieved.*

---

* In the war of 1812, the North furnished 58,552 soldiers; the South, 96,812—making a majority of 37,030 in favor of the South. Of the number furnished by the North—

Massachusetts furnished		3,110
New Hampshire	"	897
Connecticut	"	387
Rhode Island	"	637
Vermont	"	181
		5,162

While the little State of South Carolina furnished 5,696.
In the Mexican war,

Massachusetts furnished		1,047
New Hampshire	"	1
The other New England States		0,000
		1,048

The whole number of troops contributed by the North to the Mexican war was 23,054; while the South contributed 43,630, very nearly double, and, in proportion to her population, four times as many soldiers as the North.

When a resolution was introduced into the Legislature of Massachusetts, tendering a vote of thanks to the heroic Lawrence for his capture of the Peacock, that pious State refused to adopt it, and declared—

"'That in a war like the present, waged without justifiable cause, and prosecuted in a manner indicating that *conquest* and ambition are its *real motives*, it is not becoming a moral and religious people to express any approbation of military and naval exploits not directly connected with the defence of our sea coast and our soil."

The effect of Mr. Lincoln's proclamation at the South was no less decisive than at the North. It remains a problem, which facts were never permitted to decide, but the solution of which may at least be approached by the logical considerations of history, to what extent the Border Slave States might have been secured to the Union by the policy of peace, and the simple energy of patience on the part of the government at Washington. As it was, the proclamation presented a new issue; it superseded that of the simple policy of secession; and it inaugurated the *second secessionary movement* of the Southern States on a basis infinitely higher and firmer, in all its moral and constitutional aspects, than that of the first movement of the Cotton States.

The proclamation was received at Montgomery with derisive laughter; the newspapers were refreshed with the Lincolniana of styling sovereign States "unlawful combinations," and warning a people standing on their own soil to return within twenty days to their "homes;" and, in Virginia, the Secessionists were hugely delighted at the strength Mr. Lincoln had unwittingly or perversely contributed to their cause. One after the other of the Border States refused the demands for their quotas in terms of scorn and defiance. Governor Rector, of Arkansas, repudiated the proclamation with an expression of concentrated defiance; Governor Magoffin, of Kentucky, replied, that that State would "furnish no troops for the wicked purpose of subduing her sister Southern States;" Governor Ellis, of North Carolina, telegraphed to Washington, "I can be no party to this wicked violation of the laws of

---

Subsequently the famous Hartford Convention was called. It assembled in the city of Hartford, on the 15th of December, 1814, and remained in session twenty days. It made a report accompanied by a series of resolutions. The following is a part of the report, as adopted:

"In cases of deliberate, dangerous, and palpable infractions of the Constitution, affecting the sovereignty of a State and the liberties of the people, *it is not only the right, but the duty, of each State to interpose its authority for their protection in the manner best calculated to secure that end.* When emergencies occur which are either beyond the reach of judicial tribunals, or too pressing to admit of the delay incident to their forms, States, which have no common umpire, must be *their own judges and execute their own decisions.*"

This is the doctrine which the South had always held from the beginning, and for which the South is now pouring out her blood and treasure

this country, and especially to this war which is being waged upon a free and independent people;" Governor Jackson, of Missouri, replied directly to Mr. Lincoln, "Your requisition in my judgment, is illegal, unconstitutional, and revolutionary and, in its objects, inhuman and diabolical;" and even the unspirited governor of Virginia, John Letcher, constrained by the policy of the time-server to reflect the changes which had become apparent to him in the uprising indignation of the people, ventured upon a remonstrance to President Lincoln, reminding him that his proclamation was "not within the purview of the Constitution or the act of 1795." The only Southern governor that signified any degree of submission to the proclamation was the notorious Thomas Holladay Hicks, of Maryland; he gave verbal assurances to Mr. Lincoln that that State would supply her quota and give him military support; but, at the same time, with an art and effrontery that only a demagogue could attain, he published a proclamation to the people of Maryland, assuring them of his neutrality, and promising that an opportunity would be given them, in the election of congressmen, to determine, of their own free wil', whether they would sustain the old Union, or assist the Southern Confederacy.

On the 17th day of April, the Virginia Convention passed an ordinance of secession. It was an important era in the history of the times. It gave the eighth State to the Southern Confederacy. The position of Virginia was a commanding one with the other Border States; she started, by her act of secession, the second important movement of the revolution; and she added to the moral influence of the event by the fact, that she had not seceded on an issue of policy, but on one of distinct and practical constitutional right, and that too in the face of a war, which had become absolutely inevitable and was frowning upon her own borders.

Virginia had been chided for her delay in following the Cotton States out of the Union, and, on the other hand, when she did secede, she was charged by the Northern politicians with being inconsistent and having kept bad faith in her relations with the Federal government. Both complaints were equally without foundation. The record of the State was singularly explicit and clear.

The Virginia Resolutions of '98 and '99 had for sixty years constituted the text-book of the State Rights politicians of the South. The doctrine of State sovereignty was therein vindicated and maintained, and the right and duty of States, suffering grievances from unjust and unconstitutional Federal legislation, to judge of the wrongs, as well as of "the mode and measure of redress," were made clear. The Virginia platform, as thus laid down in the elder Adams' time, was adopted by the "Strict Constructionist" party of that day, and has been reasserted ever since. Mr. Jefferson, the founder of the Democratic party in this country, was elected upon this platform, and his State Rights successors all acknowledged its orthodoxy. Whenever there arose a conflict between Federal and State authority, the voice of Virginia was the first to be heard in behalf of State Rights. In 1832-33, when the Tariff and Nullification controversy arose, Virginia, though not agreeing with South Carolina as to the particular remedy to which she resorted, yet assured that gallant State of her sympathy, and, at the same time, reasserted her old doctrines of State Rights. Her gallant and patriotic governor, John Floyd, the elder, declared that Federal troops should not pass the banks of the Potomac to coerce South Carolina into obedience to the tariff laws, unless over his dead body. Her Legislature was almost unanimously opposed to the coercion policy, and a majority of that body indicated their recognition of the right of a State to secede from the Union. The voice of Virginia was potential in settling this controversy upon conditions to which the Palmetto State could agree with both honor and consistency. At every stage of the agitation of the slavery question in Congress and in the Northern States, Virginia declared her sentiments and her purposes in a manner not to be misunderstood by friend or foe. Again and again did she enter upon her legislative records, in ineffable characters, the declaration that she would resist the aggressive spirit of the Northern majority, even to the disruption of the ties that bound her to the Union.

With almost entire unanimity, Virginia had resolved in legislative council, in 1848, that she would not submit to the passage of the Wilmot proviso, or any kindred measure. From the date of the organization of the Anti-Slavery party, her people, of all parties, had declared that the election of an Abolitionist to the Presidency would be a virtual declaration of war against the South on the part of the North, and that Virginia and every other Slave State ought to resist it as such. The Legislature that assembled a few weeks after Lincoln's election declared in effect, with only four dissenting voices, that the interests of Virginia were thoroughly identified with those of the other Southern States, and that any intimation, from any source, that her people were looking to any combination in the last resort other than union with them, was unpatriotic and treasonable.

The sovereign Convention of Virginia, elected on the 4th of February, 1861, for a long time lingered in the hope that the breach that had taken place in the Union might be repaired by new constitutional guaranties. Nevertheless, that body, before it had yet determined to pass an ordinance of secession—while it was, in fact, hopeful that the Union would be saved through the returning sanity of the Northern people—adopted unanimously the following resolution:

> "The people of Virginia recognize the American principle, that government is founded in the consent of the governed, and the right of the people of the several States of this Union, for just cause, to withdraw from their association under the Federal government, with the people of the other States, and to erect new governments for their better security; and they never will consent that the Federal power, which is, in part, their power, shall be exerted for the purpose of subjugating the people of such States to the Federal authority."

The entire antecedents of Virginia were known to Mr. Lincoln and his Cabinet. They knew that she was solemnly pledged, at whatever cost, to separate from the Union in the very contingency they had brought about—namely, the attempt to subjugate her sister States of the South. They knew that the original "Union men," as well as the original Secessionists, were committed beyond the possibility of recantation to resistance to the death of any and every *coercive* measure of the Federal government. Nevertheless, Mr. Lincoln and his advisers had the temerity to make a call upon the State of Virginia to furnish her quota of seventy-five thousand men to subjugate the seceded States. They had but little right to be surprised at the course taken by the State, and still less to charge it with inconsistency or perfidy.

It was expected that Maryland might follow the heroic course of Virginia, and but two days after the secession of the latter State, there were indications in Maryland of a spirit of emulation of the daring and adventurous deeds that had been enacted South of the Potomac. On the 19th of April the passage of Northern volunteers, on their way to Washington, was intercepted and assailed by the citizens of Baltimore, and for more than two weeks the route through that city was effectually closed to Mr. Lincoln's mercenaries. The Baltimore "riot," as it was called, was one of the most remarkable collisions of the times. A number of Massachusetts volunteers, passing through Baltimore in horse cars, found the track barricaded near one of the docks by stones, sand, and old anchors thrown upon it, and were compelled to attempt the passage to the depot, at the other end of the city, on foot. They had not advanced fifteen paces after leaving the cars when they found their passage blocked by a crowd of excited citizens, who taunted them as mercenaries, and flouted a Southern flag at the head of their column. Stones were thrown by a portion of the crowd, when the troops presented arms and fired. The crowd was converted into an infuriated mob; the fire was returned from a number of revolvers; the soldiers were attacked with sticks, stones, and every conceivable weapon, and in more than one instance their muskets were actually wrung from their hands by desperate and unarmed men. Unable to withstand the gathering crowd, and bewildered by their mode of attack, the troops pressed along the street confused and staggering, breaking into a run whenever there was an opportunity to do so, and turning at intervals to fire upon the citizens who pursued them. As they reached the depot they found a crowd already collected there and gathering from every point in the city. The other troops of the Massachusetts regiment who had preceded them in the horse cars had been pursued by the people along the route, and the soldiers did not hesitate to stretch themselves at full length on the floors of the cars, to avoid the missiles thrown through the windows. The scene that ensued at the depot was terrific. Taunts, clothed in the most fearful language, were hurled at the troops by the panting crowd who, almost breathless with running, pressed up to the windows, presenting knives and revolvers, and cursing up in the faces of the soldiers. A wild cry was raised on the platform, and a dense crowd rushed out, spreading itself along the railroad track, until for a mile it was black with the excited, rushing mass. The crowd, as they went, filled the track with obstructions; the police who, throughout the whole affair, had contended for order with the most devoted courage, followed in full run removing the obstructions; as far as the eye could reach the track was crowded with the pursuers and pursued, a struggling and shouting mass of human beings. In the midst of the excitement the train moved off; and as it passed from the depot a dozen muskets were fired by the soldiers into the people that lined the track, the volley killing an estimable citizen who had been drawn to the spot only as a spectator. The results of the riot were serious enough: two of the soldiers were shot; several of the citizens had been killed, and more than twenty variously wounded.

The excitement in Baltimore continued for weeks; the bridges on the railroad to the Susquehanna were destroyed; the regular route of travel broken up, and some twenty or twenty-five thousand Northern volunteers, on their way to Washington, detained at Havre de Grace, a portion of them only managing to reach their destination by the way of Annapolis. On the night of the day of the riot, a mass-meeting was held in Monument Square, and was addressed by urgent appeals for the secession of Maryland, and speeches of defiance to the Lincoln government. Governor Hicks, alarmed by the display of public sentiment, affected to yield to it. He addressed the crowd in person, condemning the coercive policy of the government, and ending with the fervid declaration, " I will suffer my right arm to be torn from my body before I will raise it to strike a sister State." The same man, in less than a month thereafter, when Maryland had fallen within the grasp of the Federal government, did not hesitate to make a call upon the people for four regiments of volunteers to assist that government in its then fully declared policy of a war of invasion and fell destruction upon the South.

In the city of St. Louis there were collisions between the citizens and soldiery as well as in Baltimore; but in Missouri the indications of sympathy with the South did not subside or allow themselves to be choked by spectral fears of the " crucial experiment of secession"—they grew and strengthened in the face of all the Federal power could do.

The riots in Maryland and Missouri were, however, only incidents in the history of the period in which they occurred That history is occupied with far more important and general events, indicating the increased and rapid preparations, North and South, for war; the collection of resources, and the policy and spirit in which the gathering contest was to be conducted.

Mr. Lincoln had, on the 19th of April, published his proclamation, declaring the ports of the Southern Confederacy in a state of blockade, and denouncing any molestation of Federal vessels on the high seas as piracy. The Provisional Congress at Montgomery had formerly recognized the existence of war with the North, and letters of marque had been issued by the Confederate authority. The theatre of the war on land was indicated in Virginia. General Lee, who had resigned a commission as colonel of cavalry in the old United States army, was put in command of all the Confederate States forces in Virginia.

That State was the particular object of the rancor of the government at Washington, which proceeded to inaugurate hostilities on her territory by two acts of ruthless vandalism. On the 19th day of April the Federals evacuated Harper's Ferry, after an attempt to destroy the buildings and machine-shops there, which only partially succeeded—the armory buildings being destroyed, but a train to blow up the machine-shop failed, and a large quantity of valuable machinery was uninjured. On the succeeding day, preparations were made for the destruction of the Navy Yard at Norfolk, while Federal reinforcements were thrown into Fortress Monroe. The work of vandalism was not as fully completed as the enemy had designed, the dry-dock, which alone cost several millions of dollars, being but little damaged; but the destruction of property was immense, and attended by a terrible conflagration, which at one time threatened the city of Norfolk.

All the ships in the harbor, excepting the old frigate the United States, were set fire to and scuttled. They were the Pennsylvania, the Columbus and Delaware, the steam-frigate Merrimac (she was only partially destroyed), the sloops Germantown and Plymouth, the frigates Raritan and Columbia, and the brig Dolphin. The Germantown was lying at the wharf under a large pair of shears, which were thrown across her decks by cutting loose the guys. The ship was nearly cut in two and sunk at the wharf. About midnight an alarm was given that the Navy Yard was on fire. A sickly blaze, that seemed neither to diminish nor increase, continued for several hours. Men were kept busy all night transferring every thing of value from the Pennsylvania and Navy Yard to the Pawnee and Cumberland, and both vessels were loaded to their lower ports. At length four o'clock came, and with it flood-tide. A rocket shot up from the Pawnee, and then, almost in an instant, the whole front of the Navy Yard seemed one vast sheet of flame. The next minute streaks of flame flashed along the rigging of the Pennsylvania and the other doomed ships, and soon they were completely wrapped in the devouring element. The harbor was now one blaze of light. The remotest objects were distinctly visible. The surging flames leaped and roared with mad violence, making their hoarse wrath heard at the distance of several miles. The people of Hampton, even those who lived beyond, saw the red light, and thought all Norfolk was on fire. It was certainly a grand though terrible spectacle to witness. In the midst of the brilliance of the scene, the Pawnee with the Cumberland in tow, stole like a guilty thing through the harbor, fleeing from the destruction they had been sent to accomplish.

The Lincoln government had reason to be exasperated towards Virginia. The second secessionary movement, commenced by that State, added three other States to the Southern Confederacy. Tennessee seceded from the Union, the 6th of May; on the 18th day of May, the State of Arkansas was formally admitted into the Southern Confederacy; and on the 21st of the same month, the sovereign Convention of North Carolina, without delay, and by a unanimous vote, passed an ordinance of secession.

The spirit of the rival governments gave indications to discerning minds of a civil war of gigantic proportions, infinite consequences, and indefinite duration. In every portion of the South, the most patriotic devotion was exhibited. Transportation companies freely tendered the use of their lines for transportation and supplies. The presidents of the Southern railroads consented not only to reduce their rates for mail service and conveyance for troops and munitions of war, but voluntarily proffered to take their compensation in bonds of the Confederacy, for the purpose of leaving all the resources of the government at its disposal for the common defence. Under the act of the Provisional Congress authorizing a loan, proposals issued for the subscription of five millions of dollars were answered by the prompt subscription of more than eight millions by its own citizens; and not a bid was made under par. Requisitions for troops were met with such alacrity that the number in every instance, tendering their services, exceeded the demand. Under the bill for public defence, one hundred thousand volunteers were authorized to be accepted by the Confederate States government 'for a twelve months' term of service. The gravity of age and the zeal of youth rivalled each other to be foremost in the public service; every village bristled with bayonets; large forces were put in the field at Charleston, Pensacola, Forts Morgan, Jackson, St. Philip, and Pulaski; while formidable numbers from all parts of the Confederacy were gathered in Virginia, on what was now becoming the immediate theatre of the war. On the 20th day of May, the seat of government was removed from Montgomery, Alabama, to Richmond, Virginia, and President Davis was welcomed in the latter city with a burst of genuine joy and enthusiasm, to which none of the military pageants of the North could furnish a parallel.

It had been supposed that the Southern people, poor in manufactures as they were, and in the haste of preparation for the mighty contest that was to ensue, would find themselves but illy provided with arms to contend with an enemy rich in the means and munitions of war. This disadvantage had been provided against by the timely act of one man. Mr. Floyd, of Virginia, when Secretary of War under Mr. Buchanan's administration, had by a single order effected the transfer of 115,000 improved muskets and rifles from the Springfield armory and Watervliet arsenal to different arsenals at the South. Adding to these the number of arms distributed by the Federal government to the States in preceding years of our history, and those purchased by the States and citizens, it was safely estimated that the South entered upon the war with one hun dred and fifty thousand small-arms of the most approved modern pattern and the best in the world.

The government at Washington rapidly collected in that city a vast and motley army. Baltimore had been subdued; the route through it was restored; and such were the facilities of Northern transportation, that it was estimated that not less than four or five thousand volunteers were transported through the former Thermopylæ of Baltimore in a single day. The first evidences of the despotic purposes of the Lincoln government were exhibited in Maryland, and the characteristics of the war that it had commenced on the South were first displayed in the crushing weight of tyranny and oppression it laid upon a State which submitted before it was conquered.

The Legislature of Maryland did nothing practical. It was unable to arm the State, and it made no attempt to improve the spirit of the people, or to make preparations for any future opportunity of action. It assented to the attitude of submission indefinitely. It passed resolutions protesting against the military occupation of the State by the Federal government, and indicating sympathy with the South, but concluding with the declaration: "under existing circumstances, it is inexpedient to call a sovereign Convention of the State at this time, or take any measures for the immediate organization or arming of the militia." The government of Abraham Lincoln was not a government to spare submission or to be moved to magnanimity by the helplessness of a supposed enemy. The submission of Maryland was the signal for its persecution. By the middle of May, her territory was occupied by thirty thousand Federal troops; her quota of troops to the war was demanded at Washington, and was urged by a requisition of her obsequious governor; the city of Baltimore was invested by General Butler of Massachusetts, houses and stores searched for concealed arms, and the liberties of the people violated, with every possible addition of mortification and insult.

In a few weeks the rapid and aggravated progression of acts of despotism on the part of the Lincoln government reached its height in Maryland. The authority of the mayor and police board of the city of Baltimore was superseded, and their persons seized and imprisoned in a military fortress; the writ of *habeas corpus* was suspended by the single and unconstitutional authority of the President; the houses of suspected citizens were searched, and they themselves arrested by military force, in jurisdictions where the Federal courts were in uninterrupted operation; blank warrants were issued for domiciliary visits; and the sanctity of private correspondence was violated by seizing the dispatches preserved for years in the telegraph offices of the North, and making them the subject of inquisition for the purpose of discovering and punishing as traitors men who had dared to reproach the Northern government for an unnatural war, or had not sympathized with its rancor and excesses.

Such was the inauguration of "the strong government" of Abraham Lincoln in Maryland, and the repetition of its acts was threatened upon the "rebel" States of the South, with the addition that their cities were to be laid in ashes, their soil sown with blood, the slaves freed and carried in battalions against their masters, and "the rebels" doomed, after their subjection, to return home to find their wives and children in rags, and gaunt Famine sitting at their firesides.

CHAPTER III.

Confidence of the North.—Characteristic Boasts.—"Crushing out the Rebellion."—Volunteering in the Northern Cities.—The New York "Invincibles."—Misrepresentations of the Government at Washington.—Mr. Seward's Letter to the French Government.—Another Call for Federal Volunteers.—Opening Movements of the Campaign.—The Federal Occupation of Alexandria.—Death of Col. Ellsworth.—Fortress Monroe.—The BATTLE OF BETHEL.—Results of this Battle.—Gen. Joseph E. Johnston.—The Upper Potomac.—Evacuation and Destruction of Harper's Ferry.—The Movements in the Upper Portion of the Valley of Virginia.—Northwestern Virginia.—The BATTLE OF RICH MOUNTAIN.—Carrock's Ford.—The Retreat of the Confederates.—General McClellan.—Meeting of the Federal Congress.—Mr. Lincoln's Message.—Kentucky.—Western Virginia.—Large Requisitions for Men and Money by the Federal Government.—Its Financial Condition.—Financial Measures of the Southern Confederacy.—Contrast between the Ideas of the Rival Governments.—Conservatism of the Southern Revolution.—Despotic Excesses of the Government at Washington.

NOTHING could exceed the boastful and unlimited expressions of confidence on the part of the Northern people, in the speedy "crushing out of the rebellion," and of contempt for the means and resources of the South to carry on any thing like a formidable war. In the light of subsequent events, these expressions and vaunts give a grotesque illustration of the ideas with which the Northern people entered upon the war.

The New York people derided the rebellion. The *Tribune* declared that it was nothing "more or less than the natural recourse of all mean-spirited and defeated tyrannies to rule or ruin, making, of course, a wide distinction between the will and power, for the hanging of traitors is sure to begin before one month is over." "The nations of Europe," it continued, 'may rest assured that Jeff. Davis & Co. will be swinging from the battlements at Washington, at least, by the 4th of July. We spit upon a later and longer deferred justice."

The New York *Times* gave its opinion in the following vigorous and confident spirit: "Let us make quick work. The 'rebellion,' as some people designate it, is an unborn tadpole. Let us not fall into the delusion, noted by Hallam, of mistaking a 'local commotion' for a revolution. A strong active 'pull together' will do our work effectually in thirty days. We have only to send a column of 25,000 men across the Potomac to Richmond, and burn out the rats there; another column of 25,000 to Cairo, seizing the cotton ports of the Mississippi; and retaining the remaining 25,000, included in Mr. Lincoln's call for 75,000 men, at Washington, not because there is need for them there, but because we do not require their services elsewhere."

The Philadelphia *Press* declared that "no man of sense could, for a moment, doubt that this much-ado-about-nothing would end in a month." The Northern people were "simply invincible." "The rebels," it prophesied, "a mere band of ragamuffins, will fly, like chaff before the wind, on our approach."

The West was as violent as the North or the East. In the States of Iowa and Wisconsin, among the infidel Dutch, no rein was drawn upon the wild fanaticism. In Illinois, too, there was a fever of morbid violence. The Chicago *Tribune* insisted on its demand that the West be allowed to fight the battle through, since she was probably the most interested in the suppression of the rebellion and the free navigation of the Mississippi. "Let the East," demanded this valorous sheet, "get out of the way; this is a war of the West. We can fight the battle, and successfully, within two or three months at the furthest. Illinois can whip the South by herself. We insist on the matter being turned over to us."

The Cincinnati *Commercial*, in commenting upon the claims of the West, remarked that "the West ought to be made the vanguard of the war"—and proceeded: "We are akin, by trade and geography, with Kentucky, Tennessee, and Missouri, and in sentiment to the noble Union patriots who have a majority of three to one in all these States. An Ohio army would be received with joy in Nashville, and welcomed in a speech of congratulation by Andrew Johnson. Crittenden and Frank Blair are keeping Kentucky and Missouri all right. The rebellion will be crushed out before the assemblage of Congress —no doubt of it."

Not a paper of influence in the North, at that time, had the remotest idea of the conflict; not a journalist who rose to the emergencies of the occasion—all was passion, rant, and bombast.

In the Northern cities, going to the war for "three months," the term of the enlistment of volunteers, was looked upon almost as a holiday recreation. In New York and Philadelphia, the recruiting offices were besieged by firemen, rowdies, and men fished from the purlieus of vice, and every sink of degradation. There appeared to be no serious realization of the war. If a man ventured the opinion that a hundred thousand Southern troops might be gathered in Virginia, he was laughed at, or answered with stories about the Adirondack sharpshooters and the New York "roughs." The newspapers declared that the most terrible and invincible army that ever enacted deeds of war might be gathered from the "roughs" of the Northern cities. Nothing could compete with their desperate courage, and nothing could withstand their furious onslaught. A regiment of firemen and congenial spirits was raised in New York, and put under command of Colonel Ellsworth, of Chicago, a youth, who had some time ago exhibited through the country a company of young men drilled in the manual and exercises of the French Zouaves, who had made himself a favorite with the ladies at the Astor House and Willard's Hotel, by his long hair, gymnastic grace, and red uniform, and who boasted of a great deal of political influence as the pet and *protégé* of President Lincoln. To the standard of this young man, and also to that of a notorious bully and marauder, by the name of Billy Wilson, flocked all the vagrant and unruly classes of the great and vicious metropolis of New York. The latter boasted, that when his regiment was moved off, it would be found that not a thief, highwayman, or pickpocket would be left in the city. The people of New York and Washington were strangely enraptured with the spectacle of these terrible and ruthless crusaders, who were to strike terror to the hearts of the Southern people. Anecdotes of their rude and desperate disposition, their brutal speeches and their exploits of rowdyism, were told with glee and devoured with unnatural satisfaction. In Washington, people were delighted by anecdotes that Ellsworth's Zouaves made a practice of knocking their officers down; that their usual address to the sentinels was, "Say, fellow, I am agoin' to leave this ranch;" that on rainy days they seized umbrellas from citizens on th streets, and knocked them in the gutter if they remonstrated; that, "in the most entire good humor," they levied contributions of boots, shoes, liquors, and cigars on tradesmen; and that the "gallant little colonel," who controlled these unruly spirits, habitually wore a bowie knife two feet long. These freaks and eccentricities were not only excusable, they were admirable: the untamed courage of the New York firemen and rowdies, said the people, were to be so useful and conspicuous in the war; and the prophecy was, that these men, so troublesome and belligerent towards quiet citizens who came in contact with them, would be the first to win honorable laurels on the field of combat.

"Billy Wilson's" regiment was held up for a long time in New York as an inimitable scarecrow to the South. The regiment was displayed on every occasion; it was frequently marched up Broadway to pay visits to the principal hotels. On one of these occasions, it was related that Billy Wilson marched the companies into the hall and spacious bar-room of the hotel, and issued the order "Attention." Attention was paid, and the bystanders preserved silence. "Kneel down," shouted the colonel. The men dropped upon their knees. "You do solemnly swear to cut off the head of every d——d Secessionist you meet during the war." "We swear," was the universal response. "The gallant souls," said a New York paper, "then returned in good order to their quarters."

The newspaper extracts and incidents given above afford no little illustration of the spirit in which the North entered upon the war, and, in this connection, belong to the faithful history of the times. That spirit was not only trivial and utterly beneath the dignity of the contest upon which the North was to enter; it betrayed a fierceness and venom, the monstrous developments of which were reserved for a period later in the progress of events.

What was partly ignorance and partly affectation on the part of the Northern press and people, in their light estimation of the war, was wholly affectation on the part of the intelligent and better informed authorities at Washington. The government had a particular object in essaying to represent the Southern revolution as nothing more than a local mutiny. The necessity was plain for balking any thing like a European recognition of the Southern Confederacy, and Mr. Seward was prompt to rank the rebellion as a local and disorganized insurrection, amounting to nothing more than a passing and incidental "change" in the history of the Union. At the time that all the resources of the government were put out to encounter the gathering armies of the South, already within a few miles of the capital, Mr. Seward, in a letter of instructions to Mr. Dayton, the recently appointed minister to France, dated the 4th of May, urged him to assure that government of the fact that an idea of a permanent disruption of the Union was absurd; that the continuance of the Union was certain, and that too as an object of "*affection!*" He wrote: "The thought of a dissolution of this Union, peaceably or by force, has never entered into the mind of any candid statesman here, and it is high time that it be dismissed by the statesmen in Europe."

The government at Washington evidently showed, by its preparations, that it was secretly conscious of the resources and determined purposes of the revolution. Another proclamation for still further increasing his military forces had been made by Mr. Lincoln on the third of May. He called for forty-odd thousand additional volunteers to enlist for the war, and eighteen thousand seamen, besides increasing the regular army by the addition of ten regiments. It is curious that these immense preparations should have attracted such little notice from the Northern public. The people and soldiers appeared to be alike hilarious and confident in the prospect of a "short, sharp, and decisive" war, that was to restore the Union, open the doors of the treasury, give promotion and fame to those desirous of gain in those particulars, and afford new opportunities to adventurers of all classes.

The first and opening movements of the Northern campaign were decided to be a forward movement from the Potomac along the Orange and Alexandria and Central roads towards Richmond, while another invading army might be thrown into the Valley of Virginia from Pennsylvania and Maryland.

The first step of the invasion of Virginia was the occupation of Alexandria, which was accomplished on the 24th of May, by throwing some eight thousand Federal troops across the Potomac, the Virginia forces evacuating the town and falling back to the Manassas Junction, where General Bonham, of South Carolina, was in command of the Confederate forces.

The invasion was accomplished under cover of the night, and with such secrecy and dispatch, that a number of Virginia cavalry troops were found, unconscious of danger, at their quarters, and were taken prisoners.

The Federal occupation of the town was attended by a dramatic incident, the heroism and chivalry of which gave a remarkable lesson to the invader of the spirit that was to oppose his progress on the soil of Virginia. In the gray of the morning, Col. Ellsworth, who, with his Fire Zouaves, had entered the town, observed a Confederate flag floating from the top of an hotel called the Marshall House, and attended by a squad of his men, determined to secure it as his prize. He found his way into the hotel, ascended the stairs, and climbed, by a ladder, to the top of the house, where he secured the obnoxious ensign. As he was descending from the trap-door, with the flag on his arm, he was confronted by Mr. Jackson, the proprietor of the hotel, who, aroused from his bed by the unusual noise, half dressed and in his shirt-sleeves, with a double-barrel gun in his hands, faced Ellsworth and his four companions with a quiet and settled determination. "This is my trophy," said the Federal commander, pointing to the flag. "And you are mine," responded the Virginian, as, with a quick aim he discharged his gun full into the breast of Colonel Ellsworth, and the next instant sank by his side a breathless corpse, from a bullet, sped through the brain, and a bayonet-thrust at the hands of one of the soldiers.

The slayer of Colonel Ellsworth was branded, in the North, as an "assassin." The justice of history does not permit such a term to be applied to a man who defended his country's flag and the integrity of his home with his life, distinctly and fearlessly offered up to such objects of honor: it gives him the name which the Southern people hastened to bestow upon the memory of the heroic Jackson—that of "martyr." The character of this man is said to have been full of traits of rude, native chivalry. He was captain of an artillery company in his town. He was known to his neighbors as a person who united a dauntless and unyielding courage with the most generous impulses. A week before his death a "Union" man from Washington had been seized in the streets of Alexandria, and a crowd threatened to shoot or hang him, when Jackson went to his rescue, threatened to kill any man who would molest him, and saved him from the vengeance of the mob. A day before the Federal occupation of the town, in a conversation in which some such movement was conjectured, his neighbors remonstrated with him about the danger of making his house a sign for the enemy's attack, by the flag which floated over it. He replied that he would sacrifice his life in keeping the flag flying—and by daybreak the next day the oath was fulfilled. He laid down his life, not in the excitement of passion, but coolly and deliberately, upon a principle, and as an example in defending the sacred rights of his home and the flag of his country. This noble act of heroism did not fail to move the hearts of the generous people of the South; a monument was proposed to the memory of the only hero of Alexandria; the dramatic story, and the patriotic example of "the martyr Jackson," were not lost sight of in the stormy excitements of the war that swept out of the mind so many incidents of its early history; and in most of the cities of the South practical evidences of regard were given in large, voluntary subscriptions to his bereaved family.

The Federal forces were not met in Alexandria with any of those demonstrations of "Union" sentiment which they had been induced, by the misrepresentations of the Northern press, to expect would hail the vanguard of their invasion of the South. The shouts and yells of the invaders fell upon the ears of a sullen people, who shut themselves up in their houses, as much to avoid the grating exultations of their enemies as contact with the rowdyism and riot that had taken possession of the streets. On coming into the town, the New York troops, particularly the Fire Zouaves, ran all over the city with their usual cry of "Hi," "Hi." Citizens closed their doors, and as the news of the tragedy at the Marshall House spread over the town, it assumed an aspect like that of the Sabbath. About the wharves and warehouses, where hitherto the life and excitement of the town had been concentrated, the silence was absolutely oppressive; and the only people to be seen were numbers of negroes, who stood about the wharves and on the street corners with frightened faces, talking in low tones to each other.

With Alexandria and Fortress Monroe in its possession, the

Federal Government held the most important passages into Virginia. General McDowell was charged with the command of the division of the forces thrown across the Potomac. General Butler was placed in command at Fortress Monroe. The town of Hampton was occupied by the Federal troops, and Newport News, at the mouth of the James River, invested by them. At Sewell's Point, some eight or ten miles distant on the other side, the Confederates had erected a powerful battery, which had proved its efficiency and strength by resisting an attack made upon it on the 19th of May, and continued for two days, by the Federal steamer Monticello, aided by the Minnesota.

The first serious contest of the war was to occur in the low country of Virginia. On the 10th of June the battle of Bethel was fought.

THE BATTLE OF BETHEL.

The Confederates, to the number of about eighteen hundred, under Colonel J. Bankhead Magruder, were intrenched at Great Bethel church, which was about nine miles on the road leading south from Hampton. A Federal force exceeding four thousand men, under General Pierce—a Massachusetts officer who was never afterwards heard of in the war—was moved towards Bethel in two separate bodies, a portion landing on the extreme side of the creek, some distance below, while the rest proceeded across the creek. The landing of the latter was effected without opposition, and presently the Federal troops, who had marched up from below, closed in on the Confederates almost simultaneously with those attacking their front.

The attack was received by a battery of the Richmond Howitzers, under command of Major Randolph; the action being commenced by a shot from the Parrott gun in our main battery aimed by himself. One of the guns of the battery being spiked by the breaking of a priming wire in the vent, the infantry supports were withdrawn, and the work was occupied for a moment by the enemy. Captain Bridges, of the 1st North Carolina regiment, was ordered to retake it. The charge of the North Carolina infantry, on this occasion, was the most brilliant incident of the day. They advanced calmly and coolly in the face of a sheet of artillery fire, and when within sixty yards of the enemy dashed on at the double quick. The Federals fell back in dismay.

The enemy continued to fire briskly, but wildly, with his artillery. At no time, during the artillery engagement, could the Confederates see the bodies of the men in the column of attack, and their fire was directed by the bayonets of the enemy. The position of the enemy was obscured by the shade of the woods on their right and two small houses on their left. The fire of the Confederates was returned by a battery near the head of the enemy's column, but concealed by the woods and the houses so effectually that the Confederates only ascertained its position by the flash of the pieces.

The earthworks were struck several times by the shots of the Federals. They fired upon us with shot, shell, spherical case, canister, and grape, from six and twelve pounders, at a distance of six hundred yards. The only injury received from their artillery was the loss of a mule. The fire on our part was deliberate, and was suspended whenever masses of the enemy were not within range. From 9 o'clock A. M. until 1:30 P. M. but ninety-eight shot were fired by us, every one of them with deliberation.

After some intermission of the assault in front, a heavy column, apparently a reinforcement or a reserve, made its appearance on the Hampton road and pressed forward towards the bridge, carrying the United States flag at its head. This column was under command of Major Winthrop, aid to General Butler. Those in advance had put on the distinctive badge of the Confederates—a white band around the cap. They cried out repeatedly, "don't fire." Having crossed the creek, they began to cheer most lustily, thinking that our work was open at the gorge, and that they might get in by a sudden rush. The North Carolina infantry, however, dispelled this illusion. Their firing was as cool as that of veterans; the only difficulty being the anxiety of the riflemen to pick off the foe, the men repeatedly calling to their officers, "May I fire? I think I can bring him."

As the enemy fell back in disorder and his final rout commenced, the bullet of a North Carolina rifleman pierced the breast of the brave Federal officer Major Winthrop, who had made himself a conspicuous mark by his gallantry on the field. "He was," says Colonel Hill, of the North Carolina regiment, in his official report of the action, "the only one of the enemy who exhibited even an approximation to courage during the whole day." The fact was, that he had fallen in circumstances of great gallantry. He was shot while standing on a log, waving his sword and vainly attempting to rally his men to the charge. His enemy did honor to his memory; and the Southern people, who had been unable to appreciate the courage of Ellsworth, and turned with disgust from his apotheosis in the North, did not fail to pay the tribute due a truly brave man to the gallant Winthrop, who, having simply died on the battle-field, without the sensational circumstances of a private brawl or a bully's adventure, was soon forgotten in the North.

During the fight at the angle of our works, a small wooden house in front was thought to give protection to the enemy. Four privates in the North Carolina regiment volunteered to advance beyond our lines and set it on fire. One of them, a youth named Henry L. Wyatt, advanced ahead of his companions, and, as he passed between the two fires, he fell pierced by a musket-ball in the forehead, within thirty yards of the house. This was our only loss in killed during the entire engagement.

The results of the battle of Bethel were generally magnified in the South. It is true that a Confederate force of some eighteen hundred men, in a contest of several hours with an enemy more than twice their numbers, had repulsed them; that the entire loss of the former was only one man killed and seven wounded, while that of the enemy, by their own acknowledgment, was thirty killed and more than one hundred wounded. The fact, however, was, that our troops had fought under the impenetrable cover of their batteries, the only instance of exposure being that of the North Carolina infantry, who, by their charge on the redoubt taken by the enemy early in the action, contributed, most of all, to the success and glory of the day. The battle had been the result of scarcely any thing more than a reconnoissance; it was by no means to be ranked as a decisive engagement, and yet it was certainly a serious and well-timed check to the foe.

In one respect, however, the result was not magnified, and

that was in its contribution of confidence and ardor to the South.. Thus regarded, it was an important event, and its effects of the happiest kind. The victory was achieved at a time when the public mind was distressed and anxious on account of the constant backward movements of our forces in Virginia, and the oft-recurring story of "surprise" and consequent disaster to our troops in the neighborhood of the enemy's lines. The surrender of Alexandria, the surprise and dispersion of a camp at Philippi by a body of Federal troops,*

---

* The disaster at Philippi was inconsiderable; but it was the subject of some recrimination at the time, and Colonel Porterfield, the Confederate commander, was subjected to a court-martial, which, in the main, exonerated him, and complimented him for his courage. Colonel Porterfield had been ordered to Grafton about the middle of May, 1861, with written instructions from General Lee to call for volunteers from that part of the State, and receive them into the service, to the number of five thousand; and to co-operate with the agents of the Baltimore and Ohio railroad; and with verbal orders to try to conciliate the people of that section, and to do nothing to offend them. Finding, soon after his arrival, that the country was in a state of revolution, and that there was a large and increasing Federal force at Camp Denison, in Ohio, opposite Parkersburg, and another in the vicinity of Wheeling, Colonel Porterfield wrote to the commanding general, that unless a strong force was sent very soon, Northwestern Virginia would be overrun.

Upon directing the captains of organized volunteer companies to proceed with their companies to Grafton, they replied that not more than twenty in companies numbering sixty were willing to take up arms on the side of the State; that the others declared, if they were compelled to fight, it would be in defence of the Union. Colonel Porterfield succeeded in a week in getting together three newly-organized companies. This force was increased by the arrival of several other companies, two of which were unarmed cavalry companies—amounting in all to about 500 infantry and 150 cavalry. These troops had been at Grafton but a few days, when, or about the 25th of May, Colonel Porterfield was reliably informed of the force of the enemy and withdrew his command to Philippi. Orders were given for the destruction of the Cheat bridge, but were not executed. The enemy's force at Grafton was about eight thousand men. On the 3d of June, through the failure of the guard or infantry pickets to give the alarm, the command at Philippi was surprised by about five thousand infantry and a battery of artillery, and dispersed in great confusion, but with inconsiderable loss of life, through the woods. The command had no equipments and very little ammunition. Such was the inauguration of the improvident and unfortunate campaign in Western Virginia.

General Garnett succeeded Colonel Porterfield in the command in Northwestern Virginia, with a much larger force (about six thousand men), but one obviously inadequate, considering the extent of the district it was expected to defend, the hostile character of the country, and the invading forces of the enemy.

and the apparently uncertain movements of our forces on the Upper Potomac, had unpleasantly exercised the popular mind, and had given rise to many rash and ignorant doubts with respect to the opening events of the war. The battle of Bethel was the first to turn the hateful current of retreat, and sent the first gleam of sunlight through the sombre shadows that had hung over public opinion in the South.

It is certain that the movements on the Upper Potomac were greatly misunderstood at the time, especially with regard to the evacuation of Harper's Ferry. General Joseph E. Johnston, who had been a quartermaster-general in the old United States service, and had resigned to take part in the defence of his native State, Virginia, had assumed command at Harper's Ferry, on the 23d of May. On the 27th of the same month, General Beauregard had relinquished his command at Charleston, being assigned to duty at Corinth, Mississippi; but, the order being recalled, he was put in command at Manassas, our forces being divided into what was known as the armies of the Potomac and of the Shenandoah. At the time General Johnston took command at Harper's Ferry, the forces at that point consisted of nine regiments and two battalions of infantry, with four companies of artillery—a force which was certainly not sufficient, when we consider that it was expected to hold both sides of the Potomac, and take the field against an invading army. After a complete reconnoissance of the place and environs, General Johnston decided that it was untenable, but determined to hold it until the great objects of the government required its abandonment.

The demonstrations of the Federal forces in the direction of the Valley of Virginia were certainly thwarted by the timely falling back of our army from Harper's Ferry to Winchester. General Patterson's approach was expected by the great route into the Valley from Pennsylvania and Maryland, leading through Winchester, and it was an object of the utmost importance to prevent any junction between his forces and those of General McClellan, who was already making his way into the upper portions of the Valley. On the morning of the 13th of June, information was received from Winchester that Romney was occupied by two thousand Federal troops, supposed to be the vanguard of McClellan's army. A detachment was dispatched by railway to check the advance of the enemy; and on the morning of the 15th, the Confederate army left Harper's Ferry for Winchester.

The next morning, after the orders were issued for the evacuation of Harper's Ferry, brought one of those wild, fearful scenes which make the desolation that grows out of war. The splendid railroad bridge across the Potomac—one of the most superb structures of its kind on the continent—was set on fire at its northern end, while about four hundred feet at its southern extremity was blown up, to prevent the flames from reaching other works which it was necessary to save. Many of the vast buildings were consigned to the flames. Some of them were not only large, but very lofty, and crowned with tall towers and spires, and we may be able to fancy the sublimity of the scene, when more than a dozen of these huge fabrics, crowded into a small space, were blazing at once. So great was the heat and smoke, that many of the troops were forced out of the town, and the necessary labors of the removal were performed with the greatest difficulty.

On the morning of the day after the evacuation of Harper's Ferry, intelligence was received that General Patterson's army had crossed the Potomac at Williamsport; also that the Federal force at Romney had fallen back. The Confederate army was ordered to gain the Martinsburg turnpike by a flank movement to Bunker's Hill, in order to place itself between Winchester and the expected advance of Patterson. On hearing of this, the enemy crossed the river precipitately. Resuming his first direction and plan, General Johnston proceeded to Winchester. There his army was in position to oppose either McClellan from the West, or Patterson from the North-east, and to form a junction with General Beauregard when necessary.

Intelligence from Maryland indicating another movement by Patterson, Colonel Jackson with his brigade was sent to the neighborhood of Martinsburg to support Colonel Stuart, who had been placed in observation on the line of the Potomac with his cavalry. On the 2d of July, General Patterson again crossed the Potomac. Colonel Jackson, pursuant to instructions, again fell back before him; but, in retiring, gave him a severe lesson. With a battalion of the Fifth Virginia Regiment and Pendleton's Battery of Field Artillery, he engaged the enemy's advance. Skilfully taking a position where the smallness of his force was concealed, he engaged them for a considerable time, inflicted a heavy loss, and retired when about to be outflanked, scarcely losing a man, but bringing off forty-five prisoners.

Upon this intelligence, the force at Winchester, strengthened by the arrival of General Bee and Colonel Elzey and the Ninth Georgia regiment, were ordered forward to the support of Jackson, who, it was supposed, was closely followed by General Patterson. Taking up a position within six miles from Martinsburg, which town the enemy had invested, General Johnston waited for him four days, hoping to be attacked by an adversary double his number. Convinced at length that the enemy would not approach him, General Johnston returned to Winchester, much to the disappointment of his troops, who, sullen and discontented, withdrew in the face of the enemy.

On the 15th of July, Colonel Stuart, who, with his cavalry, remained near the enemy, reported the advance of General Patterson from Martinsburg. He halted, however, at Bunker's Hill, nine miles from Winchester, where he remained on the 16th. On the 17th, he moved his left to Smithfield. This movement created the impression that an attack was intended on the south of the Confederate lines; but, with a clear and quick intelligence, General Johnston had penetrated the designs of the enemy, which were to hold him in check, while "the Grand Army" under McDowell was to bear down upon General Beauregard at Manassas.

In the mean time, General McClellan's army had moved southwestward from Grafton. In the progress of the history of the war, we shall meet with frequent repetitions of the lesson of how the improvident spirit of the South, in placing small forces in isolated localities, was taken advantage of by the quick strategic movements and the overwhelming numbers of the North. The first of the series of these characteristic disasters was now to befall the South.

THE BATTLE OF RICH MOUNTAIN.

The main column of Federal troops under General McClellan was estimated to be twenty thousand strong; his movements were now directed towards Beverley, with the object of getting to the rear of General Garnett, who had been appointed to the command of the Confederate forces in Northwestern Virginia, and was occupying a strong position at Rich Mountain, in Randolph county.

The strength of General Garnett's command was less than five thousand infantry, with ten pieces of artillery, and four companies of cavalry. The disposition of these forces was in the immediate vicinity of Rich Mountain. Col. Pegram occupied the mountain with a force of about sixteen hundred men and some pieces of artillery. On the slopes of Laurel Hill, General Garnett was intrenched with a force of three thousand infantry, six pieces of artillery and three companies of cavalry.

On the 5th of July, the enemy took a position at Bealington, in front of Laurel Hill, and a day or two afterwards a large force appeared in front of Rich Mountain.

On the morning of the 11th instant, General Garnett received a note from Colonel Pegram at Rich Mountain, stating that his pickets had that morning taken a prisoner, who stated that there were in front of Rich Mountain nine regiments of seven thousand men and a number of pieces of artillery; that General McClellan had arrived in camp the evening before, and had given orders for an attack the next day; that General Rosecrans had started a night before with a division of the army three thousand strong, by a convenient route, to take him in the rear, while McClellan was to attack in front; that he had moved a piece of artillery and three hundred men to the point by which General Rosecrans was expected, and that he had requested Colonel Scott, with his regiment, to occupy a position on the path by which the enemy must come. As soon as General Garnett received this note, he sent a written order to Colonel Scott to move to the point indicated by Colonel Pegram, and to defend it at all hazards.

The attack on Colonel Pegram was met with the most gallant resistance. The fight lasted nearly three hours. The enemy advanced by a pathless route through the woods, the whole division moving in perfect silence through the brush, laurel, and rocks, while the rain poured down upon them in torrents. The expectation however of surprising the little force on the mountain was disappointed. As the enemy advanced, our artillery, posted on the top of the mountain, opened upon them, but with little effect, as their lines were concealed by the trees and brushwood. The earth of the mountain seemed to tremble under the thunders of the cannon. The tops of immense trees were cut off by our fire, which was aimed too high; the crash of the falling timber mingled with the roar of the cannon, and as our artillery again and again belched forth its missives of destruction, it seemed as if the forest was riven by living streams of lightning. While the cannonading progressed, an incessant fire of musketry was kept up in the woods, where the sharpshooters, wet to the skin in the rain, kept the advancing lines of the enemy at bay. For more than two hours the little army of Colonel Pegram maintained its ground. Its situation, however, was hopeless. Finding himself with three thousand of the enemy in his rear and five thousand in front, Colonel Pegram endeavored to escape with his command, after a small loss in the action. One part of the command, under Major Tyler, succeeded in escaping; the other, about five hundred in number, were compelled to surrender, when it was found that General Garnett had evacuated Laurel Hill. Among the prisoners taken by the enemy was Colonel Pegram himself. Thrown from his horse, which was wounded and had become unmanageable, he refused to surrender his sword to his captors, and a messenger had to ride six miles to find an officer to receive it from the hands of the ill-starred commander.

When Gen. Garnett heard of the result of the engagement at Rich Mountain, he determined to evacuate Laurel Hill as soon as night set in and retire to Huttonsville by the way of Beverley. This design was baffled, as Col. Scott with his regiment had retreated beyond Beverley towards Huttonsville, without having blocked the road between Rich Mountain and Beverley.* General Garnett was compelled by this untoward

---

* It is proper to state, that there was some controversy as to the precise orders given to Colonel Scott. That officer published a card in the newspapers

circumstance, and by the mistaken execution of another order by which the road was blocked from Beverley towards Laurel Hill, instead of that between the former place and Rich Mountain, to retreat by a mountain road into Hardy county.

The retreat was conducted in good order, amid distresses and trials of the most extraordinary description. The road was barely wide enough for a single wagon. In the morning, the army arrived at a camp on the Little Cheat, and after resting on the grass in the rain a few hours, took up their dreary line of march through the forest. On the morning of the second day of the retreat, soon after leaving the camp on the branch of the Cheat River, the pursuing enemy fell upon the rear of the distressed little army, and skirmishing continued during the day. Four companies of the Georgia regiment were cut off.

At one of the fords, a sharp conflict ensued, in which the enemy were held at bay for a considerable time.

This action, known as that of Carrock's Ford, more than retrieved the disasters of the defeat. It was a deep ford, rendered deeper than usual by the rains, and here some of the wagons became stalled in the river and had to be abandoned.

The enemy were now close upon the rear, which consisted of the 23d Virginia regiment; and the artillery ; and as soon as the command had crossed, Colonel Taliaferro commanding the 23d was ordered to occupy the high bank on the right of the ford with his regiment and artillery. On the right, this position was protected by a fence; on the left, only by low bushes; but the hill commanded the ford and the approach to it by the road, and was admirably selected for a defence. In a few minutes, the skirmishers of the enemy were seen running along the opposite bank, which was low and skirted by a few trees, and were at first taken for the Georgians, who were known to have been cut off, but our men were soon undeceived, and with a simultaneous cheer for "Jeff. Davis" by the whole command, they opened upon the enemy.

The enemy replied with a heavy fire from their infantry and artillery. A large force was brought to the attack, but the

---

at the time, relieving himself from censure and showing that he occupied on the day of the battle the position to which he was peremptorily ordered by General Garnett at the instance of Colonel Pegram.

continued and well-directed fire of the Confederates kept them from crossing the river, and twice the enemy was driven back some distance from the ford. They again, however, came up with a heavy force and renewed the fight. The fire of their artillery was entirely ineffective, although their shot and shell were thrown very rapidly, but they all flew over the heads of the Confederate troops, without any damage except bringing the limbs of the trees down upon them.

After continuing the fight until nearly every cartridge had been expended, and until the artillery had been withdrawn by General Garnett's orders, and as no part of his command was within sight or supporting distance, as far as could be discovered, or, as was afterwards ascertained, within four miles of the ford, Col. Taliaferro, after having sustained a loss of about thirty killed and wounded, ordered the regiment to retire—the officers and men manifesting decided reluctance at being withdrawn.

The loss to the enemy in this gallant little affair must have been quite considerable, as they had, from their own account, three regiments engaged. The people in the neighborhood reported a heavy loss, which they stated the enemy endeavored to conceal by transporting the dead and wounded to Bealington in covered wagons, permitting no one to approach them.

At the second ford, about half-past one o'clock in the day, Gen. Garnett was killed by almost the last fire of the enemy. On reaching at this ford the opposite bank of the stream, Gen. Garnett desired one company from the 23d Virginia regiment to be formed behind some high drift wood. He stated that he would in person take charge of them, and did so—the company being the Richmond Sharpshooters, Capt. Tompkins. In a few minutes, Capt. Tompkins and all his men, but ten, came up to the regiment, stating that Gen. Garnett only wanted ten men. The inference was palpable—he had taken an extreme near position to the enemy. Very soon the firing commenced in the rear where Gen. Garnett was, and immediately the horse of the general came galloping past without a rider. He fell just as he gave the order to the skirmishers to retire, and one of them was killed by his side.

At the second ford, where Gen. Garnett was killed, the enemy abandoned the pursuit, and the command under Col.

Ramsey reached Monterey and formed a junction with Gen Jackson.

The actual reverses of the retreat consisted of some thirty-odd killed and wounded, a number missing, many of whom afterwards reached the command, and the loss of its baggage, a portion of which was used in blocking the road against the enemy's artillery. The conflict and the retreat, the hunger and fatigue of the men, many of whom dropped from the ranks from sheer exhaustion, were unequalled by any thing that had yet occurred in the war. Its success appeared as extraordinary as its hardships and privations. Surrounded by an army of twenty thousand men, without supplies, in a strange country, and in the midst of continuous and drenching rains, it was a wonder that the little army of three thousand men should have escaped annihilation. The command had marched sixty hours, resting only five hours, and had endured a march through the forest without food for men or horses.

Gen. McClellan announced to the government at Washington a signal victory. He summed up the results of the battle on the mountain and his pursuit of the retreating army as two hundred killed and wounded, a thousand taken prisoners, the baggage of the entire command captured, and seven guns taken. "Our success," he wrote to Washington, "is complete, and Secession is killed in this country."

The affair of Rich Mountain was certainly a serious disaster; it involved the surrender of an important portion of North-western Virginia; but with respect to the courage and discipline of our troops, it had exhibited all that could be desired, and the successful retreat was one of the most remarkable in history. It is certain that the unskilful disposition of our troops, as well as their inadequate numbers, had contributed to the success of the enemy, and doubts are admissible whether more advantage might not have been taken of the position at Carrock's Ford, with proper supports, considering its extraordinary advantages of defence, and how long it had been held against the forces of the pursuing enemy by a single regiment.

A feeling of deep sympathy, however, was felt for the unfortunate commander, whose courage, patriotic ardor, and generous, because unnecessary, exposure of his person to the bullets of the enemy, commended his memory to the hearts of his countrymen.

Whatever might have been the depression of the public mind of the South by the Rich Mountain disaster, it was more than recovered by news from other quarters. The same day that the unfavorable intelligence from Rich Mountain reached the government at Richmond, the telegraph brought, by a devious route, the news of the battle of Carthage in Missouri. The blow given to the enemy at this distant point, was the first of the brilliant exploits which afterwards made the Missouri campaign one of the most brilliant episodes of the war. It had gone far to retrieve the fortunes of an empire that was hereafter to be added to the Southern Confederacy, and assure the promise that had been made in the proclamation of the gallant Gen. Price of that State—" a million of such people as the citizens of Missouri were never yet subjugated, and, if attempted, let no apprehension be felt for the result." But of this hereafter.

On the anniversary of the Fourth of July, the Federal Congress met at Washington. Galusha A. Grow, a Pennsylvania Abolitionist, and an uncompromising advocate of the war, was elected Speaker of the House. The meeting of this Congress affords a suitable period for a statement of the posture of political affairs, and of the spirit which animated the North, with respect to existing hostilities.

In his message, Mr. Lincoln denounced the idea of any of the States preserving an armed neutrality in the war, having particular reference to the continued efforts of Governor Magoffin, of Kentucky, to maintain a condition of neutrality on the part of that State. Mr. Lincoln declared that if armed neutrality were permitted on the part of any of the States, it would soon ripen into disunion; that it would build impassable walls along the line of separation; and it would tie the hands of the Unionists, while it would free those of the Insurrectionists, by taking all the trouble from Secession, except that which might be expected from the external blockade. Neutrality, he said, gave to malcontents disunion without its risks, and was not to be tolerated, since it recognized no fidelity to the Constitution or obligation to the Union.

Kentucky was not unreasonably accounted a part of the

Northern government. But with an outrage of the plainest doctrines of the government, and a practical denial not only of every thing like the rights of States, but even of their territorial integrity, the Northwestern portion of Virginia, which had rebelled against its State government, was taken into the membership of the Federal Union as itself a State, with the absurd and childish addition of giving to the rebellious counties the name of "Virginia." A Convention of the disaffected Northwestern counties of Virginia had been held at Wheeling, on the 13th day of May, and after a session of three days, decided to call another Convention, to meet on the 11th of June, subsequent to the vote of the State on the Ordinance of Secession. The Convention reorganized the counties as a member of the Federal Union: F. W. Pierpont was elected governor; and W. T. Willie and the notorious John S. Carlile, both of whom had already signalized their treason to their State by their course in the Convention at Richmond, were sent as representatives of "Virginia" to the United States Senate, in which absurd capacity they were readily received.

The message of the President gave indications of a determined and increased prosecution of hostilities. It called for an army of four hundred thousand men, and a loan of four hundred millions of dollars. This call was a curious commentary upon the spirit and resources of the people, who it had been thought in the North would be crushed out by the three months' levies before the Federal Congress met in July to decide upon what disposition should be made of the conquered States.

The statements of Mr. Lincoln's fiscal secretary were alarming enough; they showed a state of the treasury unable even to meet the ordinary expenditures of the government, and its resources were now to be taxed to the last point of ingenuity to make for the next fiscal year the necessary provision of four hundred and eighty millions of dollars, out of an actual revenue the first quarter of which had not exceeded five millions. The ordinary expenditures of the Federal government for the fiscal year ending June 30th, 1862, were estimated at eighty millions of dollars; the extraordinary expenditures, on the basis of increased military operations, at four hundred millions. To meet these large demands of the civil and war service, Secretary

Chase confessed to a receipt of but five millions per quarter from the "Morrill" tariff, showing that at this rate of the receipt of customs, the income of the government would be twenty millions per year against nearly five hundred millions of prospective outlay.

It was proposed in this financial exigency to levy specific duties of about thirty-three per cent. on coffee, tea, sugar, molasses, and syrup, which might yield twenty millions a year; it was hoped by some modification of the Morrill tariff, with respect to other articles, to increase its productiveness from twenty to thirty-seven millions; the revenue from the sale of public lands was estimated at three millions; and it was timidly proposed that a tax should be levied upon real property of one-third or one-fifth of one per cent., to produce twenty millions additional. Thus by means of—

The Tariff,	$37,000,000
Tea, Sugar, and Coffee,	20,000,000
Public Lands,	3,000,000
Direct Taxes,	20,000,000
Producing a total of	$80,000,000

The Northern government proposed to eke out the means of meeting its ordinary expenses, leaving the monstrous balance of four hundred millions of dollars to be raised by a sale of bonds.

The financial complications of the government of Mr. Lincoln were in striking contrast with the abundant and easy means which the Southern Confederacy had, at least so far, been able to carry on the war. The latter had been reduced to a paper currency, but it had for the basis of its currency the great staple of cotton,* which in the shape of a produce loan was practically pledged to the redemption of the public debt

---

* The whole cotton crop of America, in 1860, was 4,675,770 bales and of this, 3,697,727 bales were exported, and 978,043 bales used at home. England alone took 2,582,000 bales, which amounted to about four-fifths of her entire consumption. The cotton-fields of the Southern States embrace an area of 500,000 square miles, and the capital invested in the cultivation of the plant amounts to $900,000,000. Seventy years ago, the exports of our cotton were only 420 bales—not one-tenth of the amount furnished by several countries to England. Now, the South furnishes five-sevenths of the surplus cotton product of the entire world

Prospects were entertained of a speedy raising of the blockade, the disappointment of which, at a later day, drove the Confederacy to other expedients of revenue, in a war tax, &c.; but, at the time of the comparison of the financial condition of the two governments, the Confederate currency was accounted quite as good as gold, as the cotton and tobacco once in the market would afford the Southern government the instant means to discharge every cent of its indebtedness.

The Federal Congress commenced its work in a spirit that essentially tended to revolutionize the political system and ideas of the North itself. It not only voted to Mr. Lincoln the men and supplies he asked for, but the first days of its session were signalized by a resolution to gag all propositions looking towards peace, or any thing else than a prosecution of the war; by another, to approve the acts done by the President without constitutional authority, including his suspension of the *habeas corpus*; and by the introduction of a bill to confiscate the property of " rebels."

The pages of history do not afford a commensurate instance of the wide opposition in the social and political directions of two nations who had so long lived in political union and intercourse as the North and the South. While the latter was daily becoming more conservative and more attached to existing institutions,* the North was as rapidly growing discontented,

---

* A type of the conservatism of the Southern revolution—its attachment to the past—was vividly displayed in the adoption of its national ensign, a blue union with a circle of stars, and longitudinal bars, red, white, and red, in place of "the stripes" of the flag of the old government. The present Confederate flag was balloted for in the Provisional Congress, and was selected by a majority of votes out of four different models. At the time of the early session of Congress at Montgomery, the popular sentiment was almost unanimous, and very urgent, that the main features of the old Federal Constitution should be copied into the new government, and that to follow out and give expression to this idea, the flag should be as close a copy as possible of the Federal ensign. A resolution was introduced in the Provisional Congress to the effect that the flag should be as little different as possible from that of the Federal government; which resolution was vigorously opposed by Mr. Miles, of South Carolina, who was then chairman of the Flag Committee. The design recommended by Mr. Miles, but voted down, has since been adopted as the battle flag of Generals Johnston and Beauregard. It is a blue *saltier* (or Maltese cross), with inner rows of stars, on a red field—the emblem of the *saltier* (*saltire*, to eap) being appropriately that of progress and power. The two other competing designs, from which our present flag was selected, were, one, an almost

restless, radical, and revolutionary. The people of the North had passed the stage of pure Democracy, and inaugurated military despotism. They, in effect, had changed their form of government, while vainly attempting to preserve their territorial ascendency. They charged the South with attempting revolution, when it was only fighting for independence; while they, themselves, actually perpetrated revolution rather than forego the advantages of a partial and iniquitous Union. The South, in the midst of a war of independence—a war waged not to destroy, but to preserve existing institutions—was recurring to the past, and proposing to revive conservative ideas rather than to run into new and rash experiments.

The war had already developed one great moral fact in the North of paramount interest. It was the entire willingness of the people to surrender their constitutional liberties to any government that would gratify their political passions.

This peculiarity of the condition of Northern society, was more significant of its disintegration and revolutionary destiny than all the other circumstances and consequences of the war combined, in loss of trade, prostration of commerce, and poverty and hunger of the people. It was the corruption of the public virtue. The love of constitutional liberty was degraded to political hatreds. While these were gratified, the Northern people were willing to surrender their liberties to their panderers at Washington. Without protest, without opposition, in silent submission, or even in expressions stimulating and encouraging the despot who stript them of their rights, to still further excesses, they had seen every vestige of constitutional liberty swept away, while they imagined that their greed of resentment towards the South was to be satisfied to its fill. They had seen the liberties of the people strangled, even in States remaining in the Union. They had seen the writ of *habeas corpus* denied, not only by the minions of Abraham Lincoln in Maryland, but by the commanding officers of Forts Hamilton and Lafayette. They had seen, not only the rights of free speech, but the sanctity even of private correspondence, violated by the seizure

---

exact reproduction of the Federal stars and stripes, the only variation being that of a blue stripe, and the other a simple blue circle or rim, on a red field. The consideration that determined the selection of the present flag was its similarity to that of the old government.

of dispatches in their own telegraph offices. They had seen the law of the drum-head not only established in Baltimore, but measures to subvert their own municipal liberties inaugurated by a system of military police for the whole Federal Union. They had suffered without protestation these monstrous violations of the Constitution under which they professed to live. They had not only suffered, but had indorsed them. They had not only done this, but they had applauded in this government of Abraham Lincoln violations of honor, morality, and truth, more infamous than excesses of authority.

CHAPTER IV.

The "Grand Army" of the North.—General McDowell.—The Affair of Bull Run.—An Artillery Duel.—THE BATTLE OF MANASSAS.—"On to Richmond."—Scenery of the Battle-field.—Crises in the Battle.—Devoted Courage of the Confederates.—THE ROUT.—How the News was received in Washington.—How it was received in the South.—General Bee.—Colonel Bartow.—The Great Error.—General Johnston's Excuses for not advancing on Washington.—INCIDENTS OF THE MANASSAS BATTLE.

THE month of July found confronting the lines of the Potomac two of the largest armies that this continent had ever seen. The confidence of the North in the numbers, spirit, and appointments of its "Grand Army" was insolent in the extreme. It was thought to be but an easy undertaking for it to march to Richmond, and plant the Stars and Stripes in Capitol Square. An advance was urged not only by the popular clamor of "On to Richmond," but by the pressure of extreme parties in Congress; and when it was fully resolved upon, the exhilaration was extreme, and the prospect of the occupation of Richmond in ten days was entertained with every variety of public joy.

Nothing had been left undone to complete the preparations of the Northern army. In numbers it was immense; it was provided with the best artillery in the world; it comprised, besides its immense force of volunteers, all the regulars east of the Rocky Mountains, to the number of about ten thousand, collected since February, in the city of Washington, from Jefferson Barracks, from St. Louis, and from Fortress Monroe. Making all allowances for mistakes, we are warranted in saying that the Northern army consisted of at least fifty-five regiments of volunteers, eight companies of regular infantry, four of marines, nine of regular cavalry, and twelve batteries, forty-nine guns. This army was placed at the command of one who was acknowledged to be the greatest and most scientific general in the North—General McDowell. This officer had a reputation in the army of being a stoic philosopher—a reputation sought after by a certain number of West Point pupils.

General Beauregard was fully informed of the movements of

McDowell. The vaunting and audacious declaration of the enemy's purpose to force his position, and press on to Richmond, was met by firm and busy preparations for the crisis. It was no mean crisis. It was to involve the first important shock of arms between two peoples who, from long seasons of peace and prosperity, had brought to the struggle more than ordinary resources and splendors of war.

The decisive battle was preceded by the important affair of Bull Run, a brief sketch of which, as a precursor to the events of the 21st of July, furnishes an intelligent introduction to the designs of the enemy, and alike to the complicated plan and glorious issue of the great battle that, through the sultry heats of a whole day, wrestled over the plains of Manassas.

Bull Run constitutes the northern boundary of that county which it divides from Fairfax; and on its memorable banks, about three miles to the northwest of the junction of the Manassas Gap with the Orange and Alexandria railroad, was fought the gallant action of the 18th of July. It is a small stream, running in this locality, nearly from west to east, to its confluence with the Occoquan River, about twelve miles from the Potomac, and draining a considerable scope of country, from its source in Bull Run Mountain to within a short distance of the Potomac at Occoquan. Roads traverse and intersect the surrounding country in almost every direction. The banks of the stream are rocky and steep, but abound in long-used fords. At Mitchell's Ford, the stream is about equidistant between Centreville and Manassas, some six miles apart.

Anticipating the determination of the enemy to advance on Manassas, General Beauregard had withdrawn his advanced brigades within the lines of Bull Run. On the morning of the 17th of July our troops rested on Bull Run, from Union Mill's Ford to the Stone Bridge, a distance of about eight miles. The next morning the enemy assumed a threatening attitude. Appearing in heavy force in front of the position of General Bonham's brigade, which held the approaches to Mitchell's Ford, the enemy, about the meridian, opened fir with several 20-pounder rifle guns from a hill over one and half miles from Bull Run. At first, the firing of the enemy was at random; but, by half-past 12 P. M., he had obtained the range of our position, and poured into the brigade a shower of shot, but without injury to us in men, horses, or guns. Our fire was reserved, and our troops impatiently awaited the opportune moment.

In a few moments, a light battery was pushed forward by the enemy, whereupon Kemper's battery, which was attached to Bonham's brigade, and occupied a ridge on the left of the Centreville road, threw only six solid shot, with the remarkable effect of driving back both the battery and its supporting force. The unexpected display of skill and accuracy in our artillery held the advancing column of the enemy in check, while Kemper's pieces and support were withdrawn across Mitchell's Ford, to a point previously designated, and which commanded the direct approaches to the ford.

In the mean time, the enemy was advancing in strong columns of infantry, with artillery and cavalry, on Blackburn's Ford, which was covered by General Longstreet's brigade. The Confederate pickets fell back, silently, across the ford before the advancing foe. The entire southern bank of the stream, for the whole front of Longstreet's brigade, was covered at the water's edge by an extended line of skirmishers. Taking advantage of the steep slopes on the northern bank of the stream, the enemy approached under shelter, in heavy force, within less than one hundred yards of our skirmishers. Before advancing his infantry, the enemy maintained a fire of rifle artillery for half an hour; then he pushed forward a column of over three thousand infantry to the assault, with such a weight of numbers as to be repelled with difficulty by the comparatively small force of not more than twelve hundred bayonets, with which Brigadier-general Longstreet met him with characteristic vigor and intrepidity. The repulse of this charge of the enemy was, as an exhibition of the devoted courage of our troops, the most brilliant incident of the day. Not one yard of intrenchment or one rifle-pit protected the men at Blackburn's Ford, who, with rare exceptions, were, on that day, the first time under fire, and who, taking and maintaining every position ordered, exceeded in cool, self-possessed, and determined courage the best-trained veterans. Twice the enemy was foiled and driven back by our skirmishers and Longstreet's reserve companies. As he returned to the contest with increased numbers, General Longstreet had been reinforced from Early's brigade with two regiments of infantry and two pieces of artillery. Unable to effect a passage of the stream, the enemy kept up a scattering fire for some time. The fire of musketry was soon silenced, and the affair became one of artillery. The enemy was superior in the character as well as in the number of his weapons, provided with improved munitions and every artillery appliance, and, at the same time, occupying the commanding position. The results of the remarkable artillery duel that ensued were fitting precursors to the achievements of the twenty-first of July in this unexpectedly brilliant arm of our service. In the onset, our fire was directed against the enemy's infantry, whose bayonets, gleaming above the tree-tops, alone indicated their presence and force. This drew the attention of a battery placed on a high, commanding ridge, and the duel commenced in earnest. For a time, the aim of the adversary was inaccurate, but this was quickly corrected, and shot fell and shells burst thick and fast in the very midst of our battery. From the position of our pieces and the nature of the ground, their aim could only be directed by the smoke of the enemy's artillery; how skilfully and with what execution this was done can only be realized by an eye-witness. For a few moments, the guns of the enemy were silenced, but were soon reopened. By direction of General Longstreet, his battery was then advanced, by hand, out of the range now ascertained by the enemy, and a shower of spherical case, shell, and round-shot flew over the heads of our gunners. From this new position our guns fired as before, with no other aim than the smoke and flash of their adversaries' pieces, and renewed and urged the conflict with such signal vigor and effect, that gradually the fire of the enemy slackened, the intervals between their discharges grew longer and longer, finally to cease; and we fired a last gun at a baffled flying foe, whose heavy masses in the distance were plainly seen to break and scatter in wild confusion and utter rout, strewing the ground with cast-away guns, hats, blankets, and knapsacks, as our parting shell was thrown among them.

Thus ended the brilliant action of Bull Run. The guns engaged in the singular artillery conflict on our side were three six-pounder rifle pieces and four ordinary six-pounders, all of

Walton's battery—the Washington Artillery of New Orleans. Our casualties were unimportant—fifteen killed and fifty-three wounded. The loss of the enemy can only be conjectured; it was unquestionably heavy. In the cursory examination, which was made by details from Longstreet's and Early's brigades, on the 18th of July, of that portion of the field immediately contested and near Blackburn's Ford, some sixty-four corpses were found and buried, and at least twenty prisoners were also picked up, besides one hundred and seventy-five stands of arms and a large quantity of accoutrements and blankets.

The effect of the day's conflict was to satisfy the enemy that he could not force a passage across Bull Run in the face of our troops, and led him into the flank movement of the 21st of July and the battle of Manassas.

THE BATTLE OF MANASSAS.

General Scott having matured his plan of battle, ordered General McDowell to advance on Manassas on Sunday, the 21st of July—three days after the repulse at Bull Run. The movement was generally known in Washington; Congress had adjourned for the purpose of affording its members an opportunity to attend the battle-field, and as the crowds of camp followers and spectators, consisting of politicians, fashionable women, idlers, sensation-hunters, editors, &c., hurried in carriages, omnibuses, gigs, and every conceivable style of vehicle across the Potomac in the direction of the army, the constant and unfailing jest was, that they were going on a visit to Richmond. The idea of the defeat of the Grand Army, which, in show, splendid boast, and dramatic accessaries, exceeded any thing that had ever been seen in America, seems never to have crossed the minds of the politicians who went prepared with carriage-loads of champagne for festal celebration of the victory that was to be won, or of the fair dames who were equipped with opera-glasses to entertain themselves with the novel scenes of a battle and the inevitable rout of "rebels." The indecencies of this exhibition of morbid curiosity and exultant hate are simply unparalleled in the history of civilized nations. Mr Russell, correspondent of the London *Times*, an eye-witness of the scene, describes the concourse of carriages and gayly-dressed spectators in the rear of the army on the morning of the battle of Manassas as like a holiday exhibition on a race-course.

The scene was an extraordinary one. It had a beauty and grandeur, apart from the revolting spectacle of the indecent and bedizened rabble that watched from a hill in the rear of the army the dim outlines of the battle and enjoyed the nervous emotions of the thunders of its artillery. The gay uniforms of the Northern soldiers, their streaming flags and glistening bayonets, added strange charms to the primeval forests of Virginia. No theatre of battle could have been more magnificent in its addresses to the eye. The plains, broken by a wooded and intricate country, were bounded as far as the eye could reach to the west by the azure combs of the Blue Ridge. The quiet Sabbath morning opened upon the scene enlivened by moving masses of men; the red lights of the morning, however, had scarcely broken upon that scene, with its landscapes, its forests, and its garniture, before it was obscured in the clouds of battle. For long intervals nothing of the conflict was presented, to those viewing it at a distance, but wide and torn curtains of smoke and dust and the endless beat of the artillery.

Orders had been issued by McDowell for the Grand Army to be in motion by two o'clock on the morning of the twenty-first, and *en route* for their different positions in time to reach them and be in position by the break of day. It was also ordered that they should have four days' rations cooked and stored away in their haversacks—evidently for the purpose of gaining Manassas and holding it, until their supplies should reach them by the railroad from Alexandria. Thus stood the arrangements of the Northern forces on the evening preceding the battle of the twenty-first.

It is a remarkable circumstance of the battle of Manassas, that it was fought on our side without any other plan than to suit the contingencies arising out of the development of the enemy's designs, as it occurred in the progress of the action. Several plans of battle had been proposed by General Beauregard, but had been defeated by the force of circumstances. He had been unwilling to receive the enemy on the defensive line of Bull Run, and had determined on attacking him at

Centreville. In the mean time, General Johnston had been ordered to form a junction of his army corps with that of General Beauregard, should the movement, in his judgment, be advisable. The best service which the army of the Shenandoah could render was to prevent the defeat of that of the Potomac. To be able to do this, it was necessary for General Johnston to defeat General Patterson or to elude him. The latter course was the most speedy and certain, and was, therefore, adopted. Evading the enemy by the disposition of the advance guard under Colonel Stuart, our army moved through Ashby's Gap to Piedmont, a station of the Manassas Gap railroad. Hence, the infantry were to be transported by the railway, while the cavalry and artillery were ordered to continue their march. General Johnston reached Manassas about noon on the twentieth, preceded by the 7th and 8th Georgia regiments and by Jackson's brigade, consisting of the 2d, 4th, 5th, 27th and 33d Virginia regiments. He was accompanied by General Bee, with the 4th Alabama, the 2d and two companies of the 11th Mississippi. The president of the railroad had assured him that the remaining troops should arrive during the day.

General Johnston, being the senior in rank, necessarily assumed command of all the forces of the Confederate States then concentrating at Manassas. He, however, approved the plans of General Beauregard, and generously directed their execution under his command. It was determined that the two forces should be united within the lines of Bull Run, and thence advance to the attack of the enemy, before Patterson's junction with McDowell, which was daily expected. The plan of battle was again disconcerted. In consequence of the untoward detention on the railroad of some five thousand of General Johnston's forces that had been expected to reach Manassas prior to the battle, it became necessary, on the morning of the twenty-first, before daylight, to modify the plan accepted, to suit the contingency of an immediate attack on our lines by the main force of the enemy, then plainly at hand. It thus happened that a battle ensued, different in place and circumstance from any previous plan on our side.

Our effective force of all arms, ready for action on the field on the eventful morning, was less than thirty thousand men

Our troops were divided into eight brigades, occupying the defensive line of Bull Run. Brigadier-general Ewell's was posted at the Union Mill's Ford; Brigadier-general D. R. Jones' at McLean's Ford; Brigadier-general Longstreet's at Blackburn's Ford; Brigadier-general Bonham's at Mitchell's Ford; Colonel Cocke's at Ball's Ford, some three miles above, and Colonel Evans, with a regiment and battalion, formed the extreme left at the Stone Bridge. The brigades of Brigadier-general Holmes and Colonel Early were in reserve in rear of the right.

In his entire ignorance of the enemy's plan of attack, General Beauregard was compelled to keep his army posted along the stream for some eight or ten miles, while his wily adversary developed his purpose to him. The subsequent official reports of McDowell and his officers show that that commander had abandoned his former purpose of marching on Manassas by the lower routes from Washington and Alexandria, and had resolved upon turning the left flank of the Confederates.

The fifth division of his Grand Army, composed of at least four brigades, under command of General Miles, was to remain at Centreville, in reserve, and to make a false attack on Blackburn's and Mitchell's Fords, and thereby deceive General Beauregard as to its intention. The first division, composed of at least three brigades, commanded by General Tyler, was to take position at the Stone Bridge, and feign an attack upon that point. The third division, composed of at least three brigades, commanded by Heintzelman, was to proceed as quietly as possible to the Red House Ford, and there remain, until the troops guarding that ford should be cleared away. The second division, composed of three or four brigades, commanded by Hunter, was to march, unobserved by the Confederate troops, to Sudley, and there cross over the run and move down the stream to the Red House Ford, and clear away any troops that might be guarding that point, where he was to be joined by the third or Heintzelman's division. Together, these two divisions were to charge upon, and drive away any troops that might be stationed at the Stone Bridge, when Tyler's division was to cross over and join them, and thus produce a junction of three formidable divisions of the

Grand Army across the run, for offensive operations against the forces of General Beauregard, which the enemy expected to find scattered along the run for seven or eight miles—the bulk of them being at and below Mitchell's Ford, and so situated as to render a concerted movement by them utterly impracticable.

Soon after sunrise, the enemy appeared in force in front of Colorel Evans' position at the Stone Bridge, and opened a light cannonade. The monstrous inequality of the two forces at this point was not developed. Colonel Evans only observed in his immediate front the advance portion of General Schenck's brigade of General Tyler's division and two other heavy brigades. This division of the enemy's forces numbered nine thousand men and thirteen pieces of artillery—Carlisle's and Ayres' batteries—that is, nine hundred men and two six-pounders confronted by nine thousand men and thirteen pieces of artillery, mostly rifled.

A movement was instantly determined upon by General Beauregard to relieve his left flank, by a rapid, determined attack with his right wing and centre on the enemy's flank and rear at Centreville, with precautions against the advance of his reserves from the direction of Washington.

In the quarter of the Stone Bridge, the two armies stood for more than an hour engaged in slight skirmishing, while the main body of the enemy was marching his devious way through the "Big Forest," to cross Bull Run some two miles above our left, to take our forces in flank and rear. This movement was fortunately discovered in time for us to check its progress, and ultimately to form a new line of battle nearly at right angles with the defensive line of Bull Run.

On discovering that the enemy had crossed the stream above him, Colonel Evans moved to his left with eleven companies and two field-pieces to oppose his advance, and disposed his little force under cover of the wood, near the intersection of the Warrenton turnpike and the Sudley road. Here he was attacked by the enemy in immensely superior numbers.

The enemy beginning his detour from the turnpike, at a point nearly half-way between Stone Bridge and Centreville, had pursued a tortuous, narrow track of a rarely used road, through a dense wood, the greater part of his way until near the Sudley road. A division under Colonel Hunter, of the Federal regular army, of two strong brigades, was in the advance, followed immediately by another division, under Colonel Heintzelman of three brigades, and seven companies of regular cavalry, and twenty-four pieces of artillery—eighteen of which were rifled guns. This column, as it crossed Bull Run, numbered over sixteen thousand men, of all arms, by their own accounts.

Burnside's brigade—which here, as at Fairfax Court-house, led the advance—at about 9.45 A. M., debouched from a wood in sight of Evans' position, some five hundred yards distant from Wheat's Louisiana battalion. He immediately threw forward his skirmishers in force, and they became engaged with Wheat's command. The Federalists at once advanced, as they report officially, the 2d Rhode Island regiment volunteers, with its vaunted battery of six thirteen-pounder rifle guns. Sloan's companies of the 4th South Carolina were then brought into action, having been pushed forward through the woods. The enemy, soon galled and staggered by the fire, and pressed by the determined valor with which Wheat handled his battalion, until he was desperately wounded, hastened up three other regiments of the brigade and two Dahlgren howitzers, making in all quite three thousand five hundred bayonets and eight pieces of artillery, opposed to less than eight hundred men and two six-pounder guns.

Despite the odds, this intrepid command, of but eleven weak companies, maintained its front to the enemy for quite an hour, and until General Bee came to their aid with his command.

General Bee moving towards the enemy, guided by the firing, had selected the position near the now famous "Henry House," and formed his troops upon it. They were the 7th and 8th Georgia under Colonel Bartow, the 4th Alabama, 2d Mississippi, and two companies of the 11th Mississippi regiments, with Imboden's battery. Being compelled, however, to sustain Colonel Evans, he crossed the valley, and formed on the right and somewhat in advance of his position. Here the joint force, little exceeding five regiments, with six field-pieces, held the ground against about fifteen thousand Federal troops. A fierce and destructive conflict now ensued—the fire was withering on both sides, while the enemy swept our short, thin lines with their numerous artillery, which, according to their official reports, at this time consisted of at least ten rifle guns and four howitzers. For an hour did these stout-hearted men, of the blended commands of Bee, Evans, and Bartow, breast an unintermitting battle-storm, animated surely by something more than the ordinary courage of even the bravest men under fire.

Two Federal brigades of Heintzelman's division were now brought into action, led by Rickett's superb light battery of six ten-pounder rifle guns, which, posted on an eminence to the right of the Sudley road, opened fire on Imboden's battery. At this time, confronting the enemy, we had still but Evans' eleven companies and two guns—Bee's and Bartow's four regiments, the two companies 11th Mississippi under Lieutenant-colonel Liddell, and the six pieces under Imboden and Richardson. The enemy had two divisions of four strong brigades, including seventeen companies of regular infantry, cavalry, and artillery, four companies of marines, and twenty pieces of artillery. Against this odds, scarcely credible, our advance position was still for a while maintained, and the enemy's ranks constantly broken and shattered under the scorching fire of our men; but fresh regiments of the Federals came upon the field, Sherman's and Keyes' brigades of Tyler's division, as is stated in their reports, numbering over six thousand bayonets, which had found a passage across the Run, about eight hundred yards above the Stone Bridge, threatened our right.

Heavy losses had now been sustained on our side, both in numbers and in the personal worth of the slain. The 8th Georgia regiment had suffered heavily, being exposed, as it took and maintained its position, to a fire from the enemy, already posted within a hundred yards of their front and right, sheltered by fences and other cover. The 4th Alabama also suffered severely from the deadly fire of the thousands of muskets which they so dauntlessly confronted under the immediate leadership of the chivalrous Bee himself.

Now, however, with the surging mass of over fourteen thousand Federal infantry pressing on their front and under the incessant fire of at least twenty pieces of artillery, with the fresh brigades of Sherman and Keyes approaching—the latter already in musket range—our lines gave back, but under orders from General Bee.

As our shattered battalions retired, the slaughter was deplorable. They fell back in the direction of the Robinson House, under the fires of Heintzelman's division on one side, Keyes' and Sherman's brigades of Tyler's division on the other, and Hunter's division in their rear, and were compelled to engage the enemy at several points on their retreat, losing both officers and men, in order to keep them from closing in around them. Under the inexorable stress of the enemy's fire the retreat continued. The enemy seemed to be inspired with the idea that he had won the field; the news of a victory was carried to the rear, and, in less than an hour thereafter, the telegraph had flashed the intelligence through all the cities in the North, that the Federal troops were completing their victory, and premature exultations ran from mouth to mouth in Washington.

If the enemy had observed the circumstances and character of this falling back of a portion of our lines, it would have been enough to have driven him in consternation from the field. With the terrible desperation that had sustained them so long in the face of fivefold odds and the most frightful losses, our troops fell back sullenly; at every step of their retreat staying, by their hard skirmishing, the flanking columns of the enemy.

The retreat was finally arrested just in rear of the Robinson House by the energy and resolution of General Bee, assisted by the support of the Hampton Legion, and the timely arrival of Jackson's brigade of five regiments. A moment before, General Bee had been well-nigh overwhelmed by superior numbers. He approached General Jackson with the pathetic exclamation, "General, they are beating us back;" to which the latter promptly replied, "Sir, we'll give them the bayonet." General Bee immediately rallied his over-tasked troops with the words, "There is Jackson standing like a stone wall. Let us determine to die here, and we will conquer."

In the mean time, the crisis of the battle and the full development of the enemy's designs had been perceived by our

generals. They were yet four miles away from the immediate field of action, having placed themselves on a commanding hill in rear of General Bonham's left, to observe the movements of the enemy. There could be no mistake now of the enemy's intentions, from the violent firing on the left and the immense clouds of dust raised by the march of a large body of troops from his centre. With the keenest impatience, General Beauregard awaited the execution of his orders of the morning, which were intended to relieve his left flank by an attack on the enemy's flank and rear at Centreville. As the continuous roll of musketry and the sustained din of the artillery announced the serious outburst of the battle on our left flank, he anxiously, but confidently, awaited similar sounds of conflict from our front at Centreville. When it was too late for the effective execution of the contemplated movement, he was informed, to his profound disappointment, that his orders for an advance had miscarried.

No time was to be lost. It became immediately necessary to depend on new combinations, and to meet the enemy on the field upon which he had chosen to give us battle. It was plain that nothing but the most rapid combinations and the most heroic and devoted courage on the part of our troops could retrieve the field, which, according to all military conditions, appeared to be positively lost.

About noon, the scene of the battle was unutterably sublime. Not until then could one of the present generation, who had never witnessed a grand battle, have imagined such a spectacle. The hill occupied in the morning by Generals Beauregard, Johnston, and Bonham, and their staffs, placed the whole scene before one—a grand, moving diorama. When the firing was at its height, the roar of artillery reached the hill like that of protracted thunder. For one long mile the whole valley was a boiling crater of dust and smoke. Occasionally the yells of our men, in the few instances in which the enemy fell back, rose above the roar of artillery. In the distance rose the Blue Ridge, to form the dark background of a most magnificent picture.

The condition of the battle-field was now, at the least, desperate. Our left flank was overpowered, and it became necessary to bring immediately up to their support the reserves not

already in motion. Holmes' two regiments and battery of
artillery, under Captain Lindsey Walker, of six guns, and
Early's brigade, were immediately ordered up to support on
left flank. Two regiments from Bonham's brigade, with Kem
per's four six-pounders, were also called for, and Generals
Ewell, Jones (D. R.), Longstreet, and Bonham were directed
to make a demonstration to their several fronts to retain and
engross the enemy's reserves, and any forces on their flank, and
at and around Centreville.

Dashing on at headlong gallop, General Johnston and General
Beauregard reached the field of action not a moment too
soon. They were instantly occupied with the reorganization
of the heroic troops, whose previous stand in stubborn and
patriotic valor has nothing to exceed it in the records of history.
It was now that General Johnston impressively and
gallantly charged to the front, with the colors of the 4th
Alabama regiment by his side. The presence of the two
generals with the troops under fire, and their example, had the
happiest effect. Order was soon restored. In a brief and
rapid conference, General Beauregard was assigned to the
command of the left, which, as the younger officer, he claimed
while General Johnston returned to that of the whole field.

The battle was now re-established. The aspect of affairs
was critical and desperate in the extreme.

Confronting the enemy at this time, General Beauregard's
forces numbered, at most, not more than six thousand five
hundred infantry and artillerists, with but thirteen pieces of
artillery, and two companies of Stuart's cavalry.

The enemy's force now bearing hotly and confidently down
on our position—regiment after regiment of the best-equipped
men that ever took the field—according to their own official
history of the day, was formed of Colonels Hunter's and
Heintzelman's divisions, Colonels Sherman's and Keyes' brigades
of Tyler's division, and of the formidable batteries of
Ricketts, Griffin, and Arnold regulars, and 2d Rhode Island,
and two Dahlgren howitzers—a force of over twenty thousand
infantry, seven companies of regular cavalry, and twenty-
four pieces of improved artillery. At the same time, perilous,
heavy reserves of infantry and artillery hung in the
distance, around the Stone Bridge, Mitchell's, Blackburn's, and

Union Mill's Fords, visibly ready to fall upon us at any moment.

Fully conscious of the portentous disparity of force, General Beauregard, as he posted the lines for the encounter, spoke words of encouragement to the men to inspire their confidence and determined spirit of resistance. He urged them to the resolution of victory or death on the field. The men responded with loud and eager cheers, and the commander felt reassured of the unconquerable spirit of his army.

In the mean time, the enemy had seized upon the plateau on which Robinson's and the Henry houses * are situated—the position first occupied in the morning by General Bee, before advancing to the support of Evans—Ricketts' battery of six rifle guns, the pride of the Federalists, the object of their unstinted expenditure in outfit, and the equally powerful regular light battery of Griffin, were brought forward and placed in immediate action, after having, conjointly with the batteries already mentioned, played from former positions with destructive effect upon our forward battalions.

About two o'clock in the afternoon, General Beauregard gave the order for the right of his line, except his reserves, to advance to recover the plateau. It was done with uncommon resolution and vigor, and at the same time Jackson's brigade pierced the enemy's centre with the determination of veterans and the spirit of men who fight for a sacred cause; but it suffered seriously. With equal spirit the other parts of the line made the onset, and the Federal lines were broken and swept back at all points from the open ground of the plateau. Rallying soon, however, as they were strongly reinforced by fresh regiments, the Federals returned, and, by the weight of numbers, pressed our lines back, recovered their ground and guns, and renewed the offensive.

By this time, between half-past 2 and 3 o'clock, P. M., our reinforcements pushed forward, and directed by General Johnston to the required quarter, were at hand just as General Beauregard had ordered forward to a second effort, for the recovery of the disputed plateau, the whole line, including his

---

* These houses were small wooden buildings, occupied at the time, the one by the Widow Henry and the other by the free negro Robinson.

reserve, which, at this crisis of the battle, the commander felt called upon to lead in person. This attack was general, and was shared in by every regiment then in the field, including the 6th (Fisher's) North Carolina regiment, which had just come up. The whole open ground was again swept clear of the enemy, and the plateau around the Henry and Robinson houses remained finally in our possession, with the greater part of the Ricketts and Griffin batteries. This part of the day was rich with deeds of individual coolness and dauntless conduct, as well as well-directed, embodied resolution and bravery, but fraught with the loss to the service of the country of lives of inestimable preciousness at this juncture. The brave Bee was mortally wounded at the head of the 4th Alabama and some Mississippians, in the open field near the Henry house; and, a few yards distant, Colonel Bartow had fallen, shot through the heart. He was grasping the standard of his regiment as he was shot, and calling the remnants of his command to rally and follow him. He spoke after receiving his mortal wound, and his words were memorable. To the few of his brave men who gathered around him he said, "They have killed me, but never give up the field." The last command was gallantly obeyed, and his men silenced the battery of which he died in the charge. Colonel Fisher had also been killed. He had fallen at the head of the torn and thinned ranks of his regiment.

The conflict had been awfully terrific. The enemy had been driven back on our right entirely across the turnpike, and beyond Young's Branch on our left. At this moment, the desired reinforcements arrived. Withers' 18th regiment of Cocke's brigade had come up in time to follow the charge. Kershaw's 2d and Cash's 8th South Carolina regiments arrived soon after Withers', and were assigned an advantageous position. A more important accession, however, to our forces was at hand. A courier had galloped from Manassas to report that a Federal army had reached the line of the Manassas Gap railroad, was marching towards us, and was then about three or four miles from our left flank. Instead, however, of the enemy, it was the long-expected reinforcements. General Kirby Smith, with some seventeen hundred infantry of Elzey's brigade of the Army of the Shenandoah and Beckham's battery, had reached Manassas, by railroad, at noon. His forces were instantly marched across the fields to the scene of action.

The flying enemy had been rallied under cover of a strong Federal brigade, posted on a plateau near the intersection of the turnpike and the Sudley-Brentsville road, and was now making demonstrations to outflank and drive back our left, and thus separate us from Manassas. General Smith was instructed by General Johnston to attack the right flank of the enemy, now exposed to us. Before the movement was completed, he fell severely wounded. Colonel Elzey, at once taking command, proceeded to execute it with promptness and vigor, while General Beauregard rapidly seized the opportunity, and threw forward his whole line.

About 3.30 P. M., the enemy, driven back on their left and centre, and brushed from the woods bordering the Sudley road, south and west from the Henry house, had formed a line of battle of truly formidable proportions, of crescent outline, reaching, on their left, from the vicinity of Pittsylvania (the old Carter mansion), by Matthew's and in rear of Dogan's, across the turnpike near to Chinn's house. The woods and fields were filled with their masses of infantry and their carefully preserved cavalry. It was a truly magnificent, though redoubtable spectacle, as they threw forward in fine style, on the broad gentle slopes of the ridge occupied by their main lines, a cloud of skirmishers, preparatory for another attack.

Colonel Early, who, by some mischance, did not receive orders until 2 o'clock, which had been sent him at noon, came on the ground immediately after Elzey, with Kemper's 7th Virginia, Hay's 7th Louisiana, and Barksdale's 13th Mississippi regiments. This brigade, by the personal direction of General Johnston, was marched by the Holkham house, across the fields to the left, entirely around the woods through which Elzey had passed, and under a severe fire, into a position in line of battle near Chinn's house, outflanking the enemy's right.

The enemy was making his last attempt to retrieve the day. He had re-formed to renew the battle, again extending his right with a still wider sweep to turn our left. Colonel Early was ordered to throw himself directly upon the right flank of the enemy, supported by Colonel Stuart's cavalry and Beckham's battery. As Early formed his line, and Beckham's pieces played upon the right of the enemy, Elzey's brigade, Gibbons' 10th Virginia, Lieut.-colonel Stuart's 1st Maryland, and Vaughan's 3d Tennessee regiments, and Cash's 8th and Kershaw's 2d South Carolina, Withers' 18th and Preston's 28th Virginia, advanced in an irregular line, almost simultaneously. The charge made by General Beauregard in front, was sustained by the resolute attack of Early on the right flank and rear. The combined attack was too much for the enemy. He was forced over the narrow plateau made by the intersection of the two roads already mentioned. He was driven into the fields, where his masses commenced to scatter in all available directions towards Bull Run. He had lost all the artillery which he had advanced to the last scene of the conflict; he had no more fresh troops to rally on, and there were no combinations to avail him to make another stand. The day was ours. From the long-contested hill from which the enemy had been driven back, his retreating masses might be seen to break over the fields stretching beyond, as the panic gathered in their rear. The rout had become general and confused; the fields were covered with black swarms of flying soldiers, while cheers and yells taken up along our lines, for the distance of miles, rung in the ears of the panic-stricken fugitives.

THE ROUT.

Early's brigade, meanwhile, joined by the 19th Virginia regiment, of Cocke's brigade, pursued the now panic-stricken fugitive enemy. Stuart, with his cavalry, and Beckham had also taken up the pursuit along the road by which the enemy had come upon the field that morning; but, soon cumbered by prisoners who thronged the way, the former was unable to attack the mass of the fast-fleeing, frantic Federals. The want of a cavalry force of sufficient numbers made an efficient pursuit a military impossibility.

But the pressure of close and general pursuit was not necessary to disorganize the flight of the enemy. Capt. Kemper pursued the retreating masses to within range of Cub Run Bridge. Upon the bridge, a shot took effect upon the horses of a team that was crossing. The wagon was overturned directly in the centre of the bridge, and the passage was completely obstructed. The Confederates continued to play their artillery upon the train carriages and artillery wagons, and these were reduced to ruins. Cannons and caissons, ambulances and train-wagons, and hundreds of soldiers rushed down the hill into a common heap, struggling and scrambling to cross the stream and get away from their pursuers.

The retreat, the panic, the heedless, headlong confusion was soon beyond a hope. Officers with leaves and eagles on their shoulder-straps, majors and colonels who had deserted their comrades, passed, galloping as if for dear life. Not a field-officer seemed to have remembered his duty. The flying teams and wagons confused and dismembered every corps. For three miles, hosts of the Federal troops—all detached from their regiments, all mingled in one disorderly rout—were fleeing along the road. Army wagons, sutler's teams, and private carriages choked the passage, tumbling against each other amid clouds of dust, and sickening sights and sounds. Hacks containing unlucky spectators of the late affray were smashed like glass, and the occupants were lost sight of in the *debris*. Horses, flying wildly from the battle-field, many of them in death agony, galloped at random forward, joining in the stampede. Those on foot who could catch them rode them bareback, as much to save themselves from being run over as to make quick time.

Wounded men lying along the banks—the few either left on the field or not taken to the captured hospitals—appealed, with raised hands, to those who rode horses, begging to be lifted behind; but few regarded such petitions. Then, the artillery, such as was saved, came thundering along, smashing and overpowering every thing. The regular cavalry joined in the *mêlée*, adding to its terrors, for they rode down footmen without mercy. One of the great guns was overturned and lay amid the ruins of a caisson. Sights of wild and terrible agony met the eye everywhere. An eye-witness of the scene describes the despairing efforts of an artilleryman, who was running between the ponderous fore and after wheels of his gun-carriage, hanging on with both hands and vainly striving to jump upon the ordnance. The drivers were spurring the horses; he could not cling much longer, and a more agonized expression never fixed the features of a drowning man. The carriage bounded from the roughness of a steep hill leading to a creek; he lost his hold, fell, and in an instant the great wheels had crushed the life out of him.

The retreat did not slacken in the least until Centreville was reached. There, the sight of the reserve—Miles's brigade—formed in order on the hill, seemed somewhat to reassure the van. The rally was soon overcome by a few sharp discharges of artillery, the Confederates having a gun taken from the enemy in position. The teams and foot-soldiers pushed on, passing their own camp and heading swiftly for the distant Potomac.

The men literally screamed with rage and fright when their way was blocked up. At every shot, a convulsion, as it were, seized upon the morbid mass of bones, sinews, wood, and iron, and thrilled through it, giving new energy and action to its desperate efforts to get free from itself. The cry of "cavalry" arose. Mounted men still rode faster, shouting out, "cavalry is coming." For miles the roar of the flight might be heard. Negro servants on led-horses dashed frantically past, men in uniform swarmed by on mules, chargers, and even draught horses, which had been cut out of carts and wagons, and went on with harness clinging to their heels as frightened as their riders. "We're whipped," "we're whipped," was the universal cry. The buggies and light wagons tried to pierce the rear of the mass of carts, which were now solidified and moving on like a glacier; while further ahead the number of mounted men increased, and the volume of fugitives became denser.

For ten miles, the road over which the Grand Army had so lately passed southward, gay with unstained banners, and flushed with surety of strength, was covered with the fragments of its retreating forces, shattered and panic-stricken in a single day.

It is impossible to conceive of a more deplorable spectacle than was presented in Washington as the remnants of the army came straggling in. During Sunday evening, it had been supposed in the streets of the Federal city that its army had won a decisive and brilliant victory. The elation was extreme. At each echo of the peals of the cannon, men were seen on the street leaping up and exclaiming—"There goes another hundred of the d——d rebels." The next morning the news of defeat was brought by the tide of the panic-stricken fugitives. One of the boats from Alexandria came near being sunk by the rush of the panic-stricken soldiers upon its decks. Their panic did not stop with their arrival in Washington. They rushed to the depot to continue their flight from Washington. The government was compelled to put it under a strong guard to keep off the fugitives who struggled to get on the Northern trains. Others fled wildly into the country. Not a few escaped across the Susquehanna in this manner, compelling the negroes they met to exchange their clothes with them for their uniforms. For four or five days, the wild and terror-stricken excitement prevailed. Many of the fugitives, with garments nearly torn from them, and covered with the blood of their wounds, thronged the streets with mutinous demonstrations. Others, exhausted with fatigue and hunger, fear and dismay upon their countenances, with torn clothing, covered with dust and blood, were to be seen in all quarters of the city, lying upon the pavements, cellar-doors, or any other spot that offered them a place for the repose which nature demanded. Many of them had nothing of the appearance of soldiers left except their besmeared and tattered uniforms. They did not pretend to observe any order, nor did their officers seem to exercise the least authority over them. Some recounted to horror-stricken audiences the bloody prowess of the Confederate troops. The city of Washington was for days in trembling expectation of the advance of the Confederate army, flushed with victory and intent upon planting its flag upon the summits of the Northern capital.

We had, indeed, won a splendid victory, to judge from its fruits within the limits of the battle-field. The events of the battle of Manassas were glorious for our people, and were thought to be of crushing effect upon the *morale* of our hitherto confident and overweening adversary. Our loss was considerable. The killed outright numbered 369; the wounded, 1,483; making an aggregate of 1,852. The actual loss of the enemy will never be known; it may now only be conjectured. Their abandoned dead, as they were buried by our people where they fell, unfortunately were not enumerated, but many parts of the field were thick with their corpses, as but few battle-fields have ever been. The official reports of the enemy are expressly silent on this point, but still afford us data for an approximate estimate. Left almost in the dark, in respect to the losses of Hunter's and Heintzelman's divisions—first, longest, and most hotly engaged—we are informed that Sherman's brigade—Tyler's division—suffered in killed, wounded, and missing, 609; that is about 18 per cent. of the brigade. A regiment of Franklin's brigade—Gorman's—lost 21 per cent. Griffin's (battery) loss was 30 per cent.; and that of Keyes' brigade, which was so handled by its commander, as to be exposed to only occasional volleys from our troops, was at least 10 per cent. To these facts add the repeated references in the reports of the more reticent commanders, to the "murderous" fire to which they were habitually exposed—the "pistol range" volleys, and galling musketry, of which they speak, as scourging their ranks, and we are warranted in placing the entire loss of the Federalists at over 4,500 in killed, wounded, and prisoners, 28 pieces of artillery, about 5,000 muskets, and nearly 500,000 cartridges; a garrison flag and 10 colors were captured on the field or in the pursuit. Besides these, we captured 64 artillery horses, with their harness, 26 wagons, and much camp equipage, clothing, and other property, abandoned in their flight.

The news of our great victory was received by the people of the South without indecent exultations. The feeling was one of deep and quiet congratulation, singularly characteristic of the Southern people. A superficial observer would have judged Richmond, the Confederate capital, spiritless under the news. There were no bells rung, no bonfires kindled, no exultations of a mob, and none of that parade with which the North had exploited their pettiest successes in the opening of the war. But there was what superficial observation might not have apprehended and could not have appreciated—a deep, serious, thrilling enthusiasm, which swept thousands of hearts, which was too solemn for wild huzzas, and too thoughtful to be uttered in the eloquence of ordinary words. The tremulous tones of deep emotion, the silent grasp of the hand, the faces of men catching the deep and burning enthusiasm of unuttered feelings from each other, composed an eloquence to which words would have been a mockery. Shouts would have marred the solemnity of the general joy. The manner of the reception of the news in Richmond was characteristic of the conservative and poised spirit of our government and people. The only national recognition of the victory was the passage of resolutions in the Provisional Congress, acknowledging the interposition and mercies of Providence in the affairs of the Confederacy, and recommending thanksgiving services in all the churches of the South on the ensuing Sabbath.

The victory had been won by the blood of many of our best and bravest, and the public sorrow over the dead was called upon to pay particular tributes to many of our officers who had fallen in circumstances of particular gallantry. Among others, Gen. Bee, to whose soldierly distinction and heroic services on the field justice was never fully done, until they were especially pointed out in the official reports, both of General Johnston and General Beauregard, had fallen upon the field. The deceased general was a graduate of West Point. During the Mexican war, he had served with marked distinction, winning two brevets before the close of the war; the last that of captain, for gallant and meritorious conduct in the storming of Chapultepec. His achievements since that time in wars among the Indians were such as to attract towards him the attention of his State; and in his dying hand, on the field in which he fell, he grasped the sword which South Carolina had taken pride in presenting him.

Colonel Francis S. Bartow, of Georgia, who had fallen in the same charge in which the gallant South Carolinian had received his death-wound, was chairman of the Military Committee of the Provisional Congress, and that body paid a public tribute of more than usual solemnity and eloquence to his memory.*

---

* An eloquent tribute was paid to the memory of Colonel Bartow in Congress by Mr. Mason, of Virginia, in which some interesting recitals were given of Colonel Bartow's short, but brilliant experiences of the camp. The following extract is indicative of a spirit of confidence, which was peculiarly characteristic of the officers and men alike of our army:

"While in camp, and before the advance of Patterson's column into Virginia, but while it yet hovered on the border in Maryland, watched closely by Johnston's army, I said, casually, to Colonel Bartow, 'The time is approaching when your duties will call you to meet Congress at Richmond, and I look to the pleasure of travelling there with you.' He replied, 'I don't think I can go; my duties will detain me here.' I told him that if a battle was fought between the two armies, it certainly was not then imminent, and I thought his service in Congress, and especially as chairman of the Military

The results of the victory of Manassas were, on the first days of its full announcement, received in the South as indicative of a speedy termination of the war. The advance of our army on Washington was impatiently expected. A few days passed, and it became known to the almost indignant disappointment of the people, that our army had no thoughts of an advance upon the Northern capital, and was content to remain where it was, occupying the defensive line of Bull Run.

Much has been said and written in excuse of the palpable and great error, the perniciousness of which no one doubted after its effects were realized, of the failure of the Confederate army to take advantage of its victory, and press on to Washington, where for days there was nothing to oppose them but

---

Committee, would be even more valuable to the country in Congress, than in the field. After a pause, and with a beaming eye, he said: 'No, sir; I shall never leave this army, until the battle is fought and won.' And, afterwards, while the two armies lay in front of each other, the enemy at Martinsburg, and Johnston with his command at Bunker Hill, only seven miles apart—the enemy we knew numbered some twenty-two thousand men, while on our side we could not present against them half that number, and the battle hourly expected. His head-quarters under a tree in an orchard, and his shelter and shade from a burning sun the branches of that tree, and his table a camp chest—I joined him at dinner. Little is, of course, known of the views and purposes of a general in command, but it was generally understood that Johnston was then to give the enemy battle, should he invite it. In conversation on the chances of the fight, I said to Bartow, 'of the spirit and courage of the troops I have no doubt, but the odds against you are immense.' His prompt reply was, 'they can never whip us. We shall not count the odds. We may be exterminated, but never conquered. I shall go into that fight with a determination never to leave the field alive, but in victory, and I know that the same spirit animates my whole command. How, then, can they whip us?'

"Am I here to tell you how gallantly and truthfully he made that vow good on the bloody plain at Manassas, and how nobly the troops under his command there redeemed the pledge made for them? The 'battle was fought and won,' as he vowed at Bunker Hill, and he sealed in death his first promise in the field of war. Will you call this courage—bravery? No, no. Bartow never thought of the perils of the fight. Bravery, as it is termed, may be nothing more than nervous insensibility. With him the incentives to the battle-field were of a far different type. The stern and lofty purpose to free his country from the invader; the calm judgment of reason, paramount on its throne, overruling all other sensations; resolution and will combined to the deed, the consequence to take care of itself. There is the column of true majesty in man. Such was Bartow, and such will impartial history record him. He won immortality in Fame, even at the threshold of her temple."

an utterly demoralized army, intent upon a continuance of their flight at the approach of our forces. In his official report, General Johnston insists that "no serious thoughts" were ever entertained of advancing against the capital, as it was considered certain that the fresh troops within the works were, in number, quite sufficient for their defence; and that if not, General Patterson's army would certainly reinforce them soon enough. This excuse takes no account of the utterly demoralized condition of the Northern forces at Washington; and the further explanations of the inadequate means of our army in ammunition, provisions, and transportation are only satisfactory excuses, why the toil of pursuit was not undertaken immediately after the battle, and do not answer with complete satisfaction the inquiry why an advance movement was not made within the time when means for it might have been furnished, and the enemy was still cowed, dispirited, and trembling for his safety in the refuges of Washington.

The fact is, that our army had shown no capacity to understand the extent of their fortunes, or to use the unparalleled opportunities they had so bravely won. They had achieved a victory not less brilliant than that of Jena, and not more profitable than that of Alma. Instead of entering the gates of Sebastopol from the last-named field, the victors preferred to wait and reorganize, and found, instead of a glorious and unresisting prey, a ten months' siege.

The lesson of a lost opportunity in the victory of Manassas had to be repeated to the South with additions of misfortune. For months the world was to witness our largest army in the field confronting in idleness and the demoralizations of a stationary camp an enemy already routed within twenty miles of his capital; giving him the opportunity not only to repair the shattered columns of his Grand Army, but to call nearly half a million of new men into the field; to fit out four extensive armadas; to fall upon a defenceless line of sea-coast; to open a new theatre of war in the West and on the Mississippi, and to cover the frontiers of half a continent with his armies and navies.

INCIDENTS OF THE BATTLE.

A friend, Captain McFarland, who did service in the battle of Manassas as a private in Captain Powell's Virginia cavalry, has furnished us with a diary of some thrilling incidents of the action. We use a few of them in Captain McFarland's words:

"At 8 A. M. we proceeded to take position as picket guard and videttes in a little clump of timber, about three quarters of a mile, directly in front of the Confederate earth-works at Mitchell's Ford. The picket consisted of twelve infantry and three cavalry. Having secured our horses, we lay down in the edge of the timber, and with our long-range rifles commenced to pick off such of the enemy as were sufficiently presumptuous to show themselves clear of the heavy timber which crowned the distant hill. In a short time, the enemy, being very much annoyed by our sharp-shooting, ran out from the woods, both in our front and on the left, two rifle pieces, and threw their conical shells full into our covert. The pickets, however, were not dislodged. But two of our horses became frantic from the whistling and explosion of the shells, and we found it necessary to remove them. Just at this moment, a detachment of the enemy's cavalry came dashing down the road, but halted before they came within range of the muskets of the infantry. The enemy then commenced a heavy firing with artillery on our earth-works at the ford, and we retired beyond Bull Run.

In the mean time, the thunder of battle was heard on our left, and from the heights above the stream could be seen the smoke from the scene of the conflict, which, as it shifted position, showed the varying tide of conflict. Occasionally, a small white cloud of smoke made its appearance above the horizon, indicating the premature explosion of a bomb-shell; while, at painfully regular intervals, the dull, heavy report of the enemy's thirty-two pounder told us that its position remained unassailed. In the mean time, the infantry in the trenches at Mitchell's Ford were impatiently awaiting the vainly looked-for advance upon our breastworks. The enemy threw their shells continuously into this locality, but during the whole day killed only three men, and these were standing up contrary to orders. This position was commanded by the brave Brigadier-general M. L. Bonham, of South Carolina.

About 11 o'clock, the cavalry were ordered to ride to the main field of action, in the vicinity of the Stone Bridge. We set off at a dashing gallop, throwing down fences and leaping ditches, in our eagerness to participate in the then raging conflict. In crossing an open field, I was, with Lieutenant Timberlake, riding at the head of a detachment, consisting of Captain Wickham's light-horse troop, and Captain E. B. Powell's company of Fairfax cavalry, when a shell was thrown at the head of the column from a rifle piece stationed at the distance of not less than two miles, and as, hurrying onward, we leaned down upon our horses, the hurtling missile passed a few inches above us, burying itself harmlessly in the soft earth on our left.

On arriving near the scene of action, we took position below the Lewis house, under cover of an abruptly rising hill. Here we remained stationary for about an hour. The enemy in the mean time, knowing our position, endeavored to dislodge us with their shells, which for some time came hissing over our heads, and exploded harmlessly in our rear. Finally, however, they lowered their guns sufficiently to cause their shot to touch the crest of the hill, and *ricochet* into our very midst, killing one man, besides wounding several, and maiming a number of horses. But we still retained our position amid the noise of battle, which now became terrific.

From the distance came the roar of the enemy's artillery, while near by our field-pieces were incessantly vomiting their showers of grape and hurling their small shell into the very teeth of the foe. At intervals, as regiments came face to face, the unmistakable rattle of the musketry told that the small-arms of our brave boys were doing deadly work. At times, we could hear wild yells and cheers which rose above the din, as our infantry rushed on to the charge. Then followed an ominous silence, and I could imagine the fierce but quiet work of steel to steel, until another cheer brought me knowledge of the baffled enemy.

Meanwhile, our reinforcements were pouring by, and pressing with enthusiastic cheers to the battle-field. On the other hand, many of our wounded were borne past us to the rear. One poor fellow was shot through the left cheek; as he came past me, he smiled, and muttered with difficulty, "Boys, they've spoilt my beauty." He could say no more, but an expression of acute pain flitted across his face, and shaking his clenched fist in the direction of the foe, he passed on. Another came by, shot in the breast. His clothing had been stripped from over his ghastly wound, and at every breath, the warm life-blood gushed from his bosom. I rode up to him, as, leaning on two companions, he stopped for a moment to rest. "My poor fellow," said I, "I am sorry to see you thus." "Yes! yes," was his reply, "they've done for *me* now, but my father's there yet! our army's there yet! our cause is there yet!" and raising himself from the arms of his companions, his pale face lighting up like a sunbeam, he cried with an enthusiasm I shall never forget, "and Liberty's there yet!" But this spasmodic exertion was too much for him, a purple flood poured from his wound, and he swooned away. I was enthusiastic before, but I felt then as if I could have ridden singly and alone upon a regiment, regardless of all but my country's cause.

Just then, the noble Beauregard came dashing by with his staff, and the cry was raised, that part of Sherman's battery had been taken. Cheer after cheer went up from our squadrons. It was taken up and borne along the whole battle-field, until the triumphant shout seemed one grand cry of victory. At this auspicious moment, our infantry who had been supporting the batteries were ordered to rise and charge the enemy with the bayonet. With terrific yells, they rushed upon the Federal legions with an impetuosity which could not be withstood, and terror-stricken, they broke and fled like deer from the cry of wolves. Our men followed hard upon them, shouting, and driving their bayonets up to the hilt in the backs of such of the enemy as by ill luck chanced to be hindmost in the flight.

At this moment, one of Gen. Beauregard's aids rode rapidly up and spoke to Col. Radford, commander of our regiment of Virginia cavalry, who immediately turned to us and shouted, "Men, now is our time!" It was the happiest moment of my life. Taking a rapid gallop, we crossed Bull Run about three-quarters of a mile below the Stone Bridge, and made for the rear of the now flying enemy. On we dashed, with the speed of the wind, our horses wild with excitement, leaping fences, ditches, and fallen trees, until we came opposite to the house of Mrs. Spindle, which was used by the enemy as a hospital, and in front of which was a small cleared space, the fence which inclosed it running next the timber. Leaping this fence, we debouched from the woods with a demoniacal yell, and found ourselves on the flank of the enemy.

The remnant of Sherman's battery was passing at the time, and thus we threw ourselves between the main body of the enemy and Sherman's battery, which, supported by four regiments of infantry, covered the retreat of the Federal army. Our regiment had divided in the charge, and our detachment now consisted of Capt. Wickham's cavalry, Capt. E. B. Powell's troop of Fairfax cavalry, the Radford Rangers, Capt. Radford, the whole led by Col. Radford.

Our onslaught was terrific. With our rifles and shot-guns, we killed forty-nine of the enemy the first discharge, then drawing our sabres, we dashed upon them, cutting them down indiscriminately.

With several others, I rode up to the door of the hospital in which a number of terrified Yankees had crowded for safety, and as they came out, we shot them down with our pistols. Happening at this moment to turn round, I saw a Yankee soldier in the act of discharging his musket at the group stationed around the door. Just as he fired, I wheeled my horse, and endeavored to ride him down, but he rolled over a fence which crossed the yard. This, I forced my horse to leap, and drawing my revolver, I shouted to him to stop; as he turned, I aimed to fire into his face, but my horse being restive, the ball intended for his brain, only passed through his arm, which he held over his head, and thence through his cap. I was about to finish him with another shot (for I had vowed to spare no prisoners that day), when I chanced to look into his face. He was a beardless boy, evidently not more than seventeen years old. I could not find it in my heart to kill him, for he plead piteously; so seizing him by the collar, and putting my horse at the speed, leaping the fence, I dragged him to our rear-guard.

Just at this moment, I saw that the enemy had unlimbered two field-pieces, and were preparing to open upon us. Capt. Radford was near me, and I pointed to the cannon. He dashed the spurs into his horse, and shouted, "Charge the battery." But only twenty of our men were near, the rest having charged the rear of the main body of the flying Federals. Besides this, the cannon were supported by several regiments of infantry. We saw our situation at a glance, and determined to retreat to the enemy's flank. We were very close to the battery, and as I wheeled my horse, I fired a shot from my revolver at the man who was aiming the piece. He reeled, grasped at the wheel, and fell. I had thrown myself entirely on the left side of my horse, my foot hanging upon the croup of the saddle, and the grape consequently passed over me. Capt. Radford was in advance of me, his horse very unruly, plunging furiously. As I rode up, he uttered a cry, and put his hand to his side. At this instant, we came to a fence, and my horse cleared it with a bound. I turned to look for Capt. Radford, but he was not visible. A grape-shot had entered just above the hip, and tearing through his bowels, passed out of his left side. He fell from his steed, which leaped the fence, and ran off. The captain was found afterwards by some of Col. Munford's cavalry. He lived till sunset, and died in great agony. By this discharge were killed, besides Capt. R., a lieutenant, two non-commissioned officers, and five privates.

Having gained the flank of the enemy, I dismounted and fired for some time with my rifle into the passing columns. Suddenly I found myself entirely alone, and remounting, I rode back until I found Col. Munford's column drawn up in the woods. Not being able to find my own company, I returned to the pursuit.

Kemper's battery had dashed upon the horror-stricken foe, and opened on their rear, which was covered by the remainder of Sherman's battery, including the thirty-two pound rifle-gun, known as "Long Tom." The havoc produced was terrible. Drivers were shot from their horses, torn to pieces by the shells and shot. Cannon were dismounted, wheels smashed, horses maimed, and the road strewn with the dead. This completed the rout, and the passage of Cub Run was blocked by wagons and caissons being driven into the fords above and below the bridge, and upon the bridge itself.

The route taken by the flying enemy was blocked with dead. I saw Yankees stone-dead, without a wound. They had evidently died from exhaustion or sheer fright. Along the route we found the carriage of Governor Sprague of Rhode Island, and in it his overcoat, with several baskets of champagne. The necks of the bottles were snapped in a trice, and we drank to our victory. But our delight and pride can scarcely be imagined, when we found "Long Tom," whose whistling shells had been falling continually among us from early dawn. It was hauled back to Bull Run amid the shouts of our men, and particularly Kemper's artillery boys, who acted so well their part in causing the Federals to abandon it.

* * * * * * * * The following morning, in the dark drizzling rain, I rode over the field of battle. It was a sorrowful and terrible spectacle to behold, without the stirring excitements of battle to relieve the horrors of the ghastly heaps of dead that strewed the field. At a distance, some portions of the field presented the appearance of flower-gardens, from the gay colors of the uniforms, turbans, &c., of the dead Zouaves. The faces of many of the dead men were already hideously swollen, blotched, and blackened, from the effects of the warm, wet atmosphere of the night.

In a little clump of second-growth pines, a number of wounded had crawled for shelter. Many of our men were busy doing them offices of kindness and humanity. There was one New York Zouave who appeared to be dying; his jaws were working, and he seemed to be in great agony. I poured some water down his throat, which revived him. Fixing his eyes upon me, with a look of fierce hatred, he muttered, "You d——d rebel, if I had a musket I would blow out your infernal soul." Another pale youth was lying in the wet undergrowth, shivering in the rain, and in the cold of approaching death. He was looking wistfully towards a large, warm blanket spread across my saddle, and said in his halting, shivering breath, "I'm so cold." I spread the blanket over him, and left him to that end of his wretchedness which could not be far distant.

CHAPTER V.

Results of the Manassas Battle in the North.—General Scott.—McClellan, "the Young Napoleon."—Energy of the Federal Government.—The Bank Loan.—Events in the West.—The MISSOURI CAMPAIGN.—Governor Jackson's Proclamation.—Sterling Price.—The Affair of Booneville.—Organization of the Missouri forces.—The BATTLE OF CARTHAGE.—General McCulloch.—The BATTLE OF OAK HILL.—Death of General Lyon.—The Confederate Troops leave Missouri.—Operations in Northern Missouri.—General Harris.—General Price's march towards the Missouri.—The Affair at Drywood Creek.—The BATTLE OF LEXINGTON.—The Jayhawkers.—The Victory of "the Five Hundred."—General Price's Achievements.—His Retreat and the necessity for it.—Operations of General Jeff. Thompson in Southeastern Missouri.—The Affair of Fredericktown.—General Price's passage of the Osage River.—Secession of Missouri from the Federal Union.—Fremont superseded.—The Federal forces in Missouri demoralized.—General Price at Springfield.—Review of his Campaign.—SKETCH OF GENERAL PRICE.—Coldness of the Government towards him.

THE Northern mind demanded a distinguished victim for its humiliating defeat at Manassas. The people and government of the North had alike flattered themselves with the expectation of possessing Richmond by midsummer; their forces were said to be invincible, and their ears were not open to any report or suggestion of a possible disaster. On the night of the 21st of July, the inhabitants of the Northern cities had slept upon the assurances of victory. It would be idle to attempt a description of their disappointment and consternation on the succeeding day.

The Northern newspapers were forced to the acknowledgment of a disaster at once humiliating and terrible. They assigned various causes for it. Among these were the non-arrival of General Patterson and the incompetence of their general officers. The favorite explanation of the disaster was, however, the premature advance of the army under General Scott's direction; although the fact was, that the advance movement had been undertaken from the pressure of popular clamor in the North.

The clamor was now for new commanders. It came from the army and the people indiscriminately. The commander-in-chief, General Scott, was said to be impaired in his faculties by age, and it was urged that he should be made to yield the command to a younger and more efficient spirit. The railing accusations against General Scott were made by Northern journals that had, before the issue of Manassas, declared him to be the "Greatest Captain of the Age," and without a rival among modern military chieftains. It was thought no alleviation of the matter that he was not advised, as his friends represented, of the strength of "the rebels." It was his business to have known it, and to have calculated the result.

General Scott cringed at the lash of popular indignation with a humiliation painful to behold. He was not great in misfortune. In a scene with President Lincoln, the incidents of which were related in the Federal House of Representatives by General Richardson, of Illinois, he declared that he had acted "the coward," in yielding to popular clamor for an advance movement, and sought in this wretched and infamous confession the mercy of demagogues who insulted his fallen fortunes.

The call for a "younger general" to take command of the Federal forces was promptly responded to by the appointment of General G. B. McClellan to the command of the Army of the Potomac. The understanding on both sides of the line was, that General Scott was virtually superseded by the Federal government, so far as the responsibility of active service was concerned, though he retained his nominal position and pay as lieutenant-general and commander-in-chief of the Army of the United States. The unfortunate commander experienced the deep humiliation and disgrace of being adjudged incompetent by the North, whose cause he had unnaturally espoused, and whose armies he had sent into the field as invaders of the land of his birth. The retribution was righteous. No penalties of fortune were too severe for a general who had led or directed an army to trample upon the graves of his sires and to despoil the homes of his kindred and country.

General McClellan had been lifted into an immense popularity by his successes in Northwestern Virginia, in the affair of Rich Mountain and the pursuit of General Garnett, which Northern exaggeration had transformed into great victories. For weeks he had been the object of a "sensation." His name was displayed in New York, on placards, on banners, and in newspaper headings, with the phrase, "McClellan—two victories in one day." The newspapers gave him the title of "the Young Napoleon," and in the South the title was derisively perpetuated. He was only thirty-five years of age—small in stature, with black hair and moustaches, and a remarkable military precision of manner. He was a pupil of West Point, and had been one of the American Military Commission to the Crimea. When appointed major-general of volunteers by Governor Dennison, of Ohio, he had resigned from the army, and was superintendent of the Ohio and Mississippi railroad, a dilapidated concern. There is no reason to suppose that the man who was appointed to the responsible and onerous command of the Army of the Potomac was any thing more than the creature of a feeble popular applause.

A leading Southern newspaper had declared, on the announcement of the complete and brilliant victory at Manassas, "the independence of the Confederacy is secured." There could not have been a greater mistake. The active and elastic spirit of the North was soon at work to repair its fortunes; and time and opportunity were given it by the South, not only to recover lost resources, but to invent new. The government at Washington displayed an energy which, perhaps, is the most remarkable phenomenon in the whole history of the war: it multiplied its armies; it reassured the confidence of the people; it recovered itself from financial straits which were almost thought to be hopeless, and while the politicians of the South were declaring that the Federal treasury was bankrupt, it negotiated a loan of one hundred and fifty millions of dollars from the banks of New York, Philadelphia, and Boston, at a rate but a fraction above that of legal interest in the State of New York.

While the North was thus recovering its resources on the frontiers of Virginia and preparing for an extension of the campaign, events were transpiring in the West which were giving extraordinary lessons of example and encouragement to the Southern States bordering on the Atlantic and Gulf. These events were taking place in Missouri. The campaign in that State was one of the most brilliant episodes of the war one of the most remarkable in history, and one of the most fruitful in the lessons of the almost miraculous achievements of a people stirred by the enthusiasm of revolution. To the direction of these events we must now divert our narrative.

THE MISSOURI CAMPAIGN.

The riots in St. Louis, to which reference has already been made, were the inaugurating scenes of the revolution in Missouri. The Federal government had commenced its programme of subjugation with a high hand. On the 10th of May, a brigade of Missouri militia, encamped under the law of the State for organizing and drilling the militia, at Camp Jackson, on the western outskirts of St. Louis, had been forced to surrender unconditionally on the demand of Captain (afterwards General) Lyon of the Federal Army. In the riots excited by the Dutch soldiery in St. Louis, numbers of citizens had been murdered in cold blood; a reign of terror was established; and the most severe measures were taken by the Federal authority to keep in subjection the excitement and rage of the people. St. Louis was environed by a line of military posts; all the arms and ammunition in the city were seized, and the houses of citizens searched for concealed munitions of war. The idea of any successful resistance of Missouri to the Federal power was derided. "Let her stir," said the Lincolnites, "and the lion's paw will crush out her paltry existence."

The several weeks that elapsed between the fall of Fort Sumter and the early part of June were occupied by the Secessionists in Missouri with efforts to gain time by negotiation and with preparations for the contest. At length, finding further delay impossible, Governor Jackson issued his proclamation, calling for fifty thousand volunteers. At the time of issuing this proclamation, on the 13th of June, 1861, the governor was advised of the purpose of the Federal authorities to send an effective force from St. Louis to Jefferson City, the capital of the State. He determined, therefore, to move at once with the State records to Booneville, situated on the south bank of the Missouri, eighty miles above Jefferson City. Before his departure from the latter place, he had conferred upon Sterling Price the position of major-general of the army of Missouri, and had also appointed nine brigadier-generals. These were Generals Parsons, M. L. Clark, John B. Clark, Slack, Harris, Stein, Rains, McBride, and Jeff. Thompson.

There was at the time of the issuance of this proclamation no military organization of any description in the State. Perhaps, there had not been a militia muster in Missouri for twelve or fifteen years, there being no law to require it. The State was without arms or ammunition. Such was her condition, when, with a noble and desperate gallantry that might have put to blush forever the stale and common excuse of "helplessness" for a cringing submission to tyranny, the State of Missouri determined alone and unaided to confront and resist the whole power of the North, and to fight it to the issue of liberty or death.

Orders were issued by General Price, at Jefferson City, to the several brigadiers just appointed, to organize their forces as rapidly as possible, and send them forward to Booneville and Lexington.

On the 20th June, General Lyon and Colonel F. P. Blair, with seven thousand Federal troops, well drilled and well armed, came up the river by vessels, and debarked about five miles below Booneville. To oppose them there the Missourians had but about eight hundred men, armed with ordinary rifles and shot-guns, without a piece of artillery, and with but little ammunition. Lyon's command had eight pieces of cannon and the best improved small-arms. The Missourians were commanded by Colonel Marmaduke, a graduate of West Point. Under the impression that the forces against him were inconsiderable, he determined to give them battle; but, upon ascertaining their actual strength, after he had formed his line, he told his men they could not reasonably hope to defend the position, and ordered them to retreat. This order they refused to obey. They declared that they would not leave the ground without exchanging shots with the enemy. The men remained on the field, commanded by their captains and by Lieutenant-colonel Horace Brand. A fight ensued of an hour and a half or more; the result of which was the killing and wounding of upwards of one hundred of the enemy, and a loss of three Missourians killed and twenty-five or thirty wounded, several of whom afterwards died. "The barefoot rebel militia," as they were sneeringly denominated, exhibited a stubbornness on the field of their first fight which greatly surprised their enemy, and, overpowered by his numbers, they retreated in safety, if not in order.

Governor Jackson and General Price arrived at Booneville, from Jefferson City, on the 18th June. Immediately after his arrival, General Price was taken down with a violent sickness, which threatened a serious termination. On the 19th, he was placed on board a boat for Lexington, one of the points at which he had ordered troops to be congregated. This accounts for his absence from the battle of Booneville.

A portion of the Missouri militia engaged in the action, from two hundred and fifty to three hundred in number, took up their line of march for the southwestern portion of the State, under the direction of Governor Jackson, accompanied by the heads of the State Department and by General J. B. Clark and General Parsons. They marched some twenty-five miles after the fight of the morning, in the direction of a place called Cole Camp, to which point it happened that General Lyon and Colonel Blair had sent from seven hundred to one thousand of their "Home Guard," with a view of intercepting the retreat of Jackson. Ascertaining this fact, Governor Jackson halted his forces for the night within twelve or fifteen miles of Camp Cole. Luckily, an expedition for their relief had been speedily organized south of Cole Camp, and was at that very moment ready to remove all obstructions in the way of their journey. This expedition, consisting of about three hundred and fifty men, was commanded by Colonel O'Kane, and was gotten up, in a few hours, in the neighborhood south of the enemy's camp. The so-called "Home Guards," consisting almost exclusively of Germans, were under the command of Colonel Cook, a brother of the notorious B. F. Cook, who was executed at Charlestown, Virginia, in 1859, as an accomplice of John Brown, in the Harper's Ferry raid. Colonel O'Kane approached the camp of the Federals after the hour of midnight. They had no pickets out, except in the direction of Jackson's forces, and he consequently succeeded in completely surprising them. They were encamped in two large barns, and were asleep when the attack was made upon them at daybreak. In an instant, they were aroused, routed, and nearly annihilated; two hundred and six of them being killed, a still larger number wounded, and upwards of one hundred taken prisoners. Colonel Cook and the smaller portion of his command made their escape. The Missourians lost four men killed and fifteen or twenty wounded. They captured three hundred and sixty-two muskets; thus partially supplying themselves with bayonets, the weapons for which they said they had a particular use in the war against their invaders. Of this success of the Missouri "rebels" there was never any account published, even in the newspapers of St. Louis.

Having been reinforced by Col. O'Kane, Governor Jackson proceeded with his reinforcements to Warsaw, on the Osage river in Benton county, pursued by Col. Totten of the Federal army, with fourteen hundred men, well armed and having several pieces of artillery. Upon the receipt of erroneous information as to the strength of Jackson's forces, derived from a German who escaped the destruction of Camp Cole, and perhaps, also, from the indications of public sentiment in the country through which he marched, Col. Totten abandoned the pursuit and returned to the army under Gen. Lyon, at Booneville. Jackson's forces rested at Warsaw for two days, after which they proceeded to Montevallo, in Vernon county, where they halted and remained for six days, expecting to form a junction at that point with another column of their forces that had been congregated at Lexington, and ordered by Gen. Price to the southwestern portion of the State.

That column was under the command of Brigadier-generals Rains and Slack, and consisted of some twenty-five hundred men. Col. Prince, of the Federal army, having collected a force of four or five thousand men from Kansas, with a view of cutting them off, Gen. Price ordered a retreat to some point in the neighborhood of Montevallo. Gen. Price, still very feeble from his recent severe attack of sickness, started with one hundred men to join his forces. His object was to draw his army away from the base-line of the enemy, the Missouri river, and to gain time for the organization of his army. The column from Lexington marched forward, without blankets or clothing of any kind, without wagons, without tents, and, indeed, without any thing usually reckoned among the comforts of an army. They had to rely for subsistence on the country through which they passed—a friendly country it is true, but they had but little time to partake of hospitalities on their march, being closely pursued by the enemy. On the night of the 3d of July, the column from Lexington formed a junction with Jackson's forces in Cedar county.

That night, under orders from Governor Jackson, all the men belonging to the districts of brigadier-generals then present, reported respectively to their appropriate brigadier-generals for the purpose of being organized into companies, battalions, regiments, brigades, and divisions. The result was, that about two thousand reported to Brig.-gen. Rains, six hundred to Brig.-gen. Slack, and about five hundred each to Brigadier-generals J. B. Clark and Parsons; making an entire force of about three thousand six hundred men. Some five or six hundred of the number were, however, entirely unarmed; and the common rifle and the shot-gun constituted the weapons of the armed men, with the exception of the comparatively few who carried the muskets taken in the fight at Cole Camp. The army was organized by 12 o'clock, the 4th of July, and in one hour thereafter, it took up the line of march for the southwest.

Before leaving, Governor Jackson received intelligence that he was pursued by Gen. Lyon, coming down from a northeasterly direction, and by Lane and Sturgis from the northwest, their supposed object being to form a junction in his rear, with a force sufficiently large to crush him. He marched his command a distance of twenty-three miles by nine o'clock on the evening of the 4th, at which hour he stopped for the night. Before the next morning, he received authentic intelligence that a column of men, three thousand in number, had been sent out from St. Louis on the southwestern branch of the Pacific railroad for Rolla, under the command of Gen. Sigel, and that they had arrived at the town of Carthage, immediately in his front, thus threatening him with battle in the course of a few hours. Such was the situation of the undisciplined, badly-armed Missouri State troops, on the morning of the 5th of July; a large Federal force in their rear, pressing upon them, while Sigel in front intercepted their passage. But they were cheerful and buoyant in spirit, notwithstanding the perilous position in which they were placed. They resumed their march at two o'clock on the morning of the 5th, and proceeded, without halting, a distance of ten miles. At 10 o'clock A. M., they approached a creek within a mile and a half of the enemy, whose forces were in line of battle under Sigel, in the open prairie, upon the brow of a hill, and in three detachments, numbering nearly three thousand men.

THE BATTLE OF CARTHAGE.

The Missourians arrived on their first important battle-field with a spirit undiminished by the toil of their march and their sufferings. The men were suffering terribly for water, but could find none, the enemy being between them and the creek. The line of battle was formed with about twelve hundred men as infantry, commanded by Brigadier-generals J. B. Clark, Parsons, and Slack, and the remainder acting as cavalry under Brigadier-general Rains, the whole under the command of Governor Jackson. The infantry were formed, and placed in line of battle six hundred yards from the enemy, on the brow of the hill fronting his line. The cavalry deployed to the right and left, with a view of charging and attacking the enemy on his right and left wing, while the infantry were to advance from the front. Sigel had eight pieces of cannon. The Missourians had a few old pieces, but nothing to charge them with. While their cavalry were deploying to the right and left, Sigel's batteries opened upon their line with grape, canister, shell, and round-shot. The cannon of the Missourians replied as best they could. They were loaded with trace-chains, bits of iron, rocks, &c. It was difficult to get their cavalry up to the position agreed upon as the one from which a general charge should be commenced upon the foe. Sigel would turn his batteries upon them whenever they came in striking distance, causing a stampede among the horses, and subjecting the troops to a galling fire. This continued to be the case for an hour and thirty-five minutes. Owing to the difficulty of bringing the horses into position, the brigadier-generals ordered the infantry to charge the enemy, the cavalry to come up at the same time in supporting distance. They advanced in double-quick, with a shout, when the enemy retreated across Bear Creek, a wide and deep stream, and then destroyed the bridge over which they crossed. Sigel's forces retreated along the bank of the creek a distance of a mile or a mile and a half, and formed behind a skirt of timber. The Missourians had to cross an open field, exposed to a raking fire, before they could reach the corner of the woods, beyond which the enemy had formed. A number of the cavalry dismounted and acted with the infantry, thus bringing into active use nearly all the small-arms brought upon the field. They rushed to the skirt of timber, and opened vigorously upon the enemy across the stream, who returned the fire with great spirit. For the space of an hour, the fire on each side was incessant and fierce. The Missourians threw a quantity of dead timber into the stream, and commenced crossing over in large numbers, when the enemy again abandoned his position and started in the direction of Carthage, eight miles distant. A running fight was kept up all the way to Carthage, Sigel and his forces being closely pursued by the men whom they had expected to capture without a fight. At Carthage, the enemy again made a stand, forming an ambuscade behind houses, wood-piles, and fences. After a severe engagement there of some forty minutes, he retreated under cover of night in the direction of Rolla. He was pursued some three or four miles, till near nine o'clock, when the Missourians were called back and ordered to collect their wounded. They camped at Carthage that night (July 5), on the same ground that Sigel had occupied two nights before. The little army had done a brilliant day's work. They had fought an enemy from 10 A. M. to 9 P. M., killing and wounding a considerable number of his men, and driving him twelve miles on the route of his retreat. They afterwards ascertained that he continued to march all night, and did not halt till eleven o'clock the next day, nearly thirty miles from Carthage. The casualties of the day cannot be given with accuracy. The Missourians lost between forty and fifty killed, and from one hundred and twenty-five to one hundred and fifty wounded. The loss of the enemy was estimated at from one hundred and fifty to two hundred killed, and from three hundred to four hundred wounded—his killed and wounded being scattered over a space of upwards of ten miles. The Missourians captured several hundred muskets, which were given to their unarmed soldiers. The victory of Carthage had an inspiriting effect upon the Missourians, and taught the enemy a lesson of humility which he did not soon forget. It awakened the Federal commanders in Missouri to a sense of the magnitude of the work before them. When Sigel first got sight of the forces drawn up against him, he assured his men that there would be no serious conflict. He said they were coming into line like a worm-fence, and that a few grape, canister, and shell thrown into their midst, would throw them into confusion, and put them to flight. This accomplished, he would charge them with his cavalry and take them prisoners, one and all. But after carefully observing their movements for a time, in the heat of the action, he changed his tone. "Great God," he exclaimed, "was the like ever seen! Raw recruits, unacquainted with war, standing their ground like veterans, hurling defiance at every discharge of the batteries against them, and cheering their own batteries whenever discharged. Such material, properly worked up, would constitute the best troops in the world." Such was the testimony of Gen. Sigel, who bears the reputation of one of the most skilful and accomplished officers in the Federal service.

The next day, July 6th, General Price arrived at Carthage, accompanied by Brigadier-general McCulloch of the Confederate army, and Major-general Pierce of the Arkansas State forces, with a force of nearly two thousand men. These important arrivals were hailed with joy by the Missourians in camp. They were happy to see their beloved general so far restored to health as to be able to take command; and the presence of the gallant Generals McCulloch and Pierce with an effective force gave them an assurance, not to be mistaken, of the friendly feeling and intention of the Confederate government towards the State of Missouri.

On the 7th, the forces at Carthage, under their respective commands, took up the line of march for Cowskin Prairie, in McDonald county, near the Indian nation. It turned out that Lyon, Sturgis, Sweeny, and Sigel, instead of pursuing their foe, determined to form a junction at Springfield. The forces of Price and McCulloch remained at Cowskin Prairie for several days, organizing for the work before them. General Price received considerable reinforcements; making the whole numerical strength of his command about ten thousand. More than one half of the number, however, were entirely unarmed. Price, McCulloch, and Pierce decided to march upon Springfield, and attack the enemy where he had taken his position in force. To that end, their forces were concentrated at Cassville, in Barry county, according to orders, and from that point they proceeded in the direction of Springfield, ninety miles distant, General McCulloch leading the advance.

Upon his arrival at Crane Creek, General McCulloch was informed by his pickets that the Federals had left Springfield, and were advancing upon him in large force, their advanced guard being then encamped within seven miles of him. For several days there was considerable skirmishing between the pickets of the two armies in that locality. In consequence of information of the immense superiority of the enemy's force, General McCulloch, after consultation with the general officers, determined to make a retrograde movement. He regarded the unarmed men as incumbrances, and thought the unorganized and undisciplined condition of both wings of the army suggested the wisdom of avoiding battle with the disciplined enemy upon his own ground, and in greatly superior numbers.

General Price, however, entertained a different opinion of the strength of the enemy. He favored an immediate advance. This policy being sustained by his officers, General Price requested McCulloch to loan a number of arms from his command for the use of such of the Missouri soldiers as were unarmed, believing that, with the force at his command, he could whip the enemy. General McCulloch declined to comply with the request, being governed, no doubt, by the same reasons which had induced him to decline the responsibility of ordering an advance of the whole command.

On the evening of the day upon which this consultation occurred, General McCulloch received a general order from General Polk, commander of the Southwestern division of the Confederate army, to advance upon the enemy in Missouri. He immediately held another consultation with the officers of the two divisions, exhibited the order he had received, and offered to march at once upon Springfield, upon condition that he should have the chief command of the army. General Price replied, that he was not fighting for distinction, but for the defence of the liberties of his countrymen, and that it mattered but little what position he occupied. He said that he was ready to surrender not only the command, but his life as a sacrifice to the cause. He accordingly did not hesitate, with a magnanimity of which history presents but few examples in military leaders, to turn over the command to General McCulloch, and to take a subordinate position in a contest in which, from the first, he was assured of victory.

On taking command, General McCulloch issued a general order, that all the unarmed men should remain in camp, and all those furnished with arms should get their guns in condition for service, provide themselves with fifty rounds of ammunition, and get in readiness to take up the line of march by twelve o'clock at night. The army was divided into three columns: the first commanded by General McCulloch, the second by General Pierce, and the third by General Price. They took up the line of march at the hour named, leaving the baggage train behind, and proceeded in the direction of Springfield. The troops were in fine condition and in excellent spirits, expecting to find the enemy posted about eight miles from their camp, on the Springfield road, where the natural defences are very strong, being a series of eminences on either side of the road. They arrived at that locality about sunrise, carefully approached it, and ascertained that the enemy had retired the previous afternoon. They followed in pursuit that day a distance of twenty-two miles, regardless of dust and heat; twelve miles of the distance without a drop of water—the troops having no canteens.

The weary army encamped on the night of the 8th at Big Spring, one mile and a half from Wilson's Creek, and ten miles and a half south of Springfield. Their baggage trains having been left behind, and their beef cattle also, the troops had not eaten any thing for twenty-four hours, and had been supplied with only half rations for ten days previous. In this exigency, they satisfied the cravings of hunger by eating green corn, without a particle of salt or a mouthful of meat. The wardrobe of the soldiers on that night was thus humorously described by one of the number: "We had not a blanket, not a tent, nor any clothes, except the few we had on our backs, and four-fifths of us were barefooted. Billy Barlow's dress at a circus would be decent in comparison with that of almost any one, from the major-general down to the humblest private."

On the next day, the army moved to Wilson's Creek, and there took up camp, that they might be convenient to several large fields from which they could supply themselves with green corn, which, for two days, constituted their only repast.

Orders were issued by General McCulloch to the troops to get ready to take up the line of march to Springfield by nine o'clock P. M., with a view of attacking the enemy at four different points at daybreak the next morning. His effective force, as stated by himself, was five thousand three hundred infantry, fifteen pieces of artillery, and six thousand horsemen, armed with flint-lock muskets, rifles, and shot-guns.

After receiving the order to march, the troops satisfied their hunger, prepared their guns and ammunition, and got up a dance before every camp-fire. When nine o'clock came, in consequence of the threatening appearance of the weather, and the want of cartridge-boxes to protect the ammunition of the men, the order to march was countermanded, the commanding general hoping to be able to move early the next morning. The dance before the camp-fires was resumed and kept up until a late hour.

THE BATTLE OF OAK HILL.

The next morning, the 10th of August, before sunrise, the troops were attacked by the enemy, who had succeeded in gaining the position he desired. General Lyon attacked them on their left, and General Sigel on their right and in their rear. From each of these points batteries opened upon them. General McCulloch's command was soon ready. The Missourians, under Brigadier-generals Slack, Clark, McBride, Parsons, and Rains, were nearest the position taken by General Lyon with his main force. General Price ordered them to move their artillery and infantry rapidly forward. Advancing a few hundred yards, he came upon the main body of the enemy on the left, commanded by General Lyon in person. The infantry and artillery, which General Price had ordered to follow him, came up to the number of upwards of two thousand, and opened upon the enemy a brisk and well-directed fire. Woodruff's battery opened to that of the enemy under Captain Totten, and a constant cannonading was kept up between these batteries during the action. Hebert's regiment of Louisiana volunteers and McIntosh's regiment of Arkansas mounted riflemen were ordered to the front, and, after passing the battery, turned to the left, and soon engaged the enemy with the regiments deployed. Colonel McIntosh dismounted his regiment, and the two marched up abreast to the fence around a large corn-field, where they met the left of the enemy already posted. A terrible conflict of small-arms took place here. Despite the galling fire poured upon these two regiments, they leaped over the fence, and, gallantly led by their colonels, drove the enemy before them back upon the main body. During this time, the Missourians, under General Price, were nobly sustaining themselves in the centre, and were hotly engaged on the sides of the height upon which the enemy was posted. Some distance on the right, General Sigel had opened his battery upon Churchill's and Green's regiments, and had gradually made his way to the Springfield road, upon each side of which the Confederates were encamped, and had established their battery in a strong position. General McCulloch at once took two companies of the Louisiana regiment which were nearest to him at the time, and marched them rapidly from the front and right to the rear, with orders to Colonel McIntosh to bring up the remainder. When they arrived near the enemy's battery, they found that Reid's battery had opened upon it, and that it was already in confusion. Advantage was taken of this, and soon the Louisianians gallantly charged upon the guns and swept the cannoneers away. Five guns were here taken, and Sigel's forces completely routed. They commenced a rapid retreat with a single gun, pursued by some companies of the Texas regiment and a portion of Colonel Major's Missouri regiment of cavalry. In the pursuit, many of the enemy were killed and his last gun captured. Having cleared their right and rear, it became necessary for the Confederate forces to direct all their attention to the centre, where General Lyon was pressing upon the Missourians with all his strength. To this point, McIntosh's regiment under Lieutenant-colonel Embry, and Churchill's regiment on foot, Gratiot's regiment, and McRae's battalion, were sent to their aid. A terrible fire of musketry was now kept up along the whole line of the hill upon which the enemy was posted. Masses of infantry fell back and again rushed forward. The summit of the hill was covered with the dead and the wounded. Both sides were fighting with desperation for the field. Carroll's and Green's regiments, led gallantly by Captain Bradfute, charged Totten's battery; but the whole strength of the enemy were immediately in the rear, and a deadly fire was opened upon them. At this critical moment, when the fortunes of the day seemed to be at the turning-point, two regiments of General Pierce's brigade were ordered to march from their position, as reserves, to support the centre. Reid's battery was also ordered to move forward, and the Louisiana regiment was again called into action on the left of it. The battle then became general, and probably, says General McCulloch, in his official report, "no two opposing forces ever fought with greater desperation; inch by inch the enemy gave way, and were driven from their position. Totten's battery fell back—Missourians, Arkansans, Louisianians, and Texans pushed forward—the incessant roll of musketry was deafening, and the balls fell thick as hailstones; but still our gallant Southerners pushed onward, and, with one wild yell, broke upon the enemy, pushing them back, and strewing the ground with their dead. Nothing could withstand the impetuosity of our final charge. The enemy fled, and could not again be rallied."

Thus ended the battle of Oak Hill, or of Wilson's Creek, as Gen. Sigel called it in his official report to the Federal authorities. It lasted about six hours. The force of the enemy was stated at from nine to ten thousand, and consisted for the most part of well-disciplined, well-armed troops, a large portion of them belonging to the old United States army. They were not prepared for the signal defeat which they suffered. Their loss was supposed to be about two thousand in killed, wounded, and prisoners. They also lost six pieces of artillery, several hundred stand of small-arms, and several of their standards. Major-general Lyon, their chief-in-command, was killed, and many of their officers were wounded—some of them high in rank. Gen. McCulloch, in his official report, stated the entire loss on the part of his command at two hundred and sixty-five killed, eight hundred wounded, and thirty missing. Of these, the Missourians, according to Gen. Price's report, lost one hundred and fifty-six killed, and five hundred and seventeen wounded.

The victory was won by the determined valor of each division of the army. The troops from Texas, Arkansas, and Louisiana bore themselves with a gallantry characteristic of their respective States. The Missouri troops were mostly undisciplined, but they had fought with the most desperate valor, never failing to advance when ordered. Repeatedly, during the action, they retired from their position, and then returned to it with increased energy and enthusiasm—a feat rarely performed by undisciplined troops. The efficiency of the double-barrel shot-gun and the walnut-stock rifle, was abundantly demonstrated—these being the only arms used by the Missourians in this fight, with the exception of the four hundred muskets captured from the enemy on the two occasions already named.

Gen. Lyon, at the head of his regulars, was killed in an attempt to turn the wing mainly defended by the arms of the Missourians. He received two small rifle-balls or buckshot in the heart, the one just above the left nipple, the other immediately below it. He had been previously wounded in the leg. His surgeon came in for his body, under a flag of truce, after the close of the battle, and Gen. Price sent it in his own wagon. But the enemy, in his flight, left the body unshrouded in Springfield. The next morning, August 11th, Lieut.-col. Gustavus Elgin and Col. R. H. Mercer, two of the members of Brigadier-general Clark's staff, caused the body to be properly prepared for burial. He was temporarily interred at Springfield, in a metallic coffin procured by Mrs. Phelps, wife of John S. Phelps, a former member of the Federal Congress from that district, and now an officer in the Lincoln army. A few days afterwards, the body was disinterred and sent to St. Louis, to await the order of his relatives in Connecticut.

The death of Gen. Lyon was a serious loss to the Federals in Missouri. He was an able and dangerous man—a man of the times, who appreciated the force of audacity and quick decision in a revolutionary war. To military education and talents, he united a rare energy and promptitude. No doubts or scruples unsettled his mind. A Connecticut Yankee, without a trace of chivalric feeling or personal sensibility—one of those who submit to insult with indifference, yet are brave on the field—he was this exception to the politics of the late regular army of the United States, that he was an unmitigated, undisguised, and fanatical Abolitionist.

Shortly after the battle of Oak Hill, the Confederate army returned to the frontier of Arkansas, Generals McCulloch and Price having failed to agree upon the plan of campaign in Missouri.

In northern Missouri, the bold and active demonstrations of Gen. Harris had made an important diversion of the enemy in favor of Gen. Price. These demonstrations had been so successfully made, that they diverted eight thousand men from the support of Gen. Lyon, and held them north of the river until after the battle of Oak Hill, thus making an important contribution to the glorious issue of that contest.

The history of the war presents no instance of a more heroic determination of a people to accomplish their freedom, than that exhibted by the people of northern Missouri. Occupying that portion of the State immediately contiguous to the Federal States of Kansas, Iowa, and Illinois, penetrated by two lines of railroads, intersecting at right angles, dividing the country north and south, east and west—which lines of railroads were seized and occupied by the enemy, even before the commencement of hostilities; washed on every side by large, navigable rivers in possession of the enemy; exposed at every point to the inroads of almost countless Federal hosts, the brave people of northern Missouri, without preparation or organization, did not hesitate to meet the alternative of war, in the face of a foe confident in his numbers and resources.

On the 21st June, 1861, a special messenger from Governor Jackson overtook, at Paris, Monroe county, Thomas A. Harris, who was then *en route* as a private soldier to the rendezvous at Booneville. The messenger was the bearer of a commission by which Thomas A. Harris was constituted Brigadier-general of the Missouri State Guard, and assigned to the duty of organizing the forces for the defence of that portion of the State north of the Missouri river. The commission was accompanied by orders from Gen. Sterling Price. At the date of the delivery of the commission and orders, the affair at Booneville had transpired, and the governor and Gen. Price, with such of the forces as had been hastily collected, were, as already stated, in full retreat before the enemy in the direction of southwestern Missouri.

Gen. Harris was without any organized force whatever; without military supplies of any kind; without money, or any authorized agent to pledge the credit of the State. He commenced recruiting an army in the face of the enemy. At a public meeting, called by him, he delivered a stirring and patriotic address, caused the oath of allegiance to the South to be administered to himself in the most public and impressive manner, and, in turn, administered the same oath to fifty-three men, and organized them into a company, directing them to return to their homes, collect their private arms, and join him without delay. When we consider that this bold action was within three hours' march of an enemy in force, and that it invited his bitter resentment, we can rightly appreciate the heroism and self-sacrificing patriotism of the participators.

A false report of the approach of the enemy caused the evacuation of the town of Paris, where quite a number of unarmed troops had assembled. General Harris retired into a stronghold in the knobs of Salt River. He was a brigadier-general, with a command of *three men*, and a few officers whom he had appointed upon his staff. Here, without blankets, tents, or any kind of army equipments, he commenced the organization of a guerrilla force, which was destined to render important service in the progress of the war in Missouri.

Gen. Harris adopted the policy of secretly organizing his force, the necessity for such secrecy being constantly induced by the continued presence and close proximity of the enemy. The fact, however, that Gen. Lyon was moving to the southwest in pursuit of Gen. Price, caused him to attempt a diversion, which was successful, as has been stated, in holding a large Federal force north of the Missouri river. Although the active duties of a guerrilla campaign necessarily involved a delay in organization, yet Gen. Harris was successful in raising a force of two thousand seven hundred and thirty men in the very face of the enemy, and in crossing them over the river; and after a march of sixty-two miles, in twenty-eight hours, he united his command with Gen. Price in time to participate in the memorable battle of Lexington. To follow Gen. Price's command, to that battle-field we must now turn.

Late in August, Gen. Price, abandoned by the Confederate forces, took up his line of march for the Missouri river, with an armed force of about four thousand five hundred men, and seven pieces of cannon. He continued to receive reinforcements from the north side of the Missouri river.

Hearing that the notorious trio of Abolition bandits, Jim Lane, Montgomery, and Jenison, were at Fort Scott, with a marauding force of several thousand, and not desiring them to get into his rear, he detoured to the left from his course to the Missouri river, marching directly to Fort Scott for the purpose of driving them up the river. On the 7th of September, he met with Lane about fifteen miles east of Fort Scott, at a stream called Drywood, where an engagement ensued which lasted for an hour and a half, resulting in the complete rout of the enemy. Gen. Price then sent on a detachment to Fort Scott, and found that the enemy had evacuated the place. He continued his march in the direction of Lexington, where there was a Federal army strongly intrenched, under the command of Col. Mulligan.

Gen. Fremont, who had been appointed by the Federal government to take command in the Missouri department, had inaugurated the campaign with a brutality towards his enemy a selfish splendor in his camp, and a despotism and corruption more characteristic of an Eastern satrap than an American commander in the nineteenth century. He had published a proclamation absolutely confiscating the estates and slave property of "rebels," which measure of brutality was vastly pleasing to the Abolitionists of the North, who recognized the extinction of negro slavery in the South as the essential object of the war, but was not entirely agreeable to the government at Washington, which was not quite ready to declare the extremity to which it proposed to prosecute the war.

On the 10th of September, just as General Price was about to encamp with his forces for the day, he learned that a detachment of Federal troops were marching from Lexington to Warrensburg to seize the funds of the bank in that place, and to arrest and plunder the citizens of Johnson county, in accordance with General Fremont's proclamation and instructions. Although his men were greatly fatigued by several days' continuous and rapid marching, General Price determined to press forward, so as to surprise the enemy, if possible, at Warrensburg. After resting a few hours, he resumed his march at sunset, and continued it without intermission till two o'clock in the morning, when it became evident that the infantry, very few of whom had eaten any thing for twenty-four hours, could march no further. He then halted them, and went forward with the greater portion of his mounted men, till he came, about daybreak, within view of Warrensburg, where he ascertained that the enemy had hastily fled about midnight, burning the bridges behind him. A heavy rain commenced about the same time. This circumstance, coupled with the fact that his men had been fasting for more than twenty-four hours, constrained General Price to abandon the pursuit of the enemy that day. His infantry and artillery having come up, he encamped at Warrensburg, where the citizens vied with each other in feeding his almost famished soldiers.

A violent storm delayed the march next morning till the hour of ten o'clock. General Price then pushed rapidly forward, still hoping to overtake the enemy. Finding it impossible to do this with his infantry, he again ordered a detachment of mounted men to move forward, and placing himself at their head, continued the pursuit to within two and a half miles of Lexington, where he halted for the night, having learned that the enemy's forces had all gone within the city.

THE BATTLE OF LEXINGTON.

About daybreak the next morning, a sharp skirmish took place between the Missouri pickets and the enemy's outposts. A general action was threatened, but General Price, being unwilling to risk an engagement when a short delay would make success, in his estimation, perfectly certain, fell back two or three miles, and awaited the arrival of his infantry and cavalry. These having come up, he advanced upon the town, driving in the Federal pickets, until he came within a short distance of the city. Here the enemy's forces attempted to make a stand, but they were speedily driven from every position, and com pelled to take shelter within their intrenchments. The enemy having strongly fortified the college building, the Missourians took their position within easy range of it, and opened a brisk fire from Bledsoe's and Parsons' batteries. Finding, after sunset, that his ammunition, the most of which had been left behind in the march from Springfield, was nearly exhausted, and that his men, most of whom had not eaten any thing in thirty-six hours, required rest and food, General Price withdrew to the Fair Ground, and encamped there. His ammunition wagons having been at last brought up, and large reinforcements having come in, he again moved into town on the 18th, and commenced the final attack upon the enemy's works. Brigadier-general Rains' division occupied a strong position on the east and northeast of the fortifications, from which position an effective cannonading was kept up on the enemy by Bledsoe's battery, and another battery commanded by Capt. Churchill Clark, of St. Louis. General Parsons took his position southwest of the works. Skirmishers and sharpshooters were sent forward from both of these divisions to harass and fatigue the enemy, and cut them off from water on the north, east, and south of the college, and did great service in the accomplishment of the purposes for which they were detached. Colonel Congreve Jackson's division, and a part of General Stein's, were posted near General Rains and General Parsons as a reserve.

Shortly after entering the city on the 18th, Colonel Rives, who commanded the fourth division in the absence of General Slack, led his regiment and Colonel Hughes' along the river bank to a point immediately beneath and west of the fortifications, General McBride's command and a portion of General Harris's having been ordered to reinforce him. Colonel Rives, in order to cut off the enemy's means of escape, proceeded down the bank of the river to capture a steamboat which was lying immediately under their guns. Just at this moment, a heavy fire was opened upon him from a large dwelling-house, known as Anderson's house, on the summit of the bluff, which the enemy was occupying as a hospital, and from which a white flag was flying. Several companies of General Harris's command and the soldiers of the fourth division, who had won much distinction in previous battles, immediately rushed upon and took the place. The important position thus secured was within one hundred and twenty-five yards of the enemy's intrenchments. A company from Colonel Hughes' regimen then took possession of the boats, one of which was freighted with valuable stores. General McBride's and General Harris's divisions meanwhile stormed and occupied the bluffs immediately north of Anderson's house. The position of these heights enabled the assailants to harass the enemy so greatly, that, resolving to regain them, he made upon the house a successful assault, and one, said General Price, which would have been honorable to him had it not been accompanied by an act of savage barbarity, the cold-blooded and cowardly murder of three defenceless men who had laid down their arms, and surrendered themselves as prisoners. The position thus retaken by the enemy was soon regained by the brave men who had been driven from it, and was thenceforward held by them to the very end of the contest.

The heights on the left of Anderson's house were fortified by our troops with such means as were at their command. On the morning of the 20th, General Price caused a number of hemp bales to be transported to the river heights, where movable breastworks were speedily constructed out of them. The demonstrations of the artillery, and particularly the continued advance of the hempen breastworks, attracted the attention and excited the alarm of the enemy, who made many daring attempts to drive back the assailants. They were, however, repulsed in every instance by the unflinching courage and fixed determination of men fighting for their homes. The hempen breastworks, said General Price, were as efficient as the cotton bales at New Orleans. In these severe encounters, McBride's and Slack's divisions, and Colonel Martin Green and his command, and Colonel Boyd and Major Winston and their commands, were warmly commended for their gallant conduct.

About two o'clock in the afternoon of the 20th, and after fifty-two hours of continuous fighting, a white flag was displayed by the enemy on that part of his works nearest to Col. Green's position, and shortly afterwards another was displayed opposite to Colonel Rives' position. General Price immediately ordered a cessation of all firing, and sent forward his staff officers to ascertain the object of the flag and to open negotiations with the enemy, if such should be his desire. It was agreed that the Federal forces should lay down their arms and surrender themselves prisoners of war.

The entire loss of the Missourians in this series of battles was but twenty-five killed and seventy-two wounded. The enemy's loss was considerably larger, but cannot be stated here with accuracy. The visible fruits of the victory to the Missourians were great: about three thousand five hundred prisoners—among whom were Cols. Mulligan, Marshall, Peabody, White, Grover, Major Van Horn, and one hundred and eighteen other commissioned officers; five pieces of artillery and two mortars; over three thousand stand of infantry arms, a large number of sabres, about seven hundred and fifty horses, many sets of cavalry equipments, wagons, teams, some ammunition, more than $100,000 worth of commissary stores, and a large amount of other property. In addition to all this, General Price obtained the restoration of the great seal of the State, of the public records, and about $900,000 of which the bank at Lexington had been robbed, in accordance with Fremont's instructions. General Price caused the money to be returned at once to the bank.

In his official report of the battle of Lexington, General Price paid a high compliment to the command that had achieved such rich and substantial fruits of victory. "This victory," he wrote, "has demonstrated the fitness of our citizen soldiery for the tedious operations of a siege, as well as for a dashing charge. They lay for fifty-two hours in the open air, without tents or covering, regardless of the sun and rain, and in the very presence of a watchful and desperate foe, manfully repelling every assault and patiently awaiting my orders to storm the fortifications. No general ever commanded a braver o better army. It is composed of the best blood and bravest men of Missouri."

During the siege, quite a number of citizens came in from the neighboring country, and fought, as they expressed it, "on their own hooks." A participator in the battle tells an anecdote of an old man, about sixty years of age, who came up daily from his farm, with his walnut-stock rifle and a basket of provisions, and went to work just as if he were engaged in hauling rails or some other necessary labor of his farm. He took his position behind a large stump upon the descent of the hill on which the fortification was constructed, where he fired with deadly aim during each day of the siege.

When the surrender was made, and the forces under Colonel Mulligan stacked their arms, General Price ordered that they were not to be insulted by word or act, assigning as the reason therefor, that they had fought like brave men, and were entitled to be treated as such. When Colonel Mulligan surrendered his sword, General Price asked him for the scabbard. Mulligan replied that he had thrown it away. The general, upon receiving his sword, returned it to him, saying, he disliked to see a man of his valor without a sword. Mulligan refused to be paroled, upon the ground that his government did not acknowledge the Missourians as belligerents. While awaiting his exchange, Colonel Mulligan and his wife became the guests of General Price, the general surrendering to them his carriage, and treating them with the most civil and obliging hospitality. The captive colonel and his lady were treated by all the officers and soldiers of the Missouri army with a courtesy and kindness which they seemed to appreciate.

After the first day's conflict at Lexington, while General Price was encamped at the Fair Grounds near the city, awaiting reinforcements and preparing the renewal of the attack, an episode occurred at some distance from the city, in which the Missourians again had the satisfaction of inflicting a terrible chastisement upon the bandits of the Lane and Montgomery organization.

Gen. Price was informed that four thousand men under Lane and Montgomery were advancing from the direction of St. Joseph, on the north s'de of the Missouri river, and Gen. Sturgis, with fifteen hundred cavalry, was also advancing from the Hannibal and St. Joseph railroad, for the purpose of relieving the forces under Mulligan. About twenty-five hundred Missourians, under the immediate command of Col. Saunders, were, at the same time, hurrying to the aid of Gen. Price, from the same direction with the Lane and Montgomery Jayhawkers; and having reached the run at Blue Mills, thirty miles above Lexington, on the 17th September, crossed over their force, except some five hundred men, in a ferry-boat. While the remainder were waiting to cross over, the Jayhawkers attacked the five hundred Missourians on the north bank of the river. The battle raged furiously for one hour on the river bottom, which was heavily timbered and in many places covered with water. The Missourians were armed with only shot-guns and rifles, and taken by surprise: no time was given them to call back any portion of their force on the south side of the river; but they were from the counties contiguous to Kansas, accustomed in the border wars since 1854 to almost monthly fights with the Kansas "Jayhawkers," under Lane, and were fired with the most intense hatred of him and of them. Gen. D. R. Atchison, former President of the United States Senate, and well known as one of the boldest leaders of the State Rights party in Missouri, had been sent from Lexington by Gen. Price to meet our troops under Col. Saunders, and hasten them on to his army. He was with the five hundred, on the north side of the river, when they were attacked, and by his presence and example cheered them in the conflict. Charging the "Jayhawkers," with shouts of almost savage ferocity, and fighting with reckless valor, the Missourians drove the enemy back a distance of ten miles, the conflict becoming a hand-to-hand fight, between detached parties on both sides. At length, unable to support the fearful fire of the Missourians at the short distance of forty yards, the enemy broke into open flight. The loss of the Jayhawkers was very considerable. Their official report admitted one hundred and fifty killed and some two hundred wounded. The entire loss of the Missourians was five killed and twenty wounded. The intelligence of this brilliant victory of "the five hundred," was received with shouts of exultation by Price's army at Lexington.

On the second day after the battle of Blue Mills, Col. Saunders, with his command, joined the army at Lexington, and fought gallantly till the surrender of the Federal garrison. In the mean time, Sturgis with his cavalry appeared on the river bank opposite Lexington, expecting to cross over in the boats of Mulligan, and reinforce him to the extent of fourteen hundred men. It happened, however, that on the day before his arrival, Gen. Price's forces had captured all of the enemy's boats and Gen. Sturgis ascertaining this fact, retreated precipi tately in the direction from which he came. Gen. Price had sent across the river two thousand men under Gen. Parsons, to meet the forces under Gen. Sturgis, and they succeeded in capturing all the tents and camp equipage of that distinguished Yankee commander. The tents were most acceptable to the Missourians, as they were the first they had obtained in the war, except one hundred and fifty taken at Springfield. Gen. Sturgis did not stop in his flight for three days and three nights.

The capture of Lexington had crowned Gen. Price's command with a brilliant victory, and so far, the Missouri campaign had proceeded, step by step, from one success to another. It was at this period, however, that Gen. Price found his position one of the greatest emergency. After the victory of Lexington, he received intelligence that the Confederate forces, under Generals Pillow and Hardee, had been withdrawn from the southeastern portion of the State. Gen. McCulloch had retired to Arkansas. In these circumstances, Gen. Price was left with the only forces in Missouri, to confront an enemy seventy thousand strong, and being almost entirely without ammunition, he was reduced to the necessity of making a retrograde movement.

Before leaving Springfield, Gen. Price had made arrangements for an ample supply of ammunition, then at Jacksonsport, Arkansas, to be sent to him in Missouri, Gen. McCulloch promising to send a safe escort for it. Gen. McCulloch subsequently declined to furnish the escort and stopped the train, assigning as the reason therefor that, under the circumstances then existing, it would be unsafe to send it, and that Gen. Price would be compelled to fall back from the Missouri river, before the overwhelming forces of the enemy moving against him under the direction of Gen. Fremont.

Having no means of transportation, except for a limited number of men, and surrounded by circumstances of the most painful and unlooked-for misfortune, Gen. Price was compelled to disband a considerable portion of his forces. No occasion could be more fraught with mortifying reflections to the brave, generous, and hopeful spirit of such a commander as Gen. Price. He had marched from success to success; he had raised a force from hundreds to tens of thousands; his army had been swelled to twenty-three thousand during his stay at Lexington, not enumerating ten thousand volunteers who had collected on the north bank of the Missouri about the period when he commenced a retreat, compelled by emergencies which the most daring valor could no longer hope to surmount. Gen. Price advised all who could not accompany him to take care of such arms as they had, to cherish a determined spirit, and to hold themselves in readiness for another opportunity to join his standard.

In southeastern Missouri, the operations of the partisan, Jeff. Thompson, in connection with Gen. Hardee's command, had attracted some public notice from its adventure, and some incidents of interest. But the campaign in the Ozark mountains was not productive of any important or serious results. Gen. Thompson and his "Swamp Fox Brigade" gave many rash illustrations of daring in the face of the enemy. At one time he burnt an important railroad bridge within fifty miles of the city of St. Louis, which was swarming with Federal troops. On a march towards Fredericktown, with a force of twelve hundred men, Gen. Thompson encountered a Federal force numbering ten thousand men, which he engaged with such skill and courage as to check the enemy's pursuit and move his little force out of danger. The feat showed extraordinary military skill, when we consider that the small force was extricated with only twenty killed, while the loss of the enemy was counted by hundreds; and that his pursuit was baffled only from the impression of a large force opposed to him, which was given by the skilful disposition of ambuscades.

Gen. Price commenced his retreat about the 27th of September. He sent his cavalry forward, and directed them to make a demonstration in the neighborhood of Georgetown, fifty miles from Lexington, where Fremont was concentrating his forces with a view of surrounding him. With Sturgis on the north side of the river, Lane on the west, and himself on the east, each advancing upon Lexington, Fremont expected to cut off and capture the entire force of the Missourians. Gen. Price supplied his mounted men with provisions for several days, and directed them to make demonstrations on each of the divisions of the Federals, so as to gain time for the safe retreat of his infantry and artillery. By this means, he succeeded in deceiv ing the enemy as to his real purpose; inducing Fremont, Lane, and Sturgis to believe that he was about to attack each of them. Each of them fell back, and Fremont commenced ditching.

In the mean time, Price's infantry and artillery were making the best time they could towards the south. They had to encounter a very serious obstacle in crossing streams swollen by the recent rains. The whole command, fifteen thousand strong, crossed the Osage river in two common flat-boats, constructed for the occasion by men who could boast of no previous experience either as graduates of military schools, or even as bridge builders.

Subsequently, General Fremont was fifteen days engaged in crossing at the same place, upon his pontoon bridges. The superiority of the practical man of business, over the scientific engineer and "pathfinder," was demonstrated to the great satisfaction of the Missourians.

Gen. Price continued his retreat to Neosho, at which place the Legislature had assembled, under a proclamation from Governor Jackson.

At Neosho, Gen. Price again formed a junction with Gen. McCulloch, at the head of five thousand men. The Legislature had passed the Ordinance of Secession, and elected delegates to the Provisional Congress of the Southern Confederacy; and here Gen. Price had the satisfaction of firing one hundred guns in honor of the formal secession of Missouri from the United States, to which his services in the field had more than any thing else contributed.

Gen. McCulloch remained a day or two in Neosho, and then fell back with his forces to Cassville. Price remained ten days in Neosho, and then retreated also to Cassville, and from Cassville to Pineville, in McDonald county.

Meanwhile, General Fremont, with his grand army of sixty thousand men, equipped in the most splendid and costly manner, had concentrated his forces at Springfield, throwing forward an advance of ten thousand men under Gen. Sigel to Wilson's Creek. The Missouri forces at Springfield, under th command of Col. Taylor, were ordered by General Price to fall back upon the approach of the enemy; but in leaving the town they encountered Fremont's body-guard, three times their own number, armed with Colt's rifles and commanded by Col. Zagonyi. A conflict ensued, in which fifty of the enemy were killed, and twenty-five captured, including a major. The loss of the Missourians was one killed and three wounded.

At Pineville, General Price made preparations to receive Fremont, determined not to abandon Missouri without a battle. His troops were enthusiastic and confident of success, notwithstanding the fearful superiority of numbers against them. They were in daily expectation of being led by their commander into the greatest battle of the war, when they received the unexpected intelligence that Fremont had been superseded as commander of the Federal forces. This event had the effect of demoralizing the Federal forces to such an extent, that their numbers would have availed them nothing in a fight with their determined foe. The Dutch, who were greatly attached to Fremont, broke out into open mutiny, and the acting officers in command saw that a retreat from Springfield was not only a wise precaution, but an actual necessity. They accordingly left that town in the direction of Rolla, and were pursued by Gen. Price to Oceola. From Oceola, Gen. Price fell back to Springfield, to forage his army and obtain supplies; and here, for the present, we must leave the history of his campaign. We have now traced that history to a period about the first of December.

From the 20th of June to the 1st of December, General Price's army marched over 800 miles, averaging ten thousand men during the time. What they accomplished, the reader will decide for himself, upon the imperfect sketch here given. They fought five battles, and at least thirty skirmishes, in some of which from fifty to hundreds were killed on one side or the other. Not a week elapsed between engagements of some sort. They started without a dollar, without a wagon or team, without a cartridge, without a bayonet-gun. On the first of September, they had about eight thousand bayonet-guns, fifty pieces of cannon, four hundred tents, and many other articles needful in an army; for nearly all of which they were indebted to their own strong arms in battle and to the prodigality of the enemy in providing more than he could take care of in his campaign.

Notwithstanding the great exposure to which the Missouri

troops were subjected, not fifty died of disease during their six months' campaign, and but few were on the sick list at the close of it. The explanation is, that the troops were all the time in motion, and thus escaped the camp fever and other diseases that prove so fatal to armies standing all the time in a defensive position.

SKETCH OF GENERAL PRICE.

The man who had conducted one of the most wonderful campaigns of the war—Sterling Price—was a native of Virginia. He was born about the year 1810 in Prince Edward county, a county which had given birth to two other military notabilities—General John Coffee, the "right-hand man" of General Jackson in his British and Indian campaigns, and General Joseph E. Johnston, already distinguished as one of the heroes of the present war.

Sterling Price emigrated to Missouri, and settled in Charlton county, in the interior of that State, in the year 1830, pursuing the quiet avocations of a farmer.

In the year 1844, Mr. Price was nominated by his party as a candidate for Congress, and was elected by a decided majority. He took his seat in December, 1845; but having failed to receive the party nomination in the following spring, he resigned his seat and returned home. His course in this respect was dictated by that conscientious integrity and high sense of honor which have ever distinguished him in all the relations of life. He argued that his defeat was caused either by dissatisfaction with his course on the part of his constituents, or else by undue influences which had been brought to bear upon the people by ambitious aspirants for the seat, who could labor to a great advantage in their work in supplanting an opponent who was attending to his duties at a distance from them. If the former was the case, he was unwilling to misrepresent his constituents, who, he believed, had the right to instruct him as to the course he should pursue; if the latter, his self-respect would not allow him to serve a people who had rejected him without cause, while he was doing all in his power to advance their interests.

At the time of Mr. Price's retirement from Congress, hostilities had broken out between the United States and Mexico, and volunteers from all parts of the South were flocking to the defence of their country's flag. Mr. Jefferson Davis, of Mississippi, bred a soldier, who, like Mr. Price, was serving his first term in Congress, resigned his seat about the same time, and was soon marching at the head of a Mississippi regiment to the field, from which he was destined to return loaded with many honors. So, too, did a brave Missouri regiment call to its head her own son, who had just doffed his civil robes to enter a new and untried field of duty and honor. The regiment to which Col. Price was attached was detailed for duty in what is now the Territory of New Mexico. It was by his own arms that that province was subdued, though not without several brilliant engagements, in which he displayed the same gallantry that has so distinguished him in the present contest.

Soon after the close of the Mexican war, a violent political excitement broke out in Missouri. The slavery agitation had received a powerful impetus by the introduction into Congress of the Wilmot Proviso and other sectional measures, whose avowed object was to exclude the South from any portion of the territory which had been acquired principally by the blood of Southern soldiers. The people of the South became justly alarmed at the spread of Abolitionism at the North, and no people were more jealous of any encroachment upon the rights of the South than the citizens of Missouri, a majority of whose leading statesmen were as sound on the slavery question as those of Virginia or South Carolina. In order to cause Col. Benton, who had become obnoxious to a large portion of the Democratic party by his course on the Texas question, the Wilmot Proviso, and other measures of public policy, to resign his seat, and for the purpose of casting the weight of the State against the surging waves of Abolitionism, a series of resolutions, commonly known as the "Jackson resolutions," was introduced into the Senate at the session of 1848–9, by Claiborne F. Jackson, the present governor of Missouri, which passed both houses of the General Assembly. These resolutions were substantially the same as those introduced the year before, by Mr. Calhoun, into the Senate of the United States. From the Legislature Col. Benton appealed to the people, and made a vigorous canvass against the Jackson resolutions throughout the whole State, marked by extraordinary ability and bitterness towards their author and principal supporters. The sixth resolution, which pledged Missouri to "co-operate with her sister States in any measures they might adopt," to defend their rights against the encroachments of the North, was the object of his special denunciation and his most determined opposition. He denounced it as the essence of nullification, and ransacked the vocabulary of billingsgate for coarse and vulgar epithets to apply to its author and advocates. But his herculean efforts to procure the repeal of the resolutions proved abortive. Colonel Benton was defeated for the Senate the next year by a combination of Democrats and State-Rights Whigs; and the Jackson resolutions remain on the statute book unrepealed to this day. Their author is governor of the State; their principal supporters are fighting to drive myrmidons of Abolitionism from the soil of Missouri; and how nobly the State has redeemed her pledge to "co-operate with her sister States," the glorious deeds of her hardy sons, who have fought her battles almost single-handed, who have struggled on through neglect and hardship and suffering without ever dreaming of defeat, afford the most incontestible evidence.

In the canvass of 1852, the Anti-Benton Democrats put forward Gen. Sterling Price as their choice for the office of governor, and the Bentonites supported Gen. Thomas L. Price, at that time lieutenant-governor, and now a member of Lincoln's Congress and a brigadier-general in Lincoln's army. The Anti-Bentonites triumphed, and the nomination fell on Gen. Sterling Price, who, receiving the vote of the whole Democratic party, was elected by a large majority over an eloquent and popular whig, Colonel Winston, a grandson of Patrick Henry.

The administration of Gov. Price was distinguished for an earnest devotion to the material interests of Missouri. At the expiration of his term of office, he received a large vote in the Democratic caucus for the nomination for United States senator, but the choice fell on Mr. James Green.

In the Presidential election of 1860, in common with Major Jackson, who was the Democratic candidate for governor, and a number of other leading men of his party, Ex-Governor

Price supported Mr. Douglas for the Presidency, on the ground that he was the regular nominee of the Democratic party. He moreover considered Mr. Douglas true to the institutions of the South, and believed him to be the only one of the candidates who could prevent the election of the Black Republican candidate. The influence of these men carried Missouri for Douglas.

Upon the election of Abraham Lincoln, the Border States were unwilling to rush into dissolution until every hope of a peaceful settlement of the question had vanished. This was the position of Missouri, to whose Convention *not a single Secessionist was elected*. Governor Price was elected from his district as a Union man, without opposition, and, on the assembling of the Convention, was chosen its President. The Convention had not been in session many weeks before the radicalism of the Black Republican administration, and its hostility to the institutions of the South, became manifest to every unprejudiced mind. The perfidy and brutality of its officers in Missouri were particularly observable, and soon opened the eyes of the people to the true objects of the Black Republican party. The State authorities decided upon resistance to the Federal government; the Governor issued his proclamation for volunteers; and of the forces raised under this call, who were denominated the Missouri State Guard, Governor Price was appointed major-general, and took the field.

The period of history has scarcely yet arrived for a full appreciation of the heroic virtues of the campaign in Missouri, especially as illustrated in the character of the chieftain whom no personal jealousies could distract or unmerited slights turn from the single course of duty and devotion to his country. He had given the government at Richmond a valuable, but distasteful lesson in the conduct of the war. He did not settle down complacently into one kind of policy, refusing to advance because he was on the defensive, but he sought the enemy wherever he could find him, fought him when ready, and retreated out of his way when not prepared. His policy was both offensive and defensive, and he used the one which might be demanded by the exigencies of his situation. He was something better than a pupil of West Point—he was a general by nature, a beloved commander, a man who illustrated the Ro man simplicity of character in the nineteenth century. His troops not only loved him, they were wildly and enthusiastically devoted to him. His figure in the battle-field, clothed in a common brown linen coat, with his white hair streaming in the wind, was the signal for wild and passionate cheers, and there was not one of his soldiers, it was said, but who was willing to die, if he could only fall within sight of his commander.

It is not improbable that had General Price been supported after the battle of Lexington, he would have wrung the State of Missouri from the possession of the enemy. He was forced by untoward circumstances, already referred to, to turn back in a career just as it approached the zenith of success, and he could have given no higher proof of his magnanimity than that he did so without an expression of bitterness or a word of recrimination. He bore the cold neglect of the government at Richmond and the insulting proposition which President Davis was compelled by popular indignation to abandon, to place over him, as major-general in his department, a pupil of West Point his inferior in rank, with philosophic patience and without any subtraction from his zeal for his country. When his officers expressed resentment for the injustice done him by the government, he invariably checked them: stating that there should be no controversies of this kind while the war lasted, and that he was confident that posterity would do him justice. He was more than right; for the great majority of his living countrymen did him justice, despite the detractions of jealousy in Richmond.

CHAPTER VI.

The Campaign in Western Virginia.—General Wise's Command.—Political Influences in Western Virginia.—The Affair of Scary Creek.—General Wise's Retreat to Lewisburg.—General Floyd's Brigade.—The Affair at Cross Lanes.—Movements on the Gauley.—The Affair of Carnifax Ferry.—Disagreement between Generals Floyd and Wise.—The Tyrees.—A Patriotic Woman.—Movements in Northwestern Virginia.—General Lee.—The Enemy intrenched on Cheat Mountain.—General Rosecrans.—Failure of General Lee's Plan of Attack.—He removes to the Kanawha Region.—The Opportunity of a Decisive Battle lost.—Retreat of Rosecrans.—General H. R. Jackson's Affair on the Greenbrier.—The Approach of Winter.—The Campaign in Western Virginia abandoned.—The Affair on the Alleghany.—General Floyd at Cotton Hill.—His masterly Retreat.—Review of the Campaign in Western Virginia.—Some of its Incidents.—Its Failure and unfortunate Results.—Other Movements in Virginia.—The Potomac Line.—The BATTLE OF LEESBURG.—Overweening Confidence of the South.

WE must return here to the narrative of the campaign in Virginia. The campaign in the western portion of the State was scarcely more than a series of local adventures, compared with other events of the war. It was a failure from the beginning—owing to the improvidence of the government, the want of troops, the hostile character of the country itself, and a singular military policy, to which we shall have occasion hereafter to refer.

General Wise, of Virginia, was appointed a brigadier-general without an army. He rallied around him at Richmond a number of devoted friends, and explained to them his views and purposes. Cordially favoring his plans, they went into the country, and called upon the people to rally to the standard of General Wise, and enable him to prevent the approach of the enemy into the Kanawha Valley.

About the first of June, General Wise left Richmond for the western portion of the State, accompanied by a portion of his staff. At Lewisburg, he was joined by several companies raised and organized in that region. From this point, he proceeded to Charleston, in the Kanawha Valley, where he undertook, with his rare and characteristic enthusiasm, to rally the people to the support of the State. A number of them joined his command; but the masses continued apathetic, owing to a number of adverse influences, prominent among which was the political position of George W. Summers, the most influential politician of Western Virginia, the leader of the "Union" men in the State Convention, and a prominent delegate to the Peace Conference at Washington.

This person threw the weight of his great influence in opposition to the uprising of the people. He advised them to a strict neutrality between the public enemy and the supporters of the Confederate government. Notwithstanding all the appeals made to his patriotism, he maintained an attitude of indifference, and, by reason of the high estimation in which he was generally held by the community in which he lived, as a wise and sagacious man, he succeeded in neutralizing the greater portion of Kanawha and the adjoining counties.

Despite, however, the obstacles in his way, General Wise succeeded in raising a brigade of two thousand five hundred infantry, seven hundred cavalry, and three battalions of artillery. Of this force, western Virginia furnished about three-fifths and the east about two-fifths. On his arrival at Charleston, General Wise found C. G. Tompkins in command of a number of companies, chiefly from Kanawha and the adjacent counties. These forces, combined with those of the Wise Legion, amounted to about four thousand men.

General Wise, anxious to give an assurance of support to the strong Southern sentiment reported to exist in Gilmer and Calhoun, sent an expedition into those counties to repress the excesses of the Union men. In the mean time, the enemy had landed considerable forces at Parkersburg and Point Pleasant on the Ohio river, and had military possession of the neighboring country. His superior facilities for raising troops in the populous States of Ohio and Indiana, and his ample means of transportation by railroad through those States, and by the navigation of the Ohio and Kanawha rivers, enabled him, in a short space of time, to concentrate a large force, with adequate supplies and munitions of war, in the lower part of the Kanawha Valley.

About the middle of July, the enemy advanced up the river into the county of Putnam, and, on the 17th, Captain Patton (afterwards Colonel Patton), with a small force, met and repulsed three regiments of the enemy at Scary Creek, in Put nam county, taking prisoners Cols. Norton and Villiers of the Ohio troops, and Cols. Woodroof and Neff of the Kentucky troops. The enemy retired, and our forces remained in possession of the field. On the evening of the day of the action, General Wise sent down two regiments under Colonels Tompkins and McCausland to reinforce the troops at Scary. Upon arriving at the opposite side of the river, they found that the enemy had fallen back to his main forces under the command of General Cox.

Being unprepared to hold the position, not having the adequate supplies of men and munitions of war, the Confederates fell back in the direction of Charleston. Capt. Patton had been dangerously wounded in the action, and could not be removed from the place. Col. Norton, one of the Federal officers captured, was also wounded. He and Capt. Patton were placed in the same house, Col. Norton entering into an arrangement by which Capt. Patton was to be released by the enemy in exchange for himself. Gen. Cox, on his arrival, repudiated the understanding. He, however, released Capt. Patton on parole as soon as he had partially recovered from his wound.

After the action of Scary, the enemy's forces, which had been largely increased, steadily advanced up the valley both by land and water. Gen. Wise, however, was ready to offer battle to the enemy, and was confident of his ability to repulse him. But just about this time the news of the disaster to Gen. Garnett's command at Rich Mountain reached the Kanawha Valley, and put a new aspect upon military operations in that section. The consequences of this disaster exposed the little army of Gen. Wise to imminent peril. He was in danger of being cut off in the rear by several roads from the northwest, striking the Kanawha road at various points between Lewisburg and Gauley Bridge. Under these circumstances, Gen. Wise determined to fall back with his entire force to Lewisburg, a distance of one hundred miles. This he did in good order, destroying the bridges behind him, and reaching Lewisburg about the first of August. Remaining in that vicinity some ten days, laboriously engaged in organizing his brigade, and supplying it, as far as possible, with arms and the essential materials for an active campaign, he announced himself as again prepared to take up the line of advance.

About this time, General Floyd arrived at the Greenbrier White Sulphur Springs with a brigade of three regiments of infantry and a battalion of cavalry. He had been ordered, in the first instance, to proceed with his command to Jackson River, with a view to the relief of the retreating forces of Gen. Garnett; but, on his arrival at the Sweet Springs from Southampton, Virginia, Gen. Floyd's direction was changed by authority to the Kanawha Valley. After consultation between Generals Floyd and Wise in Greenbrier county, the former, who was the ranking officer, resumed his march westward, the latter following in a few days.

Gen. Floyd commenced to skirmish with the enemy's pickets at Tyree's, on the west side of the Sewell Mountain, driving them back to their command, five miles distant, with a loss of four killed and seven wounded. Upon his approach, the army retreated from Locust Lane to Hamilton's, near Hawk's Nest, Floyd's command advancing and occupying the camp of the Federals the next night. The Wise Legion also came up and occupied the same ground. The two commands then advanced to Dogwood Gap, where the road from Summersville intersects the turnpike from Lewisburg to Charleston. There two pieces of artillery were posted to keep open the line, and prevent a flanking movement from Cox's command *via* Carnifax Ferry, where there was reported to be a Federal force of several thousand. The main command then moved down to Pickett's Mills, near Hamilton's, within a few miles of the enemy's camp. At this point, information was obtained that the rear of the Confederates was threatened by Matthews' and Tyler's commands, which had occupied Carnifax Ferry (on the Gauley river), and Cross Lanes, a few miles distant therefrom. Gen. Floyd at once ordered his brigade to strike tents, and at half-past one o'clock in the morning he took up the line of march, with the view of engaging the forces of his assailants, whose object was to cut off his trains and fall upon his rear.

Gen. Wise's command was left at Pickett's Mills to hold the turnpike, and prevent a flank movement from Hawk's Nest, where the main body of Cox's forces were stationed on New River, seven miles east of Gauley Bridge.

Floyd's brigade proceeded by a rapid march, and reached Carnifax Ferry about noon of the same day. On his arrival there, he learned that the enemy had drawn in his commands at Cross Lanes and Carnifax Ferry, in anticipation of an attack at Hawk's Nest. Gen. Floyd proceeded at once to raise the boats which the enemy had sunk in the river at the ferry, and to construct other boats for crossing the river immediately, so as to occupy the strong positions which the enemy had held on the opposite side of the Gauley. In the short space of twenty-four hours, he had constructed a small batteau to carry some ten men, and had raised a ferry-boat capable of carrying fifty men and transporting his wagons, and had succeeded in ferrying over all of his infantry and two pieces of artillery. He then undertook to transport his cavalry, when an accident occurred which caused the loss of the ferry-boat and four men. The boat capsized and was drawn over the rapids. By this accident, Gen. Floyd's command was severed, most of his cavalry and four pieces of artillery being left on the eastern side of the stream, while his infantry and a small portion of his cavalry had reached the opposite shore. The stream had been so swollen by recent rains as to render ferrying extremely hazardous. Gen. Floyd, from the western side, ordered the quarter-master across the river to build boats on the other side, and to convey a message to Gen. Wise informing him of the condition of the command.

In twenty-four hours, a boat was built and launched from the west side of the river, and the remainder of the artillery and cavalry and such wagons as were needful were passed over. In the mean time, Gen. Floyd was engaged in strengthening his position. His scouts were thrown out in the direction of Gauley Bridge, by way of the Summersville and Gauley turnpike, and they reported the advance of the enemy in considerable strength from Gauley, in the direction of Cross Lanes. The next evening, the enemy had advanced to Cross Lanes, within two miles of Floyd's camp. The Federal officers had heard of the casualty at the ferry, and their "Union" friends in the neighboring country had reported to them that but two hundred of the infantry and cavalry had succeeded in crossing over.

Col. Tyler, who commanded the Federals, was confident of the capture of the whole force on the western side of the river. He was sadly disappointed. Gen. Floyd had drawn up his forces in line of battle on the evening of Sunday, August 25th, and prepared for an attack. His pickets had closely scented the enemy's position. Keeping his men in line of battle all night, at four o'clock the next morning he ordered an advance upon the enemy, whose strength was estimated at from fifteen hundred to two thousand. The order was promptly obeyed. The several Virginia regiments marched by the respective routes assigned them, and succeeded in completely surprising the Federals. Col. Tyler's line of pickets did not extend more than two or three hundred yards from his camp in the direction of Carnifax Ferry. His men were found preparing their breakfasts of green corn and fresh beef—roasting their corn by the fire and broiling their beef on sharp sticks. They were encamped in separate divisions, the rear being very near the church, in the direction of Ganley, in which building Col. Tyler had taken up his quarters. Their pickets were drawn in, and the division nearest to Floyd's forces took position behind a fence, where, for a time, they stubbornly resisted the attack. They were soon dislodged, and the whole command pushed over the hills, where they broke into the most disgraceful flight, the advance of which was conspicuously led by their colonel and field-officers. The flight was one of wild consternation, many of the enemy not only throwing away their arms, but divesting themselves of hats and coats to accelerate their flight, which was continued on an uninterrupted stretch for twelve or fifteen miles.

The commander of the Federals, Col. Tyler, was an Ohio man, and was familiar with the topography of the country he had come to invade, having visited it for years in the character of a fur-dealer. On his advent in the Kanawha Valley as the commander of an invading regiment, the coarse jest was made in some of the Northern papers that he would "drive a snug business" in *rebel skins*. The joke was turned against him by the Virginia soldiers at Cross Lanes, when they captured all the baggage of the Federal command, including the colonel's shirts, who had thus narrowly escaped with his own skin. As the flying enemy dashed on, the colonel led the retreat at a considerable distance ahead of it. One of his staff, a major, in leaping a fence got his horse astride it, and had to leave him there, trusting to the fleetness of his own heels for safety.

In the affair at Cross Lanes, the enemy's loss in killed, wounded, and prisoners was about two hundred. That on our side in killed and wounded did not exceed a dozen men.

Gen. Floyd proceeded to strengthen his position on the Gauley. Having succeeded in throwing his forces between Cox and Rosecrans, he set to work to bring up ten days' supplies in advance, intending to throw a portion of his command into the Kanawha Valley below Cox, with a view of cutting off his retreat. Having secured supplies sufficient to justify an advance movement, Gen. Floyd was about this time apprised of the approach of Rosecrans, by way of Suttonsville, with a large force for the relief of Cox. On the evening previous to the contemplated advance of the Confederates against Cox, about three o'clock of the 10th of September, Rosecrans, by a rapid march of sixteen miles, threw his entire force of ten regiments and several heavy batteries of artillery about Floyd's intrenchments, and commenced a vigorous attack.

The successful resistance of this attack of the enemy, in the neighborhood of Carnifax Ferry, was one of the most remarkable incidents of the campaign in Western Virginia. The force of Gen. Floyd's command was 1,740 men, and from three o'clock in the afternoon until nightfall, it sustained, with unwavering determination and the most brilliant success, an assault from an enemy between eight and nine thousand strong, made with small-arms, grape, and round-shot, from howitzers and rifled cannon.

Upon the close of the contest for the night, Gen. Floyd determined at once to cross the Gauley river, and take position upon the left bank—Gen. Wise having failed to reinforce him, and it being only a question of time when he would be compelled to yield to the superiority of numbers. The retreat across the river was accomplished by aid of a hastily constructed bridge of logs, about four feet wide, without the loss of a gun, or any accident whatever. In a continued firing upon us, by cannon and small-arms, for nearly four hours, only twenty of our men had been wounded and none killed. We had repulsed the enemy in five distinct and successive assaults, and had held him in complete check until the river was placed between him and the little army he had come in the insolent confidence of overwhelming numbers to destroy. The loss fo the enemy had been considerable, Col. Lytle, of Cincinnati, and a number of other Federal officers, having fallen in their attempts to rally their men to a successful charge. The whole loss of the enemy cannot be stated here; it was very serious, by the admission of the Cincinnati *Commercial*, and other Federal newspapers; it, unquestionably, must have amounted to several hundred in killed and wounded. Gen. Floyd was wounded by a musket-shot in the arm. His flag, which was flying at head-quarters, and his tent were riddled with balls.

At the time that information had reached Gen. Floyd of the advance of the enemy towards his position, he had dispatched orders to Gen. Wise for reinforcements, which he failed to procure. In his official report of the action, Gen. Floyd wrote to the War Department at Richmond: "I am very confident that I could have beaten the enemy and marched directly to the Valley of the Kanawha, if the reinforcements from Gen. Wise's column had come up when ordered, and the regiments from North Carolina and Georgia could have reached me before the close of the second day's conflict. I cannot express the regret which I feel at the necessity, over which I had no control, which required that I should recross the river. I am confident that if I could have commanded the services of five thousand men, instead of eighteen hundred, which I had, I could have opened the road directly into the Valley of the Kanawha." Referring to the correspondence between himself and Gen. Wise, in which the latter had declined to send forward reinforcements, Gen. Floyd indicated to the government the urgent necessity of shaping the command in the Valley of the Kanawha, so as to insure in the future that unity of action, upon which alone can rest any hope of success in military matters.

While Gen. Floyd was at Carnifax Ferry, Gen. Wise marched down to Big Creek, in Fayette county, where the enemy were in considerable force, fortified his position, and offered them battle. He hoped to obtain a position upon the flank of the enemy, and with that view, sent Col. Anderson and his regiment by an obscure county road, but did not succeed in his object. Meanwhile, with two regiments of infantry and a battery of artillery, Gen. Wise remained within a quarter of a mile of the enemy. A sharp skirmish took place, the enemy opening upon Wise's forces with artillery, doing no execution, however. The artillery of the Wise Legion replied, throwing shell, with some effect, into the enemy's lines. But the attempt to bring on a general engagement was unsuccessful, the enemy declining the offer of battle.

Gen. Floyd retreated in good order from Carnifax Ferry to the summit of Big Sewell Mountain, where he remained for three days, when, in accordance with the decision of a council of officers called by him, he ordered a retreat to Meadow Bluff, a position which, it was said, guarded all the approaches to Lewisburg and the railroad. Gen. Wise, however, who had fallen back with Gen. Floyd to Big Sewell, declined to retreat to Meadow Bluff, and proceeded to strengthen his position, which he named Camp "Defiance."

The enemy had advanced to Tyree's—a well-known public house, on the turnpike-road, in Fayette county. This country tavern had been kept for a number of years by an ancient couple, whose fidelity and services to the South were remarkable. Of the courage and adventure of Mrs. Tyree, many well-authenticated anecdotes are told. Her husband, though a very old man, had gone into the ranks of the Confederate army at the commencement of the war. The enemy, who were well-advised of the enthusiastic attachment of Mrs. Tyree to the cause of the State of Virginia, soon made her an object of their annoyances. Their first attempt was to take away the only horse the old woman had. A Federal soldier came to her house, caught her horse without her knowledge, and was about to ride him off, when she discovered the thief and demanded his business. The soldier replied that he was directed to take the horse for the purpose of "jayhawking." The words were scarcely out of his mouth, when Mrs. Tyree knocked him down with a billet of wood, stretching the ambitious "jayhawker" almost lifeless upon the ground. The horse, for further security, was locked up in the old woman's smoke-house.

On another occasion, a file of Federal soldiers proceeded to the premises of Mrs. Tyree, with the intention of driving off her cow. Discovering them, she asked what they intended to do with her cow. "We intend to drive it to camp for a beef," was the reply. Instantly, wrenching a gun from the hands of one of the soldiers, Mrs. Tyree deliberately declared that she would shoot the first man who attempted to drive the cow from her premises. "The rest of you may then kill me," she said, "if you think proper." The soldiers were baffled, and Mrs. Tyree's cow was saved.

A few nights afterwards, a number of soldiers surrounded her house, under the shelter of which was herself, her daughter, and a few faithful servants, without any male protector whatever. They ordered the family to leave, as they intended to burn the house. Mrs. Tyree positively refused to leave the house, very coolly locked all the doors, and told them if they intended to burn the building, to apply the torch without further ceremony, as she and her family were resolved to be consumed with it. The villains, hesitating at such a work of fiendish assassination, were forced to leave without putting their threat into execution. The heroic spirit of such a woman, not only protected her household, but furnished many interesting incidents to the campaign in her neighborhood, which it is not now the time to relate. It is to be regretted that her home was left within the lines of the enemy.

Having traced to a certain period, the operations in the Valley of the Kanawha, we must turn to note the movements of the army in northwestern Virginia.

After the retreat of Gen. Garnett from Rich Mountain, and the death of that officer, Gen. Lee was appointed to succeed him, and, with as little delay as possible, to repair to the scene of operations. The most remarkable circumstance of this campaign was, that it was conducted by a general who had never fought a battle, who had a pious horror of guerrillas, and whose extreme tenderness of blood induced him to depend exclusively upon the resources of strategy, to essay the achievement of victories without the cost of life.

Gen. Lee took with him reinforcements, making his whole force, in conjunction with the remnant of Gen. Garnett's army that had fallen back from Rich Mountain to Monterey, about sixteen thousand men. Early in August, Gen. Lee reached with his command the neighborhood of Cheat Mountain, on the Staunton and Parkersburg turnpike, and found it strongly fortified by the enemy. The position was known to be an exceedingly strong one, and not easily turned. Nevertheless, Gen. Lee was confident that he would be able by strategic movements to dislodge the enemy from his stronghold, capture his forces, and then march his victorious army into the heart of northwestern Virginia, releasing the people there from the fetters with which, for two months, they had been bound. The prospect of such a conquest of the enemy was eminently pleasant. Rosecrans* was the ranking officer in northwestern Virginia, but Gen. Reynolds was in command of the troops on Cheat Mountain and in its vicinity, his force being estimated at from ten to twelve thousand men.

Gen. Lee felt his way cautiously along the road leading from Huntersville to Huttonsville, in the county of Randolph, and reaching Valley Mountain, he halted for some time, arranging his plans for attacking the enemy, who were about eight miles below him, in Randolph county, at Crouch's, in Tygart's Valley River, five or six thousand strong. His plans were arranged so as to divide his forces for the purpose of surrounding the enemy. After great labor and the endurance of severe hardships on the mountain spurs, where the weather was very cold, he succeeded in getting below the enemy, on Tygart's Valley River, placing other portions of his forces on the spurs of the mountain immediately east and west of the enemy, and marching another portion of his troops down the Valley River close to the enemy. The forces were thus arranged in position for making an attack upon the enemy at Crouch's, and remained there for some hours. It was doubtless in the plan of Gen. Lee for his forces to remain in position until the consummation of another part of his plan, viz. that some fifteen hundred of Gen. H. R. Jackson's forces stationed at Greenbrier

---

* Gen. Rosecrans is of German descent, a native of Ohio, and a graduate of West Point. He had devoted much study to chemistry and geology, and resided some time in Charleston, Kanawha, prosecuting some researches into the mineral riches of that region. He was also employed in some capacity for a time by some of the coal companies or some of the coal-oil manufacturers there. His last enterprise, previous to the war, was the establishment of an oil manufactory in Cincinnati. In this he failed pecuniarily. The war was a timely event to him, and his military education gave him a claim to consideration. In the South, he was esteemed as one of the best generals the North had in the field; he was declared by military critics, who could not be suspected of partiality, to have clearly out-generalled Lee in western Virginia, who made it the entire object of his campaign to "surround" the Dutch general; and his popular manners and amiable deportment towards our prisoners, on more than one occasion, procured him the respect of his enemy.

River should march around another position of the enemy, at the celebrated Cheat Mountain Pass, on the Staunton and Parkersburg road, where he was five or six thousand strong. Jackson's forces did march around this position, under command of Col. Rust, of Arkansas, through extraordinary difficulties and perils and under circumstances of terrible exhaustion. The troops had to ascend the almost perpendicular mountain sides, but finally succeeded in obtaining a position in front of and to the west of the enemy. The attack of this force upon the enemy on Cheat Mountain was understood to be, in the plan of Gen. Lee, a signal for the attack by his forces upon the enemy at Crouch's. Col. Rust, however, discovered the enemy on the mountain to be safely protected by block-houses and other defences, and concluding that the attack could not be made with any hope of success, ordered a retreat. The signal was not given according to the plan of Gen. Lee, and no attack was made by his forces, which retreated without firing a gun back to Valley Mountain.

It is understood that Gen. Lee did not expect Col. Rust to make an attack with any certainty or even probability of success; his purpose being for Col. Rust to hold the enemy in position at Cheat Mountain Pass, while he was engaging them at Crouch's. The fact, however, is, that Cheat Mountain Pass was, by the nearest road to Crouch's, ten miles distant; and there are strong reasons for believing that, if Gen. Lee had made the attack upon the enemy at the latter position, they would have been captured to a man, notwithstanding the failure to hold the forces in check at Cheat Mountain. Such was the impression of the Federals themselves. If the enemy had been captured at Crouch's, a march of ten miles down the Valley River by Gen. Lee would have brought his forces in the rear of the enemy at Huttonsville, cutting off his supplies, and, with Jackson on the other side, compelling him to the necessity of surrender.

It is to be regretted that Gen. Lee failed to make the attack at Crouch's, and to realize the rich results of his well-matured plan. Had he defeated the enemy at Crouch's, he would have been within two days' march of the position from which Gen. Garnett had retreated, and could have held Rosecrans in check, who was at that time making his way to Carnifax Ferry to

oppose Floyd. There is reason to believe that if Gen. Lee had not allowed the immaterial part of his plan to control his action, a glorious success would have resulted, opening the whole northwestern country to us, and enabling Floyd and Wise to drive Cox with ease out of the Kanawha Valley. Regrets, however, were unavailing now. Gen. Lee's plan, finished drawings of which were sent to the War Department at Richmond, was said to have been one of the best-laid plans that ever illustrated the consummation of the rules of strategy, or ever went awry on account of practical failures in its execution.

Having failed in his plans for dislodging the enemy from Cheat Mountain, and thus relieving northwestern Virginia of his presence, Gen. Lee determined to proceed to the Kanawha region, with a view of relieving Generals Floyd and Wise, and possibly driving the enemy to the extreme western borders of Virginia. Accordingly, in the latter part of September, he ordered the principal portion of his command to take up a line of march in that direction.

It has already been stated that Gen. Floyd had fallen back with his forces to Meadow Bluff, while Gen. Wise stopped to the east of the summit of Big Sewell. In this position Gen. Lee found them on his arrival. He took up his head-quarters with Gen. Floyd, and, after examining his position, proceeded to Sewell, where Gen. Wise still remained in front of the enemy. He decided to fortify Wise's position. Gen. Floyd's command, except a garrison at Meadow Bluff, returned to Big Sewell. He had been largely reinforced since he had left the Gauley river. The position on Big Sewell was made exceedingly strong by a breastwork extending four miles.

The whole Confederate force here under the command of Gen. Lee was nearly twenty thousand. This formidable army remained for twelve or fifteen days within sight of the enemy, each apparently awaiting an attack from the other. Thus the time passed, when, one morning, Gen. Lee discovered, much to his surprise, that the enemy he had been so long hesitating to attack no longer confronted him. Rosecrans had disappeared in the night, and reached his old position on the Gauley, thirty-two miles distant, without annoyance from the Confederate army. Thus the second opportunity of a decisive battle in western Virginia was blindly lost, Gen. Lee making no attempt to follow up the enemy who had so skilfully eluded him; the excuses alleged for his not doing so being mud, swollen streams, and the leanness of his artillery horses.

In withdrawing from the Cheat Mountain region, Gen. Lee had left a force of some twenty-five hundred men at Greenbrier River, and, while he was playing at strategy in the Kanawha valley, this little force had achieved a signal victory over an apparently overwhelming force of the enemy. The force on the Greenbrier at the foot of Cheat Mountain was under command of Gen. H. R. Jackson, of Georgia. A small force had also been left on the Alleghany Mountain, at Huntersville, and perhaps other localities in that region.

On the 3d of October, the enemy, thinking that he might strike a successful blow, in the absence of Gen. Lee and the larger portion of his command, came down from Cheat Mountain, five thousand strong, and attacked Jackson's position on the Greenbrier. The attack was gallantly repulsed. The most unusual and brilliant incident of the battle was the conduct of our pickets, who held the entire column of the enemy in check for nearly an hour, pouring into the head of it a galling fire not withdrawing until six pieces of artillery had opened briskly upon them, and full battalions of infantry were outflanking them on the right, and then retiring in such order, and taking such advantage of the ground, as to reach their camp with but a trifling loss.

The action was continued by a severe artillery engagement, when, after four hours' interchange of fire, in which we could not bring more than five pieces into action to return the fire of the enemy's eight, he began to threaten seriously our front and right, by heavy masses of his infantry. He had been repulsed at one point of the so-called river (in fact, a shallow stream, about twenty yards in width), by the 3d Arkansas regiment. As the designs of his column were fully developed, the 12th Georgia regiment were ordered to take position near the stream, while a battery commanded by Capt. Shumaker was directed to open fire upon the same column. The encounter was of but short duration. In a short time, the unmistakable evidences of the enemy's rout became apparent. Distinctly could their officers be heard, with words of mingled command, remonstrance, and entreaty, attempting to rally their battalions into line, and to bring them to the charge, but they could not be induced to re-form their broken ranks, nor to emerge from the cover of the woods, in the direction of our fire. Rapidly, and in disorder, they returned into the turnpike, and soon thereafter the entire force of the enemy, artillery, infantry, and cavalry, retreated in confusion along the road and adjacent fields.

The engagement lasted from seven in the morning to half-past two o'clock in the afternoon, at which time the enemy, who had come with artillery to bombard and demoralize the small force of Confederates; with infantry to storm their camp; with cavalry to rout and destroy them, and *with four days' cooked rations* in his haversacks, to prosecute a rapid march either towards Staunton, or towards Huntersville, was in precipitate retreat back to his Cheat Mountain fastnesses. His loss in killed and wounded was estimated at from two hundred and fifty to three hundred. That of the Confederates was very inconsiderable, not exceeding fifty in all.

The approaching rigors of a winter in the mountains, gave warning of a speedy termination of the campaign in western Virginia, in which, in fact, we had no reason to linger for any fruits we had gained. The campaign was virtually abandoned by the government, in recalling Gen. Lee shortly after he had allowed the opportunity of a decisive battle with Rosecrans to escape him. He was appointed to take charge of the coast defences of South Carolina and Georgia. Gen. Wise was ordered to report to Richmond; Gen. Loring was sent with his command to reinforce Gen. T. J. Jackson ("Stonewall"), at Winchester; and Gen. H. R. Jackson was transferred to duty in the South. With the exception of Gen. Floyd's command, which still kept the field in the region of the Gauley, and a force of twelve hundred men on the Alleghany Mountain, the Confederate forces were withdrawn from western Virginia, after the plain failure of the campaign, and in the expectation that the rigors of the advancing winter season would induce the enemy to retire from the mountains to the Ohio.

The last incident of battle in the campaign was a brilliant one. On the 13th of December, the whole of the enemy's forces, under Gen. Reynolds, were brought out to attack the position commanded by Col. Edward Johnson, of Georgia, with his little force on the Alleghany. The enemy had been conducted to our position by a guide, a Union man. The Federals, on the flank, where the principal attack was made, numbered fully two thousand. They were gallantly met by our troops, who did not exceed three hundred at this time, being a portion of Hansborough's battalion, the 31st Virginia. These were reinforced by a few companies of Georgia troops, who came up with a shout, and joining the troops who had been forced back by overwhelming numbers, pressed upon the enemy with a desperate valor, and drove him from his almost impenetrable cover of fallen trees, brush, and timber. Many of the officers fought by the side of their men, and the enemy was pushed down the mountain, but with serious loss to the gallant little command. In describing the conduct of his men, Col. Johnson wrote to the War Department, "I cannot speak in terms too exaggerated of the unflinching courage and dashing gallantry of those five hundred men, who contended from a quarter past 7 A. M., until a quarter to 2 P. M., against an immensely superior force of the enemy, and finally drove them from their position and pursued them a mile or more down the mountain." The casualties in this small force amounted to twenty killed and ninety-six wounded.

Gen. Floyd was the last of the Confederate generals to leave the field of active operations in western Virginia. After the retreat of Rosecrans from Sewell Mountain, Gen. Floyd, at his own request, was sent with his brigade, by way of Richard's Ferry and Raleigh and Fayette Court House, to Cotton Hill, on the west side of the Kanawha. Here he again confronted Rosecrans and his whole force, encamped at Hamilton's, at Hawk's Nest, at Tompkins' farm, and at Stodin's, near the falls. Cotton Hill is in Fayette county, on the Kanawha, opposite the mouth of the Gauley; the Raleigh and Fayette turnpike passes over the hill, crossing the Kanawha river at the ferry below the falls, where it intersects the Kanawha turnpike leading from Lewisburg to Charleston. From the position of Cotton Hill, the several camps of Rosecrans referred to could be distinctly seen, stretching to the distance of several miles. Gen. Floyd reached this point after a fatiguing march of eleven days, and occupied the landings of all the approaches to his position, at Bougen's Ferry, Matthews' Ferry, Montgomery's Ferry at the falls, and Loop Creek. For three weeks, he continued to challenge the enemy to battle, firing at him across the river, annoying him considerably, cutting off his communication with the Valley of the Kanawha, and holding in check his steamboats, which ran up to Loop Creek shoals at high tides. For several days, the communication of the Federals, between their corps on the opposite sides of the Gauley, was entirely suspended. Gen. Floyd continued to challenge, insult, and defy the enemy with his little six-pounders at Cotton Hill, while Rosecrans, before he would accept the challenge made to his already superior numbers, waited for heavy reinforcements from the Ohio.

At last, being largely reinforced by the way of Charleston, Rosecrans planned an attack upon Cotton Hill, and moved by several distinctly indicated routes, namely, Miller's, Montgomery's, and Loop Creek Ferries, all concentrating at Fayetteville, nine miles from Cotton Hill. He expected the most brilliant results from his overpowering numbers and well-conceived designs, and was confident of cutting off the retreat of Floyd and capturing his command. His force was fifteen thousand men; that of Floyd did not exceed four thousand effective men, his ranks having been reduced by sickness, and the old story of promised reinforcements never having been realized to him. In these circumstances, Gen. Floyd made a retreat, the success of which was one of the most admirable incidents of a campaign, which he, at least, had already distinguished by equal measures of vigor, generalship, and gallantry. He effected his retreat in perfect order, fighting the enemy for twenty miles, and bringing off his force, including sick, with a loss of not more than five or six men. In this loss, however, was Col. Croghan, of Kentucky, a gallant young officer, and a son of the late Col. Croghan, who had obtained historical distinction in the Northwestern campaign of the War of 1812. The enemy, after pursuing Gen. Floyd for twenty miles, turned back in the direction of Fayette Court House, leaving him to retire at his leisure to southwestern Virginia. It was from here that Gen. Floyd was transferred by the government to the now imposing theatre of war in Tennessee and Kentucky.

A minuter history of the campaign in western Virginia than

the plan of our work admits, would enable us to cite many instances of individual gallantry and self-sacrifice. They would show the good conduct of small parties of Confederates on many occasions. In concluding the narrative of the general events of the war in western Virginia, we may add a very brief mention of some of these occurrences, which were only incidents of the campaign, which did not affect its general results, but which showed instances of gallantry that, on a larger scale of execution, might have accomplished very important results.

While the enemy had possession of the Kanawha Valley, Col. J. Lucius Davis' cavalry, of the Wise Legion, was sent to Big Coal River, thirty-five miles from Fayette Court House. On reaching Big Coal, they gave rapid chase to a marauding party of Federals, and overtook them at Tony's Creek, where a fight took place on the 11th September, which resulted in the total rout of the enemy, with a loss of about fifty killed and wounded, about the same number of prisoners, and the capture of all his provisions, munitions, &c. The Confederates sustained no loss whatever. The action lasted three hours, the remnant of the enemy having been pursued to a point within twelve miles of Charleston. The cavalry returned with their trophies, after having traversed, in twenty-four hours, a distance of seventy-five or eighty miles over steep mountain trails, bridle-paths, and rocky fords. Col. J. Lucius Davis, in his report of the affair, speaks of Lieut.-col. Clarkson as the hero of the expedition.

On the 25th September, Col. J. W. Davis, of Greenbrier, at the head of two hundred and twenty-five militia of Wyoming, Logan, and Boone counties, were attacked at Chapmansville, by an Ohio regiment commanded by Col. Pratt. The militia fought well, and were forcing the enemy from the field, when their gallant leader, Col. Davis, received a desperate, and as was thought at the time, a mortal wound. This unfortunate circumstance reversed the fortune of the field. The militia retreated and the enemy returned to the field. Col. Davis was taken by the Ohio troops, and remained in their hands till his partial recovery from his wounds, when he was paroled. The troops under Col. Davis lost but two killed and two wounded, while the loss of the Ohio troops in killed and wounded ex ceeded fifty, from the best information Col. D. was able to obtain.

Col. Jenkins' cavalry rendered efficient service in the Kanawha Valley, and kept the enemy all the time uneasy. On the 9th November, they made a gallant dash into the town of Guyandotte, on the Ohio river, and routed the forces of the enemy stationed there, killing and wounding a number of them, and taking nearly one hundred prisoners. Federal reinforcements afterwards came up to the town, and on the pretence that the Confederates had been invited to attack it by resident Secessionists, gratified a monstrous and cowardly revenge by firing the larger portion of the town, although many of the inhabitants had come out to meet them on the banks of the river, waving white flags and signifying the most unqualified submission. Women and children were turned into the street, many of them being forced to jump from the windows of their houses to escape the flames.

We have already adverted to the causes which contributed to make the campaign in western Virginia a failure. The cause which furnished the most popular excuse for its ineffectiveness—the disloyalty of the resident population—was, perhaps, the least adequate of them all. That disloyalty has been hugely magnified by those interested, in finding excuses in it for their own inefficiency and disappointment of public expectation. While Maryland, Kentucky, and other regions of the South, which not only submitted to Lincoln, but furnished him with troops, were not merely excused, but were the recipients of overflowing sympathy, and accounted by a charitable stretch of imagination "sister States" of the Southern Confederacy, an odium, cruelly unjust, was inflicted upon western Virginia, despite of the fact that this region was enthralled by Federal troops, and, indeed, had never given such evidences of sympathy with the Lincoln government as had been manifested both by Maryland and Kentucky in their State elections, their contributions of troops, and other acts of deference to the authorities at Washington. It is a fact, that even now, "Governor" Pierpont, the creature of Lincoln, cannot get one-third of the votes in a single county in western Virginia. It is a fact, that the Northern journals admit that in a large portion of this country, it is unsafe for Federal troops to show themselves unless in large bodies

The unfortunate results of the campaign in western Virginia abandoned to the enemy a country of more capacity and grandeur than, perhaps, any other of equal limits on this continent; remarkable for the immensity of its forests, the extent of its mineral resources, and the vastness of its water-power, and possessing untold wealth yet awaiting the coal-digger, the salt dealer, and the manufacturer.

While the events referred to in the foregoing pages were transpiring in western Virginia, an inauspicious quiet, for months after the battle of Manassas, was maintained on the lines of the Potomac. A long, lingering Indian summer, with roads more hard and skies more beautiful than Virginia had seen for many a year, invited the enemy to advance. He steadily refused the invitation to a general action; the advance of our lines was tolerated to Munson's Hill, within a few miles of Alexandria, and opportunities were sought in vain by the Confederates, in heavy skirmishing, to engage the lines of the two armies. The gorgeous pageant on the Potomac, which, by the close of the year, had cost the Northern people three hundred millions of dollars, did not move. The "Young Napoleon" was twitted as a dastard in the Southern newspapers. They professed to discover in his unwillingness to fight the near achievement of their independence, when, however the fact was, the inactivity of the Federal forces on the northern frontier of Virginia only implied that immense preparations were going on in other directions, while the Southern people were complacently entertained with the parades, reviews, and pompous idleness of an army, the common soldiery of which wore white gloves on particular occasions of holiday display.

THE BATTLE OF LEESBURG.

The quiet, however, on the lines of the Potomac was broken by an episode in the month of October, which, without being important in its military results, added lustre to our arms. The incident referred to was the memorable action of Leesburg, in which a small portion of the Potomac army drove an enemy four times their number from the soil of Virginia, killing and taking prisoners a greater number than the whole Confederate force engaged.

Gen. Stone having been persuaded that no important force of the Confederates remained along the Upper Potomac, and in obedience to orders from head-quarters, commenced his passage of the river on Sunday, the 20th of October, at Harrison's Island, a point of transit about six miles above Edwards' Ferry, and nearly an equal distance from Leesburg. A force of five companies of Massachusetts troops, commanded by Col. Devins, effected a crossing at the ferry named above, and, a few hours thereafter, Col. Baker, who took command of all the Federal forces on the Virginia side, having been ordered by Stone to push the Confederates from Leesburg and hold the place, crossed the river at Conrad's Ferry, a little south of Harrison's Island.

The brigade of Gen. Evans (one of the heroic and conspicuous actors in the bloody drama of Manassas), which had occupied Leesburg, consisted of four regiments, viz.: the 8th Virginia, the 13th, the 17th, and the 18th Mississippi. Having a position on Goose Creek, they awaited the approach of the overwhelming numbers of the enemy, the force which he had thrown across the river being between seven and eight thousand strong. The enemy had effected a crossing both at Edwards' Ferry, and Ball's Bluff, and preparations were made to meet him in both positions. Lieut.-col. Jenifer, with four of the Mississippi companies, confronted the immediate approach of the enemy in the direction of Leesburg; Col. Hunton, with his regiment, the 8th Virginia, was afterwards ordered to his support, and, about noon, both commands were united, and became hotly engaged with the enemy in their strong position in the woods.

Watching carefully the action, Gen. Evans saw the enemy were constantly being reinforced, and at half-past two o'clock P. M., ordered Col. Burt to march his regiment, the 18th Mississippi, and attack the left flank of the enemy, while Colonels Hunton and Jenifer attacked him in front. On arriving at his position, Col. Burt was received with a tremendous fire from the enemy, concealed in a ravine, and was compelled to divide his regiment to stop the flank movement of the enemy.

At this time, about three o'clock, finding the enemy were in large force, Gen. Evans ordered Col. Featherston, with his regiment, the 17th Mississippi, to repair, at double quick, to the support of Col. Burt, where he arrived in twenty minutes, and the action became general along the whole line of the Confederates, and was hot and brisk for more than two hours.

The Confederates engaged in the action numbered less than eighteen hundred men; the 13th Mississippi, with six pieces of artillery, being held in reserve. The troops engaged on our side fought with almost savage desperation. The firing was irregular. Our troops gave a yell and volley; then loaded and fired at will for a few minutes; then gave another yell and volley. For two hours, the enemy was steadily driven near the banks of the Potomac. The Federal commander, Col. Baker, had fallen at the head of his column, and his body was with difficulty recovered by his command. As the enemy continued to fall back, Gen. Evans ordered his entire force to charge and drive him into the river.

The rout of the enemy near the bluffs of the river was appalling. The crossing of the river had gone on until seven thousand five hundred men, according to the report of Gen. Stone, were thrown across it. Some of these never saw the field of battle. They had to climb the mud of the bluff, dragging their dismounted arms after them, before they could reach the field, expecting to find there a scene of victory. The difficult ascent led them to a horrible Golgotha. The forces that had been engaged in front were already in retreat; behind them rolled the river, deep and broad, which many of them were never to repass; before them glared the foe.

The spectacle was that of a whole army retreating, tumbling, rolling, leaping down the steep heights—the enemy following them, killing and taking prisoners. Col. Devins, of the 15th Massachusetts regiment, left his command, and swam the river on horseback. The one boat in the channel between the Virginia shore and the island was speedily filled with the fugitives. A thousand men thronged the banks. Muskets, coats, and every thing were thrown aside, and all were desperately trying to escape. Hundreds plunged into the rapid current, and the shrieks of the drowning added to the horror of sounds and sights. The Confederates kept up their fire from the cliff above. All was terror, confusion, and dismay One of the Federal officers, at the head of some companies, charged up the hill. A moment later, and the same officer, perceiving the hopelessness of the situation, waved a white handkerchief and surrendered the main body of his regiment. Other portions of the column surrendered, but the Confederates kept up their fire upon those who tried to cross, and many, not drowned in the river, were shot in the act of swimming.

The last act of the tragedy was the most sickening and appalling of them all. A flat-boat, on returning to the island, was laden with the mangled, the weary, and the dying. The quick and the dead were huddled together in one struggling, mangled mass, and all went down together in that doleful river, never again to rise.

The Northern newspapers, with characteristic and persistent falsehood, pretended that the Leesburg affair was nothing—a mere reconnoissance, in which the Federals accomplished their object—a skirmish, in which they severely punished the "rebels"—an affair of outposts, in which they lost a few men, nothing like so many as the "rebels," &c. But the truth at last came out, stark and horrible. The defeat of Leesburg was named in the Federal Congress as "most humiliating," "a great national calamity," and as another laurel added to the chaplet of the "rebellion."

The Federal soldiers who had suffered most severely in this action were from New York, Massachusetts, and Pennsylvania. They had given an exhibition of cowardice, quite equal, in degree at least, to its display at Manassas. There were no instances among them of desperate stubbornness, of calm front, of heroic courage. There was but one tint of glory to gild the bloody picture, and that was in the circumstance of the fall of their gallant commander, Col. Baker, who had been shot several times through the body, and, at last, through the head, in his desperate and conspicuous effort to rally his broken forces.

Col. Baker was United States senator from Oregon. He had served with distinction in the Mexican war; was since a member of Congress from Missouri; emigrated to California, where he long held a leading position at the bar, and, being disappointed in an election to Congress from that State, removed to Oregon, where he was returned United States senator to Washington. In the opening of the war, he raised what was called a "California" regiment, recruited in New York and New Jersey, and at the last session of the Federal Congress had distinguished himself by his extreme views of the subjugation of the South, and its reduction to a "territorial" condition. He was a man of many accomplishments, of more than ordinary gifts of eloquence, and, outside of his political associations, was respected for his bravery, chivalry, and address.

Our loss in the action of Leesburg, out of a force of 1,709 men, was 153 in killed and wounded. The loss of the enemy was 1,300 killed, wounded, and drowned; 710 prisoners captured, among them twenty-two commissioned officers; besides 1,500 stand of arms and three pieces of cannon taken. This brilliant victory was achieved on our side by the musket alone, over an enemy who never ventured to emerge from the cover, or to expose himself to an artillery fire.

The battle of Leesburg was followed by no important consequences on the Potomac. It was a brilliant and dramatic incident; it adorned our arms; and it showed a valor, a demonstration of which, on a grander scale and in larger numbers, might easily have re-enacted on a new field the scenes of Manassas. But, like the Manassas victory, that of Leesburg bore no fruits but those of a confidence on the part of the South, which was pernicious, because it was overweening and inactive, and a contempt for its enemy, which was injurious, in proportion as it exceeded the limits of truth and justice, and reflected the self-conceits of fortune.

CHAPTER VII.

The Position and Policy of Kentucky in the War.—Kentucky Chivalry.—Reminiscences of the "Dark and Bloody Ground."—Protection of the Northwest by Kentucky.—How the Debt of Gratitude has been repaid.—A Glance at the Hartford Convention.—The Gubernatorial Canvass of 1859 in Kentucky.—Division of Parties.—Other Causes for the Disloyalty of Kentucky.—The "Pro-Slavery and Union" Resolutions.—The "State Guard."—General Buckner.—The Pretext of "Neutrality," and what it meant.—The Kentucky Refugees.—A Reign of Terror.—Judge Monroe in Nashville.—General Breckinridge.—Occupation of Columbus by General Polk.—The Neutrality of Kentucky first broken by the North.—General Buckner at Bowling Green.—Camp "Dick Robinson."—The "Home Guard."—The Occupation of Columbus by the Confederates explained.—Cumberland Gap.—General Zollicoffer's Proclamation.—The Affair of Barboursville.—"The Wild-Cat Stampede."—The Virginia and Kentucky Border.—The Affair of Piketon.—Suffering of our Troops at Pound Gap.—The "Union Party" in East Tennessee.—Keelan, the Hero of Strawberry Plains.—The Situation on the Waters of the Ohio and Tennessee.—THE BATTLE OF BELMONT.—Weakness of our Forces in Kentucky.—General Albert Sidney Johnston.—Inadequacy of his Forces at Bowling Green.—Neglect and Indifference of the Confederate Authorities.—A Crisis imminent.—Admission of Kentucky into the Southern Confederacy.

IF, a few months back, any one had predicted that in an armed contest between the North and the South, the State of Kentucky would be found acting with the former, and abetting and assisting a war upon States united with her by community of institutions, of interests, and of blood, he would, most probably, in any Southern company in which such a speech was adventured, have been hooted at as a fool, or chastised as a slanderer. The name of Kentucky had been synonymous with the highest types of Southern chivalry; her historical record was adorned by the knightly deeds, the hardy adventures, the romantic courage of her sons; and Virginia had seen the State which she had peopled with the flower of her youth grow up, not only to the full measure of filial virtue, but with the ornament, it was thought, of even a prouder and bolder spirit than flowed in the blood of the Old Dominion.

War discovers truths in the condition of society which would never otherwise have been known. It often shows a spirit of devotion where it has been least expected; it decides the claims of superior patriotism and superior courage often in favor of communities which have laid less claim to these qualities than others; and it not infrequently exposes disloyalty, rottenness, or apathy on the part of those who had formerly superior reputation for attachment to the cause which they are found to desert or to assail.

It is not to be supposed for a moment, that while the position of Kentucky, like that of Maryland, was one of reproach, it is to mar the credit due to that portion of the people of each, who, in the face of instant difficulties, and at the expense of extraordinary sacrifices, repudiated the decision of their States to remain under the Federal government, and expatriated themselves, that they might espouse the cause of liberty in the South. The honor due such men is in fact increased by the consideration that their States remained in the Union, and compelled them to fly their homes, that they might testify their devotion to the South and her cause of independence. Still, the justice of history must be maintained. The demonstrations of sympathy with the South on the part of the States referred to—Maryland and Kentucky—considered either in proportion to what was offered the Lincoln government by these States, or with respect to the numbers of their population, were sparing and exceptional; and although these demonstrations on the part of Kentucky, from the great and brilliant names associated with them, were perhaps even more honorable and more useful than the examples of Southern spirit offered by Maryland, it is unquestionably, though painfully true, that the great body of the people of Kentucky were the active allies of Lincoln, and the unnatural enemies of those united to them by lineage, blood, and common institutions.

A brief review of some of the most remarkable circumstances in the history of Kentucky is not inappropriate to the subject of the existing war.

Kentucky has been denominated "the Dark and Bloody Ground" of the savage aborigines. It never was the habitation of any nation or tribe of Indians; but from the period of the earliest aboriginal traditions to the appearance of the whit man on its soil, Kentucky was the field of deadly conflict between the Northern and Southern warriors of the forest.

When, shortly after the secession of the American colonies

from the British empire, this contested land was penetrated by the bold adventurous white men of Carolina and Virginia, who constituted the third party for dominion, its title of the "Dark and Bloody Ground" was appropriately continued. And when, after the declaration of American independence, Great Britain, with a view to the subjugation of the United States, formed an alliance with the Indian savages, and assigned to them the conduct of the war upon all our western frontier, the territory of Kentucky became still more emphatically the Dark and Bloody Ground. Nor did the final treaty of peace between Great Britain and the United States bring peace to Kentucky. The government of Great Britain failed to fulfil its obligations to surrender the western posts from which their savage allies had been supplied with the munitions of war, but still held them, and still supplied the Indians with arms and ammunition, inciting them to their murderous depredations upon the western border.

This hostile condition continued in Kentucky until the celebrated treaty of Jay, and the final victory over the savage enemy achieved by General Wayne, and the consequent treaty of peace which he concluded with them in 1795. By this treaty of peace, the temple of Janus was closed in Kentucky for the first time in all her history and tradition.

The battles in these wars with the savage enemy were not all in Kentucky, nor were they for the defence of the territory of her people only, but chiefly for the defence of the inhabitants of Ohio, who were unable to protect themselves against their barbarous foes. How this debt has been paid by the descendants of these Ohio people, the ravages of the existing war sufficiently demonstrate.

Peace was continued in Kentucky for about twenty years. There were commotions and grand enterprises which we cannot even mention here. But they were all terminated by the purchase of Louisiana by Mr. Jefferson in 1803. The ratification of the treaty by which this vast southern and western dominion was acquired at the price of fifteen millions of dollars, was opposed by the Northern politicians, whose descendants now seek to subjugate the people of the South, at the cost of a thousand millions of dollars, and of a monstrous, unnatural, and terrible expenditure of blood.

In the war of 1812 with Great Britain, the surrender of Hull having exposed the Michigan Territory and all the northern border of Ohio to the invasion of the British and the savages, who were now again the allies of that government, Kentucky sent forth her volunteers for the defence of her assailed Northern neighbors; and when so many of her gallant sons were sacrificed upon the bloody plains of Raisin, the Legislature of Kentucky requested the governor of the State to take the field, and at the head of his volunteer army to go forth and drive back the enemy. The request was promptly complied with. It was the army of Kentucky that expelled the savages from all Ohio and Michigan, and pursuing them into Canada, achieved over them and the British upon the Thames a victory more important than had been yet won upon land in that war, thus giving peace and security to Ohio and all the northwestern territory, whose people were confessedly powerless for their own defence.

It is these people, protected by the arms and early chivalry of Kentucky, who have now made her soil the Dark and Bloody Ground of an iniquitous civil war, waged not only upon a people bearing the common name of American citizens, but upon the eternal and sacred principles of liberty itself. In these references to the early history of Kentucky we must be brief. In indicating, however, the lessons of rebuke they give to the North with respect to the existing war, we must not omit to mention that in the war of 1812, in which Kentucky covered herself with such well-deserved and lasting glory, the New England States stood with the enemy, and the body of their politicians had resolved upon negotiation with Great Britain for a separate peace, and had, in fact, appointed a Convention to be assembled at Hartford, to carry into effect what would have been virtually a secession from the United States, and the assumption of neutrality between the belligerents, if not an alliance with the public enemy. These facts are not fully recorded in history, but they might be well collected from the public documents and journals of the day. Indeed, they are well known to men yet living in our land. The schemes of the New England traitors were defeated only by the battle of Orleans, and the consequent treaty of peace. Upon the happening of these events, the conspirators abandoned their

Convention *projet*, and denied that they had ever contemplated any thing revolutionary or treasonable. The whole matter was suffered to pass into oblivion. The conspirators were treated by the government and people of the United States as William the Third treated those around his throne who, within his knowledge, had conspired against him, and had actually served the public enemy of England. It was known in each case that the conspirators were controlled by their selfish interests, and that the best mode of managing them, was to cause them to see that it was to their interest to be faithful to their government. It needs no comment to indicate with what grace the vehement denunciation of the secession of the Southern States from a Union which had been prostituted alike to the selfishness of politicians and the passion of fanatics, comes from a people who had been not only domestic rebels, but allies to the foreign enemy in the war of 1812.

In tracing the political connections of Kentucky in the present war, it will be sufficient for our purposes to start at the election of its governor in 1859. Down to that period the body of the partisans now upholding the Lincoln government had been an emancipation party in the State. This party had lately suffered much in popularity. In the election of 1859, they determined to consult popularity, and took open pro-slavery ground. The State Rights candidate (Magoffin) was elected.

By their adroit movement, however, the Anti-State Rights party had made some advance in the confidence of the people, which availed them in the more important contests that followed. In the Presidential election of 1860 they supported Mr. Bell, and thus succeeded in their object of gaining the ascendency in the councils of the State. Emancipationists were urged to support Mr. Bell, upon the ground that from his antecedents and present position they had more to expect from him than from his principal competitor in the race in Kentucky, while the people at large were persuaded to support Mr. Bell as the candidate of the friends of "the Union, the Constitution, and the Laws."

The Anti-State Rights party (at least they may be known for the present by this convenient denomination), succeeded in carrying the State by a large plurality. They commenced at an early day to combat the movements of secession in the

South. Popular assemblies and conventions were called to pledge themselves to the support of the Union in every contingency. The party, as represented in these assemblies, united all the friends of Mr. Bell, and the great body of those of Mr Douglas and of Mr. Guthrie. By this combination an organization was effected which was able to control and direct public opinion in the subsequent progress of events.

It is certainly defective logic, or, at best, an inadequate explanation, which attributes the subserviency of a large portion of the people of Kentucky to the views of the Lincoln government to the perfidy of a party or the adroitness of its management. However powerful may be the machinery of party, it certainly has not the power of belying public sentiment for any considerable length of time. The persistent adhesion of a large portion of the Kentucky people to the Northern cause must be attributed to permanent causes; and among these were, first, an essential unsoundness on the slavery question, under the influences of the peculiar philosophy of Henry Clay, who, like every great man, left an impress upon his State which it remained for future even more than contemporary generations to attest; and, second, the mercenary considerations of a trade with both North and South, to which the State of Kentucky was thought to be especially convenient. These suggestions may at least assist to the understanding of that development of policy in Kentucky which we are about to relate.

On the meeting of the Legislature of Kentucky, after the election of Lincoln, the party in the interest of the North succeeded in obtaining the passage by that body of a singular set of resolutions, which, by a curious compost of ideas, were called "pro-slavery and Union" resolutions. They denounced secession, without respect to any cause which might justify the measure, deprecated any war between the North and the South, and avowed the determination of Kentucky to occupy in such an event a position of perfect neutrality.

At its regular session in 1859–'60, the Legislature had organized an active body of volunteer militia, denominated the State Guard, and General Buckner had been appointed its highest officer. This army, as it might be called, was found to consist of the finest officers and best young men in the State

It was necessarily, by the provisions of the Constitution, under the command of the governor; but as Governor Magoffin was supposed to be a Southern Rights man, and the fact appearing that nearly all of the State Guard were favorable to the same cause, and that they could not be made the soldiers of the despotic government of the North, he was in effect deprived of their command, and measures were taken for forcing out of their hands the public arms with which they had been furnished, and for the organization of a new corps, to be commanded by the officers and partisans of Abraham Lincoln. In the mean time, as if to make their professed determination of neutrality effective, the Legislature proceeded to arm with muskets their "Home Guards," as their new army was called. With this programme before the people, the Legislature took a recess, probably to await the progress of events, when the mask of neutrality might be thrown off, and their real purposes might safely be announced to the people.

Gov. Magoffin's refusal to furnish troops to answer the requisition of the Federal government (to which reference has already been made in another part of this work), appeared at the time to meet with the approval of the entire people of Kentucky. The enemies of the South acquiesced in the decision of the governor only until the period arrived when the farce of neutrality might be conveniently broken, and the next step ventured, which would be union with the North. With the pretence of neutrality, and the seductive promises of a trade with both belligerents, which would enrich Kentucky and fill her cities with gold, a considerable portion of the people were held blinded or willingly entertained, while the purposes of the Lincoln government with respect to their State were being steadily fulfilled.

In the election of members of the Congress called by Lincoln to meet in special session on the 4th of July, 1861, men of Northern principles were elected from every district in Kentucky save one; and in the same condition of the public mind, the members of the Legislature were elected in August, the result being the return of a large majority of members ostensibly for the purpose of maintaining the ground of neutrality, but with what real designs was soon discovered. The election of the Lincoln rulers having been thus accomplished, the measures all the time contemplated and intended were easily put in course of execution. In a short time every State Rights newspaper was suspended; every public man standing in defence of the South was threatened with arrest and prosecution; and the raising of a volunteer corps for the defence of the South was totally suppressed.

Immediately after the declaration of war by the Lincoln government, a number of young men in Kentucky, actuated by impulses of patriotism, and attesting the spirit of the ancient chivalry of their State, had commenced raising volunteer companies in the State for the Confederate service. They passed South in detachments of every number. This emigration was at first tolerated by the Unionists, if not actually desired by them, for the purpose of diminishing the opposition in the State to their sinister designs. By the removal of its members, and by the acts of the Legislature already mentioned, the admirable army of the "State Guard of Kentucky" was totally disorganized, and the command of it virtually taken from Governor Magoffin and General Buckner, and placed in the hands of the political partisans of the Lincoln government. General Buckner could not long occupy such a position, and therefore, as soon as practicable, he resigned his office, renounced the Lincoln government, and placed himself under the Confederate flag. The value of his accession to the Southern cause was justly appreciated, and he was speedily appointed a brigadier-general in the provisional army of the Confederacy.

The encouragement to emigration was not long continued by the party in power in Kentucky. It was determined by the Lincoln government to make examples of the small party remaining in Kentucky who sympathized with the South, and to arrest at once every public and influential man in the State known to be hostile to the North, or to the despotic purposes of the government at Washington. Ex-Governor Morehead was at a dead hour of the night arrested in his own house, a few miles from Louisville, in the presence of his afflicted family, by the Lincoln police, and hurried through the city and over the river, and out of his State and district, in violation of all law; and the benefit of the writ of *habeas corpus* was practically denied him in a mode which, at any period in the last two hundred years, would have aroused all England into commotion. The high-handed act, it might have been supposed, would have aroused Kentucky also to a flame of indignation at any other period since it became the habitation of white men. The people, however, seemed to be insensible, and the outrage was allowed to pass with no public demonstration of its disapproval. Encouraged by its experience of the popular subserviency in Kentucky to its behests, it was in convenient time determined by the Lincoln government to arrest or drive off from the State every prominent opponent of its despotic authority. It was determined at Louisville that John C. Breckenridge, late Vice-President of the United States, Col. G. W. Johnson, a prominent citizen, T. B. Monroe, Jr., Secretary of State, William Preston, late Minister to Spain, Thomas B. Monroe, Sr., for about thirty years District Judge of the United States, Col. Humphrey Marshall, ex-member of Congress, and a distinguished officer in the Mexican war, Capt. John Morgan (since "the Marion" of Kentucky), and a number of other distinguished citizens in different parts of the State, should be arrested at the same hour, and consigned to prison, or driven from their homes by the threats of such a fate. It is supposed that some of the Lincoln men, and perhaps some officers of the government, preferred the latter alternative, especially in respect to some of the individuals named. However this may be, it happened that all of them escaped, some in one direction, and some in another.

The venerable Judge Monroe, on his arrival at Bowling Green, whence he was on his next day's journey to pass out of his State and his district, executed in duplicate, and left to be transmitted by different modes of conveyance, his resignation of the office of Judge of the United States for Kentucky; and in conformity to the general expectation at the time, he placed upon historic record the declaration of his expatriation of himself from the dominion of the despotic government of Lincoln, and adopted himself a citizen of the Southern Confederacy. The proceedings occurred in the Confederate Court of Nashville on the 3d of October. The scene of the renunciation of allegiance to the government that would have enslaved him, by this venerable jurist, who had been driven from a long-cherished home, and was now on his way to the State of Virginia, whose honored soil held the sacred ashes of a dozen generations of his ancestors, was one of peculiar augustness and interest. The picture of the scene alone was sufficient to illustrate and adorn the progress of a great revolution. It was that of a venerable patriot, a man of one of the greatest historical names on the continent, just escaped from the minions of the despot, who had driven him from a State in which he had lived, the light of the law, irreproachable as a man, beloved by his companions, honored by his profession, and venerable in years, voluntarily and proudly abjuring an allegiance which no longer returned to him the rights of a citizen, but would have made him an obsequious slave; and with all the dignity of one thus honored and respected, and conscious of his rectitude, appearing in the presence of a Confederate court of justice, and with the pure eloquence of truth, offering the remaining years of his life to the service of the new government, which had arisen as the successor of the old Union, as it was in its purer and brighter days.

Mr. Breckenridge reached Nashville by a very circuitous route, a few days after his departure from Lexington, and after a brief sojourn in the former place, proceeded to Bowling Green, and there entered into a compact with a number of his old constituents who had taken refuge in the camp of General Buckner, that they would take up their arms in defence of the rights and liberties of their country, and never lay them down till the invader was driven from the soil of Kentucky. Shortly afterwards, he received the appointment of brigadier-general in the army of the Confederate States, and was assigned to the command of a brigade of his fellow-citizens of Kentucky. Col. Humphrey Marshall received, at the same time, the appointment of brigadier-general, and was assigned to the district of southeastern Kentucky and southwestern Virginia. Colonel Johnson was subsequently chosen Provisional Governor of Kentucky by the friends of the Confederate government in that State.

To reconcile the people of Kentucky to the Lincoln government, its partisans had told them at the outset that they had the right to insist upon the strict observance of neutrality. As events progressed, they ascribed the violation of Kentucky's neutrality to the acts of the Southern government, in the face of facts about which there can be no dispute. The facts are, that the Federal forces were preparing to take possession of Columbus and Paducah, regarding them as important positions; and because Gen. Polk anticipated them and got prior possession of Columbus, they charged the Confederates with the responsibility of the first invasion of Kentucky. The Federals had commissioned Gen. Rouseau, at Louisville, to raise a brigade for the invasion of the South, but while the recruits were enlisted in Louisville, the camp was kept at Jeffersonville, on the Indiana side of the river, until the Lincoln commander became satisfied that the temper of the people of Louisville would tolerate a parade of Northern soldiers on their streets. Then, and not till then, were the Northern soldiers boldly marched across the State in the direction of Nashville. Gen. Buckner took possession of the railroad, and stationed himself at Bowling Green, in Southern Kentucky, about thirty miles from the Tennessee line. The partisans of Lincoln, still determined to blind the people by all sorts of false representations, established a camp called "Dick Robinson," near Lexington, and there made up an army comprised of recruits from Ohio, vagabonds from Kentucky, and Andrew-Johnson men from Tennessee. They insisted that no invasion was contemplated, that their forces were merely a "Home Guard" organization of a purely defensive character. They did not hesitate, however, to rob the arsenals of the United States of their muskets, bayonets, and cannon, and place them at the disposal of such infamous leaders as George D. Prentice, Tom Ward, and Garrett Davis. With these arms, "Dick Robinson's" camp was replenished, and at this memorable spot of the congregation of the most villanous characters, an army was raised in Kentucky for the invasion of the South.

The causes which led to the occupation of Kentucky by the Confederate States were plain and abundant. Finding that their own territory was about to be invaded through Kentucky, and that many of the people of that State, after being deceived into a mistaken security, were unarmed, and in danger of being subjugated by the Federal forces, the Confederate armies were marched into that State to repel the enemy, and prevent their occupation of certain strategic points which would have given them great advantages in the contest—a step which was justified, not only by the necessities of self-defence on the part of the Confederate States, but also by a desire to aid the people of Kentucky. It was never intended by the Confederate government to conquer or coerce the people of that State; but, on the contrary, it was declared by our generals that they would withdraw their troops if the Federal government would do likewise. Proclamation was also made of the desire to respect the neutrality of Kentucky, and the intention to abide by the wishes of her people, as soon as they were free to express their opinions.

Upon the occupation of Columbus by the Confederates, in the early part of September, the Legislature of Kentucky adopted resolutions calling upon them, through Governor Magoffin, to retire. General Polk, who was in command of the Confederates at Columbus, had already published a proclamation, clearly explaining his position. He declared in this proclamation, that the Federal government having disregarded the neutrality of Kentucky, by establishing camps and depots of armies, and by organizing military companies within their territory, and by constructing a military work on the Missouri shore, immediately opposite and commanding Columbus, evidently intended to cover the landing of troops for the seizure of that town, it had become a military necessity, involving the defence of the territory of the Confederate States, that the Confederate forces should occupy Columbus in advance.

The act of Gen. Polk found the most abundant justification in the history of the concessions granted to the Federal government by Kentucky ever since the war began. Since the election of Lincoln, she had allowed the seizure in her ports (Paducah) of property of citizens of the Confederate States. She had, by her members in the Congress of the United States, voted supplies of men and money to carry on the war against the Confederate States. She had allowed the Federal government to cut timber from her forests for the purpose of building armed boats for the invasion of the Southern States. She was permitting to be enlisted in her territory troops, not only from her own citizens, but from the citizens of other States, for the purpose of being armed and used in offensive warfare against the Confederate States. At camp "Dick Robinson," in the county of Garrard, it was said that there were already ten thousand troops, in which men from Tennessee, Ohio, Indiana, and Illinois were mustered with Kentuckians into the service of the United States, and armed by the government for the avowed purpose of giving aid to the disaffected in one of the Confederate States, and of carrying out the designs of that government for their subjugation. When Gen. Polk took possession of Columbus, he found that the enemy, in formidable numbers, were in position on the opposite bank of the river, with their cannon turned upon Columbus, that many of the citizens had fled in terror, and that not a word of assurance of safety or protection had been addressed to them.

In reply to the demand made through Governor Magoffin for the withdrawal of the Confederate troops from Kentucky, Gen. Polk offered to comply on condition that the State would agree that the troops of the Federal government be withdrawn simultaneously, with a guaranty (which he would give reciprocally for the Confederate government) that the Federal troops should not be allowed to enter, or occupy any part of Kentucky in the future. This proposition for a simultaneous withdrawal of forces, was derided by the partisans of Lincoln in Kentucky and elsewhere.

Gen. Polk had taken possession of Columbus on the 4th of September. The Federals were then occupying Paducah, at the mouth of the Tennessee river. The town of Cairo, at the mouth of the Ohio, had been previously occupied by a strong Federal force. New Madrid, on the Missouri side of the Mississippi, was occupied by Southern troops under the command of Gen. Jeff. Thompson.

Early in the summer, it was known that the Federals were threatening the invasion of East Tennessee by way of Cumberland Gap. To counteract their designs, the Confederate government sent Brigadier-general Zollicoffer, with a force of several thousand men, by way of Knoxville, East Tennessee, to the point threatened. On the 14th September, Gen. Zollicoffer telegraphed Governor Magoffin, of Kentucky, as follows: "The safety of Tennessee requiring, I occupy the mountain passes at Cumberland, and the three long mountains in Kentucky. For weeks, I have known that the Federal commander at Hoskins' Cross Roads was threatening the invasion of East Tennessee, and ruthlessly urging our people to destroy our own road and bridges. I postponed this precautionary movement until the despotic government at Washington, refusing to recognize the neutrality of Kentucky, has established formidable camps in the centre and other parts of the State, with the view, first to subjugate your gallant State, and then ourselves. Tennessee feels, and has ever felt, towards Kentucky as a twin-sister; their people are as one people in kindred, sympathy, valor, and patriotism. We have felt, and still feel, a religious respect for Kentucky's neutrality. We will respect it as long as our safety will permit. If the Federal force will now withdraw from their menacing position, the force under my command shall immediately be withdrawn."

At the same time Gen. Zollicoffer issued an order setting forth that he came to defend the soil of a sister Southern State against an invading foe, and that no citizen of Kentucky was to be molested in person or property, whatever his political opinions, unless found in arms against the Confederate government, or giving aid and comfort to the enemy by his counsels. On the 19th September, a portion of Gen. Zollicoffer's command advanced to Barboursville, in Kentucky, and dispersed a camp of some fifteen hundred Federals, without any serious struggle. He continued to advance cautiously in the direction of Somerset, driving the enemy before him. A large Federal force, chiefly from Ohio and Indiana, was sent forward to meet him. This expedition was speedily brought to a disgraceful and ruinous conclusion. Before getting near enough to Zollicoffer to confront him, Gen. Schoepff, the commander of the Yankee expedition, was induced to believe that Gen. Hardee was advancing from Bowling Green on his flank. What was known as the "Wild Cat Stampede" ensued. The retreat of the panic-stricken soldiers, which for miles was performed at the double-quick, rivalled the agile performances at Bull Run. For many miles the route of the retreat was covered with broken wagons, knapsacks, dead horses, and men who had sunk by the wayside from exhaustion. The flight of the Federals was continued for two days, although there was no enemy near them. Such was the result of the first expedition sent to capture Zollicoffer and to invade the South by way of Cumberland Gap.

Another design of the Federals was to invade southwestern

Virginia from eastern Kentucky, by way of Prestonsburg and Pound Gap, with the view of seizing upon the salt-works and lead-mines in this portion of Virginia, and of cutting off railroad communication between Richmond and Memphis. To thwart this design, there was raised in the neighborhood of Prestonsburg a force little exceeding a thousand men, who were placed under the command of Col. Williams. To capture the "rebels" at Prestonsburg, a considerable force was sent after them under the command of Gen. Nelson, of Kentucky. This somewhat notorious officer reported to the Lincoln government that his expedition had been brilliantly successful; his command, according to his account, having fallen upon the "rebels" at Piketon, captured upwards of a thousand of them, killed five hundred, or more, wounded a great number, and scattered the few remaining ones like chaff before the wind. This announcement caused intense joy in Cincinnati, and, indeed, throughout the North; but the rejoicings were cut suddenly short by the authentic account of the affair at Piketon, which occurred on the 8th of November, and in which the Confederates lost ten killed and fifteen wounded, while they ambushed a considerable body of Nelson's men on the river cliff, near that place, and killed and wounded hundreds of them. Owing to the superior force of the Federals, however, Col. Williams' little command fell back to Pound Gap.

He had not more than 1,010 men, including sick, teamsters, and men on extra duty. He described the little army that had held in check an apparently overwhelming force of the enemy, as an "unorganized, half-armed, and barefooted squad." He wrote to Richmond: "We want good rifles, clothes, greatcoats, knapsacks, haversacks, and canteens; indeed, every thing almost except a willingness to fight. Many of our men are barefooted, and I have seen the blood in their tracks as they marched."

There had long been unpleasant indications on the Tennessee border of disloyalty to the South. In what was called East Tennessee there was reported to be a strong "Union" party. This section was inhabited by an ignorant and uncouth population squatted among the hills. The Union faction in East Tennessee was the product of the joint influences of three men, differing widely in tastes, habits of thought, and political opinion, but concurring in a blind and bigoted devotion to the old Federal government. These men were Andrew Johnson, William G. Brownlow, and T. A. R. Nelson. The first of these was a man who recommended himself to the ignorant mountain people of Tennessee by the coarseness and vulgarity of his manners; but beneath his boorish aspect he had a strong native intellect, was an untiring political schemer, and for more than twenty years had exercised a commanding control over the rude mountaineers of Tennessee, who for an equal length of time had held the balance of power between the old Whig and Democratic parties in that State, voting first with one and then with the other political organization. Brownlow, "the parson," the haranguer of mobs in churches and at the hustings, and who, by his hatred of Andrew Johnson, had once made himself an ultra pro-slavery oracle of the Methodist Church, found Unionism so strong an element of popular partisan strength in East Tennessee, that he was forced to co-operate with his old enemy. The sincerest and most respectable of the trio was Nelson, an accomplished orator, a poet and dreamer besides, having no likeness to the people among whom he resided but in his apparel, and passing most of his time in the secluded occupations of a scholar, in which vocation he was both profound and classical. There could be no stranger combination of talent and character than in these three men, who had been brought together by a single sympathy in opposition to the cause of the South.

The Union party in Tennessee was for a long time occult; its very existence was for a considerable period a matter of dispute among Southern politicians; but it only awaited the operations of the enemy in Kentucky to assist and further their designs by a sudden insurrection among themselves. Their demonstrations were, however, premature. Early in November there was a conspiracy formed on the part of the Unionists for burning all the bridges on the East Tennessee and Virginia and Georgia and Tennessee railroads. The designs of the conspirators were consummated in part by the destruction of two or three bridges in East Tennessee, and of one in Georgia. The bridge across the Holston, at Strawberry Plains, on the East Tennessee and Virginia road, was saved by the heroic and self-sacrificing act of an humble individual, named Edward

Keelan, at that time the sole guard at the place. He fought the bridge-burning party—more than a dozen in number—with such desperation and success, that they were forced to retire without accomplishing their object. One of the party was killed, and several badly wounded. Keelan was wounded in a number of places. Upon the arrival of friends, a few minutes after the occurrence, he exclaimed to them, "They have killed me, but I have saved the bridge." Luckily the wounds did not prove mortal, and the hero of Strawberry Plains still lives.

The Federal expedition to Pound Gap was of the same character with all the other invasions from the northwestern territory in this contest. The troops were from Ohio and other northwestern States, the occupiers of the lands bountifully granted by Virginia to the Federal government, and by that government liberally distributed among the ancestors of the people attempting the invasion of Virginia and the South. This territory had been won by a Virginia army, composed of volunteers from this State and from the district of Kentucky, then a part of the Old Dominion. The bold and successful enterprise of George Rogers Clark in the conquest of all that western territory, constitutes one of the most romantic and brilliant chapters of the history of the Revolution.

We turn from the operations on the Kentucky and Virginia border, which were in effect abandoned by the enemy, to the more active theatre of the war in Kentucky, in the neighborhood of the waters of the Ohio and Tennessee. It was to these waters that the enemy in fact transferred his plans of invasion of the South through Kentucky and Tennessee, by means of amphibious expeditions, composed of gunboats and land forces. Further on in the course of events we shall find the front of the war on the banks of the Tennessee instead of those of the Potomac, and we shall see that a war which the Southern people supposed lingered on the Potomac, was suddenly transferred, and opened with brilliant and imposing scenes on the Western waters. But it is not proper to anticipate with any comment the progress of events.

Gen. Polk had been completing his works for the defence of Columbus. While thus engaged, he was assailed on the 7th November by the enemy in strong force from Cairo.

THE BATTLE OF BELMONT.

Before daybreak on the morning of the 7th of November, Gen. Polk was informed that the enemy, who were under the command of Gen. Grant, had made their appearance in the river with gunboats and transports, and were landing a considerable force on the Missouri shore, five or six miles above Belmont, a small village. Gen. Pillow, whose division was nearest the point immediately threatened, was ordered to cross the river and to move immediately with four of his regiments to the relief of Col. Tappan, who was encamped at Belmont.

Our little army had barely got in position, when the skirmishers were driven in, and the shock took place between the opposing forces. The enemy were numerous enough to have surrounded the little Confederate force with triple lines. Several attempts were made by the enemy's infantry to flank the right and left wings of the Confederates; but the attempt on the right was defeated by the deadly fire and firm attitude of that wing, composed of the regiments of Colonels Russell and Tappan, the 13th Arkansas and the 9th Tennessee, commanded by Col. Russell, as brigade commander. The attempt to turn the left wing was defeated by the destructive fire of Beltzhoover's battery and Col. Wright's regiment, aided by a line of felled timber extending obliquely from the left into the bottom. The two wings of the line stood firm and unbroken for several hours, but the centre, being in the open field, and greatly exposed, once or twice faltered.

About this time, Col. Beltzhoover reported to Gen. Pillow that his ammunition was exhausted: Col. Bell had previously reported his regiment out of ammunition, and Col. Wright that one battalion of his regiment had exhausted its ammunition. The enemy's force being unchecked, and now emerging into the edge of the field, Gen. Pillow ordered the line to use the bayonet. The charge was made by the whole line, and the enemy driven back into the woods. But his line was not broken, and he kept up a deadly fire, and being supported by his large reserve, the Confederate line was forced back to its original position, while that of the enemy advanced. The charge was repeated the second and third time, forcing the enemy's line heavily against his reserve, but with like result. Finding it impossible longer to maintain his position without reinforcements and ammunition, Gen. Pillow ordered the whole line to fall back to the river-bank. In this movement his line was more or less broken and his corps mingled together, so that when they reached the river-bank they had the appearance of a mass of men rather than an organized corps.

The field was to all appearances lost. Reinforcements, however, had been sent for, and at the critical time when our forces were being driven to the river, a regiment, the 2d Tennessee, commanded by Col. Walker, which had crossed the river, came to their support. The opportunity was seized by Gen. Pillow to engage afresh, with this timely addition to his force, the advance of the enemy, while he made a rapid movement up the river-bank, with the design of crossing through the fallen timber, turning the enemy's position and attacking him in the rear.

As Gen. Pillow advanced the main body of his original force in broken order up the river, to a point where he could cross through the fallen timber to make the flank movement, he was joined by two other regiments ordered by Gen. Polk to his support. These fresh troops were placed under command of Col. Marks, of the 11th Louisiana. He was directed to lead the advance in double-quick time through the woods, and to the enemy's rear, and to attack him with vigor. Col. Russell, with his brigade, was ordered to support the movement.

It was with great reluctance that Gen. Polk lessened the force assigned to the immediate defence of Columbus, as an attack in his rear was every moment apprehended. It was obvious, however, from the yielding of our columns to the heavy pressure of the masses of the enemy's infantry, and the fierce assaults of their heavy battery, that further reinforcements were necessary to save the field. Gen. Cheatham was ordered to move across the river in advance of his brigade, to rally and take command of the portions of the regiments within sight on the shore, and to support the flank movement ordered through Col. Marks.

About this time the enemy had fired our tents, and advancing his battery near the river-bank, opened a heavy fire on the steamers which were transporting our troops, in some instances driving shot through two of them at the same time. Captain Smith's Mississippi battery was ordered to move to the river-bank, opposite the field of conflict, and to open upon the enemy's position. The joint fire of this battery and the heavy guns of the fort was for a few moments terrific. The enemy's battery was silenced, and it could be seen that they were taking up their line of march for their boats.

The Federals, however, had scarcely put themselves in motion, when they encountered Col. Marks first, and afterwards Gen. Cheatham, on their flank. The conjuncture was decisive. The enemy finding himself between two fires, that of Smith's artillery in front, and of Col. Marks' and Russell's column in the rear, after a feeble resistance, broke and fled in disorder.

Satisfied that the attack on Columbus for some reason had failed, Gen. Polk had crossed the river, and ordered the victorious commands to press the enemy to their boats. The order was obeyed with alacrity. The pursuit was continued until our troops reached the point where the enemy had made his surgical head-quarters, and depository of stores, of ammunition, baggage, &c. Here our troops found a yard full of knapsacks, arms, ammunition, blankets, overcoats, mess-chests, horses, wagons, and dead and wounded men, with surgeons engaged in the duties of their profession. The enemy's route of retreat was strewn likewise with many of these articles, and abundantly with blood, dead, and wounded men. "The sight along the line of the retreat," says an observer on the field, "was awful. The dead and wounded were at every tree. Some crawled into the creeks to get water, and died there."

On coming in sight of the enemy's gunboats and transports, our troops, as they arrived, were ordered to move as rapidly as possible through the cornfields to the bank of the river. The bank was thus lined for a considerable distance by our troops, who were ordered, as the boats passed up the river, to give the enemy their fire. The fire was hot and destructive. On the boats all was dismay. Under the fire from the bank, the Federals rushed to the opposite side of the boats, and had to be forced back by the bayonet to prevent capsizing. Many of the soldiers were driven overboard by the rush of those behind them. They did not take time to unloose the cables, but cut all loose, and were compelled to run through the fire of sharpshooters lining the bank for more than a mile.

The day which at one time had been so inauspicious to our arms, closed upon a signal triumph. In his official report of the battle, Gen. Pillow declared, that no further evidence were needed to assure the fact, that "the small Spartan army" which withstood the constant fire of three times their number for nearly four hours (a large portion of them being without ammunition), had acted with extraordinary gallantry, than the length and character of the conflict, the great inequality of numbers, and the complete results that crowned the day.

That our loss should be severe in such a conflict might be expected. The list of our killed, wounded, and missing numbered 632. The loss of the enemy was stated in the official reports of our generals to have been more than treble ours. Of this, we had the most abundant evidence in the incidents of the field, in his flight, and his helpless condition, when assailed in his crowded transports with the fire of thousands of deadly rifles.

The victory of Belmont was esteemed as one of the most brilliant triumphs of the war.* In his congratulatory order, Gen. Albert Sydney Johnston, who had been appointed to

---

* The government at Washington, with a characteristic falsehood, stubborn to every other consideration but that of sustaining the spirits of its people, claimed the affair at Belmont as a victory to Northern arms. It is curious, and to some degree amusing, to notice the manner of this misrepresentation, and the gloze and insinuation by which it was effected in the Northern official reports of the battle. Gen. Grant, in his official report, declared that he had driven the Confederates to the river, burnt their camps, &c. So far, his report was ostentatiously fine, but not untrue. It has been shown, however, that the scale of battle was completely turned by a flank movement of our forces in heavy numbers, which routed the enemy, and converted his early successes of the morning into an ignominious defeat. In the Northern official reports of the battle, this portion of the day was dismissed with refreshing brevity and nonchalance. After describing in the most glowing terms his victory in pressing the Confederates to the river, Gen. Grant wrote to his friends, who communicated the letter to the newspapers, "on our return, *stragglers that had been left in our rear* fired into us, and more recrossed the river." In his official report, the flank movement of the Confederates, that was *the* event of the day and had decided it, was alluded to in a single sentence of casual mention, "The rebels recrossed the river, and *followed in the rear to our place of debarkation.*" Instances of this style and effrontery of falsehood abounded in all the Northern official reports of the events of the war; the above is furnished only as a characteristic specimen.

command in the Western Department, and had established his head-quarters at Bowling Green, declared: "This was no ordinary shock of arms; it was a long and trying contest, in which our troops fought by detachments, and always against superior numbers. The 7th of November will fill a bright page in our military annals, and be remembered with gratitude by the sons and daughters of the South."

Despite the victory of Belmont, our situation in Kentucky was one of extreme weakness and entirely at the mercy of the enemy, if he had not been imposed upon by false representations of the number of our forces at Bowling Green. When Gen. Johnston was about to assume command of the Western Department, the government charged him with the duty of deciding the question of occupying Bowling Green, Kentucky, which involved not only military, but political considerations. At the time of his arrival at Nashville, the action of the Legislature of Kentucky had put an end to the latter consideration by sanctioning the formation of companies menacing Tennessee, by assuming the cause of the government at Washington, and by abandoning the neutrality it professed; and, in consequence of their action, the occupation of Bowling Green became necessary as an act of self-defence, at least in the first step.

About the middle of September, Gen. Buckner advanced with a small force of about four thousand men, which was increased by the 15th of October to twelve thousand, and though other accessions of force were received, it continued at about the same strength until the end of November, measles and other diseases keeping down the effective force. The enemy's force then was reported to the War Department at fifty thousand, and an advance was impossible.

Our own people were as much imposed upon as were the enemy, with respect to the real strength of Gen. Johnston's forces, and while they were conjecturing the brilliant results of an advance movement, the fact was that inevitable disasters might have been known by the government to have been in store for the Southern cause in Kentucky and Tennessee, and to be awaiting only the development of a crisis. The utter inadequacy of Gen. Johnston's forces was known to the government. The authorities at Richmond appeared to hope for results without the legitimate means for acquiring them; to look for relief from vague and undefined sources; and to await, with dull expectation, what was next to happen. While the government remained in this blank disposition, events marched onward. It is easily seen, as far as our narrative has gone, that our troops had shown a valor that was invincible against largely superior numbers of the enemy; that had given striking illustrations of endurance in circumstances of the greatest adversity and suffering; and that promised with absolute certainty, as far as its agency could go, the achievement of our independence. It is hereafter to be seen that this valor and devotion, great as they were, could yet not withstand an enemy superior in force, when his numbers were multiplied indefinitely against them; that they could not resist armaments to which, for want of defences, they could only offer up useless sacrifices of life; and that some other agency than the natural spirit and hardihood of men was necessary in the conduct of a war, in the nineteenth century, against a nation which had given such unquestionable proofs, as the North had, of quick and abundant resource, mental activity, and unflagging hope.

It remains but to add here, mention of the political connection which was scarcely more than nominally effected between Kentucky and the Confederate States. On the 18th November, the opponents of the Lincoln rule in Kentucky assembled in Convention, at Russellville, in the southern part of the State, for the purpose of organizing a provisional government for Kentucky, and for taking steps for her admission into the Southern Confederacy. On the 20th November, the Convention unanimously agreed upon a report, presenting in a strong light the falseness of the State and Federal Legislature, and concluded with the declaration that "the people are hereby absolved from all allegiance to said government, and that they have the right to establish any government which to them may seem best adapted to the preservation of their lives and liberty." George W. Johnson, of Scott county, was chosen governor. Commissioners were appointed to negotiate with the Confederate government for the earliest admission of Kentucky into the government of the Confederate States. The embassy of the commissioners to Richmond was successful, and before the middle of December, Kentucky was duly recognized as one of the States of the Southern Confederacy.

CHAPTER VIII.

Prospects of European Interference.—The selfish Calculations of England.—Effects of the Blockade on the South.—Arrest by Capt. Wilkes of the Southern Commissioners.—The Indignation of England.—Surrender of the Commissioners by the Lincoln Government.—Mr. Seward's Letter.—REVIEW OF AFFAIRS AT THE CLOSE OF THE YEAR 1861.—Apathy and Improvidence of the Southern Government.—Superiority of the North on the Water.—The Hatteras Expedition.—The Port Royal Expedition.—The Southern Privateers.—Their Failure.—Errors of Southern Statesmanship.—"King Cotton."—Episodes of the War.—The Affair of Santa Rosa Island.—The Affair of Dranesville.—Political Measures of the South.—A weak and halting Policy.—The Spirit of the War in the North.—Administration of the Civil Polity of the Southern Army.—The Quarter-master's Department.—The Hygiene of the Camps.—Ravages of the Southern Army by Disease.—The Devotion of the Women of the South.

SINCE the commencement of the war, the South had entertained prospects of foreign interference, at least so far as to involve the recognition of her government by England and France, and the raising of the blockade. Such prospects, continued from month to month, had an unhappy effect in weakening the popular sentiment of self-reliance, in turning the attention of the people to the result of external events, and in amusing their attention with misty illusions.

These prospects were vain. By the close of the year, the South had learned the lesson, that the most certain means of obtaining injury, scorn, and calumny from foreign people, was to attempt their conciliation or to seek their applause, and that not until she had proved herself independent of the opinions of Europe, and reached a condition above and beyond the help of England and France, was she likely to obtain their amity and justice.

It had been supposed in the South, that the interest of Europe in the staples of cotton and tobacco would effect a raising of the blockade, at least by the fall of the year. The statistics on these subjects were thought to be conclusive. France derived an annual revenue of $38,000,000 from her monopoly of the tobacco trade; and Great Britain and her people, a revenue of $350,000,000 per annum from American cotton. Five millions of souls, in England, were interested in one way or the other in the cotton manufacture; and the South calculated, with reason, that the blockade would be raised by foreign intervention, rather than that one-sixth of the population of the British Isles would be permitted to be thrown out of employment by a decree or fulmination of the Yankee government at Washington.

Among the statesmen of Great Britain, however, a different calculation prevailed, and that was, as long as the possible contingencies of the future held out the least hope of avoiding the alternative of war with the Washington government, to strain a point to escape it. It was argued, that it would be cheaper for England to support, at the public expense, five millions of operatives, than to incur the cost, besides the unpleasantness of an embroilment in American affairs; and it was in this spirit of selfish calculation—the results of which were stated by Lord Palmerston in the declaration, that the "necessities" of England had not reached that point to require her to interfere, in any manner, in the American war—that it was ultimately decided by the British government to maintain her neutrality with reference to the blockade, as well as other incidents of the war.

About the fall of the year, the South had begun to feel severely the effects of the blockade. Supplies of the usual goods, and even provisions, were becoming scarce. The evils were augmented every day in the results of a baneful spirit of speculation, which indulged in monstrous extortions and corrupted the public spirit, making opportunities for mercenary adventure out of the distresses and necessities of the country. There was great suffering among the poor, and especially among refugees, who had fled to the cities from districts occupied by the enemy.

The resources of the South were such, however, that any thing like famine or actual starvation, of any portion of the people, was not to be apprehended. The changes which happened in the circumstances and pursuits of people, were not always as unfortunate as they appeared, and, in the end, not unfrequently proved an advantage to them and to the prosperity of the country. Many new enterprises were started; many sources of profitable labor were sought out; and many instances of the diversion of popular industry were occasioned, which promised to become of permanent advantage in developing the resources of the country in minerals and manufactures, and introducing provision crops on an enlarged scale in the Cotton States of the Confederacy.

In the month of December occurred an event which promised the most fortunate consequences to the South, with respect to foreign intervention and her release from the blockade. The Confederate government had deputed Mr. James M. Mason, of Virginia, and Mr. John Slidell, of Louisiana, commissioners, respectively, to England and France. They had escaped the blockade at Charleston on a Confederate vessel, and arriving at the neutral port of Havana, had left there on the 7th day of December in a British mail-steamer, the Trent, commanded by Capt. Moir. The next day after leaving port, the British vessel, while in the Bahama channel, was intercepted by the Federal steam-frigate, San Jacinto, Commander Wilkes, being brought to by a shotted gun, and boarded by an armed boat's crew. The persons of the commissioners and their secretaries, Messrs. Eustis and Macfarland, were demanded; they claimed the protection of the British flag, and refused to leave it except at the instance of actual physical force, which Lieut. Fairfax, who had boarded the vessel, then declared he was ready to use. The Trent was an unarmed steamer, and as resistance was hopeless, the commissioners were surrendered, under a distinct and passionate protest against a piratical seizure of ambassadors under a neutral flag.

This outrage done by a Federal vessel to the British flag, when it was learned in the South, was welcome news, as it was thought certain that the British government would resent the insult, and as the boastful and exultant tone in the North, over the capture of the commissioners, appeared to make it equally certain that the government at Washington would not surrender its booty. War between England and the North was thought to be imminent. Providence was declared to be in our favor; the incident of the Trent was looked upon almost as a special dispensation, and it was said, in fond imagination, that on its deck and in the trough of the weltering Atlantic the key of the blockade had at last been lost.

These prospects were disappointed by the weakness of the government at Washington, in surrendering the commissioners and returning them to the British flag. The surrender was an exhibition of meanness and cowardice unparalleled in the political history of the civilized world, but strongly characteristic of the policy and mind of the North. The people of the North had, at first, gone into raptures over the arrest of the commissioners; the newspapers designated it as "worth more than a victory in the field;" the hospitalities of the city of New York were offered by its common council to Capt. Wilkes, and a dinner was given him by leading citizens of Boston, in honor of his brave exploit in successfully capturing, from the deck of an unarmed mail-steamer, four unarmed passengers. The government at Washington had given every indication of its approval of the arrest. The compliments of the Cabinet had been tendered to Capt. Wilkes, and a proposition introduced into Congress to distinguish his piratical adventure by a public vote of thanks. The subjects of the capture were condemned to close cells in Fort Warren.

Despite all this manifest indorsement by the government of the legality and value of the arrest of the commissioners, Mr. Seward did not hesitate to surrender them when the alternative of war with Great Britain was indicated to him, in the dispatches of that government demanding, in very simple and stern terms, the reparation of the outrage that had been committed upon its flag.

In a letter to Mr. Adams, the representative of the Washington government at London, Mr. Seward had advised him to make no explanations, as the Washington Cabinet thought it better that the ground taken by the British government should first be made known to them. The ground of its claims was never furnished by the British government. Its demand for reparation and apology was entirely naked, and evidently disdained to make a single argument on the law question. With unexampled shamelessness, Mr. Seward made the plea himself for the surrender of the commissioners; he argued that they could not be the subjects of a judicial proceeding to determine their status, because the vessel, the proper subject of such a proceeding, had been permitted to escape; and with a contemptible affectation of alacrity to offer, from a returning sense of justice, what all the world knew had been extorted from the alarms of cowardice, he declared that he "cheerfully" surrendered the commissioners, and did so in accordance with long-established American doctrine.

In surrendering the commissioners, the Washington government took the opportunity to declare its reassured hopes of the Union, and to express its contempt for the Southern revolution. In his letter to Earl Russell, Mr. Seward took particular pains to declare, that " the safety of the Union did not require the detention of the captured persons ;" that an " effectual check" had been put to the " existing insurrection," and that its " waning proportions" made it no longer a subject of serious consideration.

The declaration was false and affected, but it contained an element of truth. There is no doubt that, at the time it was made, the power of the revolution in the South was declining ; and a rapid survey of the political posture, and of events transpiring in the latter half of the year 1861, affords painful evidence of relaxation on the part of the Confederate government, and of instances of weakness and abuse that the people, who had pledged every thing and endured every thing in a contest for freedom, had no right to expect.

REVIEW OF AFFAIRS AT THE CLOSE OF THE YEAR 1861.

The justice of history compels us to state that two causes—the overweening confidence of the South in the superior valor of its people, induced by the unfortunate victory of Manassas, and the vain delusion, continued from month to month, that European interference was certain, and that peace was near at hand, conspired, about this time, to reduce the Southern cause to a critical condition of apathy.

Western Virginia had been abandoned to the enemy almost with indifference, and with an apathetic confidence in an army that was in danger of becoming demoralized, and in the prospects of European interference, which were no brighter than formerly, except in imagination, the South carelessly observed the immense preparations of the North, by sea and land, to extend the area of the contest from the coasts of Carolina to the States on the Mississippi, and to embrace her whole territory with the lengthening arms of the war.

While the enemy was busy making his immense naval prep

arations against our sea-coast, and building scores of gunboats on the upper Mississippi to drive our armies out of Kentucky and Tennessee, the Southern government had shown the most extraordinary apathy; the spirit of our armies was evidently decaying, and abuses of extraordinary magnitude had crept into the civil administration of our affairs. No corresponding activity was manifested by us in the line of naval enterprise adopted by the enemy. Means were not wanting for at least some emulation in this respect. Large appropriations had been made by Congress for the construction of gunboats and objects of river defence; the State of Virginia had turned over to the Confederate government the best navy-yard on the continent, and two armories with their machinery; and with the means and appliances at Gosport and Richmond, it is not doubted that, with proper activity, the government might have created a considerable fleet.

The North had improved the advantage of its possession of a navy by increasing its numbers. Nearly a hundred vessels of different descriptions were purchased by it, and fleets of gunboats fitted out for operations on the coast and rivers. Two naval expeditions had already, before the close of the year, been sent down the Carolina coast, and without accomplishing much, had given serious indications of what was to be expected from this arm of the service on the slight fortifications of our ocean frontier.

On the 29th of August, a naval expedition from Fortress Monroe, under command of Commodore Stringham and Major-general Butler, had reduced the two forts at Hatteras Inlet, and had signalized their victory by the capture of fifteen guns and 615 prisoners, among whom was Commodore Barron, the Confederate officer in command.

The capture of Port Royal, on the South Carolina coast, on the 7th of November, by the bombardment of Forts Walker and Beauregard, gave to the enemy a point for his squadrons to find shelter, and a convenient naval depot. The attack was made on the 7th of November, by a Federal fleet, numbering fifteen war-steamers and gunboats, under command of Capt. Dupont, flag-officer of the south Atlantic blockading squadron. The attack was easily successful by the bombardment of the forts at the entrance of the sound. It may be imagined how inefficient our defences must have been, when the fact is, that they yielded after a bombardment which continued precisely four hours and thirty minutes; the condition of Fort Walker at this time being, according to the official report of General Drayton, who was in command, "all but three of the guns in the water front disabled, and only five hundred pounds of powder in the magazine." But these were only the first lessons of the enemy's power and our improvidence in defences, that were to be taught us on the coast.

The privateering service had yielded us but poor fruits. The Savannah, the first of the privateers, was captured, and her crew treated as pirates, at least so far as to load them with irons, and confine them in felons' cells. With the exception of the Sumter (an awkwardly rigged bark) and one or two others, the privateers of the South were pretty closely confined within their own harbors and rivers by the blockading fleets. The "militia of the seas," that, it was predicted in the early part of the war, would penetrate into every sea, and find splendid prizes in the silk ships of China, and the gold-freighted steamers of California, had proved but an inconsiderable annoyance to the extensive commercial marine of the North; it had captured during the year but fifty prizes in smacks, schooners, and small merchantmen, and by this time the South had learned that its privateering resources were about as delusive as that other early and crude expectation of adventitious aid in the war—the power of "King Cotton."

It is curious, indeed, how the early expectations of the manner and conduct of a war are disappointed by the progress of its events, and its invariable law of success in the stern competitions of force, without reference to other circumstances. It was said, at the beginning of the war, that, while cotton would "bring Europe to its knees," the Southern privateers would cut up the commerce of the North, and soon bring the mercenary and money-making spirits of that section to repentance. Neither result was realized. At the close of the year 1861, the South appeared to be fully convinced that it was waging a war in which it could no longer look for aid to external and adventitious circumstances; that it could no longer hope to obtain its independence from European interference, or from cotton, or from the annoyances of its privateers, or from the rupture of a financial system in the North; and that it had no other resource of hope but in the stern and bloody trials of the battle-field.

Beyond the events briefly sketched in this and the foregoing chapters, there were some incidents which were interesting as episodes in the progress of the war, up to the close of the year 1861, to which a full reference has been impossible in a work which professes to treat only the material parts of the important campaigns of the year.

The most interesting of these was probably the attack on Santa Rosa Island, in the harbor of Pensacola, on the night of the 8th October, and the storming, by picked companies from the Mississippi, Alabama, Georgia, Louisiana, and Florida regiments, of the camp which had been made on the island by the notorious Billy Wilson Zouaves. Landing from steamers and flats on the enemy's shore, within sight of his fleet, the small band of Confederates marched some three or four miles in the darkness of the night over an unknown and almost impassable ground, killing the enemy's pickets, storming his intrenched camp, driving off the notorious regiment of New York bullies, with their colonel flying at their head, and burning every vestige of their clothing, equipage, and provisions. This action was rendered remarkable by an instance of disgusting brutality on the part of the enemy—the murder of our wounded who had been left on the field on account of the necessity of rapidly retiring with our small force, before the enemy could rally from his surprise. Of thirteen dead bodies recovered, eleven were shot through the head, having, at the same time, disabling wounds on the body. This fact admits of but one inference.

The affair of Dranesville, on the line of the Potomac, had given a sharp and unexpected lesson to our immoderate confidence. This action occurred on the 22d day of December. Our whole force engaged was nearly 2,500 men, composed of Virginia, South Carolina, Kentucky, and Alabama troops, under command of Gen. Stuart. The expedition, which was attended by a train of wagons intended for foraging purposes, fell in with the enemy near Dranesville. On the appearance of the enemy, the 11th Virginia regiment charged them with a yell, and drove them back to their lines within sight of Dranesville. Here the enemy rallied. In the confusion which ensued, the 1st Kentucky regiment fired upon the South Carolina troops, mistaking them for the enemy. Discovering his mistake, Colonel Taylor, of the 1st Kentucky, moved cautiously through the woods. Coming in sight of another regiment, and prompted to unusual caution by his previous mistake, he shouted to their commander to know who he was. "The colonel of the 9th," was the reply. "Of what 9th?" "Don't shoot," said the Yankees; "we are friends—South Carolinians." "On which side are you?" asked Col. Taylor. "For the Union," now shouted the Federals; at the same instant pouring a murderous volley into the ranks of the Kentuckians. The engagement now became general. The Federals had the advantage of position and largely superior numbers. Their field batteries swept our lines, and several regiments of their infantry, protected by the ground, had advanced within one hundred yards of us, keeping the air full of minié-balls. After sustaining the fire for some time, our troops were compelled to fall back. The retreat was executed in good order, as the enemy did not attempt any pursuit. Our loss on the field from which we were repulsed was about two hundred in killed and wounded. The next day, reinforcements having reached Gen. Stuart, the enemy had drawn off from the locality of the battle-field, and declined any further engagement.

The affair at Dranesville was no serious disaster, but it was a significant warning, and, in this respect, it had an importance beyond the size of the engagement and its immediate results. The Yankees were learning to stand fire, and, out of the material which was raw at Bull Run, McClellan was making troops who were no longer contemptible, and who were perceptibly improving in discipline, stanchness, and soldierly qualities.

Of the political measures adopted by the South in furtherance of the objects of the war, but a few words need be said. They are justly described as weak and halting responses to the really vigorous acts of the Northern government in its heartless, but strong and effective prosecution of the war. Whil the Washington government protected itself against disaffected persons and spies by a system of military police, extending over the whole North, the Provisional Congress, at Richmond, was satisfied to pass a law for the deportation of "alien enemies," the execution of which afforded facilities to the egress of innumerable spies. The Washington government had passed a law for the confiscation of the property of "rebels." The Congress at Richmond replied, after a weak hesitation, by a law sequestrating the property of alien enemies in the South, the operations of which could never have been intended to have effect; for, by future amendments in the same Congress, the law was soon emasculated into a broad farce. The Washington government was actually collecting an army of half a million of men. The Richmond Congress replied to the threat of numbers, by increasing its army, on paper, to four hundred thousand men; and the Confederate government, in the midst of a revolution that threatened its existence, continued to rely on the wretched shift of twelve months' volunteers and raw militia, with a population that, by the operation of conscription, could have been embodied and drilled into an invincible army, competent not only to oppose invasion at every point of our frontier, but to conquer peace in the dominions of the enemy.

The universal mind and energy of the North had been consolidated in its war upon the South. The patriotism of the nation was broadly invoked; no clique arrogated and monopolized the control of affairs; no favorites closed up against the million outside the avenues of patronage, of honor, and of promotion. It was a remarkable circumstance that the North had, at all stages of the war, adopted the best means for securing specific results. The popularity of Fremont, with the half million "Wide Awakes" of the North, was used to bring an army into the field. The great ship-broker of New York, Morgan, and the great ship-owner, Vanderbilt, were patronized to create a navy. In the army, the popularity of Banks, Butler, Grant, and Baker were employed equally with the science of McClellan, Buell, and Halleck.* It had been thus that the

---

* The two most conspicuous Federal generals in the operations of the West were Generals Buell and Halleck. Don Carlos Buell was a native of Ohio. He had served in the Mexican war with distinction, having been twice brevetted for gallant conduct—the last time as major in the battle of Churubusco, in which he was severely wounded. At the close of the Mexican war, he was

Federal government had united the whole North, brought an army of half a million men into the field, and swelled the proportions of the war far beyond any expectations of the world.

The policy of monotonous defence had been perseveringly pursued by the authorities of the Confederacy. On the side of the enemy, it had more than repaired the damage inflicted upon them in many brilliant battles, and had left them at perfect leisure, in the very presence of our forces, to devise, mature, and make trial of any plan of campaign or assault which they thought expedient. A large portion of Virginia and important regions on the Southern seaboards were now occupied by the enemy, who would never have ventured forth to such distances, if they had been menaced nearer home. The strictly defensive policy was sustained by elaborate arguments.

---

appointed assistant adjutant-general, with rank of captain, but relinquished his rank in line in 1851. As a commander, he was courageous, energetic, and methodical, and he obtained the respect of the South for his chivalric disposition, his courteous behavior to prisoners, and his uniform recognition of the laws and amenities of civilized warfare.

Gen. Henry Wager Halleck, before the war, had been but little known, and that only as the author of some military works, and a prominent land lawyer, deeply versed in Mexican titles, at the bar of San Francisco, California. He was a pupil of West Point, and had been brevetted captain for meritorious services in California during the Mexican war. He was appointed Secretary of State of the province of California in the military government of Generals Kearney, Mason, and Riley, and was a member of the Convention to form and one of the committee to draft the State Constitution of California in 1849. He subsequently disappeared from public attention, and occupied himself with his innumerable Mexican clients in California as a lawyer and land speculator.

A correspondent gives the following account of the personnel of General Halleck: "In the field he is hardly the same person who might have been seen quietly gliding from the Planters' House to head-quarters in St. Louis. He does not look a whit more military in appearance, but looks, in his new and rich, though plain uniform, as if he were in borrowed clothes. In truth, he bears a most striking resemblance to some oleaginous Methodist parson dressed in regimentals, with a wide, stiff-rimmed black felt hat sticking on the back of his head, at an acute angle with the ground. His demeanor in front of his tent is very simple and business-like. When on horseback, his Wesleyan character is more and more prominent. He neither looks like a soldier, rides like one, nor does he carry the state of a major-general in the field, but is the impersonation of the man of peace. His face is large, tabular, and Teutonic; his eyes a kind of indistinct gray, not without expression, but of that deep welling kind that only reveal the emotion without indicating its character."

It is not within the design of our work to canvass the logical value of these arguments; but it is to recognize as a fact the natural and almost universal impression made upon the popular mind of the South, that it could not be good generalship which left the enemy at perfect leisure to mature all his preparations for aggression; and that it could not be a glorious system of warfare, which never ventured an aggressive movement, and which decimated its armies by inaction.

In the administration of the civil polity of the Southern army, as distinguished from its command, there were abuses and defects which were constant subjects of newspaper comment.

In the Quarter-master's department, however, the results accomplished by the energy of its directors were little less than surprising, and received the marked commendation of a committee of the Provisional Congress, appointed to inquire into the civil polity of the army. That the immense army now in the service of the Confederate States, suddenly collected, men and officers generally inexperienced in camp life and military duty, should be clothed, armed, and moved with the facility of a permanent organization, was not to be expected; and yet, with but few exceptions, this result was accomplished. Major Alfred M. Barbour, of Virginia, was appointed Chief Quarter-master of the army of the Potomac, our principal *corps d'armée* in the field; and his remarkable resources of judgment, his vast energy, and his untiring devotion to his extensive duties in the field, contributed most important results in the emergencies of the many sudden and rapid movements of our forces in Virginia, in the remarkable campaign in that State of the spring of 1862. Such contributions to the public service are not to be depreciated by the side of more visible, and, in the popular mind, more brilliant achievements of the war. The labors of the Quarter-master's department penetrate the entire military establishment, breathe life into the army, nurture its growth, and give it strength and efficiency in the field; vigilant, prepared, and present, it moves unnoticed amid the stirring events of the field, and obscured by the dust and smoke of the combat, it remains unobserved even while collecting the fruits of victory.

The most distressing abuses were visible in the ill-regulated hygiene of our camps. The ravages of disease among the army in Virginia were terrible; the accounts of its extent were suppressed in the newspapers of the day, and there is no doubt that thousands of our brave troops disappeared from notice without a record of their end, in the nameless graves that yet mark the camping grounds on the lines of the Potomac, and among the wild mountains of Virginia.

Our camps were scourged with fever, pneumonia, and diarrhœa. The armies on the Potomac and in western Virginia suffered greatly—those troops in Cheat Mountain and in the vicinity of the Kanawha Valley most intensely. The wet and changeable climate, the difficulty of transportation, exposure to cold and rain without tents, the necessary consequence of the frequent forward and retrograde movements, as well as the want of suitable food for either sick or well men, produced most of the sickness, and greatly aggravated it after its accession.

The regulations, requiring reports from the regiments as to the number of sick, their diseases, and the wants of the medical station, were, but in few instances, complied with. The result of this neglect was, that upon a change of position in the army, it was the unhappy consequence that the number of sick greatly exceeded that indicated by the reports. They were hurried to the rear, where the accommodations, both as to food, shelter, and medical attendance, being all insufficient, there was great suffering and great mortality.

The suffering of our army evoked, on the part of the Southern people, demonstrations of patriotic devotion and generosity, such, perhaps, as the world had never seen. The patriotism of our citizens at home was manifested in unremitting efforts to supply the wants and relieve the sufferings of the soldiers, sick and well. The supply of money, clothing, and hospital stores, from this voluntary and generous source, is estimated in millions of dollars.* It was the most cheering indication

---

* The following contributions (estimated in money) were listed at the Passport Office, in Richmond, during the last three months of the year 1861. The list comprises almost exclusively the donations made to the army of the Potomac. Of the voluntary supplies sent to the army in Missouri, Arkansas, and Kentucky, there is no account whatever; but, as the same patriotic devotion animated our people everywhere, there is no reason to doubt that an equal

of the spirit of our people in the cause of independence. The women of the country, with the tenderness and generosity of their sex, not only loaded railroad cars with all those appliances for the comfort of the sick which their patriotic ingenuity could devise, but also came to the rescue in clothing those who were well and bearing arms in the field. They made large pecuniary contributions, took charge of the hospitals established by the States, and, as matrons of those institutions, carried cleanliness and comfort to the gallant soldier, far from home and kindred. A committee of the Provisional Congress placed on record the thanks of the country to the women of the South, for their works of patriotism and public charity, and declared that the government owed them "a public acknowledgment of their faithfulness in the glorious work of effecting our independence."

amount of clothing, stores, &c., had been sent to those troops. With this calculation, the whole amount of contributions for the last quarter of the year 1861 could not have fallen short of three millions of dollars:

North Carolina,	$325,417
Alabama,	317,600
Mississippi,	272,670
Georgia,	244,885
South Carolina,	137,206
Texas,	87,800
Louisiana,	61,950
Virginia,	48,070
Tennessee,	17,000
Florida,	2,350
Arkansas,	950
	$1,515,898

CHAPTER IX.

Prospects of the Year 1862.—The Lines of the Potomac.—General Jackson's Expedition to Winchester.—The BATTLE OF MILL SPRINGS IN KENTUCKY.—General Crittenden.—Death of General Zollicoffer.—Sufferings of Crittenden's Army on the Retreat.—Comparative Unimportance of the Disaster.—The BATTLE OF ROANOKE ISLAND.—Importance of the Island to the South.—Death of Captain Wise.—Causes of the Disaster to the South.—Investigation in Congress.—Censure of the Government.—Interviews of General Wise with Mr. Benjamin, the Secretary of War.—Mr. Benjamin censured by Congress, but retained in the Cabinet.—His Promotion by President Davis.—Condition of the Popular Sentiment.

The year 1862 was to bring in a train of disasters to the South. Taking a brief glance at the lines of the Potomac, we shall thereafter have to find the chief interest of the war in other directions—in the West and on the seacoast.

In December last, Gen. Thomas F. Jackson was sent from Gen. Johnston's line to Winchester with a force at his disposal of some ten thousand men. Had the same force been placed at the command of Gen. Jackson in early autumn, with the view to an expedition to Wheeling, by way of the Winchester and Parkersburg road, the good effects would, in all probability, have shown themselves in the expulsion of the Federals from northwestern Virginia.

On the 1st of January, 1862, Gen. Jackson marched with his command from Winchester to Bath, in Morgan county, and from the latter place to Romney, where there had been a large Federal force for many weeks, and from which point they had committed extensive depredations on the surrounding country. Gen. Jackson drove the enemy from Romney and the neighboring country without much fighting. His troops, however, endured the severest hardships in the expedition. Their sufferings were terrible in what was the severest portion of the winter. They were compelled at one time to struggle through an almost blinding storm of snow and sleet, and to bivouac at night in the forests, without tents or camp equipage. Many of the troops were frozen on the march, and died from exposure and exhaustion.

The heroic commander, whose courage had been so brilliantly illustrated at Manassas, gave new proofs of his iron will in this expedition and the subsequent events of his campaign in the upper portion of the valley of Virginia. No one would have supposed that a man, who, at the opening of the war, had been a professor in a State military institute—that at Lexington, Virginia—could have shown such active determination and grim energy in the field. But Gen. Jackson had been brought up in a severer school of practical experience than West Point, where he had graduated twenty years before; he had served in the memorable campaign from Vera' Cruz to Mexico; and an iron will and stern courage, which he had from nature, made him peculiarly fitted to command.* But we must wait for a subsequent period to refer again to Gen. Jackson's operations in the Valley, or to other portions of the campaign in Virginia.

---

* At the siege of Vera Cruz, Jackson commanded a battery, and attracted attention by the coolness and judgment with which he worked his guns, and was promoted first lieutenant. For his conduct at Cerro Gordo, he was brevetted captain. He was in all Scott's battles to the city of Mexico, and behaved so well that he was brevetted major for his services. To his merits as a commander he added the virtues of an active, humble, consistent Christian, restraining profanity in his camp, welcoming army colporteurs, distributing tracts, and anxious to have every regiment in his army supplied with a chaplain. He was vulgarly sneered at as a fatalist; his habits of soliloquy were derided as superstitious conversations with a familiar spirit; but the confidence he had in his destiny was the unfailing mark of genius, and adorned the Christian faith, which made him believe that he had a distinct mission of duty in which he should be spared for the ends of Providence. Of the habits of his life the following description is given by one who knew him: "He is as calm in the midst of a hurricane of bullets as he was in the pew of his church at Lexington, when he was professor of the Institute. He appears to be a man of almost superhuman endurance. Neither heat nor cold makes the slightest impression upon him. He cares nothing for good quarters and dainty fare. Wrapped in his blanket, he throws himself down on the ground anywhere, and sleeps as soundly as though he were in a palace. He lives as the soldiers live, and endures all the fatigue and all the suffering that they endure. His vigilance is something marvellous. He never seems to sleep, and lets nothing pass without his personal scrutiny. He can neither be caught napping, nor whipped when he is wide awake. The rapidity of his marches is something portentous. He is heard of by the enemy at one point, and, before they can make up their minds to follow him, he is off at another. His men have little baggage, and he moves, as nearly as he can, without incumbrance. He keeps so constantly in motion, that he never has a sick list, and no need of hospitals.'

THE BATTLE OF MILL SPRINGS IN KENTUCKY.

In a previous chapter, we noticed the expedition of Gen. Zollicoffer in Kentucky, and gave an account of the rout of the forces sent against him. The next expedition of the enemy against him was successful beyond their expectations.

Since the affair referred to, Gen. Zollicoffer had moved with a portion of his command to Mill Springs, on the southern bank of the Cumberland river, and soon after advanced across to Camp Beech Grove, on the opposite bank, fortifying this camp with earthworks. At Beech Grove, he placed five regiments of infantry, twelve pieces of artillery, and several hundred cavalry, and at Mill Springs he had two regiments of infantry and several hundred cavalry. About the first of January, Major-general Crittenden arrived and took the command, having been advanced, by President Davis, from a captaincy in the Federal army to a major-generalship in the Confederate army.

Our position at Beech Grove had but few advantages. From the face of the country in front there was a very bad range for artillery, and it could not be of very material benefit against an attacking infantry force; and, considering the extent of the front line and the number of works to be defended, there was within the camp an insufficient force. At the same time, for several weeks, bare existence in the camps was very precarious, from want of provisions and forage. Regiments frequently subsisted on one-third rations, and this very frequently of bread alone. Wayne county, which was alone productive in this region of Kentucky, had been exhausted, and the neighboring counties of Tennessee could furnish nothing for the support of the army. Only corn could be obtained for the horses and mules, and this in such small quantities that often cavalry companies were sent out on unshod horses which had eaten nothing for two days. The condition of the roads and the poverty of the intervening section rendered it impossible to transport from Knoxville, a distance of one hundred and thirty miles. The enemy from Columbia commanded the Cumberland river, and only one boat was enabled to come up with supplies from Nashville. With the channel of communication closed, the position became untenable without attack.

In these straits, when the entire army at Mill Springs had been reduced to a single ration of beef per day, and a half ration of corn, the latter eaten as parched corn, and not issued as meal, news reached Gen. Crittenden of an advance movement of the enemy, both from Columbia and from Somerset. On the 17th of January it was ascertained that a large Federal force, under Gen. Thomas, was moving on the road from Columbia, and, on the evening of that day, was camped about ten miles from Beech Grove. It was also ascertained that other reinforcements were moving from the direction of Columbia, under command of Gen. Schoëpff, and that the junction of these two forces was intended for an attack on Camp Beech Grove.

Under these circumstances, Gen. Crittenden determined to attack Gen. Thomas's force in his camp. The decision, which was sanctioned by a council of war, was a most adventurous one. It was proposed, with an effective force of four thousand men, to attack an enemy in his intrenchments, at least ten thousand strong; it is true, however, that a defence of our intrenchments was impracticable, and that to have awaited the enemy there, would only have given him time to have effected a junction of his forces. This consideration, however, gives but an imperfect vindication of the impetuous adventure determined upon by Gen. Crittenden. The fact was, that the avenues of retreat were open to our little army, and could only have been cut off by the enemy's crossing above and below Mill Springs.

In perfect silence, at midnight, the march began. The brigade of Gen. Zollicoffer moved in front. In the gray dawn, about six o'clock, two miles from their camp, the pickets of the enemy fired upon our advanced cavalry. The morning of the 19th was dark and rainy—a fit day for a sabbath battle. The 15th Mississippi regiment, in line of battle, was steadily advanced, under the constant fire of the enemy. The charge of Gen. Zollicoffer's brigade, in which this gallant regiment earned the most conspicuous distinction of the day, soon became impetuous. The Mississippi troops fought with a devotion never excelled by the soldiers of any battle-field; nearly half of the regiment (it numbered only 440) fell in the action; at times they fought with the enemy at ten or twelve paces, and, in one of their sweeping and exultant charges, for fifty yards, dashed over the dead bodies of Yankees. The enemy was steadily driven back before the charge of Gen. Zollicoffer's command. Already he was ascending the last hill to its crest, where the heaviest firing told the battle raged. He sent for reinforcements, and the brigade of Gen. Carrol was ordered up. In another moment, it was announced that Gen. Zollicoffer was killed. He had fallen on the crest of the hill, the stronghold of the enemy, which he had almost driven them from, and which once gained, the day was ours.

Gen. Zollicoffer fell very near the camp of the enemy. He was with Col. Battle's Tennessee regiment, this and the Mississippi regiment being the chief participants in the action, and in the ranks of which were his own home friends, born and brought up around him at Nashville. In front, and concealed in the woods, was a regiment of Kentucky renegades, commanded by Col. Fry. By some mistake, probably that of the Kentuckians for a regiment of his own command, Gen. Zollicoffer got very near them. Col. Fry was at the right of his regiment. Gen. Zollicoffer was within a few feet of the colonel. A gum coat concealed his uniform. The two parties mistook each other for friends, and discovered their mutual mistake almost at the same instant. One of General Zollicoffer's aids shot at Colonel Fry, but only wounded his horse. The next moment the Federal colonel fired at Zollicoffer, and the general, raising his hand to his breast, fell, pierced by several balls.

At the announcement of the death of Gen. Zollicoffer, a sudden gloom pervaded the field and depressed the Tennessee troops, who had been devotedly attached to him. Gen. Crittenden essayed all that personal example could do to retrieve the sinking fortunes of the day. He, in person, rode up to the front of the fight, in the very midst of the fire of the enemy. To gain the disputed hill, the fight was still continued. Charge after charge was driven back by the heavy forces of the enemy. After a conflict of three and a half hours, our troops commenced to give way. The pursuit was checked by several stands made by the little army, and the intrenchments at Camp Beech Grove were reached in the afternoon, with a loss on our side of about three hundred killed and wounded, and probably fifty prisoners.

The advance of the enemy arrived late in the evening before

the Confederate intrenchments, and fired upon them with shot and shell. Night closing in, put a stop to further demonstrations. Our men, tired and worn out as they were, stood behind the breastworks until midnight, when orders came for them to retreat quietly across the river. A steamer, with three barges attached, commenced the work of transportation. Cannon, baggage wagons, and horses were abandoned; every thing was lost save what our men had on their backs, and yet the whole night was consumed in getting the army over the river, which was very high at the time. The line of retreat was taken up towards Monticello, Gen. Crittenden having determined to strike for the Cumberland at the highest point where boats could land with safety, in order to be in open communication with Nashville.

The retreat was one of great distress. Many of the troops had become demoralized, and, without order, dispersed through the mountain by-ways in the direction of Monticello. "We reached Monticello," writes an officer of one of the regiments in the retreat, "at night, and then we were threatened with starvation—an enemy far more formidable than the one we left beyond the river. Since Saturday night, we had but an hour of sleep, and scarcely a morsel of food. For a whole week, we have been marching under a bare subsistence, and I have at length approached that point in a soldier's career when a handful of parched corn may be considered a first-class dinner. We marched the first few days through a barren region, where supplies could not be obtained. I have more than once seen the men kill a porker with their guns, cut and quarter it, and broil it on the coals, and then eat it without bread or salt. The suffering of the men from the want of the necessaries of life, of clothing, and of repose, has been most intense, and a more melancholy spectacle than this solemn, hungry, and weary procession, could scarcely be imagined."

The enemy invested the abandoned camp of the Confederates on the morning following the day of the battle. Gen. Schoëpff's brigade had crossed the river preparatory to the attack which Gen. Thomas had intended to make on the intrenchments on Monday. Early in the morning, the steamer used by the Confederates in effecting their retreat was discovered lying in the river, and was burnt by the shells of the enemy. They congratulated themselves that they had cut off the last hope of the escape of "the rebels." Long columns of troops filed away, and the artillery commenced to play on the intrenchments, in doubt for a moment whether their guns were replied to or not, when word came that the intrenchments were abandoned. As the enemy marched into the camp there was hardly a cheer. They had hoped to capture every man of the Confederates, and were bitterly disappointed. They secured, however, a rich spoil of victory—every thing in fact that made our poor soldiers an army. The property captured was of considerable value. It consisted of eight six-pounders and two Parrott-guns, with caissons filled with ammunition, about 100 four-horse wagons, and upwards of 1,200 horses and mules, several boxes of arms which had never been opened, and from 500 to 1,000 muskets.

The death of Gen. Zollicoffer was deeply lamented by his countrymen. It is doubtful whether the death of any man of the present generation ever produced such conspicuous grief among Tennesseeans. He was a man made of stern stuff, and possessed in a remarkable degree the confidence of his army and of the Tennessee people. He was devoted to the interests of the South, and, during a long career in Congress, was one of the few members of the Whig party who voted uniformly with Southern men on all questions involving her honor and welfare. Made a brigadier-general, he was assigned to the department of East Tennessee at an early period of the war, and had exhibited rare address and genuine courage and military talents in the administration of his responsible command. It was a melancholy mode which his army chose of testifying their appreciation of his ability as a commander, in giving up all for lost when he was shot down ; but it certainly afforded a marked testimony of their confidence in his generalship.

The body of General Zollicoffer fell into the hands of the enemy. His remains were treated by them with unusual respect. One of their officers, who had known him in Washington, asked to be permitted to see the corpse. A pistol-shot had struck him in the breast, a little above the heart. His face bore no expression such as is usually found upon those who fall in battle—no malice, no reckless hate, not even a shadow of physical pain. It was calm, placid, noble. "Poor fellow," wrote the officer who visited with respect his remains just after the battle, "I have never looked on a countenance so marked with sadness. A deep dejection had settled on it. 'The low cares of the mouth' were distinct in the droop at its corners, and the thin cheeks showed the wasting which comes through disappointment and trouble."

The reverse sustained by our arms in Southern Kentucky involved no important military consequences; and the government at Richmond found cause of congratulation in the circumstance that, if a defeat must needs have happened to it at this time, it could not have come upon it at a point of less comparative consequence than the battle-ground near Somerset, Kentucky. It was a hundred miles from the line of railroad connecting us with the great West; it was a still greater distance from Cumberland Gap, the nearest point of the Virginia line; and there intervened, on the road to Knoxville, rivers and mountain passes which an invading army could only traverse slowly and with great caution.

But a disaster to our arms was shortly to ensue, of the importance and gravity of which there could be no doubt, and with respect to which the government could find neither consolations nor excuses. While we have seen how matters stood on the Potomac in the opening of the year 1862, and what ominous indications had taken place in the West, we must now remove the attention of the reader to the sea-coast, where, along the low and melancholy scenery of the sea-border of North Carolina, one of the most extraordinary dramas of the war was to be enacted.

THE BATTLE OF ROANOKE ISLAND.

On the 21st of December, that part of North Carolina east of the Chowan river, together with the counties of Washington and Tyrrell, was, at the request of the proper authorities of North Carolina, separated from the remainder, and constituted into a military district, under Brigadier-general II. A. Wise, and attached to the command of Major-general Huger, commanding the department of Norfolk.

Immediately upon the secession of the State of North Carolina from the government of the United States, and the adoption of the Constitution of the Confederate States of America, the authorities of that State commenced the construction of fortifications at Hatteras and Oregon Inlets, and other points upon her coast, which were not completed when the State transferred her forts, arsenals, army, navy, and coast defences to the Confederate government. Shortly thereafter the attack was made upon Forts Hatteras and Clark, and they were taken, and the fortifications at Oregon Inlet were abandoned, and the armament, stores, and ammunition were removed to Roanoke Island. The enemy immediately appeared in force in Pamlico Sound, the waters of which are connected with Albemarle and Currituck sounds by means of the two smaller sounds of Croatan and Roanoke. The island of Roanoke being situated between these two latter sounds, commanding the channels of each, became, upon the fall of Hatteras and the abandonment of Oregon Inlet, only second in importance to Fortress Monroe. The island then became the key which unlocked all northeastern North Carolina to the enemy, and exposed Portsmouth and Norfolk to a rear approach of the most imminent danger.

Such was the importance of Roanoke Island. It was threatened by one of the most formidable naval armaments yet fitted out by the North, put under the command of Gen. Burnside, of Rhode Island. It might have been placed in a state of defence against any reasonable force, with the expenditure of money and labor supposed to be within the means of the government. Ample time and the fullest forewarnings were given to the government for the construction of defences, since, for a full month, Gen. Wise had represented to the government, with the most obvious and emphatic demonstrations, that the defences of the island were wholly inadequate for its protection from an attack either by land or water.

The military defences of Roanoke Island and its adjacent waters on the 8th of February, the day of its surrender, consisted of three sand forts, a battery of two 32-pounders, and a redoubt thrown across the road in the centre of the island, about seventy or eighty feet long, on the right of which was a swamp, on the left a marsh. In addition to these defences on the shore and on the island, there was a barrier of piles, extending from the east side of Fulker Shoals, towards the island. Its object was to compel vessels passing on the west of the island to approach within reach of the shore batteries; but up to the 8th of February, there was a span of 1,700 yards open opposite to Fort Bartow, the most southern of the defences, on the west side of the island.

The entire military force stationed upon the island prior to, and at the time of, the late engagement, consisted of the 8th regiment of North Carolina State troops, under the command of Col. H. M. Shaw; the 31st regiment of North Carolina volunteers, under the command of Col. J. V. Jordan; and three companies of the 17th North Carolina troops, under the command of Major G. H. Hill. After manning the several forts, on the 7th of February, there were but one thousand and twenty-four men left, and two hundred of them were upon the sick list. On the evening of the 7th of February, Brig.-gen. Wise sent from Nagg's Head, under the command of Lieut.-col. Anderson, a reinforcement, numbering some four hundred and fifty men. The whole force was under the command of Brig.-gen. Wise, who, upon the 7th and 8th of February, was at Nagg's Head, four miles distant from the island, confined to a sick-bed, and entirely disabled from participating in the action in person. The immediate command, therefore, devolved upon Col. H. M. Shaw, the senior officer present.

On the morning of the 7th of February, the enemy's fleet proceeded steadily towards Fort Bartow. In the sound between Roanoke Island and the mainland, upon the Tyrrell side, Commodore Lynch, with his squadron of seven vessels, had taken position, and at eleven o'clock the enemy's fleet, consisting of about thirty gunboats and schooners, advanced in ten divisions, the rear one having the schooners and transports in tow. The advance and attacking division again subdivided, one assailing the squadron and the other firing upon the fort with nine-inch, ten-inch, and eleven-inch shell, spherical case, a few round-shot, and every variety of rifled projectiles. The fort replied with but four guns (which were all that could be brought to bear), and after striking the foremost vessels several times, the fleet fell back, so as to mask one of the guns of the fort, leaving but three to reply to the fire of the whole fleet. The bombardment was continued throughout the day, and the enemy retired at dark. The squadron, under the command of Commodore Lynch, sustained their position most gallantly, and only retired after exhausting all their ammunition, and having lost the steamer Curlew and the Forest disabled.

In the mean time, the enemy had found a point of landing out of the reach of our field-pieces, and defended by a swamp from the advance of our infantry. The enemy having effected a landing here, our whole force took position at the redoubt or breastwork, and placed in battery their field-pieces with necessary artillerymen, under the respective commands of Captain Schemerhorn, and Lieutenants Kinney and Seldon. Two companies of the Eighth and two of the Thirty-first were placed at the redoubt to support the artillery. Three companies of the Wise Legion, deployed to the right and left as skirmishers. The remainder of the infantry were in position, three hundred yards in the rear of the redoubt, as a reserve.

The enemy landed some fifteen thousand men, with artillery, and, at 7 o'clock, A. M., of the 8th, opened fire upon the redoubt, which was replied to immediately with great spirit, and the action soon became general, and was continued without intermission for more than five hours, when the enemy succeeded in deploying a large force on either side of our line, flanking each wing. The order was then given by Col. Shaw to spike the guns in the battery, and to retreat to the northern end of the island. The guns were spiked, and the whole force fell back to the camps.

During the engagement at the redoubt, the enemy's fleet attempted to advance to Croatan Sound, which brought on a desultory engagement between Fort Bartow and the fleet, which continued up to half-after 12 o'clock, when the commanding officer was informed that the land defences had been forced, and the position of the fort turned; he thereupon ordered the guns to be disabled and the ammunition destroyed, which was done, and the fort abandoned. The same thing was done at the other forts, and the forces from all the forts were marched in good order to the camp. The enemy took possession of the redoubts and forts immediately, and proceeded in pursuit, with great caution, towards the northern end of the island in force, deploying so as to surround our forces at the camp.

Co.. Shaw had arrived with his whole force at his camp in

time to have saved his whole command, if transports had been furnished. But there were none. His situation was one of extreme exigency. He found himself surrounded by a greatly superior force upon the open island; he had no field-works to protect him; he had lost his only three field-pieces at the redoubt; and he had either to make an idle display of courage in fighting the foe at such immense disadvantage, which would have involved the sacrifice of his command, or to capitulate and surrender as prisoners of war. He determined upon the latter alternative.

The loss on our side was, killed, 23; wounded, 58; missing, 62. Our mortality list, however, was no indication of the spirit and vigor of our little army, as in its position it had but little opportunity of contest without a useless sacrifice of human life on their side. Among the killed was Captain O. Jennings Wise, of the Richmond Blues, son of General Wise, a young man of brilliant promise, refined chivalry, and a courage to which the softness of his manners and modesty of his behavior added the virtue of knightly heroism. His body, pierced by wounds, fell into the hands of the enemy, in whose camp, attended by every mark of respect, he expired. The disaster at Roanoke Island was a sharp mortification to the public. But for the unfortunate general, who was compelled to hear on a sick-bed—perhaps to witness from the windows of a sick-chamber—the destruction of his army and the death of his son, there was not a word of blame.

In a message to Congress, President Davis referred to the result of the battle at Roanoke Island as "deeply humiliating;" a committee of Congress, appointed to investigate the affair, resented the attempt to attribute a disaster, for which the government itself was notoriously responsible, to want of spirit in our troops; declared that, on the contrary, the battle of Roanoke Island was "one of the most gallant and brilliant actions of the war;" and concluded that whatever of blame and responsibility was justly attributable to any one for the defeat, should attach to Gen. Huger, in whose military department the island was, and to the Secretary of War, Judah P. Benjamin, whose positive refusal to put the island in a state of defence secured its fall. There was, in fact, but little room for the government to throw reflection upon the conduct of the troops. In the lan guage of their commanding general, "both officers and men fought firmly, coolly, efficiently, and as long as humanity would allow."

The connection of the War Department with the Roanoke Island affair, which was with difficulty dragged to light in Congress, is decidedly one of the most curious portions of the history of the war. Gen. Wise had pressed upon the government the importance of Roanoke Island* for the defence of Norfolk. He assumed the command of the post upon the 7th of January. In making a reconnoissance of the island and its defences, on the 13th January, he addressed Secretary Benjamin, and declared that the island, which was the key of all the rear defences of Norfolk, and its canals and railroads, was "utterly defenceless." On the 15th of January, Gen. Wise addressed the secretary again. He wrote that twenty-four vessels of the enemy's fleet were already inside of Hatteras Inlet, and within thirty miles of Roanoke Island; that all there was to oppose him was five small gunboats, and four small land batteries, wholly inefficient; that our batteries were not casemated; and that the force at Hatteras, independent of the Burnside expedition, was "amply sufficient to capture or pass Roanoke Island in any twelve hours."

These written appeals for aid in the defences of the island were neglected and treated with indifference. Determined to leave nothing wanting in energy of address, Gen. Wise repaired in person to Richmond, and called upon the Secretary of War, and urged, in the most importunate manner, the absolute

---

* It (Roanoke Island) was the key to all the rear defences of Norfolk. It unlocked two sounds, Albemarle and Currituck; eight rivers, the North, West, Pasquotank, the Perquimmons, the Little, the Chowan, the Roanoke, and the Alligator; four canals, the Albemarle and Chesapeake, the Dismal Swamp, the Northwest Canal, and the Suffolk; two railroads, the Petersburg and Norfolk, and the Seaboard and Roanoke. It guarded more than four-fifths of all Norfolk's supplies of corn, pork, and forage, and it cut the command of General Huger off from all its most efficient transportation. It endangers the subsistence of his whole army, threatens the navy-yard at Gosport, and to cut off Norfolk from Richmond, and both from railroad communication with the South. It lodges the enemy in a safe harbor from the storms of Hatteras, gives them a rendezvous, and large rich range of supplies, and the command of the seaboard from Oregon Inlet to Cape Henry. It should have been defended at the expense of twenty thousand men, and of many millions of dollars."—*Report of Gen. Wise.*

necessity of strengthening the defences upon that island with additional men, armament, and ammunition. Mr. Benjamin replied verbally to his appeals for reinforcements, that he had not the men to spare for his command. Gen. Wise urged upon the secretary that Gen. Huger had about 15,000 men in front of Norfolk, lying idle in camp for eight months, and that a considerable portion of them could be spared for the defence of the rear of Norfolk, and especially as his (Gen. Wise's) district supplied Norfolk and his army with nearly or quite all of his corn, pork, and forage.

The reply to all these striking and urgent appeals was a peremptory military order from Secretary Benjamin, dated the 22d of January, requiring Gen. Wise to proceed immediately to Roanoke Island. With ready military pride the unfortunate general received the orders, without a murmur in public; it being known only to his most intimate friends the circumstances under which he left Richmond on the stern and unpropitious mission which promised nothing to himself but disaster, the mistaken calumnies of the public, and death in the midst of defeat.

The facts we have referred to are of record. The committee of Congress that investigated the affair of Roanoke Island declared that the Secretary of War, Mr. J. P. Benjamin, was responsible for an important defeat of our arms, which might have been safely avoided by him; that he had paid no practical attention to the appeals of Gen. Wise; and that he had, by plain acts of omission, permitted that general and an inconsiderable force to remain to meet at least fifteen thousand men, well armed and equipped. The committee referred to was open to any justification that might have been sought by the Secretary of War, or his friends: none was offered; and the unanimous conclusion of the committee, in sharp and distinct terms, was put upon the public record, charging a Cabinet officer with a matter of the gravest offence known to the laws and the interests of the country.

The effect of war is always, in some degree, public demoralization; and the gravest charges are often lost and swallowed up in the quick and feverish excitements of such times. But whatever may have been the charities of speedy oblivion with respect to the charges against Mr. Benjamin, the public were, at least, not prepared for such an exhibition of trust and honor as was given him by the President, in actually promoting him, after the developments of the Roanoke Island disaster, and giving him the place in his cabinet of Secretary of State. Whatever may have been the merits of this act of the President, it was at least one of ungracious and reckless defiance to the popular sentiment; and from the marked event of the surrender of Roanoke Island and its consequences, we must date the period when the people had their confidence weakened in the government, and found no other repose for their trust than in the undiminished valor and devoted patriotism of the troops in the field.

CHAPTER X.

The Situation in Tennessee and Kentucky.—The affair at Woodsonville.—Death of Colonel Terry.—The Strength and Material of the Federal Force in Kentucky.—Condition of the Defences on the Tennessee and Cumberland Rivers.—The Confederate Congress and the Secretary of the Navy.—The Fall of Fort Henry.—Fort Donelson threatened.—The Army of General A. S. Johnston.—His Interview with General Beauregard.—Insensibility of the Confederate Government to the Exigency.—General Johnston's Plan of Action.—BATTLE OF FORT DONELSON.—Carnage and Scenery of the Battle-field.—The Council of the Southern Commanders.—Agreement to surrender.—Escape of Generals Floyd and Pillow.—The Fall of Fort Donelson develops the Crisis in the West.—The Evacuation of Nashville.—The Panic.—Extraordinary Scenes.—Experience of the Enemy in Nashville.—The Adventures of Captain John Morgan.—General Johnston at Murfreesboro.—Organization of a New Line of Defence South of Nashville.—The Defence of Memphis and the Mississippi.—Island No. 10.—Serious Character of the Disaster at Donelson.—Generals Floyd and Pillow "relieved from Command."—General Johnston's Testimony in favor of these Officers.—President Davis's Punctilio.—A sharp Contrast.—Negotiation for the Exchange of Prisoners.—A Lesson of Yankee Perfidy.—Mr. Benjamin's Release of Yankee Hostages.

THE unequivocal demonstrations of the Federals for an advance upon Tennessee through Kentucky, urged the Confederate government to send all the disposable forces at its command to strengthen the army of the southwestern division. Near the close of the year 1861, the Floyd Brigade and several regiments belonging to Tennessee and other Confederate States were sent from Virginia to Bowling Green, in southern Kentucky, the principal strategic point of the southwestern army. The command of that army was given, as we have seen, to General Albert Sidney Johnston.

Early in December, the Federal army occupied Muldraugh's Hill, Elizabethtown, Nolin, Bacon's Creek, and other points on the railroad, from forty to sixty miles below Louisville. Later in that month, a body of them advanced to Munfordville, on Green River, about seventy-five miles below Louisville, and about thirty-five miles above Bowling Green. A portion of this advance crossed the river at Munfordville to Woodsonville on the opposite shore, where they were attacked by the advance Confederate forces under Brig.-general Hindman and defeated with a loss of about fifty killed. The Confederates lost fou killed and nine wounded. Their conduct was marked by the most impetuous valor. On charging the enemy, Col. Terry, of the Texas Rangers, was killed in the moment of victory. In the death of Col. Terry, said General Hardee, in his official report, "his regiment had to deplore the loss of a beloved and brave commander, and the whole army one of its ablest officers." His name was placed in the front rank of the gallant sons of Texas, whose daring and devoted courage had added to the lustre of our arms and to the fruits of more than one victory.

The fight at Woodsonville was on the 17th of December. When the enemy reached that place in force, the Confederates fell back some fifteen or twenty miles, in the direction of Bowling Green. For some weeks thereafter, the whole South was excited with reports to the effect that the Federals were advancing upon Bowling Green in three columns, of 20,000 each. But the unanticipated success of the Federals in two important movements at other points within the department of General Johnston, enabled them to accomplish their object without an attack upon Bowling Green, and forced upon the Confederates the necessity of evacuating that post.

The North had collected an immense army in Kentucky, under command of Major-general Buell, a general of great skill, remarkable for the caution of his operations, but having with this quality the rare combination of energy, courage, and unwearied activity. The whole force of the Federals in Kentucky consisted of about one hundred thousand infantry, eleven thousand cavalry, and three thousand artillerists, divided into some twenty odd batteries. It is remarkable that this immense army was composed almost entirely of Western men, and that the "Yankee" proper was scarcely represented in its ranks. Of the Eastern States, only Pennsylvania had troops in Kentucky, and those comparatively few. Every Western State, with the exception of Iowa, Missouri, and Kansas, was represented by more or less regiments.

A large force of the Federals had been collected at Paducah, at the mouth of the Tennessee river, with a view to offensive operations on the water. This river was an important stream. It penetrated Tennessee and Alabama, and was navigable for steamers for two or three hundred miles. The Provisional

Congress, at Richmond, had appropriated half a million dollars for floating defences on the Tennessee and Cumberland rivers; but owing to the notorious inefficiency of the Navy Department, presided over by Mr. Mallory of Florida, who was remarkable for his obtuseness, slow method, and indifferent intellect, and whose ignorance even of the geography of Kentucky and Tennessee had been broadly travestied in Congress, both rivers were left open to the incursions of the enemy. On the Tennessee there was nothing to resist the enemy's advance up the stream but a weak and imperfectly constructed fort. The Cumberland was a still more important river, and the key to Nashville; but nothing stood in the way of the enemy save Fort Donelson, and from that point the Federal gunboats could reach Nashville in six or eight hours, and strike a vital point of our whole system of defences in the West.

On the 4th of February, the enemy's expedition up the Tennessee, under Gen. Grant, arrived at Fort Henry, the only fortification on the Tennessee river of any importance, situated near the lines of Kentucky and Tennessee, on the east bank of the stream. On the morning of the 6th, the fort was attacked.

Our works were untenable, but it concerned us to save our little army. To defend the position at the time, Gen. Tilghman, commanding division, had Col. Heiman's 10th Tennessee, Irish volunteers, eight hundred strong; Col. Drake's Mississippi volunteers, four hundred strong; Col. Hughes' Alabama volunteers, five hundred strong; and Lieut.-col. Gantt's Tennessee volunteers, cavalry, three hundred strong; one company of light artillery, commanded by Lieut. Culbertson, Confederate States artillery, and Captain Jesse Taylor's company of artillery, sixty strong, forming the garrison of Fort Henry, and manning its batteries of nine or ten guns.

A sudden rise in the river found Fort Henry, on the morning of the attack, completely surrounded by water, containing only Capt. Taylor's company of artillery. The two thousand men of all arms, who formed Gen. Tilghman's command, were half a mile off, beyond a sheet of back-water. Gen. Grant's army was on the direct road, between them and Fort Donelson, on the Cumberland, and within two miles of the fort, and already in motion to invest it. It was an embarrassing question to determine what was to be done. Gen. Tilghman's little army was in the jaws of the lion, and the question was, how could it be extricated.

Gen. Tilghman at once solved the problem, by ordering it to retreat by the upper route. He remained with his sixty men in the fort, where he was surrounded by water, and unable to get away.

A few minutes before the surrender, the scene in and around the fort exhibited a spectacle of fierce grandeur. Many of the cabins and tents in and around the fort were in flames: added to the scene were the smoke from the burning timber, and the curling but dense wreaths of smoke from the guns; the constantly recurring spattering and whizzing of fragments of crashing and bursting shells; the deafening roar of artillery; the black sides of five or six gunboats, belching fire at every port-hole; the volumes of smoke settled in dense masses along the surrounding back-waters; and up and over that fog, on the heights, the army of Gen. Grant (10,000) deploying around our small army, attempting to cut off its retreat. In the midst of the storm of shot and shell, the small force outside of the fort had succeeded in gaining the upper road, the gunboats having failed to notice their movements until they were out of reach.

To give them further time, the gallant Tilghman, exhausted and begrimed with powder and smoke, stood erect at the middle battery, and pointed gun after gun. It was clear, however, that the fort could not hold out much longer. A white flag was raised by the order of Gen. Tilghman, who remarked, " it is vain to fight longer; our gunners are disabled; our guns dismounted; we can't hold out five minutes longer." As soon as the token of submission was hoisted, the gunboats came alongside the fort and took possession of it, their crews giving three cheers for the Union. Gen. Tilghman and the small garrison of forty were taken prisoners.

The fall of Fort Henry was the signal for the direction of the most anxious attention to Fort Donelson, on the Cumberland.

We have noticed before the extreme inadequacy of Gen. Johnston's forces. It is doubtful whether he ever had over

23,000 effective troops at Bowling Green. Of these, after reinforcing Fort Donelson, he had scarcely more than eleven thousand effective men. Shortly after the disaster at Mill Springs, Gen. Beauregard had been sent from the Potomac to Gen. Johnston's line in Kentucky. At a conference which took place between the two generals, Gen. Beauregard expressed his surprise at the smallness of Gen. Johnston's forces, and was impressed with the danger of his position. There is nothing more remarkable in the history of the war than the false impressions of the people of the South as to the extent of our forces at the principal strategic point in Kentucky, and the long and apathetic toleration, by the government in Richmond, of a prospect that promised nothing but eventual disaster. On establishing himself in Bowling Green early in October, General Johnston wrote to the War Department: "We have received but little accession to our ranks since the Confederate forces crossed the line—in fact, no such enthusiastic demonstration as to justify any movements not warranted by our ability to maintain our own communications." He repeatedly called upon the government for reinforcements. He made a call upon several States of the Southwest, including Tennessee, for large numbers of troops. The call was revoked at the instance of the authorities in Richmond, who declined to furnish twelve months' volunteers with arms; and Gen. Johnston, thus discouraged and baffled by a government which was friendly enough to him personally, but insensible to the public exigency for which he pleaded, was left in the situation of imminent peril, in which Gen. Beauregard was so surprised to find him.

A memorandum was made of the conference between the two generals. In the plans of Gen. Johnston, Gen. Beauregard entirely concurred. It was determined to fight for Nashville at Donelson, and Gen. Johnston gave the best part of his army to do it, retaining only, to cover his front, fourteen thousand men, about three thousand of whom were so enfeebled by recent sickness that they were unable to march.

BATTLE OF FORT DONELSON.

On the 9th February, Gen. Pillow had been ordered to proceed to Fort Donelson and take command at that place, which it was supposed would be an immediate object of attack by Gen. Ulysses S. Grant and his combined land and naval forces. No time was lost in getting the works in defensible condition. The armament of the batteries consisted of thirteen guns of different calibres. The site of the fortification was plainly unfavorable in view of a land attack, being commanded by the heights above and below the river, and by a continuous range of hills all around the work to its rear. A line of intrenchments about two miles in extent was occupied by the troops.

On the morning of the 13th of February, Gen. Floyd, who had been stationed at Russellville, reached the fort by orders transmitted by telegraph from Gen. A. S. Johnston, at Bowling Green. Soon after his arrival, the intrenchments were fully occupied from one end to the other, and just as the sun rose the cannonade from one of the enemy's gunboats announced the opening of the conflict, which was destined to continue for several days and nights. The fire soon became general along our whole lines.

During the whole day the enemy kept up a general and active fire from all arms upon our trenches. At several points along the line he charged with uncommon vigor, but was met with a spirit of courageous resistance, which by nightfall had driven him, discomfited and cut to pieces, back upon the position he had assumed in the morning. The results of the day were encouraging. The strength of our defensive line had been pretty well tested, and the loss sustained by our forces was not large, our men being mostly under shelter in the rifle-pits.

The enemy continued his fire upon different parts of the intrenchments throughout the night, which deprived the Confederate troops of any opportunity to sleep. They lay that night upon their arms in the trenches. A more vigorous attack from the enemy than ever, was confidently expected at the dawn of day; but in this the Confederates were entirely mistaken. The day advanced, and no preparation seemed to be making for a general onset. The smoke of a large number of gunboats and steamboats on the river was observed a short distance below, and information at the same time was received within our lines of the arrival of a large number of new troops greatly increasing the strength of the enemy's forces, already said to be from twenty to thirty thousand strong.

About three o'clock in the afternoon the enemy's fleet of gunboats, in full force, advanced upon the fort and opened fire. They advanced in the shape of a crescent, and kept up a constant fire for an hour and a half. Once the boats reached a point within a few hundred yards of the fort. The effects of our shot upon the iron-cased boats were now distinctly visible. Two or three well-directed shots from the heavy guns of the fort drove back the nearest boat; several shot struck another boat, tearing her iron case and splintering her timbers, and making them crack as if by a stroke of lightning, when she, too, fell back. A third boat received several severe shocks, making her metal ring and her timbers crack, when the whole line gave way and fell rapidly back from the fire of the fort, until they passed out of range.

The incidents of the two days had all been in our favor. We had repulsed the enemy in the battle of the trenches, broken the line of his gunboats, and discomfited him on the water.

In the mean time, however, reinforcements were continually reaching the enemy; and it might have been evident from the first that the whole available force of the Federals on the western waters could and would be concentrated at Fort Donelson, if it was deemed necessary to reduce it. A consultation of the officers of divisions and brigades was called by General Floyd, to take place after dark. It was represented that it was an absolute impossibility to hold out for any length of time with our inadequate number and indefensible position; that there was no place within our intrenchments but could be reached by the enemy's artillery from their boats or their batteries; that it was but fair to infer that, while they kept up a sufficient fire upon our intrenchments to keep our men from sleep and prevent repose, their object was merely to give time to pass a column above us on the river, and to cut off our communications; and that but one course was left by which a rational hope could be entertained of saving the garrison, and that was to dislodge the enemy from his position on our left, and thus to pass our troops into the open country lying southward towards Nashville.

It was thus determined to remove from the trenches at an early hour the next morning, and attack the enemy in his position. There was, in fact, no other alternative. The enemy had been busy in throwing his forces of every arm around the Confederates, extending his line of investment entirely around their position, and completely enveloping them. Every road and possible avenue of departure was intercepted, with the certainty that our sources of supply by the river would soon be cut off by the enemy's batteries placed upon the river above us.

The sufferings of our army had already been terrible. The day of the opening of the battle (Thursday) was very cold, the mercury being only ten degrees above zero, and during the night, while our troops were watching on their arms in the trenches, it sleeted and snowed. The distance between the two armies was so slight that but few of the dead of either could be taken off, and many of the wounded who could neither walk nor crawl remained for more than two days where they fell. Some of our men lay wounded before our earth-works at night, calling for help and water, and our troops who went out to bring them in were discovered in the moonlight and fired upon by the enemy. Many of our wounded were not recovered until Sunday morning—some of them still alive, but blue with cold, and covered with frost and snow. It would have been merciful if each army had been permitted, under a flag of truce, to bring off its wounded at the close of each day; but it was not so, and they lay in the frost and sleet between the two armies—many to hear, but none to help them.

For nearly a week a large portion of our troops had been guarding their earth-works, and from the day of the battle they had been out in force night and day. Many of them in the rifle-pits froze their feet and hands. The severity of the cold was such that the clothes of many of the troops were so stiff from frozen water, that could they have been taken off, they would have stood alone.

At the meeting of general officers called by Gen. Floyd on Friday night, it was unanimously determined to cut open a route of exit, and thus to save our army. The plan of attack agreed upon and directed by Gen. Floyd was, that Gen. Pillow, assisted by Gen. Bushrod Johnson, having also under his command commanders of brigades, Col. Baldwin, commanding

Mississippi and Tennessee troops, and Col. Wharton and Col. McCausland, commanding Virginians, should, with the main body of the forces defending our left wing, attack the right wing of the enemy occupying the heights reaching to the bank of the river; that Gen. Buckner, with the forces under his command, and defending the right of our line, should strike the enemy's encampment on the Winn's Ferry road; and that each command should leave in the trenches troops to hold them.

The attack on the left was delayed, as Gen. Pillow moved out of his position in the morning. He found the enemy prepared to receive him in advance of his encampment. For two hours this principal portion of the battle-field was hotly and stubbornly contested, and strewn with piles of dead. The Federal troops in this quarter fought with a steadiness and determination rarely witnessed, and the exhibition of their courage on this field afforded a lesson to the South of a spirit that it had not expected in an enemy whose valor it had been accustomed to deride and sneer at since the battle of Manassas. The Federals did not retreat, but fell back fighting us and contesting every inch of ground. Being forced to yield, they retired slowly towards the Winn's Ferry road, Buckner's point of attack.

On this road, where Gen. Buckner's command was expected to flank the enemy, it had been forced to retire from his battery, and as the enemy continued to fall back, Gen. Buckner's troops became united with the forces of Gen. Pillow in engaging the enemy, who had again been reinforced. The entire command of the enemy had been forced to our right wing, and in front of Gen. Buckner's position in the intrenchment. The advantage was instantly appreciated. The enemy drove back the Confederates, advanced on the trenches on the extreme right of Gen. Buckner's command, getting possession, after a stubborn conflict of two hours, of the most important and commanding position of the battle-field, being in the rear of our river batteries, and, advancing with fresh forces towards our left, drove back our troops from the ground that had been won in the severe and terrible conflict of the early part of the day

The field had been won by the enemy after nine hours of conflict. Night found him in possession of all the ground that had been won by our troops in the morning, and occupying the most commanding portion of our intrenched work, to drive him from which the most desperate assaults of our troops had been unsuccessful. The enemy had been landing reinforcements throughout the day. His numbers had been augmented to eighty-two regiments. We had only about 13,000 troops, all told. Of these we had lost in three different battles a large proportion. The command had been in the trenches night and day, exposed to the snow, sleet, mud, and ice-water, without shelter, without adequate covering, and without sleep. To renew the combat with any hope of successful result was obviously vain.

A council of general officers was called at night. It was suggested that a desperate onset upon the right of the enemy's forces on the ground might result in the extrication of a considerable proportion of the command. A majority of the council rejected this proposition. Gen. Buckner remarked, that it would cost the command three-fourths its present numbers to cut its way out, and it was wrong to sacrifice three-fourths to save one-fourth; that no officer had a right to cause such a sacrifice. The alternative of the proposition was a surrender of the position and command. Gen. Floyd and Gen. Pillow, each, declared that they would not surrender themselves prisoners. The former claimed that he had a right individually to determine that he would not survive a surrender. He said that he would turn over the command to Gen. Buckner, if he (Gen. Floyd) could be allowed to withdraw his own particular brigade. To this Gen. Buckner consented. Thereupon, the command was turned over to Gen. Pillow, he passing it instantly to Gen. Buckner, declaring that "he would neither surrender the command nor himself." Col. Forrest, at the head of an efficient regiment of cavalry, was directed to accompany Gens. Floyd and Pillow in what was supposed to be an effort to pass through the enemy's lines. Under these circumstances, Gen. Buckner accepted the command. He sent a flag of truce to the enemy for an armistice of six hours, to negotiate for terms of capitulation.* Before the flag and communication

---

* The following is a correct list of the Confederate prisoners taken at Fort Donelson. The number was reported in the newspapers of the time, South

were delivered, Gens. Pillow and Floyd had retired from the garrison, and by daylight were pursuing their retreat towards Nashville, the largest portion of the command of the latter toiling in their flight along the banks of the Tennessee, but without a pursuing enemy to harass them.

The surrender of Donelson was rendered memorable by the hardest fighting that had yet occurred in the war, and by one of the most terrible and sickening battle-fields that had yet marked its devastations, or had ever appealed to the horror-stricken senses of humanity. The conflict had run through four days and four nights; in which a Confederate force not exceeding 13,000, a large portion of whom were illy armed, had contended with an army at least three times its number. The loss of the Federals was immense, and the proofs of an undeniable courage were left in the numbers of their dead on the field. In his official report of the battle, Gen. Floyd conjectures that the enemy's loss in killed and wounded reached a number beyond 5,000. The same authority gives our loss at 1,500. Both statements are only conjectural.

The scene of action had been mostly in the woods, although there were two open places of an acre or two where the fight had raged furiously, and the ground was covered with dead. All the way up to our intrenchments the same scene of death was presented. There were two miles of dead strewn thickly, mingled with fire-arms, artillery, dead horses, and the paraphernalia of the battle-field. Federals and Confederates were promiscuously mingled, sometimes grappling in the fierce death throe, sometimes facing each other as they gave and received the fatal shot and thrust, sometimes huddled in grotesque shapes, and again heaped in piles, which lay six or seven feet deep. Many of the bodies were fearfully mangled. The artillery horses had not hesitated to tread on the wounded, dying,

---

as well as North, to have been much larger: Floyd's Virginia Artillery, 34; Gray's Virginia Artillery, 59; French's Virginia Artillery, 43; Murray's Battery, 97; Cumberland Battery, 55; Fiftieth Tennessee, 485; Fourteenth Mississippi, 326; Third Mississippi, 330; Seventh Texas, 354; Twenty-sixth Mississippi, 427; Twenty-seventh Alabama, 180; Third Tennessee, 627; Tenth Tennessee, 608; Forty-second Tennessee, 494; Forty-eighth Tennessee, 249; Forty-ninth Tennessee, 450; Twenty-sixth Tennessee, 65; Second Kentucky, 136; Third Alabama, 34; Fiftieth Virginia, 10; Fifty-first Tennessee, 17 Total, 5,079.

and dead, and the ponderous artillery wheels crushed limbs and skulls. It was an awful sight to behold weak, wounded men lifting their feeble hands beneath the horses' hoofs. The village of Dover, which was within our lines, contained in every room in every house sick, wounded, or dead men. Bloody rags were everywhere, and a door could not be opened without hearing groans.

"I could imagine," says an eye-witness of the field of carnage, "nothing more terrible than the silent indications of agony that marked the features of the pale corpses which lay at every step. Though dead and rigid in every muscle, they still writhed and seemed to turn to catch the passing breeze for a cooling breath. Staring eyes, gaping mouths, clinched hands, and strangely contracted limbs, seemingly drown into the smallest compass, as if by a mighty effort to rend asunder some irresistible bond which held them down to the torture of which they died. One sat against a tree, and, with mouth and eyes wide open, looked up into the sky as if to catch a glance at its fleeting spirit. Another clutched the branch of an overhanging tree, and hung half-suspended, as if in the death-pang he had raised himself partly from the ground; the other had grasped his faithful musket, and the compression of his mouth told of the determination which would have been fatal to a foe had life ebbed a minute later. A third clung with both hands to a bayonet which was buried in the ground. Great numbers lay in heaps, just as the fire of the artillery mowed them down, mangling their forms into an almost undistinguishable mass."

The display of courage on the part of the Federal troops was unquestionable. The battle, however, was fought against us by Western men, there not being in the ranks of the enemy, as far as known, any men east of the Ohio. The Southern people, while contemning the fighting qualities of the New England "Yankee" and the Pennsylvania Dutchman, were constrained to give to the Western men credit for their bravery; and many of our own officers did not hesitate to express the opinion that the Western troops, particularly from southern Illinois, Minnesota, and Iowa, were as good fighting material as there was to be found on the continent. A Confederate officer relates a story of an extraordinary display of spirit on the field of Donelson by a regiment of Zouaves from southern Illinois—the "Egypt" regiment, as it was called. It had been completely shattered by the fire of artillery, and was scattered over the fields in what the Confederates supposed to be an irretrievable rout. A few sharp rallying words from their color-bearer, and the men, who a few minutes ago were fugitives, flocked to their colors, at the double quick, from different parts of the field, and re-formed in the very face of the advancing foe.

The fall of Fort Donelson developed the crisis in the West, which had long existed. The evacuation of Bowling Green had become imperatively necessary, and was ordered before and executed while the battle was being fought at Donelson. Gen. Johnston awaited the event opposite Nashville. The result of the conflict each day was announced as favorable. At midnight on the 15th February, Gen. Johnston received news of a glorious victory—at dawn of a defeat.

The blow was most disastrous. It involved the surrender of Nashville, which was incapable of defence from its position, and was threatened not only by the enemy's ascent of the Cumberland, but by the advance of his forces from Bowling Green. Not more than 11,000 effective men had been left under Gen. Johnston's command to oppose a column of Gen Buell, of not less than 40,000 troops, while the army from Fort Donelson, with the gunboats and transports, had it in their power to ascend the Cumberland, so as to intercept all communication with the South. No alternative was left but to evacuate Nashville or sacrifice the army.

The evacuation of Nashville was attended by scenes of panic and distress on the part of the population unparalleled in the annals of any American city. The excitement was intensified by the action of the authorities. Governor Harris mounted a horse and galloped through the streets, proclaiming to everybody the news that Donelson had fallen; that the enemy were coming and might be expected hourly, and that all who wished to leave had better do so at once. He next hastily convened the Legislature, adjourned it to Memphis, and, with the legislators and the State archives, left the town.

An earthquake could not have shocked the city more. The congregations at the churches were broken up in confusion and dismay; women and children rushed into the streets, wailing with terror; trunks were thrown from three-story windows in the haste of the fugitives; and thousands hastened to leave their beautiful city in the midst of the most distressing scenes of terror and confusion, and of plunder by the mob.

Gen. Johnston had moved the main body of his command to Murfreesboro'—a rear-guard being left in Nashville under Gen. Floyd, who had arrived from Donelson, to secure the stores and provisions. In the first wild excitement of the panic, the store-houses had been thrown open to the poor. They were besieged by a mob ravenous for spoils, and who had to be dispersed from the commissariat by jets of water from a steam fire-engine. Women and children, even, were seen scudding through the streets under loads of greasy pork, which they had taken as prizes from the store-houses. It is believed that hundreds of families, among the lower orders of the population, secured and secreted government stores enough to open respectable groceries. It was with the greatest difficulty that Gen. Floyd could restore order and get his martial law into any thing like an effective system. Blacks and whites had to be chased and captured and forced to help the movement of government stores. One man, who, after a long chase, was captured, offered fight, and was in consequence shot and badly wounded. Not less than one million of dollars in stores was lost through the acts of the cowardly and ravenous mob of Nashville. Gen. Floyd and Col. Forrest exhibited extraordinary energy and efficiency in getting off government stores. Col. Forrest remained in the city about twenty-four hours, with only forty men, after the arrival of the enemy at Edgefield. These officers were assisted by the voluntary efforts of several patriotic citizens of Nashville, who rendered them great assistance.

These shameful scenes, enacted in the evacuation of Nashville, were nothing more than the disgusting exhibitions of any mob brutalized by its fears or excited by rapine. At any rate, the city speedily repaired the injury done its reputation by a temporary panic, in the spirit of defiance that its best citizens and especially its ladies, offered to the enemy. We discover, in fact, the most abundant evidence in the Northern newspapers that the Federals did not find the "Union" sentiment that they expected to meet with in the capital of Tennessee, and that, if there were any indications whatever of such sentiment, they were "found only among the mechanics and laboring classes of the city." The merchants and business men of Nashville, as a class, showed a firm, unwavering, and loyal attachment to the cause of the South. The ladies gave instances of patriotism that were noble testimonies to their sex. They refused the visits of Federal officers, and disdained their recognition; they collected a fund of money for the especial purpose of contributing to the needs of our prisoners; and, says a recipient of the bounty of these noble women, as soon as a Confederate prisoner was paroled, and passed into the next room, he found pressed in his hands there a sum of money given him by the ladies of Nashville. Many of the most respectable of the people had been constrained to leave their homes rather than endure the presence of the enemy. The streets, which, to confirm the predictions of Northern newspapers of the welcomes that awaited the "Union" army in the South, should have been gay and decorated, presented to the enemy nothing but sad and gloomy aspects. Whole rows of houses, which, but a short while ago, were occupied by families of wealth and respectability, surrounded by all the circumstances that make homes happy and prosperous, stood vacant, and the gaze of the passer-by was met, instead of, as in former days, with fine tapestry window-curtains and neatly polished marble steps, with panes of dust-dimmed glass.

On the whole, the experience of the enemy in Nashville was vastly instructive. The fact that, wherever he had gone, he had converted lukewarm Southern districts into Secession strongholds, or had intensified the sentiment of opposition to him, was as unexpected to him as it was gratifying to us. This experience was universal in the war, from the date of the occupation of Alexandria, which had voted overwhelmingly for the Union in the preliminary stages of the revolution, and was subsequently as thoroughly Southern as any town in the Confederacy, down to the occupation of Nashville, which had at first given some signs of weak submission to its fate, and afterwards spurned its invaders with a spirit of defiance, reckless of consequences.

In the neighborhood of Nashville, the enemy was constantly

harassed by local parties of adventurers, who shot his pickets, watched his movements, and attacked detached portions of his forces at various points. The whole country rang with the exploits of the gallant and intrepid cavalier, Captain John H. Morgan and his brave men, in the vicinity of Nashville. His squadron belonged to Gen. Hardee's command, and he had been left in command of the forces at Murfreesboro to watch the movements of the Federals, which he not only did effectually, but enacted a number of daring adventures within the lines of the enemy.

Scarcely a day passed without some such exploit of Capt. Morgan and his intrepid partisans. Once he nearly succeeded in capturing a Federal general. Another day he attacked a party of scouts, and killed the captain. The next exploit was to rush into the camp of some regiment, and carry off a train of wagons. The most daring of his adventures was his sudden appearance in the rear of the enemy, entering with forty brave followers the town of Gallatin, twenty-six miles north of Nashville, on the Louisville and Nashville railroad. On entering the town, Capt. Morgan immediately seized upon the telegraph office and the depot. He had presented himself at the telegraph office, carelessly asking the operator what was the news, when that individual, never for a moment imagining who it was that addressed him, replied that there were rumors that "the rebel scoundrel" Morgan was in the neighborhood, and proceeded to illustrate his own valor by flourishing a revolver, and declaring how anxious he was to encounter the man who was creating so much uneasiness and alarm in the country. "You are now speaking to Captain Morgan" was the quiet reply of the partisan: "I am he!" At these words, the pistol dropped from the hands of the operator, who entreated the mercy of his captor. The poor fellow easily submitted to the task assigned to him of sending a dispatch, in the name of Capt. Morgan, to Prentice, the notorious editor of the Louisville *Journal*, politely offering to act as his escort on his proposed visit to Nashville. After this amusement, Capt. Morgan and his men awaited the arrival of the train from Bowling Green. In due time the train came thundering in; Capt. Morgan at once seized it, and taking five Federal officers who were passengers and the engineer of the train prisoners, he burned to cinders all of the cars, with their contents, and then filling the locomotive with turpentine, shut down all the valves, and started it towards Nashville. Before it had run eight hundred yards, the accumulation of steam caused it to explode, shivering it into a thousand atoms. Capt. Morgan then started southward with his prisoners, and made his way safely to the Confederate camp.

On another occasion, while returning alone towards Murfreesboro, Capt. Morgan encountered a picket of six of the enemy, and captured them and their arms. It was accomplished by a bold adventure. He discovered the pickets in a house, and having on a Federal overcoat, assumed a bold front, and riding up to the sergeant rebuked him for not attending properly to his duty, and ordered that the whole party should consider themselves under arrest, and surrender their arms. The soldiers, not doubting for a moment that they were addressed by a Federal officer, delivered up their muskets. As they were marched into the road, with their faces turned from their camp, the sergeant said, "We are going the wrong way, colonel." "We are not," was the reply. "I am Captain Morgan."

The name of Captain Morgan was fast becoming famous as that of a partisan leader. He was induced to abandon his present field of operations to accept promotion in the army, being appointed to a colonelcy in the regular military service, for which he had been urgently recommended by Gen. Hardee.

Since falling back to Murfreesboro, Gen. Johnston had managed, by combining Crittenden's division and the fugitives from Donelson, to collect an army of 17,000 men. His object was now to co-operate with Gen. Beauregard for the defence of the Valley of the Mississippi, on a line of operations south of Nashville. The line extending from Columbus, by way of Forts Henry and Donelson, had been lost. The disaster had involved the surrender of Kentucky, and a large portion of Tennessee to the enemy; and it had become necessary to reorganize a new line of defence south of Nashville, the object of which would be to protect the railroad system of the Southwest, and to insure the defence of Memphis and the Mississippi.

The work of putting the Mississippi river in a state of complete defence had been intrusted to General Beauregard. On abandoning Columbus, he had taken a strong position about forty-five miles below it, at Island No. 10. This locality was looked upon as the chief barrier to the progress of the Federals down the Mississippi. At the island, a bend occurs in the river of several miles extent. Around and upon this curve were located the towns of New Madrid and Point Pleasant. The distance around the bend was about thirty miles, whereas the distance across by land from Tiptonville below to the island above did not exceed five miles. It was calculated that even should the enemy hold Point Pleasant, and get possession of New Madrid by our evacuation of that post also, our communications by water to Tiptonville, and thence by land across the bend to Island No. 10, would still remain intact. The island was thought to be impregnable. It was flanked on the Missouri side by an extensive swamp, and on the other side by a lake of several miles extent, which rendered it impossible for the enemy to approach the position by land.

With this indication of the situation in the West, and the operations for the defence of Memphis and the Mississippi, to which the southward movement of Gen. Johnston towards the left bank of the Tennessee was expected to contribute, we must leave, for a short period, our narrative of the movements and events of the war in this direction.

The serious disaster at Donelson appears to have been fully appreciated by the Confederate government; and its announcement in Richmond was followed, to the surprise of the public, by a communication from President Davis to Congress, on the 11th of March, declaring the official reports of the affair incomplete and unsatisfactory, and "relieving from command" Gens. Floyd and Pillow. The main causes of dissatisfaction indicated by the President were, that reinforcements were not asked for by the commanding generals at Donelson, and that the senior generals "abandoned responsibility," by transferring the command to a junior officer. This act of President Davis was the subject of warm and protracted argument in Congress and in the newspapers. It was shown, by evidence produced before Congress, that no reinforcements had been asked for, because it was known how much the command of Gen. Johnston had already been weakened by sending Floyd's and Buckner's forces to Donelson; because an overwhelming force of the enemy was pressing on his rear; and because Gen. Johnston's troops were on the march between Bowling Green and Nashville, and could not reach Fort Donelson in time to change the fortunes of the day.

With reference to the second assignment of cause of the President's displeasure, it was agreed on all sides that the transfer of the command by the senior generals was irregular. In a letter, however, written to the President by Gen. Johnston himself, which was understood to be private and confidential, and was, therefore, wholly relieved from any suspicion of the gloze of an official report, that officer had directed no censure upon Gens. Floyd and Pillow. On the contrary, in the confidence of this private letter, he wrote to the President, "the command was irregularly transferred, and devolved on the junior general, but not apparently to avoid any just responsibility or from any want of personal or moral intrepidity;" and he expressed continued "confidence in the gallantry, the energy, and the devotion to the Confederacy," of both Gens. Floyd and Pillow, which was testified especially in the case of Gen. Floyd, by assigning him, after the fall of Donelson, to the important duty of proceeding to Chattanooga to defend the approaches towards northern Alabama and Georgia, and the communication between the Mississippi and the Atlantic. This was the private and unrestrained testimony of Gen. Johnston. With perhaps a superior military sensitiveness of "irregularity," Mr. Davis repudiated the explanations of the commanding general in the field; deprived Generals Floyd and Pillow of their commands; and offered the spectacle to the country of a President with one hand sacrificing two brave officers who had contributed to the country's glory and safety in more than one victory, for a military punctilio, and with the other elevating to the highest office in his gift a man who, as Attorney-general, Secretary of War, and, at last, Secretary of State, seemed to enjoy the monopoly of the lucre and honors of state, and who had been charged, by the official report of a general in the field, and by the deliberate and unanimous verdict of a committee of Congress, with the plain and exclusive responsibility of the disaster of Roanoke Island. The contrast between these two acts needed no addition of argument to convince the public mind that its government was not above the errors of judgment or the partialities of human affection.

The disposition of the Confederate prisoners taken at Fort Donelson gave an exhibition of vile perfidy on the part of the North, to which there is no parallel to be found in the history of civilized warfare, or in all the crooked paths of modern diplomacy. Instead of these prisoners being discharged by the North according to the understanding existing between the two governments, they were carried off into the Western interior, where they were treated with indignities and made a spectacle for mobs, who jeered at them because they did not have uniforms and warm coats, because many of the poor fellows had nothing better than horse blankets, rags, and coffee sacks around their shoulders, and because the "rebels"—whose true glory a just and generous spirit would have found in their coarse and tattered garbs and marks of patient suffering—lacked the fine and showy equipments of the Federal troops. This act of bad faith on the part of the North is remarkable enough for a full and explicit history of the circumstances in which it was committed.

Permission had been asked by the Northern government for two commissioners, Messrs. Fish and Ames, to visit their prisoners of war within the jurisdiction of the South. Our government, while denying this permission, sought to improve the opportunity by concerting a settled plan for the exchange of prisoners; and for the execution of this purpose Messrs. Conrad and Seddon were deputed as commissioners to meet those of the Northern government under a flag of truce at Norfolk.

Subsequently a letter from Gen. Wool was addressed to Gen Huger, informing him that he, Gen. Wool, had *full authority* to settle any terms for the exchange of prisoners, and asking an interview on the subject. General Howell Cobb was then appointed by the government to mediate with Gen. Wool, and to settle a permanent plan for the exchange of prisoners during the war.

In the letter to General Huger, dated the 13th of February, 1862, General Wool wrote:

"*I am alone clothed with full power* for the purpose of arranging for the exchange of prisoners. Being thus empowered, I am ready to confer with you on the subject, or the Honorable Messrs. Seddon and Conrad, or any other persons appearing for that purpose. I am prepared to arrange for the restoration of all the prisoners to their homes on fair terms of exchange, man for man, and officer for officer of equal grade, assimilating the grade of officers of the army and navy, when necessary, and agreeing upon equitable terms for the number of men or officers, of inferior grade, to be exchanged for any of higher grade when the occasion shall arrive. That all the surplus prisoners on either side be exchanged on parole, with the agreement that *any prisoners of war taken by the other party shall be returned in exchange as fast as captured,* and this system to be continued while hostilities continue.

"I would further inform you, or any other person selected for the purpose of making arrangements for the exchange of prisoners, that the prisoners taken on board of vessels, or otherwise in maritime conflict, by the forces of the United States, have been put, and are now held, only in military custody, and *on the same footing as other prisoners taken in arms.*"

The proposition, it appears, was readily accepted by our government, and a memorandum made as a basis for a cartel. It was proposed in this memorandum that the prisoners of war in the hands of each government should be exchanged, man for man, the officers being assimilated as to rank, &c.; that our privateersmen should be exchanged on the footing of prisoners of war; that any surplus remaining on either side, after these exchanges, should be released, and that hereafter, during the whole continuance of the war, prisoners taken on either side should be paroled within ten days after their capture, and delivered on the frontier of their own country.

General Wool promptly agreed to all the propositions except two. In lieu of the compensation basis of equivalents contained in one of the items of the memorandum, he proposed the cartel of equivalents adopted by Great Britain and the United States, in the war of 1812, and General Cobb accepted it.

He also objected to the provisions in another item, which required each party to pay the expense of transporting their prisoners to the frontier of the country of the prisoners. The provision met his entire approval, but he did not feel authorized, by his instructions, to incorporate it into the proposed cartel, and, therefore, desired time to consult his government on the subject.

The interview closed with the promise from General Wool that he would notify General Cobb, as soon as he could hear from his government, on that point.

On the first of March General Cobb held his second interview with him, in which he (General Cobb) proposed to enter into a *cartel*, containing the stipulations previously set forth. Gen. Wool then replied that his government would not agree to the proposition that each party should pay the expense of transporting their prisoners to the frontier, when General Cobb promptly waived it, thus leaving the cartel free from all his objections, and just what General Wool had himself proposed in his letter of the 13th February, to General Huger.

Upon this, General Wool informed General Cobb that his *government had changed his instructions*, and abruptly broke off the negotiation.

In the mean time our government, in a very curious or very foolish anticipation of the good faith of the North, had directed the discharge of the prisoners held by us as hostages for the safety and proper treatment of our privateersmen, who were confined in felons' cells and threatened with the gallows. Cols. Lee, Cogswell, and Wood, and Major Revere were sent to their own country; the remaining hostages were brought on parole from distant points to Richmond, on their way to be delivered up, at the expense of this government, and their surrender was only suspended on receipt of intelligence from General Cobb, that he saw reason to suspect bad faith on the part of the enemy.

The perfidy of the North was basely accomplished.* The

---

* This act of deception on the part of the North was but one of a long series of acts of Yankee perfidy, and of their abnegation of the rights of civilized war. When McDowell left Washington city to take Richmond, his army was supplied with handcuffs to iron rebels. After the battle of Bull Run they sent a white flag to ask permission to bury their dead. It was humanely granted. They left their dead to bury their dead, and attempted, under the protection of that white flag, to erect batteries for our destruction. On the battle-field of Manassas they unfurled a Confederate flag, and shouted to our troops not to fire upon them, that they were our friends, and then they fired upon our troops and fled. At Manassas and Pensacola they repeatedly and deliberately fired upon our hospitals, when over them a yellow flag was waving. In Hampton Roads they hung out a white flag, and then prostituted the protection it secured to them to the cowardly assassination of our brave seamen. At Newbern, in violation of the laws of war, they attempted to shell a city containing several thousand women and children, before either demanding a surrender, or giving the citizens notice of their intentions. A Kentuckian went into a Federal camp to reclaim a fugitive slave, and they tied him up

correspondence of the Federal authorities, to which we have alluded, on this subject, constitutes a chapter of diplomacy qualified to attract the scorn of all civilized and honorable nations. At the time when it was believed our government held the larger number of prisoners, the Federal government proposed to exchange all prisoners, and to place on parole, in their own country, the surplus held by either party; and our government agreed to the proposition. Before the agreement could be reduced to writing, and signed by the parties, the casualties of war, in the fall of Fort Donelson, reversed this state of things, and gave the Federal government the larger number of prisoners. With this change of things that government changed its policy, and deliberately, and perfidiously, and shamelessly receded from the propositions to which it had been distinctly committed by every obligation of truth, honor, and good faith.

While Mr. Benjamin, Secretary of War, by a curious act of supererogation was releasing our most important prisoners of war *in advance* of the conclusion of negotiations, sending them North without waiting to have them regularly and safely exchanged under a flag of truce in Norfolk harbor, the enemy were conveying the prisoners captured at Fort Donelson to Chicago and other points more distant from their homes, and were parading the officers who fell into their power through the entire breadth of the land, from western Tennessee, to Fort Warren in Boston harbor, where they were incarcerated. For the prisoners so curiously, and with such unnecessary haste, dispatched to the North by Mr. Benjamin, not a single officer taken at Fort Donelson, nor a single captive privateersman, had been restored to his home. With an excess of zeal well calcu-

---

and gave him twenty-five lashes upon his bare back, in the presence of his runaway slave. It was repeatedly proposed by the people of the South to treat such an enemy without ceremony or quarter, by hanging out the black flag, and making the war a *bellum internecinum;* but while the South debated, talked, and threatened, the North acted, availing itself of the most ferocious and brutal expedients of the war, arming the slaves, breaking faith on every occasion of expediency, disregarding flags of truce, stealing private property, ravishing women, bombarding hospitals, and setting at defiance every law of civilized warfare. Such was the perfidy and brutality of the North, to which the South responded with the puerile threat of a black flag, which was never hoisted, and which did not even serve the purposes of a scarecrow to its bold and unscrupulous enemy

lated to draw attention from his own part of the transaction, Mr. Benjamin proposed, as a retaliation upon the perfidy of the North, to discharge our own citizens who were subject to parole; but happily a counsel, which proposed to redress a wrong by an act disreputable to ourselves and in violation of what were the obligations of our own honor in the sight of the civilized world, was rejected alike by the government and the country, who were content to commit the dishonor of their enemy, without attempting to copy it under pleas of retaliation, to the justice of history and the future judgments of the world.

CHAPTER XI.

Organization of the permanent Government of the South.—The Policy of England.—Declaration of Earl Russell.—Onset of the Northern Forces.—President Davis's Message to Congress.—The Addition of New States and Territories to the Southern Confederacy.—Our Indian Allies.—The Financial Condition, North and South.—Deceitful Prospects of Peace.—Effect of the Disasters to the South.—Action of Congress.—The Conscript Bill.—Provisions vs. Cotton.—Barbarous Warfare of the North.—The Anti-slavery Sentiment.—How it was unmasked in the War.—Emancipation Measures in the Federal Congress.—Spirit of the Southern People.—The Administration of Jefferson Davis.—His Cabinet.—The Defensive Policy.—The NAVAL ENGAGEMENT IN HAMPTON ROADS.—Iron-clad Vessels.—What the Southern Government might have done.—The Narrative of General Price's Campaign resumed.—His Retreat into Arkansas.—The BATTLE OF ELK HORN.—Criticism of the Result.—Death of General McCulloch.—The BATTLE OF VALVERDE.—The Foothold of the Confederates in New Mexico.—Change of the Plan of Campaign in Virginia.—Abandonment of the Potomac Line by the Confederates.—The BATTLE OF KERNSTOWN.—Colonel Turner Ashby.—Appearance of McClellan's Army on the Peninsula.—Firmness of General Magruder.—The New Situation of the War in Virginia.—Recurrence of Disasters to the South on the Water.—The Capture of Newbern.—Fall of Fort Pulaski and Fort Macon.—Common Sense vs. "West Point."

The permanent government of the Confederate States was organized on the 22d day of February, in a season of reverses to our arms and at a dark hour in our national fortunes.

All hopes of foreign interference were positively at an end. On the meeting of the British Parliament in the early part of February, Earl Russell had declared that the blockade of the American ports had been effective from the 15th of August, in the face of the facts that the dispatches of Mr. Bunch, the English consul at Charleston, said that it was not so; and that authentic accounts and letters of merchants showed that any ships, leaving for the South, could be insured by a premium of seven and a-half to fifteen per cent. England had accepted the Treaty of Paris, and yet did not hesitate to violate the principles that had been definitely consecrated by article four of that treaty, by declaring the Federal blockade effective, for no other reason than that "considerable prudence was necessary in the American question." In the House of Commons, Mr. Gregory asserted that the non-observation of the Treaty of

Paris was a deception for the Confederate States, and an ambuscade for the interests of commerce throughout the world.

The Northern army had remained quiet on the Potomac, amusing the Southern people with its ostentatious parades and gala-day sham fights, while the government at Washington was preparing an onset all along our lines from Hatteras to Kansas. Burnside had captured Roanoke Island in the east, while Fort Henry on the Tennessee and Fort Donelson on the Cumberland had sent the echo back to Albemarle. Buffeting sleet and storm, and by forced marches, the enemy had seized Bowling Green, while Sigel fell suddenly upon Springfield; the enemy's gunboats threatened Savannah, and Gen. Butler hurried off his regiments and transports to the Gulf, for an attack *via* Ship Island upon New Orleans.

In his message to Congress, President Davis declared that the magnified proportions of the war had occasioned serious disasters, and that the effort was impossible to protect by our arms the whole of the territory of the Confederate States, seaboard and inland. To the popular complaint of inefficiency in the departments of the government, he declared that they had done all which human power and foresight enabled them to accomplish.

The increase of our territory since the opening of the war was scarcely a cause for boast. The addition of new States and Territories had greatly extended our lines of defence. Missouri had been unable to wrest from the enemy his occupancy of her soil. Kentucky had been admitted into the Confederacy only to become the theatre of active hostilities, and, at last, to be abandoned to the enemy. The Indian treaties effected by the Provisional Congress, through the mediation of Gen. Albert Pike, had secured us a rich domain, but a troublesome and worthless ally.* It was possible, however, that

---

* In December last, Col. James McIntosh was sent from Arkansas into the Cherokee Nation to chastise the rebellious Creek chief Opoth-lay-oho-la, which he did with good effect. The results of the incursion were thus enumerated by Col. McIntosh: "We captured one hundred and sixty women and children, twenty negroes, thirty wagons, seventy yoke of oxen, about five hundred Indian horses, several hundred head of cattle, one hundred sheep, and a great quantity of property of much value to the enemy. The stronghold of Opoth lay-oho-la was completely broken up and his force scattered in every direction, destitute of the simplest elements of subsistence."

in this domain there might be secured a rich inheritance for posterity. It comprised an area of more than eighty thousand square miles, diversified by mountains filled with iron, coal, and other mineral treasures, and broad-reaching plains, with the Red River running along its southern border, the Arkansas river almost through its centre, and their tributaries reticulating its entire surface.

At the time of the inauguration of our permanent government, there was, however, one aspect of our affairs of striking encouragement. It was the condition of the finances of the government. We had no floating debt. The credit of the government was unimpaired among its own people. The total expenditures for the year had been, in round numbers, $170,000,000; less than one-third of the sum expended by the enemy to conquer us, and less than the value of a single article of export—the cotton crop of the year.

In the Federal Congress it was estimated that, at the end of the fiscal year (June, 1862), the public debt of the Northern government would be about $750,000,000, and that the demands on the treasury, to be met by taxation, direct and indirect, would not be less than $165,000,000 per annum.

The problem of the Northern finances was formidable enough. It was calculated that the Federal tax would be from four to six times greater for each State than their usual assessments heretofore, and doubts were expressed, even by Northern jour-

---

The Indian Territory (not including the Osage country—its extent being unknown—nor the 800,000 acres belonging to the Cherokees, which lie between Missouri and Kansas) embraces an area of 82,073 square miles—more than fifty-two millions of acres, to wit:

The land of the Cherokees, Osages, Quapaws, Senecas, and Senecas and Shawnees, 38,105 square miles, or 24,388,800 acres.

That of the Creeks and Seminoles, 20,531 square miles, or 13,140,000 acres.

That of the Reserve Indians, and the Choctaws and Chickasaws, 23,437 square miles, or 15,000,000 acres.

Total 82,073 square miles, or 52,528,800 acres.

Its population consists of Cherokees, 23,000; Osages, 7,500; Quapaws, 320; Creeks, 13,500; Seminoles, 2,500; Reserve Indians, 2,000; Choctaws, 17,500; and Chickasaws, 4,700—making an aggregate of 71,520 souls.

This Indian country is, in many respects, really a magnificent one. It is one of the brightest and fairest parts of the great West, and only needs the development of its resources to become the equal of the most favored lands on this continent.

nals in the interest of the government, if it could be raised in any other way than by practical confiscation.

The South, however, had already lingered too long in the delusive promise of the termination of the war by the breaking down of the finances of the Northern government, and had entertained prospects of peace in the crude philosophy and calculations of the newspaper article, without looking to those great lessons of history which showed to what lengths a war might be carried despite the difficulties of finance, the confines of reason, and the restraints of prudence, when actuated by that venom and desperation which were shown alike by the people and government of the North. The very extent of the Northern expenditure should have been an occasion of alarm instead of self-complacency to the South; it showed the tremendous energy of the North and the overpowering measure of its preparation; it argued a most terrible degree of desperation; and it indicated that the North had plunged so far into the war, that there was but little sane choice between striving to wade through it, and determining to turn back with certain and inevitable ruin in its face.

Fortunately, the lessons of its late disasters were not entirely lost upon the government of the Confederate States. They happily gave fresh impulses to the authorities, and were productive of at least some new and vigorous political measures. The most important of these was a conscript bill for increasing our forces in the field. The enlargement of the proportions of the war demanded such a measure; the conflict, in which we were now engaged, extended from the shores of the Chesapeake to the confines of Missouri and Arizona.

The measures and expressions of the government plainly intimated to the people, who had been so persistently incredulous of a long war, that it had become probable that the war would be continued through a series of years, and that preparations for the ensuing campaigns should be commensurate with such a prospect. In Congress, resolutions were passed urging the planters to suspend the raising of cotton, and to plant provision crops, so as to provide for the support of the army. This change in the direction of our industry, besides increasing the capacity of the South to sustain itself, aimed a blow at the well-known selfish calculations of England to repay herself for past losses from the blockade, in the cheap prices expected from the excessive supply of two years' crops of cotton in the South. The South was not to be the only or chief loser in the diminished production of her great staple and the forced change in her industrial pursuits. For every laborer who was diverted from the culture of cotton in the South, perhaps, four times as many elsewhere, who had found subsistence in the various employments growing out of its use, would be forced also out of their usual occupations. The prospect of thus bringing ruin upon the industrial interests of other countries was not pleasing to our people or our government; although it was some consolation to know that England, especially, might yet feel, through this change of production in the South, the consequences of her folly and the merited fruits of her injustice to a people who had been anxious for her amity, and had at one time been ready to yield to her important commercial privileges.

In the growing successes of the Northern armies, the spirit of the Southern people came to the aid of their government with new power, and a generosity that was quite willing to forget all its shortcomings in the past. The public sentiment had been exasperated and determined in its resolution of resistance to the last extremity by the evidences of ruin, barbarism, and shameless atrocities that had marked the paths of the progress of the enemy. The newspapers were filled with accounts of outrages of the enemy in the districts occupied by him. By his barbarous law of confiscation, widows and orphans had been stripped of death's legacies; he had overthrown municipalities and State governments; he had imprisoned citizens without warrant, and regardless of age or sex; he had destroyed commerce, and beggared the mechanic and manufacturer; he had ripped open the knapsacks of our captured soldiery, robbing them of clothing, money, necessaries of life, and even of the instruments of their surgeons. The Southern people considered that they were opposing an enemy who had proved himself a foe to mankind, religion, and civilization.

The venomous spirit of Abolition had been free to develop itself in the growing successes of the Northern arms. It is a curious commentary on the faith of the people of the North, or rather a striking exposure of the subserviency of all the expressions of opinion on the part of that people to considerations of *expediency*, that, in the beginning of hostilities, even after the proclamation of war by President Lincoln, when it was yet thought important to affect moderation, fugitive slaves from Virginia were captured in the streets of Washington, and, by the direct authority of the Northern government, returned to their masters! A few months later, negro slaves were kidnapped from their masters by the Federal army, under the puerile and nonsensical pretence of their being "contraband of war." The anti-slavery purposes of the war rapidly developed from that point. The Northern journals declared that the excision of slavery was one of the important objects of the war; that the opportunity was to be taken in the prosecution of hostilities to crush out what had been the main cause of difference, and thus to assure the fruit of a permanent peace. In his message to the Federal Congress in December, Mr. Lincoln had hinted that "*all indispensable means*" must be employed to preserve the Union. An order was published by the War Department making it the occasion of a court-martial for any army officer to return any negro slave within his lines to his master. It was followed by the explanation of Mr. Lincoln's former hint. In an executive message to the Federal Congress, the policy of "the gradual abolishment of slavery," with the pretence of "pecuniary aid" to States adopting such policy, was advised; it was approved in the House of Representatives, by a vote of 88 to 31; and about the same time a bill was introduced into the Senate for the forcible emancipation of the negro slaves in the District of Columbia, which was subsequently passed.

These bitter exhibitions of the North had envenomed the war; its sanguinary tides rose higher; its battle-fields emulated in carnage the most desperate in modern history; flags of truce were but seldom used, and the amenities of intercourse between belligerents were often slighted by rude messages of defiance. Battles had become frequent and really bloody. But they were no longer decisive of a nation's fate. The campaign covered the whole of a huge territory, and could only be decided by complicated movements, involving great expenditure of troops and time.

The Southern people, however, were again aroused, and

nothing was wanting but wisdom, energy, and capacity on the part of the government to have inaugurated another series of brilliant achievements, such as those which rendered illustrious the first months of the war. The rush of men to the battle-field, which was now witnessed in every part of the South, was beyond all former example; and if the government had met this mighty movement of the people with a corresponding amplitude of provision and organization, the cause of the South might have been reckoned safe beyond peradventure.

Unfortunately, however, President Davis was not the man to consult the sentiment and wisdom of the people; he desired to signalize the infallibility of his own intellect in every measure of the revolution, and to identify, from motives of vanity, his own personal genius with every event and detail of the remarkable period of history in which he had been called upon to act. This imperious conceit seemed to swallow up every other idea in his mind. By what was scarcely more than a constitutional fiction, the President of the Confederate States was the head of the army; but Mr. Davis, while he made himself the supreme master of the civil administration of the government, so far as to take the smallest details within his control, and to reduce his cabinet officers to the condition of head clerks, insisted also upon being the autocrat of the army, controlling the plans of every general in the field, and dictating to him the precise limits of every movement that was undertaken. Many of our generals fretted under this pragmatism of an executive, who, instead of attending to the civil affairs of the government and correcting the monstrous abuses that were daily pointed out by the newspapers in the conduct of the departments, was unfortunately possessed with the vanity that he was a great military genius, and that it was necessary for him to dictate, from his cushioned seat in Richmond, the details of every campaign, and to conform every movement in the field to the invariable formula of "*the defensive policy.*"*

---

* The following extract of terse criticism on offensive and defensive warfare is taken from a small work written by one of Napoleon's generals in 1815, and revised in 1855. The writer could not have written with more aptitude to the existing contest, if the errors and unfortunate demonstrations of President Davis's defensive policy had been before his eyes: "The offensive is the proper character which it is essential to give to every war; it exalts the courage of

In a revolutionary leader, something more is wanted than scholarly and polished intellect. The history of the world shows that, in such circumstances, the plainest men, in point o learning and scholarship, have been the most successful, and that their elements of success have been quick apprehension, practical judgment, knowledge of human nature, and, above all, a disposition to consult the aggregate wisdom of the people, and to increase their stores of judgment, by deigning to learn from every possible source of practical wisdom within their reach.

President Davis was not a man to consult, even in the smallest matter of detail, the wisdom of others, or to relax his purposes or personal preferences, at the instance of any consideration that might compromise him in respect of conceit or punctilio. About nothing connected with the new government had the popular will been so clearly and emphatically expressed, as the necessity of a reorganization of the Cabinet. Nobody expected those offices to be permanently filled by the provisional appointees. They were put there under an emergency; in some instances simply as compliments to certain States, and without the slightest expectation that they would be imposed on the country for seven long years. Had the Union continued, and Mr. Davis been elected to the Presidency, the selection of such a Cabinet of intellectual pigmies from the nation at large would have astounded the public. The two great branches of the administration—the War and the Navy Departments— were in the hands of men who had neither the respect, nor the confidence of the public. Mr. Benjamin, the Secretary of War, had been seriously injured, by a number of doubtful official acts, in the public estimation, which never held him higher

---

the soldier; it disconcerts the adversary, strips from him the initiative, and diminishes his means. Do not wait for the enemy in your own fireplaces, go always to seek him in his own home, when you will find opportunity at the same time to live at his expense, and to strip from him his resources. In penetrating his territory, commence by acting *en masse* with all forces, and be sure that the first advantages are yours. * * * * Never adopt the defensive, unless it is impossible for you to do otherwise. If you are reduced to this sad extremity, let it be in order to gain time, to wait for your reinforcements, drill your soldiers, strengthen your alliances, draw the enemy upon bad ground, lengthen the base of his operations; and *let an ulterior design to take the offensive be without ceasing the end of all your actions.*"

than a smart, expeditious, and affable official. Mr. Mallory, the Secretary of the Navy, had, in the old government, in which he was chairman of the Senate Committee on Naval Affairs, been the butt of every naval officer in the country for his ignorance, his *sang-froid*, his slow and blundering manner, and the engrossment of his mind by provisions to provide gratifications for his social habits.

President Davis refused to concede any thing to public sentiment with reference to the reorganization of his cabinet; although it is to be remarked that the demand for change was made not by a popular clamor, which a wise ruler would have done right to disregard and to contemn, but by that quiet, conservative, and educated sentiment which no magistrate in a republican government had the right to disregard. Mr. Mallory was retained at the head of the navy; Mr. Benjamin was promoted to the Secretaryship of the State, and the only material change in the cabinet was the introduction as Secretary of War of General Randolph, of Virginia, a gentleman whose sterling personal worth made him acceptable to all parties, and promised at least some change for the better in the administration of a government that had been eaten up by servility, and had illustrated nothing more than the imperious conceit of a single man.

The Confederate Congress had passed a bill to create the office of commanding general, who should take charge of the military movements of the war. The bill was vetoed by President Davis; but, at the same time, the unsubstantial show of compliance which had been made with reference to the Cabinet was repeated with reference to the commanding general, and Mr. Davis appointed Gen. Lee to the nominal office of commanding general, the order, however, which nominated him providing that he should "act under the direction of the president." Thus it was that Mr. Davis kept in his hands the practical control of every military movement on the theatre of the war; and it was very curious, indeed, that the servile newspapers, which applauded in him this single and imperious control of the conduct of the war, were unmindful of the plain and consistent justice of putting on his shoulders that exclusive responsibility for disasters which is inseparable from the honors of practical autocracy.

We have referred to the dark period and uncompromising auspices in which the permanent government of the Confederate States was inaugurated. Across the dreary tract of disaster there were, however, sudden and fitful gleams of light, such as the undaunted courage of our troops and the variable accidents of war might give in such circumstances of misgovernment as were adverse or embarrassing to a grand scale of successes. Of these, and of the disasters mingled with them, we shall proceed to treat in the progress of the narrative of the external events of the war.

THE NAVAL ENGAGEMENT IN HAMPTON ROADS.

In the progress of the war, attention had been directed, on both sides, to different classes of naval structure, composed of iron, such as floating batteries, rams, &c. On the 12th of October, an affair had occurred near the mouth of the Mississippi river, in which a partially submerged iron ram, the Manassas, attacked the Federal blockading fleet at the head of the Passes, sinking one of them, the Preble, and driving the remainder of the fleet out of the river. This, the first of our naval exploits, was to be followed by adventures on a larger and more brilliant scale.

As far back as the month of June, 1861, the little energy displayed by the Navy Department had been employed in building a single iron-clad naval structure. In the destruction of the navy-yard at Norfolk, at the commencement of the war, the steam-frigate Merrimac had been burned and sunk, and her engine greatly damaged by the enemy. However, the bottom of the hull, boilers, and heavy and costly parts of the engine were but little injured, and it was proposed of these to construct a casemated vessel with inclined iron-plated sides and submerged ends. The novel plan of submerging the ends of the ship and the eaves of the casement was the peculiar and distinctive feature of the Virginia, as the new structure was called. It was never before adopted. The resistance of iron plates to heavy ordnance, whether presented in vertical planes or at low angles of inclination, had been investigated in England before the Virginia was commenced; but, in the absence of accurate data, the inclination of the plates of the Virginia and their thickness and form had to be determined by actual experiment.

With the completion of the Virginia, the Confederate squadron in the James river, under command of Flag-officer Franklin Buchanan, was as follows: steamer Virginia, ten guns; steamer Patrick Henry, twelve guns; steamer Jamestown, two guns; and gunboats Teazer, Beaufort, and Raleigh, each one gun—total, 27 guns.

On the morning of the 8th of March, about eleven o'clock, the Virginia left the navy-yard at Norfolk, accompanied by the Raleigh and Beaufort, and proceeded to Newport News to engage the enemy's frigates Cumberland and Congress, and their gunboats and shore batteries. On passing Sewell's Point, Capt. Buchanan made a speech to the men. It was laconic. He said: "My men, you are now about to face the enemy. You shall have no reason to complain of not fighting at close quarters. Remember, you fight for your homes and your country. You see those ships—you must sink them. I need not ask you to do it. I know you will do it."

At this time, the Congress was lying close to the batteries at Newport News, a little below them. The Cumberland was lying immediately opposite the batteries. The Virginia passed the Congress, giving her a broadside, which was returned with very little effect, and made straight for the Cumberland. In the midst of a heavy fire from the Cumberland, Congress, gunboats, and shore batteries concentrated on the Virginia, she stood rapidly on towards the Cumberland, which ship Capt. Buchanan had determined to sink with the prow of the Virginia. On board the Yankee frigate, the crew were watching the singular iron roof bearing down upon them, making all manner of derisive and contemptuous remarks, many of them aloud, and within hearing of those on board the Virginia; such as: "Well, there she comes." "What the devil does she look like?" "What in h—ll is she after?" "Let's look at that great Secesh curiosity," etc. These remarks were cut short by a discharge from the Virginia's bow gun, which swept from one end of the Cumberland's deck to the other, killing and wounding numbers of the poor deluded wretches. In a few minutes thereafter, the Virginia had struck her on her starboard bow; the crash below the water was distinctly heard, and, in fifteen minutes thereafter, the Yankee vessel, against whom an old grudge had long existed for her participation in the burning of the navy-yard, sank beneath the water, her guns being fought to the last, and her flag flying at her peak.

Just after the Cumberland sunk, Commander Tucker was seen standing down James river under full steam, accompanied by the Jamestown and Teazer. Their escape was miraculous, as they were under a galling fire of solid shot, shell, grape, and canister, a number of which passed through the vessels without doing any serious injury, except to the Patrick Henry, through whose boiler a shot passed, scalding to death four persons and wounding others.

Having sunk the Cumberland, the Virginia turned her attention to the Congress. She was some time in getting her proper position, in consequence of the shoalness of the water. To succeed in this object, Captain Buchanan was obliged to run the ship a short distance above the batteries on James river in order to wind her. During all the time her keel was in the mud, and, of course, she moved but slowly. The vessel was thus subjected twice to all the heavy guns of the batteries in passing up and down the river.

It appears that while the Virginia was engaged in getting her position, it was believed on the Congress that she had hauled off. The Yankees left their guns and gave three cheers. Their elation was of short duration. A few minutes afterwards the Virginia opened upon the frigate, she having run into shoal water. The "Southern bugaboo," into whom the broadside of the Congress had been poured without effect, not even faizing her armor, opened upon the Yankee frigate, causing such carnage, havoc, and dismay on her decks, that her colors were in a few moments hauled down. A white flag was hoisted at the gaft and half-mast, and another at the main. Numbers of the crew instantly took to their boats and landed. Our fire immediately ceased. The Beaufort was run alongside, with instructions from Captain Buchanan to take possession of the Congress, secure the officers as prisoners, allow the crew to land, and burn the ship. Lieutenant Parker, commanding the Beaufort, received the flag of the Congress and her surrender from Commander William Smith and Lieutenant Pendergrast, with the side-arms of these officers. After having delivered themselves as prisoners of war on board the Beaufort, they were allowed, at their own request, to return to the Congress to assist in removing the wounded to the Beaufort. They never returned, although they had pledged their honor to do so, and in witness of that pledge had left their swords with Lieut. Alexander, on board the Beaufort.

The Beaufort had been compelled to leave the Congress under a perfidious fire opened from the shore, while the frigate had two white flags flying, raised by her own crew. Determined that the Congress should not again fall into the hands of the enemy, Captain Buchanan remarked: "That ship must be burned," when the suggestion was gallantly responded to by Lieutenant Minor, who volunteered to take a boat and burn her. He had scarcely reached within fifty yards of the Congress, when a deadly fire was opened upon him, wounding him severely and several of his men. On witnessing this vile treachery, Captain Buchanan instantly recalled the boat, and ordered the Congress to be destroyed by hot shot and incendiary shell. The illumination of the scene was splendid; the explosion of the frigate's magazine a little past midnight, aroused persons asleep in Norfolk, and signalled to them the completeness of our victory.

In the perfidious fire from the shore, Captain Buchanan had been disabled by a severe wound in the thigh from a minié-ball, and the command of the ship had been transferred to Lieut. Catesby Jones, with orders to fight her as long as the men could stand to their guns. At this time the steam-frigate Minnesota and Roanoke, and the sailing-frigate St. Lawrence, which had come up from Old Point, opened their fire upon the Virginia. The Minnesota grounded in the North channel, where, unfortunately, the shoalness of the channel prevented the near approach of the Virginia. She continued, however, to fire upon the Minnesota, until the pilots declared that it was no longer safe to remain in that position, when she returned by the South channel (the middle ground being necessarily between the Virginia and Minnesota, and the St. Lawrence and Roanoke having retreated under the guns of Old Point), and again had an opportunity to open upon her enemy. Night falling about this time, the Virginia was anchored off Sewell's Point.

The next morning (Sunday) the contest occurred between the Monitor (the Ericsson battery) and the Virginia. The Yankee frigates, the Roanoke and St. Lawrence, had retreated to Old Point—"the apothecary shop," as it was facetiously styled by our men; and the Monitor had gone up on Saturday night to assist the Minnesota, which was still aground. The daylight revealed lying near the Minnesota the celebrated iron battery, a wonderful-looking structure that was justly compared to a prodigious "cheese-box on a plank," said "cheese-box" being of a Plutonian blackness. At 8 o'clock the Virginia ran down to engage the Monitor. The contest continued for the space of two hours, the distance between the two vessels varying from half a mile to close quarters, in which the two iron vessels were almost side to side, belching out their fire, the heavy thugs on the iron sides of each being the only effect of the terrific cannonade. Again and again the strange-looking battery, with its black, revolving cupola, fled before the Virginia. It was, as one of our officers remarked, "like fighting a ghost." Now she ran down towards Old Point, now back towards Newport News, now approached to fire, and then ran away to load. The rapidity of the movements of the Monitor gave her the only advantage which she had in the contest. The great length and draft of the Virginia rendered it exceedingly difficult to work her. Once she got aground. It was a moment of terrible suspense to the noble ship, against which the combined batteries of the Minnesota and Monitor were now directed. The shot fell like hail, the shells flew like rain-drops, and slowly, steadily she returned the fire. There lay the Minnesota with two tugs alongside. Here, there, and everywhere, was the black "cheese-box." The Virginia still fired with the same deliberate regularity as before. Presently a great white column of smoke shot up above the Minnesota, higher and higher, fuller and fuller in its volume, and beyond doubt, carried death all along her decks, for the boiler of one of the tugs had been exploded by a shot, and that great white cloud canopy was the steam thus liberated.

In fifteen minutes the Virginia had got off and was again in motion. The pilots declared that it was impossible to get nearer the Minnesota, which was believed to be entirely disabled. The Virginia had twice silenced the fire of the Monitor, and had once brushed her, narrowly missing the coveted opportunity of sinking her with her prow, and the continuation of the contest being declined by the Monitor having run into shoal water, the Virginia ceased firing at noon and proceeded to Norfolk.

She steamed back amid the cheers of victory. In the direction of Newport News could be seen the spars of the Cumberland above the river she had so long insolently barred; but of her consort there was not even a timber-head visible to tell her story. This was not all the Virginia had done. The Minnesota was disabled and riddled with shot. Within eight and forty hours the Virginia had successfully encountered the whole naval force of the enemy in the neighborhood of Norfolk, amounting to 2,890 men and 230 guns; had sunk the Cumberland, probably the most formidable vessel of her class in the Federal navy, consigning to a watery grave the larger portion of her crew of 360 men; had destroyed the crack sailing-frigate Congress, with her enormous armament; and had crippled in the action the Minnesota, one of the best steamers of the enemy's navy. Our casualties were two killed and nineteen wounded, and the Virginia had come out of the action with the loss of her prow, starboard anchor, and all her boats, with her smoke-stack riddled with balls, and the muzzles of two of her guns shot away, but with no serious damage to her wonderful armor, that had sustained a cannonade such as never before was inflicted upon a single vessel.

The exploits of the Virginia created immense excitement in the North and a marked interest in Europe, as illustrating a novel and brilliant experiment in naval architecture. As an example of the sharp and practical energy of the Northern government, and its readiness to avail itself of all means in the prosecution of the war, it may be mentioned that in five days after the occurrence of the Confederate victory in Hampton Roads, a bill was introduced into the Senate at Washington, appropriating nearly fifteen millions of dollars for the construction of additional iron-clad vessels.

In Great Britain and France, and on the Continent generally, public attention was strained to a pitch of fearful anxiety on the subject of changes in naval architecture, and their adaptation to the new exigencies that had arisen in warfare on the water. All the European governments that had a strip of sea-coast busied themselves to turn to profit the lesson the Virginia had given them. Denmark voted a million of rix dollars for the construction of iron-plated vessels, while Sweden sent its Crown Prince to assist at the trial trip of the French frigate La Couronne, the largest iron war-steamer afloat. Italy had already some very fine iron vessels-of-war, and her citizens were hard at work on others. Austria was officially informed of the revolution in warfare at sea on the very day that an imperial commission reported her huge land fortresses as defiant of every known means of assault; and the Prussians, people and government, regarded the engagement in Hampton Roads as one of " the most important events of the day."

The Confederate States government might have learned some instructive lessons from the victory achieved by the Virginia. Instead of one such vessel, we might have had ten, had the Secretary of the Navy, Mr. Mallory, possessed the ability and zeal essential to his responsible position. The cost was not a matter of the slightest consideration. A vessel built at an expense of half a million was cheap enough, when in her first essay she had destroyed thrice her value of the enemy's property. The State of North Carolina and the Confederacy had spent at least a million of dollars already in futile attempts to defend the eastern coast of that State. If that sum had been expended in building iron-clad vessels suitable to the waters on the Carolina coast, all of our disasters in that direction might have been prevented, except, perhaps, the one at Hatteras, and our ports on that portion of our coast kept open, at least partially, if not entirely. In no possibly better manner could ten or twenty millions of dollars have been expended than by augmenting the power of our infant navy.

While the Virginia was achieving her memorable victory in Hampton Roads, a battle had commenced in the extreme northwest portion of the State of Arkansas, which had but one parallel as to its duration, and probably few as to its desperate character, since the opening of the war.

It will be recollected that, in a previous chapter, we left Gen. Price about the close of the year 1861 occupying Springfield, Missouri, for the purpose of being within reach of supplies, and protecting that portion of the State from domestic depredations and Federal invasion. About the latter part of January, it became evident that the enemy were concentrating in force at Rolla, and shortly thereafter they occupied Lebanon. Believing that this movement could be for no other purpose than to attack him, and knowing that his command was inadequate for such successful resistance as the interests of the army and the cause demanded, General Price appealed to the commanders of the Confederate troops in Arkansas to come to his assistance. He held his position to the very last moment. On the 12th of February, his pickets were driven in, and reported the enemy advancing upon him in force. Gen. Price commenced retreating at once. He reached Cassville with loss unworthy of mention in any respect. Here the enemy in his rear commenced a series of attacks, running through four days. Retreating and fighting all the way to the Cross Hollows, in Arkansas, the command of Gen. Price, under the most exhausting fatigue, all that time, with but little rest for either man or horse, and no sleep, sustained themselves, and, came through, repulsing the enemy upon every occasion, with great determination and gallantry.

Gen. Van Dorn had recently been appointed to the command of the Confederate forces in the Trans-Mississippi district. A happy accord existed between him and Gen. Price, and a private correspondence that had ensued between these two military chieftains, on the occasion of Gen. Van Dorn's appointment by President Davis to take command in Arkansas and Missouri, not only showed a spirit of mutual appreciation and compliment highly honorable to both, but developed a singular similarity of views (considering that the letter of each was written without knowledge of that of the other) with reference to the conduct of the war.

Learning that Gen. Price had rapidly fallen back from Springfield before a superior force of the enemy, and was endeavoring to form a junction with the division of Gen. McCulloch at Boston Mountain, Gen. Van Dorn, who was then at Pocahontas, Arkansas, resolved to go in person to take command of the combined forces of Price and McCulloch. He reached their head-quarters on the 3d of March.

THE BATTLE OF ELK HORN.

The enemy, under the command of Gens. Curtis and Sigel, had halted on Sugar Creek, fifty-five miles distant, where, with a force variously estimated at from seventeen to twenty-four thousand, he was awaiting still further reinforcements before he would advance. Gen. Van Dorn resolved to make the attack at once. He sent for Gen. Albert Pike to join him with his command of Indian warriors, and, on the morning of the 4th of March, moved with the divisions of Price and McCulloch, by way of Fayetteville and Bentonville, to attack the enemy's camp on Sugar Creek. The whole force under his command was about sixteen thousand men.

At Bentonville, General Sigel's division, seven thousand strong, narrowly escaped a surprise and fell back, our advance skirmishing with the rear-guard to Sugar Creek, about seven miles beyond.

On the morning of the 7th of March, Gen. Van Dorn made disposition for attack. Before eleven o'clock, the action had become general. The attack was made from the north and west, the enemy being completely surrounded. About two o'clock, Gen. Van Dorn sent a dispatch to Gen. McCulloch, who was attacking the enemy's left, proposing to him to hold his position, while Price's left advance might be thrown forward over the whole line, and easily end the battle. Before the dispatch was penned, Gen. McCulloch had fallen, and the victorious advance of his division upon the strong position of the enemy's front was checked by the fall of himself and Gen. McIntosh, also, in the heat of the battle and in the full tide of success. It appears that two musket-balls, by killing the gallant McCulloch and McIntosh, had prevented us from gaining a great victory. Notwithstanding the confusion that succeeded this untimely occurrence, Gen. Van Dorn pressed forward with the attack, sustained by the resistless charges of the Missouri division. At nightfall, the enemy had been driven back from the field of battle, and the Confederates held his intrenchments and the greater part of his commissary stores, on which our half-famished men fed. Our troops slept upon their arms nearly a mile beyond the point where the enemy had made his last stand, and Gen. Van Dorn's head-quarters for the night were at the Elk Horn tavern—from which locality the battle-field derived its name. We had taken during the day seven cannon and about two hundred prisoners.

On the morning of the 8th, the enemy, having taken a strong position during the night, reopened the fight. The action soon became general, and continued until about half-past nine o'clock, by which time Gen. Van Dorn had completed his arrangements to withdraw his forces. Finding that his right wing was much disorganized, and that the batteries were, one after another, retiring from the field, with every shot expended, Gen. Van Dorn had determined to withdraw his forces in the direction of their supplies. This was accomplished with almost perfect success. The ambulances, crowded with the wounded, were sent in advance; a portion of McCulloch's division was placed in position to follow, while Gen. Van Dorn disposed of his remaining force as best to deceive the enemy as to his intention, and to hold him in check while executing it. An attempt was made by the enemy to follow the retreating column. It was effectually checked, however, and, about 2 P. M., the Confederates encamped about six miles from the field of battle, all of the artillery and baggage joining the army in safety. They brought away from the field of battle 300 prisoners, four cannon, and three baggage wagons.

Our loss in killed and wounded was stated by Gen. Van Dorn to be about six hundred, as nearly as could be ascertained, while that of the enemy was conjectured to be more than seven hundred killed and at least an equal number wounded. Gen. Curtis, in his official report, gives no statement of his loss, but simply remarks that it was heavy. The entire engagement had extended over the space of three days, the 6th, 7th, and 8th of March. The gallantry of our soldiers had been unrivalled. More than half of our troops were raw levies, armed with shot-guns and country rifles. The enemy were armed with superior guns of the latest patents, such as revolving rifles, sabre bayonets, rifled cannon, mounted howitzers, &c. Our army had forced them by inches from one position to another, and, although compelled to fall back at last, were able to make their determination good never to permit the enemy to advance South.

The Indian regiments, under Gen. Pike, had not come up in time to take any important part in the battle. Some of the red-men behaved well, and a portion of them assisted in taking a battery; but they were difficult to manage in the deafening roar of artillery, to which they were unaccustomed, and were naturally amazed at the sight of guns that ran on wheels. They knew what to do with the rifle; they were accustomed to sounds of battle as loud as their own war-whoop; and the amazement of these simple children of the forest may be imagined at the sight of such roaring, deafening, crashing monsters as twelve-pounders running around on wheels. Gen. Van Dorn, in his official report of the battle, does not mention that any assistance was derived from the Indians—an ally that had, perhaps, cost us much more trouble, expense, and annoyance, than their services in modern warfare could, under any circumstances, be worth.

In the action, the Missouri troops, from the noble veteran, who had led them so long, down to the meanest private, behaved with a courage, the fire and devotion of which never, for a moment, slackened. The personal testimony of Gen. Van Dorn to their noble conduct, was a just and magnanimous tribute. He wrote to the government at Richmond: "During the whole of this engagement, I was with the Missourians under Price, and I have never seen better fighters than these Missouri troops, or more gallant leaders than Gen. Price and his officers. From the first to the last shot, they continually rushed on, and never yielded an inch they had won; and when at last they received orders to fall back, they retired steadily and with cheers. Gen. Price received a severe wound in the action, but would neither retire from the field nor cease to expose his life to danger."

Nor is this all the testimony to the heroism of Gen. Price on the famous battle-fields of Elk Horn. Some incidents are related to us by an officer of his conduct in the retreat, that show aspects of heroism more engaging than even those of reckless bravery. In the progress of the retreat, writes an officer, every few hundred yards we would overtake some wounded soldier. As soon as he would see the old general, he would cry out, "General, I am wounded!" Instantly some vehicle was ordered to stop, and the poor soldier's wants cared for

Again and again it occurred, until our conveyances were covered with the wounded. Another one cried out, 'General, I am wounded!' The general's head dropped upon his breast, and his eyes, bedimmed with tears, were thrown up, and he looked in front, but could seen no place to put his poor soldier. He discovered something on wheels in front, and commanded: 'Halt! and put this wounded soldier up; by G—d, I will save my wounded, if I lose the whole army!' This explains why the old man's poor soldiers love him so well."

Although, in the battle of Elk Horn, our forces had been compelled to retire, and the affair was proclaimed in all parts of the North as a splendid victory of their arms, there is no doubt, in the light of history, that the substantial fruits of victory were with the Confederates. The enemy had set out on a march of invasion, with the avowed determination to subjugate Arkansas, and capture Fort Smith. But after the shock of the encounter at Elk Horn, he was forced to fall back into Missouri, leaving several hundred prisoners in our hands, and more than two thousand killed and wounded on the field. The total abandonment of their enterprise of subjugation in Arkansas is the most conclusive evidence in the world, that the Federals were worsted by Gen. Van Dorn, and that this brave and honorable commander had achieved for his country no inconsiderable success.

The fall of Gen. Ben McCulloch was esteemed as a national calamity, and, in his official report of the battle, Gen. Van Dorn declared that no success could repair the loss of the gallant dead, who had fallen on the well-fought field. Gen. McCulloch's name was already historical at the time of the breaking out of the revolution. Twenty-six years ago he served in the battle of San Jacinto, afterwards passed his time on the Texan frontier, in a succession of hardships and dangers such as few men have seen, and subsequently, in the Mexican war on the bloody field of Buena Vista, received the public and official thanks of Gen. Taylor for his heroic conduct and services.

McCulloch, as a soldier, was remarkable for his singular capacities for partisan warfare, and, in connection with Walker, Hays, and Chevallie, had originated and rendered renowned the name of "Texas Ranger." These daring adventurers did much in achieving the independence of the Texan republic, and in defending its borders from the ruthless and enterprising Camanche. In the war of the United States with Mexico, they rendered invaluable service as daring scouts, and inaugurated the best and most effective cavalry service that has ever been known in the world.

The moment Lincoln's election became known, McCulloch identified himself as an unconditional secessionist, and repaired to Texas to take part in any movement that might grow out of the presence of over 3000 United States troops in that State. He was unanimously selected by the Committee of Public Safety to raise the men necessary to compel the surrender of San Antonio, with its arsenal and the neighboring forts, four or five in number. Within four days, he had travelled one hundred and fifty miles, and stood before San Antonio with eight hundred armed men, his old comrades and neighbors. His mission succeeded. Texas looked to him with confidence as one of her strong pillars in case of war. She sent him abroad to procure arms; but, before he had fully succeeded, President Davis appointed him brigadier-general, and assigned him to the command of the Indian Territory.

He was killed in the brush on a slight elevation by one of the sharp-shooters of the enemy. He was not in uniform, but his dress attracted attention. He wore a dress of black velvet, patent-leather high-top boots, and he had on a light-colored, broad-brimmed Texan hat. The soldier who killed him, a private in an Illinois regiment, went up and robbed his body of a gold watch.

Gen. McIntosh, who had been very much distinguished all through the operations in Arkansas, had fallen on the battle-field, about the same time that McCulloch had been killed. During the advance from Boston Mountain, he had been placed in command of the cavalry brigade, and in charge of the pickets. He was alert, daring, and devoted to his duty. His kindness of disposition, with his reckless bravery, had attached the troops strongly to him, so that, after McCulloch fell, had he remained to lead them, all would have been well with the right wing; but, after leading a brilliant charge of cavalry, and carrying the enemy's battery, he rushed into the thickest of the fight again at the head of his old regiment, and was shot through the heart.

A noble boy from Missouri, Churchill Clarke, commanded a battery of artillery, and, during the fierce artillery action of the 7th and 8th, was conspicuous for the daring and skill which he exhibited. He fell at the very close of the action.

While there was, in Richmond, great anxiety to construe aright the imperfect and uncertain intelligence which had arrived there, by devious ways, from Arkansas, news reached the Southern capital of a brilliant and undoubted victory still further to the West, in the distant territory of New Mexico. This victory had been achieved weeks before the slow intelligence of it reached Richmond. Although it had taken place on a remote theatre, and was but little connected with the general fortunes of the war, the victory of Valverde had a good effect upon the spirits of the Southern people, which had been so long depressed and darkened by a baleful train of disasters.

THE BATTLE OF VALVERDE.

The Confederates marched from Mesilla, in Arizona, upon Fort Craig, about 175 miles distant, and there fought the battle and won the victory of Valverde, on the 21st of March. Gen. Sibley, with his command, numbering, rank and file, two thousand three hundred men, left Fort Thorn, eighty miles below Fort Craig, about the 12th of February. On arriving in the vicinity of Fort Craig, he learned from some prisoners, captured near the post, that Gen. Canby was in command of the Federal forces in the fort; that he had twelve hundred regular troops, two hundred American volunteers, and five thousand Mexicans, making his entire force near six thousand four hundred men. Notwithstanding this superior force, he boldly advanced, and, on the 19th, crossed the river near Fort Craig, and, making a detour of some miles, arrived on the morning of the 21st March at Valverde, on the east bank of the Rio Grande, three miles above the fort, where a large body of the enemy were stationed to receive him. It seems that all the enemy's forces, with the exception of their artillery and reserve, were upon the same side of the river to which our troops were advancing. A portion of Col. Baylor's regiment, under command of Major Pyon, numbering 250 men, were the first to engage the enemy. Alone and unsupported for one hour they held their position amid a hail of grape, canister, and round-shot. At that time they were reinforced, and the battle became general. The enemy then made an attack upon our right wing, and were repulsed. A general movement was then made upon our line with more success, a portion of our left wing being compelled to fall back and take a new position. This was about 2 o'clock. The enemy now supposed they had gained the day, and ordered their battery across the river, which was done, and the battery planted upon the bank. As soon as the battery opened General Sibley knew it had crossed, and immediately ordered a general charge, which was performed only as Texans can do it. Starting at a distance of eight hundred yards, with their Camanche war-whoop, they reserved their fire until within thirty yards of the battery, when they poured a deadly fire, with double-barrelled shot-guns and pistols, immediately into the horror-stricken ranks of their foes. They sprung into the river, and in crossing, numbers were killed. Captain Teel's battery now coming up, closed this sanguinary contest with shell and grape, as they fled down the opposite side of the river to the fort. The battle lasted nine hours. It afforded one of the most remarkable instances of valor in the war—the taking of a field-battery with shot-guns and pistols. Our loss was thirty-eight killed, and one hundred and twenty wounded; that of the enemy, as given by themselves, was three hundred killed, four or five hundred wounded, and two thousand missing. The enemy suffered the most while retreating across the river, where the slaughter was for some moments terrible.

After the victory of Valverde, the small force of Texans not being in any condition to assault Fort Craig, pressed on to Albuquerque, about ninety miles north of the battle-field. This city, the second in size and importance in the territory, having a population of seven or eight thousand, the Federals had evacuated. The victorious Confederates still pressed towards Santa Fé, the capital city of the great central plateau of interior America, which the Federals had also evacuated, and fallen back on Fort Union, about sixty miles northeast of Santa Fé, and one of the strongest fortifications in America.

Thus the Texans had marched about three hundred miles

from Mesilla, defeated the Federals and destroyed their army in a pitched battle, ejected them from their two chief cities, and driven them out of the territory to their outpost on its eastern limits.

The result of the battle of Valverde was encouraging, and the prospect was indulged that New Mexico was already conquered, and that the Confederate States held the Southern overland route to California.

Referring to the progress of the campaign in Virginia, we shall find its plans and locality widely changed, the line of the Potomac abandoned, and the long and persistent struggle of the Federals for the possession of Richmond transferred to a new but not unexpected theatre of operations.

Gen. Joseph E. Johnston had determined to change his line on the Potomac, as the idea of all offensive operations on it had been abandoned, and it had become necessary, in his opinion, that the main body of the Confederate forces in Virginia should be in supporting distance and position with the army of the Peninsula; and in the event of either being driven back, that they might combine for final resistance before Richmond.

The discretion of falling back from the old line of the Potomac was confided by President Davis entirely to the discretion of Gen. Johnston, who enjoyed a rare exemption from official pragmatism at Richmond, and was in many things very much at liberty to pursue the counsels of his own military wisdom.

For the space of three weeks before the army left its intrenchments at Manassas, preparations were being made for falling back to the line of the Rappahannock, by the quiet and gradual removal of the vast accumulations of army stores; and with such consummate address was this managed, that our own troops had no idea of what was intended until the march was taken up. The first intimation the enemy had of the evacuation of Manassas was the smoke of the soldiers' huts that had been fired by our army.

That the strategic plans of the enemy were completely foiled by the movement of Gen. Johnston, was quite evident in the tone of disappointment and vexation in which the Northern newspapers referred to the evacuation of Manassas, which, unless there had been some disconcert of their own strategy by such an event, they would have been likely to regard as a considerable advantage on their side in letting them further into the territory of Virginia.

THE BATTLE OF KERNSTOWN.

While our forces deserted the old line of the Potomac, it was determined not to leave the Valley of Virginia undefended, and the command of Gen. Jackson was left in the neighborhood of Winchester, to operate to the best advantage.

Near the town of Winchester occurred, on the 23d of March, what was known as the battle of Kernstown. The Federals were attacked by our forces under Gen. Jackson, the engagement having been brought on by the gallant Col. Ashby, who had been fighting the enemy wherever he had shown himself in the Valley. The Confederate forces amounted to six thousand men, with Capt. McLaughlin's battery of artillery and Colonel Ashby's cavalry. All the troops engaged were from Virginia, except a few companies from Maryland. It was thought that there would be but a very small force at the point of attack, but the enemy proved to be nearly eighteen thousand strong, with a considerable number of field-pieces. They occupied a rising ground, and a very advantageous position.

Gen. Banks had concluded that there was no enemy in front except Ashby's force of cavalry; that Gen. Jackson would not venture to separate himself so far from the main body of the Confederate army as to offer him battle, and under these impressions he had left for Washington. On Sunday morning, Gen. Shields, who had been left in command of the Federals, satisfied that a considerable force was before him, concentrated his whole force, and prepared to give battle. The action commenced about four o'clock in the evening, and terminated when night closed upon the scene of conflict. Our men fought with desperation until dark, when the firing on both sides ceased. During the night, Gen. Jackson decided to fall back to Cedar creek, and prepare there to make successful opposition with his small force, should the enemy advance. The enemy was left in possession of the field of battle, two guns and four caissons, and about three hundred prisoners. Our loss was about one hundred killed, and probably twice that number wounded. The loss of the enemy was certainly more than double. At one period of the fight our men had got possession of a stone wall, which formed the boundary of two fields, and dropping on their knees, had fired deadly volleys into the advancing lines of the enemy. The Confederates carried off the greater portion of the wounded up the Valley. Their retreat was conducted in perfect order; and even Gen. Shields, in his accounts of the affair, which were very much exaggerated, of course, for the purposes of popular sensation in the North, testified of the Confederates, that "such was their gallantry and high state of discipline, that at no time during the battle or pursuit did they give way to panic."

The enemy had but little reason to boast of the battle of Kernstown. In fact, the affair was without general signification. It was an attack by the Confederates, undertaken on false information, gallantly executed, and, although unsuccessful, was not disastrous. The Northern troops had made no advance in the Valley; from the Manassas line they had actually retired; nor had they any considerable body of troops this side of Centreville. Whether they would ever attempt to execute their original plan, of a march through Piedmont to Richmond, was now more than problematical.

The greater portion of our dead left on the field of battle were buried under the direction of the mayor of Winchester. Some fifty citizens collected the dead, dug a great pit on the battle-field, and gently laid the poor fellows in their last resting-place. It was a sad sight, and sadder still to see women looking carefully at every corpse to try to identify the bodies of their friends. Scarcely a family in the county but had a relative there. But their suffering did not mollify the noble Southern women of Winchester. Every feeling, testified a Federal officer who witnessed the sad and harrowing scenes of the battle-field, seemed to have been extinguished in their intense hatred of "the Yankees." "They would say, 'You may bring the whole force of the North here, but you can never conquer us,—we will shed our last drop of blood,'" &c.

Col. Ashby covered the retreat of the army, and by his tireless energy, made himself, as on many other occasions, the terror of the Yankees. The daring feats and heroic exploits of this brave officer were universal themes of admiration in the South, and were rehearsed by the people of the Valley, whe idolized him, with infinite gratification and delight. A few months before, when Winchester had been evacuated, under orders from the War Department, he had been unwilling to leave the town, and had lingered behind, watching the approach of the haughty and unprincipled foe into this ancient town of the Valley. He waited until the Federal columns had filled the streets, and, within two hundred yards of them, cheered for the Southern Confederacy, and then dashed off at full speed for the Valley turnpike. He reached it only to find his way intercepted by two of the enemy's pickets. Nothing daunted, he drew his pistol and shot down one of the pickets, and, seizing the other, dragged him off a prisoner, and brought him safely to the Confederate lines. It was adventures like these, as well as extraordinary gallantry in the field, that made the name of the brave Virginia cavalier conspicuous throughout the South, and a tower of strength with those for whose homes and firesides he had been struggling.

The personal appearance of Col. Ashby was not striking. He was of small stature. He wore a long black beard, and had dark, glittering eyes. It was not generally known that the man who performed such deeds of desperate valor and enterprise, and who was generally pictured to the imagination as a fierce, stalwart, and relentless adventurer, was as remarkable for his piety and devoutness as for his military achievements. His manners were a combination, not unusual in the truly refined spirit, of gentleness with the most enthusiastic courage. It was said of him, that when he gave his most daring commands, he would gently draw his sabre, wave it around his head, and then his clear, sounding voice would ring out the simple but thrilling words, "Follow me." In such a spirit we recognize the fine mixture of elements that the world calls heroism.

The Northern forces pursued neither the retreat of Johnston from Manassas, nor that of Jackson from Winchester. On the contrary, they withdrew the forces first advanced, and blocked the road between Strasburg and Winchester. It was known, however, about this time, that the camps at Washington had been rapidly diminished, and that McClellan had totally disappeared from the scene. At the same time an unusual confidence was expressed in the Northern journals that Richmond would now fall almost immediately into the hands of their generals. Then followed the daily announcements of fleets of transports arriving in Hampton Roads, and the vast extension of the long line of tents at Newport News. These were evident indications of the intention of the enemy to abandon for the present other projects for the capture of Richmond, so as to make his great effort on the Peninsula formed by the York and James rivers.

General Magruder, the hero of Bethel, and a commander who was capable of much greater achievements, was left to confront the growing forces on the Peninsula, which daily menaced him, with an army of seventy-five hundred men, while the great bulk of the Confederate forces were still in motion in the neighborhood of the Rappahannock and the Rapidan, and he had no assurance of reinforcements. The force of the enemy was ten times his own; they had commenced a daily cannonading upon his lines; and a council of general officers was convened, to consult whether the little army of seven thousand five hundred men should maintain its position in the face of tenfold odds, or retire before the enemy. The opinion of the council was unanimous for the latter alternative, with the exception of one officer, who declared that every man should die in the intrenchments before the little army should fall back. "By G—, it shall be so!" was the sudden exclamation of Gen. Magruder, in sympathy with the gallant suggestion. The resolution demonstrated a remarkable heroism and spirit. Our little force was adroitly extended over a distance of several miles, reaching from Mulberry Island to Gloucester Point, a regiment being posted here and there, in every gap plainly open to observation, and on other portions of the line the men being posted at long intervals, to give the appearance of numbers to the enemy. Had the weakness of Gen. Magruder at this time been known to the enemy, he might have suffered the consequences of his devoted and self-sacrificing courage; but as it was, he held his lines on the Peninsula until they were reinforced by the most considerable portion of Gen. Johnston's forces, and made the situation of a contest upon which the attention of the public was unanimously fixed as the most decisive of the war.

It is not our purpose at this time to follow up the develop

ments of the situation on the Peninsula. We must, for the present, leave affairs there in the crisis to which we have brought them, while we refer to a serious recurrence of disasters about this time on our sea-coast and rivers, where again the lesson was repeated to us of the superiority of the enemy on the water, not by any mysterious virtue of gunboats, but solely on account, as we shall show, of inefficiency and improvidence in our government.

On the 4th of March, the town of Newbern, in North Carolina, was taken by the Federals, under command of General Burnside, after a feeble resistance. The day before, the Federals had landed about ten thousand troops fifteen miles below Newbern, and at the same time had ascended the river with a fleet of gunboats, which, as they advanced, shelled the woods in every direction. The next morning the fighting was commenced at early dawn, and continued until half-past ten o'clock, when our forces, being almost completely surrounded, were compelled to retreat. All the forts on the river were abandoned. Fort Thompson was the most formidable of these. It was four miles from Newbern, and mounted thirteen heavy guns, two of them rifled 32-pounders. The guns at Fort Ellis, three miles from Newbern, were dismounted and thrown down the embankment. Fort Lane, mounting eight guns, two miles from Newbern, was blown up. In the first attack upon our lines, at 7 o'clock, the enemy had been repulsed three times successively by our infantry, with the assistance of Fort Thompson; but having flanked our forces on the right, which caused a panic among the militia, he had changed the fortunes of the day. The railroad bridge across Neuse river was not burnt until after all our troops had crossed, except those whose escape had been effectually cut off by the enemy. The Federals achieved a complete victory after a contest of very short duration, having taken about five hundred prisoners, over fifty pieces of cannon, and large quantities of arms and ammunition.

The easy defeat of the Confederate forces at Newbern, the surrender of our fortifications, on which thousands of dollars had recently been expended, and the abandonment not only of our heavy guns, but of some of our field-guns also, was a subject of keen mortification to the South. The fact was known that our force at Newbern was very inadequate—not more than five thousand—a part of whom were militia, and had been left, despite of appeals to the government for reinforcements, to encounter whatever force Gen. Burnside should choose to bring against them. Gen. Branch, who was in command of the Confederate forces, and who displayed courage and judgment, was compelled to fight at Newbern. To have given it up without a struggle, after all that had been done there, would have brought him into discredit with the government, the people, and the troops. As it was, the enemy had gained an important position within easy reach of the Wilmington and Weldon road. But few persons remained in the town. Seven trains left for Goldsboro', all crowded to overflowing by fugitive soldiers and panic-stricken people. A shell from the enemy's gunboats fell within twenty-five feet of the last train as it moved off. Women and children were overtaken by the trains many miles from Newbern, some in vehicles of various kinds, and many on foot. The panic and disorganization extended for miles, and yet there was a nobility in the determination of the population of Newbern to fly anywhere rather than court security in their homes by submission to the enemy. The town of Newbern originally contained twelve hundred people; when occupied by the enemy, it contained one hundred people, male and female, of the old population.

On the 12th day of April one year ago, the guns and mortars of the South Carolina batteries opened upon the then hostile walls of Fort Sumter. Strangely enough, the first anniversary of the event was signalized by the startling and uncomfortable announcement that Fort Pulaski, the principal defence of the city of Savannah, had surrendered to the Yankees, after a brief bombardment. The news was all the more unpleasant, from the fact that the day before the public had been informed by telegraph that the enemy's batteries had been "silenced." It seems that they were not silent until our flag was struck. The surrender was unconditional, and the garrison, consisting of more than three hundred men, four of whom had been wounded and none killed, were made prisoners of war.

Another Confederate disaster on the coast shortly ensued, in the surrender of Fort Macon. This fort, on the North Carolina coast, was surrendered on the 25th of April, after a bombardment from the enemy's land batteries of less than twelve hours. It commanded the entrance to Beaufort harbor, and was said to be the most formidable fortification on the North Carolina coast.

For these painful and almost humiliating disasters on our coast and rivers, a ready but very silly excuse was always at hand. A most pernicious and false idea appeared to have taken possession of the public mind with reference to the essential superiority of the enemy on water. A very obvious reflection of common sense dissipates the idea of any *essential* advantage which the enemy had over us on the water. The failures in our defences had been most unjustly attributed to the bugbear of gunboats, when they ought to have been ascribed to no more unavoidable causes than our own improvidence and neglect.

The suggestion of common sense is, that if it was possible to make a vessel ball-proof, it was certainly much easier to make a fortification ball-proof. The excuse had been persistently made for our lack of naval defences, that it was difficult to supply the necessary machinery, and almost impossible, with the limited means at our disposal, to construct steam-engines. But these excuses about lack of machinery and steam-engines did not apply to our land defences. No machinery was necessary; no engine was necessary; and no consultation of curved lines of naval architecture was required to make a land fortification ball-proof. The iron plate that was fitted on the side of a gunboat had only to be placed on a dead surface, to make the land fortification a match in invulnerability to the iron-plated man-of-war. This was common sense. Unfortunately, however, it was a common sense which the scientists of West Point had been unable to appreciate. While the public mind had been busy in ascribing so many of our late disasters to some essential and mysterious virtue in iron-plated boats, it seemed never to have occurred to it that it was much easier to construct iron-plated batteries on land than the iron-plated sides of a ship, besides giving the structure the power of locomotion, and that our defeats on the water, instead of being charged to "gunboats," or to "the dispensations of Providence," had been but the natural results of human neglect and human stupidity.

CHAPTER XII.

The Campaign in the Mississippi Valley.—Bombardment of Island No. 10.—The Scenes, Incidents, and Results.—Fruits of the Northern Victory.—Movements of the Federals on the Tennessee River.—The BATTLE OF SHILOH.—A "Lost Opportunity."—Death of General Albert Sidney Johnston.—Comparison between the Battles of Shiloh and Manassas.—The Federal Expeditions into North Alabama.—Withdrawal of the Confederate Forces from the Trans-Mississippi District.—General Price and his Command.—The FALL OF NEW ORLEANS.—The Flag Imbroglio.—Major-general Butler.—Causes of the Disaster.—Its Results and Consequences.—The Fate of the Valley of the Mississippi.

The last period of our narrative of events in Tennessee, left Gen. Johnston making a southward movement towards the left bank of the Tennessee river, for the objects of the defence of Memphis and the Mississippi river, and indicated the important position of Island No. 10, forty-five miles below Columbus, as still in possession of the Confederates.

This important position in the Mississippi river was defended by General Beauregard with extraordinary vigor and success against the fleet of the enemy's gunboats, under the command of Flag-officer Foote. The works were erected with the highest engineering skill, were of great strength, and, with their natural advantages, were thought to be impregnable.

The bombardment of Madrid Bend and Island No. 10 commenced on the 15th of March, and continued constantly night and day. On the 17th a general attack, with five gunboats and four mortar-boats, was made, which lasted nine hours. The attack was unsuccessful. On the first of April, General Beauregard telegraphed to the War Department at Richmond that the bombardment had continued for fifteen days, in which time the enemy had thrown three thousand shells, expending about one hundred thousand pounds of powder, with the result on our side of one man killed and none seriously wounded. The gratifying statement was also made in General Beauregard's dispatches that our batteries were entirely intact. We had disabled one of the enemy's gunboats and another was reported to be sunk, and the results of the bombardment so far as it had continued, afforded room for congratulation that the fantasy of the invincible power of Yankee gunboats would at last be dispelled, and that the miserable history of the surrender of all our forts to this power was destined to wind up in a decisive and brilliant Confederate triumph on the waters of the Mississippi. The daily bulletin from Island No. 10, for many days, represented that the enemy, after an incessant bombardment of many hours, had inflicted no injury. The people of the South were constantly assured that the place was impregnable, and that the enemy never could pass it.

The bombardment had been one of unparalleled length in the war. Every day the mortars continued to boom, and still the cannon of the island replied with dull, sullen roar, wasting shot and temper alike. The very birds became accustomed to the artificial thunder, and alighted upon the branches of trees overhanging the mortars in the sulphurous smoke. The scenes of this long bombardment are described as affording some of the most magnificent spectacles—the tongues of flame leaping from the mouths of the mortars amid a crash like a thousand thunders, and then the columns of smoke rolling up in beautiful fleecy spirals, developing into rings of exquisite proportions. It is only necessary for one to realize the sublime poetry of war, as illustrated in the remarkable scenes at Island No. 10, to imagine a dozen of these monsters thundering at once, the air filled with smoke clouds, the gunboats belching out destruction and completely hidden from sight in whirls of smoke, the shells screaming through the air with an unearthly sound, and the distant guns of the enemy sending their solid shot above and around the island, dashing the water up in glistening columns and jets of spray.

While the people of the South were induced to anticipate a decisive and final repulse of the enemy on the waters of the Mississippi, the news reached them through Northern channels that the capture of Island No. 10 had been effected on the 8th of April, and that not only had the position been weakly surrendered, but that we had saved none of our cannon or munitions, had lost our boats, and had left about six hundred prisoners on the island in the hands of the enemy.

The evacuation of the island, which was effected in the greatest precipitation—our sick being abandoned, there being no concert of action whatever between the Confederates upon the island and those occupying the shore, the latter fleeing, leaving the former to their fate—had taken place but two days after Gen. Beauregard had left command of the post for important operations to check the movements of the enemy on the Tennessee river, which were developing a design to cut off his communication in west Tennessee with the eastern and southern States. Gen. Makall had been appointed to take command of the post. He assumed it on the 5th of April, in a flaming order, in which he announced to the soldiers: "Let me tell you who I am. I am a general made by Beauregard—a general selected by Gens. Beauregard and Bragg." In the mean time, the enemy was busy, and his operations were suffered to escape the vigilance of the Confederate commander. The Federals had cut a canal across the peninsula at New Madrid, through which the steamers and several barges were taken. The undertaking was an herculean one. The canal was twelve miles long, through heavy timber, which had to be sawed off by hand four feet under water.

One of the enemy's gunboats had succeeded in passing the island in a heavy fog. On the night of the 5th of April, the enemy, with a gunboat engaged Rucker's battery. While attention was engaged with this boat, a second gunboat slipped down unperceived, except by the men at one of the batteries, who fired two shots at her without effect. The situation was now serious; the enemy had possession of the river below the island. On the night of April 6, Gen. Makall moved the infantry and Stewart's battery to the Tennessee shore, to protect the landing from anticipated attacks. The artillerists remained on the island. The enemy having effected a landing above and below the island in large force, its surrender might be considered as a military necessity. But there could be no excuse for the wretched management and infamous scenes that attended the evacuation. All our guns, seventy in number, varying in calibre from 32 to 100 pounders, rifled, were abandoned, together with our magazines, which were well supplied with powder, large quantities of shot, shell, and other munitions of war. The transports and boats were scuttled. Nothing seems to have been done properly. The guns were spiked with rat-tail files, but so imperfectly that several of them were rendered serviceable to the enemy in a very short time. The floating battery, formerly the Pelican Dock at New Orleans, of sixteen heavy guns, after being scuttled, was cut loose. At daylight it was found lodged a short distance above Point Pleasant, and taken possession of by the enemy. Four steamers afloat fell into the hands of the enemy, with all the stores on board.

The unhappy men on the island were abandoned to their fate, the Confederates on the mainland having fled with precipitation. On one of the hospital boats were a hundred poor wretches, half dead with disease and neglect. On the shore were crowds of our men wandering around among the profusion of ammunition and stores. A few of them effected their escape through the most remarkable dangers and adventures. Some trusted themselves to hastily constructed rafts, with which to float down the Mississippi, hoping to attract the attention and aid of the people living on the shore. Others gained the upper banks of the river, where, for several days and nights, they wandered, lost in the extensive cane-brakes, without food, and in severe toil. Some two or three hundred of the stragglers, principally from the forces on the mainland, succeeded in making their way to Bell's Station, on the Ohio railroad, and reached Memphis.

The disaster was considerable enough in the loss of Island No. 10; but the circumstances attending it, and the consequences in the loss of men, cannon, ammunition, supplies, and every thing appertaining to an army, all of which might possibly have been avoided, increased the regrets of the South, and swelled the triumph of her enemies. Our total loss in prisoners, including those taken on the mainland as well as those abandoned on the island, was probably not less than two thousand. The Federal Secretary of the Navy, Mr. Welles, had reason to declare, that "the triumph was not the less appreciated, because it was protracted, and finally bloodless." No single battle-field had yet afforded to the North such visible fruits of victory as had been gathered at Island No. 10.

THE BATTLE OF SHILOH.

In the mean time, the movements of the enemy on the Tennessee river were preparing the situation for one of the grandest battles that had yet been fought in any quarter of the war, or had yet illustrated the exasperation and valor of the contestants. Gen. Beauregard had determined to foil the apparent designs of the enemy to cut off his communication with the south and east, by concentrating all his available forces at and around Corinth. This town is situated at the junction of the Memphis and Charleston and the Mobile and Ohio railroads, about ninety-two miles east of Memphis.

Gen. Johnston had taken up a line of march from Murfreesboro, to form a junction of his forces with those of General Beauregard. By the 1st of April, these united forces were concentrated along the Mobile and Ohio railroad from Bethel to Corinth, and on the Memphis and Charleston railroad from Corinth to Iuka. The army of the Mississippi had received other important accessions. It was increased by several regiments from Louisiana, two divisions of Gen. Polk's command from Columbus, and a fine corps of troops from Mobile and Pensacola. In numbers, in discipline, in the galaxy of the distinguished names of its commanders, and in every article of merit and display, the Confederate army in the vicinity of Corinth was one of the most magnificent ever assembled by the South on a single battle-field.

The enemy under Gen. Grant, on the west bank of the Tennessee, had obtained a position at Pittsburg and in the direction of Savannah. An advance was contemplated by him, as soon as he could be reinforced by the army under Gen. Buell, then known to be advancing for that purpose by rapid marches from Nashville by the way of Columbus. To prevent this demonstration, it was determined by Gen. Beauregard to press the issue without delay. By a rapid and vigorous attack on Gen. Grant, it was expected he would be beaten back into his transports and the river, or captured in time to enable the Confederates to profit by the victory, and remove to the rear all the stores and munitions that would fall into their hands, in such an event, before the arrival of Gen. Buell's army on the scene. It was never contemplated, however, to retain the position thus gained and abandon Corinth, the strategic point of the campaign.

It appears to have been Gen. Beauregard's plan to have attacked the enemy in their encampments on Saturday, the 5th. He, therefore, began the movement on Thursday, but the roads were heavy, and the men could not be got into position before Saturday. Had the attack been made on that day, the first day's fighting must have ended the conflict, for the enemy could have had no hope of aid from Buell. As it was, one day was lost, and the enemy were constantly inspirited by the almost momentary expectation of the arrival of Gen. Buell. In the mean time, courier after courier was sent by Gen. Grant for Buell to hasten on.

The Confederate forces did not reach the intersection of the roads from Pittsburg and Hamburg, in the immediate vicinity of the enemy, until late on Saturday afternoon. Their march had been tedious and wearisome. The roads were narrow and traversed a densely wooded country, and a severe rain-storm had rendered them almost impassable, and had drenched our troops in bivouac.

The morning of the 6th of April (Sunday) was to usher in the bloody scenes of a memorable battle. One camp of the enemy was near Shiloh church—a rude log chapel; and another stretched away in the direction of the road leading from Pittsburg Landing on the river to Corinth. The scene of the encampment was a very beautiful and magnificent one, there being but little undergrowth, and the thin ranks of the tall forest-trees affording open views, while the interlacing of their topmost boughs made a picturesque and agreeable canopy. In a military point of view, the battle-field might be described as a broken country, presenting opportunities for a great variety of manœuvres and independent operations by comparatively small bodies of men.

On the Saturday evening preceding the Sunday fight at Shiloh, there had been considerable skirmishing on our lines. Early Sunday morning, before sunrise, Gen. Hardee, in front of the enemy's camp, made an advance upon it. The enemy was taken completely by surprise, not expecting to be attacked, under any circumstances, by our inferior force. Many of the men were undressed and in night attire, and the hot breakfasts prepared by the messes were left untouched for the entertainment of our men. A line of battle was hastily formed by the enemy, and, in the mean time, our forces were advancing in every direction. The plan of the battle on our side was to form three parallel lines—the front, centre, and rear—each line having its centre and two flanks. The rear constituted the reserve, and the artillery was distributed between the first and second lines. The front was commanded by Gen. Hardee, the centre by Gen. Bragg, and the rear by Gen. Polk—Johnston and Beauregard being with the latter.

From daylight until a little after six o'clock, the fighting was principally between the pickets and skirmishers, but, at the latter hour, a portion of our main body appearing in sight, fire opened with artillery, and for an hour or more one heard nothing but the incessant uproar of the heavy guns. Our men, though many of them were unaccustomed to the iron hail, received the onset coolly, awaiting the orders to rise from their recumbent position and advance. In due time these came, and thenceforward through the day, brave and disciplined as were the Federal troops, nothing seemed capable of resisting the desperate valor of the Confedrates. The enemy fell like chaff before the wind. Broken in ranks, they rallied behind trees and in the underbrush, only to be again repulsed and driven back.

The scenery of the battle-field was awfully sublime. Far up in the air shells burst into flame like shattered stars, and passed away in little clouds of white vapor, while others filled the air with a shrill scream, and burst far in the rear. All along the line the faint smoke of the musketry rose lightly, while, from the mouths of the cannon, sudden gusts of intense white smoke burst up all around. Every second of time had its especial tone. Bullets shredded the air, and whistled swiftly by, or struck into trees, fences, wagons, or with their peculiar "chuck" into men. Every second of time had its especial tone, and the forest, among whose branches rose the wreathing smoke, was packed with dead.

The irresistible attack of our troops was compared by Gen. Beauregard, in his official report of the battle, to "an Alpine avalanche." The enemy were driven back by a series of daring, desperate, and successful charges, the various Confederate regiments and brigades rolling rapidly forward to the sound of enthusiastic cheers. In all of these, both general and field officers displayed a bravery that amounted to sheer recklessness, frequently leading the men into the very teeth of the opposing fire. It was these inspiring examples of personal valor which made our troops invincible.

At half-past two, Gen. Johnston, the commander-in-chief of the Confederates, fell. He was leading a charge upon the third camp of the enemy. The fatal wound was inflicted by a musket-ball on the calf of his right leg, and was considered by him as only a flesh wound. Soon after receiving it, he gave an order to Governor Harris, who was acting as volunteer aid to him, who, on his return to Gen. Johnston, in a different part of the field, found him exhausted from loss of blood, and reeling in his saddle. Riding up to him, Governor Harris asked: "Are you hurt?" To which the now dying hero answered: "Yes, and I fear mortally;" and then stretching out both arms to his companion, fell from his horse, and soon after expired. No other wounds were discovered upon his person.

Prudently the information of Gen. Johnston's fall was kept from the army. But the day was already secured. Amid the roar of artillery and the cheers of the victorious army, the commander-in-chief quietly breathed his last. Our forces were successfully pushing the enemy back upon the Tennessee river. It was after six o'clock in the evening when his last position was carried. The remnant of his army had been driven in utter disorder to the immediate vicinity of Pittsburg, under the shelter of the heavy guns of his iron-clad gunboats, and the Confederates remained undisputed masters of his well-selected, admirably provided cantonments, after over twelve hours of obstinate conflict with his forces, who had been beaten from them and the contiguous covert, but only by a sustained onset of all the men we could bring into action.

The substantial fruits of our victory were immense. We were in possession of all the enemy's encampments between Owl and Lick rivers, nearly all of his field artillery, about thirty flags, colors, and standards, over three thousand prisoners, including a division commander (General Prentiss) and several brigade commanders, thousands of small-arms, an im mense supply of subsistence, forage, and munitions of war, and a large amount of means of transportation. Never, perhaps, was an army so well provided as that of the enemy, and never, perhaps, was one so completely stripped on a single battle-field. On taking possession of the enemy's encampments, there were found therein the complete muster-rolls of the expedition up the river. It appeared that we had engaged the divisions of Gens. Prentiss, Sherman, Hurlbut, McClernand, and Smith, of 9,000 men each, or at least 45,000 men. Our entire force in the engagement could not have exceeded 38,000 men. The flower of the Federal troops were engaged, being principally Western men, from the States of Illinois, Indiana, Wisconsin, and Iowa. There were also quite a number of Missourians opposed to us, who are said to have fought with great spirit, opposite Gen. Gladden's brigade, on the extreme right. These men were accustomed to lives of hardihood and adventure. The captured Federal general, Prentiss, did not hesitate to testify to General Beauregard, "You have whipped our best troops to-day."

The enemy's artillery on the field, according to Gen. Prentiss' statement, numbered in all one hundred and eight pieces, or eighteen batteries of six pieces each. Their small-arms were of every description: Minié rifles, Enfield rifles, Maynard rifles, Colt's six-shooters, common muskets, &c., all of the best quality and workmanship. The Federal equipments left nothing to be desired. Their clothing was of the best quality and abundant, and the same may be said of their supplies. An abundance of excellent coffee was found in their tents—beef, pork, butter, cheese, navy biscuit, and sugar. The famous expedition to the plains of Manassas was not better fitted out or supplied.

On Sunday night, Gen. Beauregard established his headquarters at the little church of Shiloh, and our troops were directed to sleep on their arms in the enemy's encampment. The hours, however, that should have been devoted to the refreshment of nature were spent by many of the troops in a disgraceful hunt after the spoils. The possession of the rich camp of the enemy seemed to have demoralized whole regiments. All through the night and early the next morning the hunt after the spoils was continued. Cowardly citizens and rapacious soldiers were engaged alike in the wretched work. They might be seen everywhere, plundering the tents out of which the enemy had been driven, and loading themselves down with the spoils. The omission of discipline, which permitted these scenes, is not pardonable even in the license and indulgences which generally attend the victory of an army. The spoils of a victorious army should be carefully gathered up and preserved for the use of the army itself. They are the just possession of the conqueror, are frequently of great value, and should not be lost or carried off, where they can be of use. But, more than this, nothing could be more likely to demoralize troops than the indiscriminate pillage of an enemy's camp. It creates disorganization in the army; it so far stands in the way of a vigorous pursuit of the enemy; it demoralizes the spoiler himself, and lets him down at one step from an honorable soldier to a plundering brigand. It is no wonder that the troops which confronted the enemy next morning in the vicinity of Pittsburg Landing betrayed, however bravely they fought in comparison with the enemy, a diminution of spirit and visible signs of demoralization.

Sunday night found both armies in a critical situation. Gen. Beauregard hoped, from news received by a special dispatch, that delays had been encountered by Gen. Buell in his march from Columbia, and that his main force, therefore, could not reach the field of battle in time to save Gen. Grant's shattered fugitive forces from capture or destruction on the following day. The situation of Gen. Grant was that of the most extreme anxiety to himself. The enemy had supposed that the last act of the tragedy would have been completed on Saturday evening. The reserve line of the Federals was entirely gone. Their whole army was crowded into a circuit of half to two-thirds of a mile around the landing. They had been falling back all day. The next repulse would have put them into the river, and there were not transports enough to cross a single division before the Confederates would be upon them. As the lull in the firing of the Confederates took place, and the angry rattle of musketry died upon the ears of the fugitive Federals, they supposed that the pursuing army was preparing for the grand final rush that was to crown the day's success. But Gen. Beauregard had been satisfied to pursue the enemy to the river, and to leave him under the cover of his gunboats, without an attempt to penetrate it. When it was understood that pursuit was called off, Gen. Grant could ill conceal his exultation. His anxiety was suddenly composed, and, in a tone of confidence, he exclaimed to the group of officers around him, "to-morrow they will be exhausted, and then we will go at them with fresh troops."*

He was right. Looking across the Tennessee, he could see a body of cavalry awaiting transportation over. They were said to be Buell's advance; yet they had been there an hour or two alone. Suddenly there was a rustle among the gazers. They saw the gleaming of the gun-barrels, and they caught, amid the leaves and undergrowth down the opposite side of the river, glimpses of the steady, swinging tramp of trained soldiers. A division of Buell's army was there, and was hailed with tremendous cheers by the men on the opposite bank of the river.

The enemy was reinforced on Monday morning by more troops than Gen. Beauregard could have counted upon. The divisions of Gens. Nelson, McCook, Crittenden, and Thomas, of Buell's army, had crossed the river, some 25,000 strong; also, Gen. L. Wallace's division of Gen. Grant's army had been moved up the river—making at least 33,000 fresh troops. Vigorous preparations were made by Gen. Beauregard to resist the assault, which was deemed almost certain on Monday. A hot fire of musketry opened about six o'clock in the morning from the enemy's quarter upon his advanced lines, and assured him of the junction of his forces. The battle soon raged with fury, the enemy being flushed by his reinforcements, and confident in his largely superior numbers.

---

* The evidence of a "lost opportunity" in the battle of Shiloh abundantly appeared in the statements of the Northern commanders. Gen. Prentiss is reported to have made the following statement: "Gen. Beauregard," he said, "asked me if we had any works at the river, to which I replied, 'you must consider us poor soldiers, general, if you suppose we would have neglected so plain a duty!' The truth is, however, we had no works at all. Gen. Beauregard stopped the pursuit at a quarter to six; had he used the hour still left him, he could have captured the last man on this side of the river, for Buell did not cross till Sunday night."

According to Buell's report, our shot were falling among the fugitives crouching under the river-bank when our troops were called off.

On the right and centre, the enemy were repulsed in every attempt he made with his heavy columns in that quarter of the field; on the left, however, and nearest to the point of arrival of his reinforcements, he drove forward line after line of his fresh troops, which were met with resolution and courage. Again and again our troops were brought to the charge, invariably to win the position at issue, invariably to drive back their foe. But hour by hour, thus opposed to an enemy constantly reinforced, the ranks of the Confederates were perceptibly thinned under the unceasing withering fire of the enemy. By noon, eighteen hours of hard fighting had sensibly exhausted a large number; Gen. Beauregard's last reserves had necessarily been disposed of, and the enemy was evidently receiving fresh reinforcements after each repulse; accordingly, about 1 P. M., he determined to withdraw from so unequal a conflict, securing such of the results of the victory of the day before as was then practicable.

The retreat was executed with uncommon steadiness, and the enemy made no attempt to follow. Gen. Breckinridge had been posted with his command so as to cover the withdrawal of the rest of the army. Gen. Beauregard had approached him and told him, that it might be necessary for him to sacrifice himself; for said he, "*This retreat must not be a rout!* You must hold the enemy back, if it requires the loss of your last man!" "Your orders shall be executed to the letter," said the chivalrous Breckinridge; and gathering his command, fatigued and jaded and decimated by the toils and terrors of a two days' battle, he and they prepared to devote themselves, if necessary, for the safety of the army. There, weary and hungry, they stood guard and vigil. The enemy, sorely chastised, did not indeed come as expected; but Breckinridge and his heroes deserve none the less praise.

Never did troops leave a battle-field in better order. Even the stragglers fell into the ranks, and marched off with those who had stood more steadily by their colors. The fact that the enemy attempted no pursuit indicates their condition. They had gained nothing; we had lost nothing. The Confederates left the field only after eight hours of incessant battle with a superior army of fresh troops, whom they had repulsed in every attack on their lines,—so repulsed and crippled, indeed, as to leave it unable to take the field for the campaign for which it was collected and equipped at such enormous expense, and with such profusion of all the appliances of war. The action of Monday had not eclipsed the glorious victory of the preceding day. Sunday had left the Confederate army masters of the battle-field, their adversary beaten, and a signal victory achieved after an obstinate conflict of twelve hours.

The result of the engagement was most honorable to the South, and was recognized as one of the most conspicuous triumphs to its arms. The exultations, however, of victory in the public mind were perceptibly tempered by the sad intelligence of the death of Gen. Albert Sidney Johnston.

The deceased commander had led, perhaps, one of the most eventful military lives on this continent. He was graduated at the West Point Academy in 1826, as lieutenant in the Sixth Infantry, and after serving in the Black Hawk war left the army, and in 1836 emigrated to Texas, arriving there shortly after the battle of San Jacinto. He entered the Texan army as a private soldier, and was soon promoted to succeed Gen. Felix Houston in the chief command—an event which led to a duel between them, in which Johnston was wounded. Having held the office of senior brigadier-general until 1838, he was appointed Secretary of War, and in 1839 organized an expedition against the Cherokees, who were totally routed in an engagement on the Neches. In 1840, he retired from office, and settled upon a plantation in Brazoria county. He was an ardent advocate for the annexation of Texas to the United States. In 1846, at the request of Gen. Taylor, he took the field against Mexico, as commander of the volunteer Texan rifle regiment, in which capacity he served six months. Subsequently, he was acting inspector-general to Gen. Butler, and for his services at the siege of Monterey received the thanks of his commander. In October, 1849, he was appointed paymaster by President Taylor, with the rank of major, and, upon the passage of the act of Congress authorizing the raising of additional regiments in the army, he was appointed colonel of the Second Cavalry. In the latter part of 1857, he received the command of the United States forces sent to coerce the Mormons into obedience to the Federal authority, and conducted the expedition in safety to Great Salt Lake City in the opening of the succeeding year. Since then he commanded the military district of Utah. He resigned the Federal service as soon as the intelligence of the opening of the war reached him, and, travelling from California by the overland route, reached New Orleans in August last. Proceeding to Richmond, he was appointed, on his arrival there, general, to take command of the Department of the Mississippi.

It is known that Gen. Johnston was the subject of most unjust and hasty public censure in connection with his late retreat from Bowling Green and fall of Fort Donelson. He is said, but a few days before the battle in which he fell, to have expressed the determination to discharge his duties and responsibilities to his country, according to the best convictions of his mind, and a resolution to redeem his losses at no distant day. According to the official report, he fell in the thickest of the fight.

Keen regrets were felt by the friends of Gen. Johnston on learning the circumstances of the manner of his death, as these circumstances appeared to leave but little doubt that his life might have been saved by surgical attention to his wound. His only wound was from a musket-ball that severed an inconsiderable artery in the thigh. He was probably unconscious of the wound, and never realized it until, from the loss of blood, he fell fainting and dying from his horse.

Gen. Johnston was in the natural vigor of manhood, about sixty years of age. He was about six feet in height, strongly and powerfully formed, with a grave, dignified, and commanding presence. His features were strongly marked, showing the Scottish lineage, and denoted great resolution and composure of character. His complexion, naturally fair, was, from exposure, a deep brown. His manner was courteous, but rather grave and silent. He had many devoted friends, but they had been won and secured rather by the native dignity and nobility of his character, than by his power of address.

Besides the conspicuous loss of the commander-in-chief, others had fallen whose high qualities were likely to be missed in the momentous campaign impending. Gen. Gladden, of South Carolina, had fallen, after having been conspicuous to his whole corps and the army for courage and capacity. Distinguished in Mexico, on the bloody fields of Contreras and

Churubusco, he received honorable wounds. Having become a citizen of Louisiana, and selected to command a noble brigade, he again accumulated honor upon his native State, illustrated its martial fame, served her, no less than Louisiana, with his life, and sealed the great cause with his best blood.

George M. Johnston, Provisional Governor of Kentucky, had gone into the action with the Kentucky troops. Having his horse shot under him on Sunday, he entered the ranks of a Kentucky company, commanded by Capt. Monroe, son of the venerable Judge Monroe. At night, while occupying the same tent with the captain, it occurred to him that he had not taken the oath which entitled him to be enrolled in that company. He, therefore, desired the oath to be administered, which was done with due solemnity; "and now," said the new recruit, "I will take a night's rest and be ready for a good day's fighting." Faithfully he kept his pledge, and fell mortally wounded in the thickest of the fight. In making official mention of his death, Gen. Beauregard declared that "not Kentucky alone, but the whole Confederacy had sustained a great loss in the death of this brave, upright, and able man." He was one of a family of heroes, the nephew of the dauntless chief in the battle of the Thames, and the man who, during a long public and private career, had been ever regarded one of the noblest of Kentucky chevaliers, true and worthy governor of all that was left of Kentucky.

The fearless deportment of the Confederate commanders in the action was remarkable, as they repeatedly led their commands personally to the onset upon their powerful adversary. Gen. Bragg had two horses shot under him. Gen. Breckinridge was twice struck by spent balls. Major-general Hardee had his coat rent by balls and his horse disabled, but escaped with a slight wound. Gen. Cheatham received a ball in the shoulder, and Gen. Bushrod Johnson one in the side. Gen. Bowen was wounded in the neck. Col. Adams, of the First Louisiana regulars, succeeded Gen. Gladden in the command of the right wing, and was soon after shot, the ball striking him just above the eye and coming out behind the ear. Col. Kitt Williams, of Memphis, and Col. Blythe, of Mississippi, formerly consul to Havana, were killed.

The casualties of the battle of Shiloh were terrible. In car nage, the engagement might have compared with some of the most celebrated in the world. Our loss, in the two days, in killed outright, was 1,728; wounded, 8,012; missing, 959—making an aggregate of casualties of 10,699. The loss of the enemy in killed, wounded, and prisoners, unquestionably could not have been less than 15,000.

The suffering among the large numbers of our wounded was extreme. They continued to come in from the field slowly, but it was a long and agonizing ride that the poor fellows had to endure, over twenty-two or twenty-three miles of the roughest and ruttiest road in the Southern Confederacy. The weather was horrible, and a cold northeast storm pelted mercilessly down upon them. As they were carried, groaning, from the vehicle to the floor of the hospital, or laid in the depot, it was sad to see the suffering depicted upon their pinched and pallid features. Some of them had lain on the ground, in the mud, for two nights, and were wet to the skin and shivering with chills.

In view of the immense carnage of the battle of Shiloh, it was popularly esteemed *the* great battle of the war, and was declared by the Southern newspapers to take preference over the celebrated action of Manassas. Indeed, the rank which the Manassas battle held in the history of the war, was disputed by newspaper critics on every occasion when some other action presented a larger list of casualties or more prolonged scenes of conflict. But these circumstances, by themselves, certainly afford no standard for measuring the importance and grandeur of battles. It is true that the action of Shiloh was a brilliant Confederate success. But in dramatic situation, in completeness of victory, in interesting details, and in the grand historical tragedy of the enemy's rout, no battle has yet been fought in the war equal to that of Manassas, and, so far, it must hold its place in the history of the first year of the war as its grand battle, despite the efforts of interested critics to outrank its grandeur by that of other achievements, and to do violence to the justice of history.

There was one very remarkable circumstance in the battle of Manassas, which alone must give it an interest distinguished from that of any other engagement of the war. It was that, in the army which achieved that victory, there was represented, by troops, every State then in the Southern Confederacy.

At Shiloh, the troops engaged were principally Tennesseeans, Mississippians, Alabamians, Louisianians, Floridians, Texans, Arkansians, and Kentuckians. There was also a battery of Georgians in the field. The behavior of these troops had given us additional reason for the pride so justly felt in Southern arms and Southern prowess. Each and all of them fought so bravely that no distinction can be made between corps from different States. Battles are won, by each soldier feeling that the day depends upon his own individual efforts, and, on the field of Shiloh, this spirit was displayed, unless in rare instances of cowardice, or the more numerous exceptions of demoralization by the pillage which had unfortunately been permitted of the enemy's camp.

The misrepresentations of the North, with reference to the issue of the war, found a crowning example of falsehood and effrontery in the official declaration made at Washington of the action of Shiloh as a brilliant and glorious *Federal* victory. The Lincoln government had not hesitated to keep up the spirits of the people of the North by the most audacious and flaming falsehoods, which would have disgraced even the war bulletins of the Chinese, and which have always been found to be, in nations using this expedient in war, evidences not only of imperfect civilization, but of natural cowardice. The order of the War Department at Washington, signalizing its impostured victory at Shiloh, was as disgusting in profanity as it was brazen in falsehood. It declared that at meridian of Sunday next after the receipt of this order, at the head of every regiment in the armies of the United States, there should be offered by its chaplain a prayer, giving "thanks to the Lord of Hosts for the recent manifestation of His power in the overthrow of the rebels and traitors." One of the Federal generals who was incidentally complimented in this order—H. W. Halleck—for his "success" in the Missouri campaign, had written a voluminous letter to the Washington Cabinet recommending the *policy* of representing every battle in the progress of the war as a Federal victory. A government, which Mr. Seward had declared, in his letter to the British premier on the occasion of his cringing surrender to that power of the Southern commissioners, represented "a civilized and humane nation, a Christian people," had been persuaded to stoop to a policy which even the spirit and honor of brigands might have scorned, and which is never recognized but as a weapon of the vilest and most cowardly of humanity.

Gen. Beauregard retired to Corinth, in pursuance of his original design to make that the strategic point of his campaign. The Federals had sent several expeditions into North Alabama, and had succeeded in occupying Huntsville and Decatur; but the design of these expeditions did not appear to extend further than an attempt to cripple our resources by cutting off the Memphis and Charleston railroad, which runs through these towns.

In the mean time, it was decided by the government at Richmond to remove our forces from the Trans-Mississippi district, and to unite the armies of Van Dorn and Price with such force as Gen. Beauregard already had at Corinth. The order for leaving the limits of their States was responded to by the Missouri and Arkansas troops with ready and patriotic spirit. These brave men gave an example of gallantry and devotion, in leaving their homes and soil in the possession of the enemy, to fight for other parts of the Confederacy, which was made especially conspicuous from the contrast afforded by the troops of some other States which had made unusually large pretensions to patriotism and gallantry, regiments of which had openly mutinied at being ordered beyond the limits of their State, or had marched off with evident discontent, although no enemy held their territory, or was left in possession of their homes and the treasures they contained.

The noble "State Guard" of Missouri had a better appreciation of the duties of patriotism than many of their fellow-citizens of the Confederacy, whose contracted and boastful spirit had made them louder in professions of chivalry and devotion. They followed their beloved commander without a murmur across the waters of the Mississippi, turning their backs upon their homes, for which they had fought with a gallantry and devotion unequalled by any other struggle of the war. They felt that while they were fighting for the fortunes of the Confederacy, they were also contending for the ultimate restoration of Missouri, and that they would serve their State most effectually by following promptly and cheerfully Gens Van Dorn and Price to Tennessee. Their leader had been made a major-general in the Confederate service; the tardy act of promotion having been at last done from motives of policy, after all efforts had been made in vain to wring it from the obtuse official sense of justice. His influence was used to lead the troops of Missouri to new and distant fields of service, and his noble, patriotic appeals could not but be effectual to men who loved him, who had suffered with him, and were almost as his children.*

---

* The annexed address of Gen. Price to the troops, who followed him across the Mississippi into the Confederate camp, will strike the reader as an admirable appeal. Comprehensive in its terms, Napoleonic in spirit, and glowing with patriotic fire, it challenges comparison with some of the military orders of the most celebrated commanders in history.

HEADQUARTERS, MISSOURI STATE GUARD,
Des Arc, Arkansas, April 3, 1862.

Soldiers of the State Guard:

I command you no longer. I have this day resigned the commission which your patient endurance, your devoted patriotism, and your dauntless bravery have made so honorable. I have done this that I may the better serve you, our State, and our country—that I may the sooner lead you back to the fertile prairies, the rich woodlands and majestic streams of our beloved Missouri, that I may the more certainly restore you to your once happy homes, and to the loved ones there.

Five thousand of those who have fought side by side with us under the grizzly bears of Missouri, have followed me into the Confederate camp. They appeal to you, as I do, by all the tender memories of the past, not to leave us now, but to go with us wherever the path of duty may lead, till we shall have conquered a peace, and won our independence by brilliant deeds upon new fields of battle.

Soldiers of the State Guard! veterans of six pitched battles and nearly twenty skirmishes! conquerors in them all! your country, with its "ruined hearths and shrines," calls upon you to rally once more in her defence, and rescue her forever from the terrible thraldom which threatens her. I know that she will not call in vain. The insolent and barbarous hordes which have dared to invade our soil, and to desecrate our homes, have just met with a signal overthrow beyond the Mississippi. Now is the time to end this unhappy war. If every man will but do his duty, his own roof will shelter him in peace from the storms of the coming winter.

Let not history record that the men who bore with patience the privations of Cowskin Prairie, who endured uncomplainingly the burning heats of a Missouri summer, and the frosts and snows of a Missouri winter; that the men who met the enemy at Carthage, at Oak Hills, at Fort Scott, at Lexington, and in numberless lesser battle-fields in Missouri, and met them but to

It was generally considered in the South that the victory of its arms at Shiloh fully compensated the loss of Island No. 10, and that the Mississippi river below Fort Pillow, with its rich and productive valley, might be accounted safe, with the great army at Corinth covering Memphis, and holding the enemy in check on the land. But a great disaster was to occur where it was least expected, and where it involved the most immense consequences—a disaster which was to astound the South, which was to shake the confidence of the world in the fortunes of the Confederacy, and which was to lead, by unavoidable steps, to the abandonment to the enemy of the great Valley of the Mississippi.

THE FALL OF NEW ORLEANS.

When it was known in Richmond that the Federal fleet, which had so long threatened New Orleans, had at last commenced an attack on the Mississippi river forts, Jackson and St. Philip, no uneasiness was felt for the result. The enemy's fleet, which was to be engaged in this demonstration, was of formidable size. It consisted of forty-six sail, carrying two hundred and eighty-six guns and twenty-one mortars; the whole under the command of Flag-officer Farragut, a renegade Tennessean. But it was declared, with the most emphatic confidence, that New Orleans was impregnable; the forts, Jackson and St. Philip, were considered but as the outer line of defences; vast sums of money had been expended to line the shores of the river with batteries; the city itself was occupied by what was popularly supposed to be a large and disciplined Confederate force under Gen. Lovell, and in its harbor was a fleet consisting of twelve gunboats, one iron-clad steamer, and the famous ram Manassas.

The authorities at Richmond did not hesitate to express the most unlimited confidence in the safety of New Orleans, and

---

conquer them; that the men who fought so bravely and so well at Elk Horn; that the unpaid soldiery of Missouri were, after so many victories, and after so much suffering, unequal to the great task of achieving the independence of their magnificent State.

Soldiers! I go but to mark a pathway to our homes. Follow me!
STERLING PRICE.

refused even to entertain the probability of the enemy's penetrating the outer line of defence, constituted by the river forts, which were about sixty miles below the city. General Duncan, who was said to be the best artillerist in the Confederate service, was in command of the forts. On the 23d of April he had telegraphed the most encouraging account of their condition. The bombardment had then been continued for a week with extraordinary vigor. Nearly 25,000 thirteen-inch shell had been thrown by the enemy's mortar-boats, many thousands having fallen within the fort. But, in spite of this unremitting bombardment, the works were not at all damaged; only three guns had been dismounted, and the garrison had suffered only to the extent of five killed and ten wounded.

The public were inspired with confidence of a favorable result. The citizens of New Orleans, never doubting the impregnability of the defences of their city, were occupied as usual with the avocations of business and trade. The morning succeeding the date of the encouraging telegram of General Duncan was to witness scenes of the most extraordinary consternation, and to usher in the appalling intelligence of the enemy's approach to the city.

At half-past three o'clock, on the morning of the 24th of April, the Federal fleet steamed up the river and opened on our gunboats and both the forts, Jackson and St. Philip. The fire was vigorously returned by our side, and in a very short time became perfectly furious, the enemy's fleet and our whole force being engaged. In about one hour several of the enemy's vessels passed the forts—the first one in the advance having our *night signal* flying, which protected her from the fire of our boats, until she ran up close and opened the fire herself.

The citizens of New Orleans were awakened from their dream of security to hear the tolling of the alarm bells announcing the approach of the foe. It was about 9 o'clock, on the morning of the 24th, that the intelligence was received. The whole city was at once thrown into intense commotion; every one rushed into the streets—to the public places—to head-quarters —to the City Hall—inquiring the meaning of the agitation which prevailed, the extent of the danger, and its proximity. It was soon announced, on authority, that the enemy's vessels had succeeded in passing the forts and were then on their way to the city. The number was not known, but was afterwards ascertained to amount to five heavy sloops-of-war and seven or eight gunboats.

The attempt of the enemy had been audacious, but was aided by various contingencies. The defences of the Mississippi consisted of the two forts already mentioned—Jackson and St. Philip—the former situated on the left bank, and the latter on the right bank of the river. About three-quarters of a mile below, the river had been obstructed by means of a raft consisting of a line of eleven dismasted schooners, extending from bank to bank, strongly moored, and connected together with six heavy chains. Unfortunately, a violent storm had rent a large chasm in the raft, which could not be closed in time.

It appears, too, that on the night of the attack, the river had not been lighted by fire-rafts, although General Lovell had several times requested that it should be done. Moreover, the person in charge of the signals neglected to throw up rockets on the approach of the fleet, and, by a strange coincidence, the enemy's signals, on that night, were identically the same as those used by our gunboats. The consequence was, that the advance of the enemy's vessels was not discovered until they were abreast of the forts.

The conflict between the Federal fleet and our fleet and forts, was of a desperate character. The forts opened fire from all their guns that could be brought to bear; but it was too late to produce much impression. The ships passed on, the Hartford, Commodore Farragut's flag-ship in the van, delivering broadsides of grape, shrapnell, and round-shot at the forts on either side. On arriving at this point they encountered the Confederate fleet, consisting of seventeen vessels in all, only about eight of which were armed. The Confederate gunboats carried, some of them, two guns, and others only one. Nevertheless, they fought with desperation against the enemy's overwhelming force, until they were all driven on shore and scuttled or burned by their commanders. The Manassas was not injured by the enemy's fire. She was run ashore and then sunk. The Louisiana, the great iron-clad vessel, built to compete with the success lately won by the famous Virginia, was not in good working order. She could not manœuvre, and only her three bow-guns could be used, although her full com plement consisted of eighteen. She emerged from the action totally uninjured. The broadsides of the Pensacola, delivered three times, within a distance of ten yards, failed to loosen a single fastening, or to penetrate a single plate. The forts, likewise, remained intact; but the garrisons lost 52, in killed and wounded. Commander McIntosh was desperately wounded. He and Commander Mitchell both stood on the deck of the Louisiana during the whole engagement.

Gen. Lovell arrived just in time to see the Federal fleet passing Fort St. Philip, and to witness the desperate but ineffectual attempt of the Confederate gunboats to check its progress up the river. Just at this moment, the Iroon, one of the enemy's vessels started in pursuit of the Doubloon, Gen. Lovell's boat, and was rapidly overhauling her, when the Governor Moore darted upon the Iroon, and ran into her three times. The Federal vessel managed to escape from this assault, and was again chasing the Doubloon, when the Quitman attacked her, ran into her amidships, and sank her. Thus General Lovell narrowly escaped capture. In the mean time, Captain Kennon, commanding the gunboat Governor Moore, sped down the river into the midst of the enemy's fleet, darting hither and thither, attacking first one and then another of his monstrous antagonists, until he had fired away his last round of ammunition. He then drove his vessel ashore, and applied the torch to her with his own hand. In this way the forts were eluded, the Confederate naval forces destroyed, and the great city of New Orleans placed at the mercy of the Federal squadron.

At 2 o'clock, P. M., on the 24th, General Lovell arrived at the city, having driven and ridden almost the whole way up along the levee. He was immediately called on by the mayor and many other citizens, and in reply to the inquiries of these gentlemen, stated that the intelligence already received was correct; that the enemy's fleet had passed the forts in force, and that the city was indefensible and untenable.

The hasty withdrawal of Gen. Lovell's army from the city drew upon him severe public censure; but the applications of this censure were made in ignorance of the facts, and the evidence which afterwards transpired showed that the evacuation had been made at the urgent instance of the civil authorities themselves of New Orleans, who had entreated the Confederate commander to retire from their midst, in order to save the city from the risk of bombardment. Gen. Lovell expressed a readiness and willingness to remain with all the troops under his command. But it was the undivided expression of public opinion that the army had better retire and save the city from destruction; and, accordingly, the general ordered his troops to rendezvous at Camp Moore, about seventy miles above New Orleans, on the Jackson railroad.

A demand was made by Farragut for the surrender of the command, which Gen. Lovell positively refused, but told the officer who bore the message, that if any Federal troops were landed he would attack them. Two days after he retired, it was said that the city had changed its purpose, and preferred a bombardment to occupation by the enemy. General Lovell promptly ordered a train and proceeded to New Orleans, and immediately had an interview with Mayor Monroe, offering, if such was the desire of the authorities and people, to return with his command and hold the city as long as a man and shot were left.

This offer not being accepted, it was decided that the safety of the large number of unprotected women and children should be looked to, and that the fleet would be permitted to take possession. The raw and poorly armed infantry could by this time have done nothing against the fleet.

The impression which prevailed, that General Lovell had a large army under his command, was singularly erroneous. His army had been stripped to reinforce that at Corinth, and, since the 1st of March, he had sent ten full regiments to Gen. Beauregard, besides many companies of cavalry and artillery. The morning report on the day of the evacuation of New Orleans showed his force to be about *twenty-eight hundred men*, two-thirds of whom were the volunteer and military companies which had recently been put in camp.

Notwithstanding, however, these facts, the circumstances in which Gen. Lovell agreed to evacuate the city under the persuasion of the civil authorities, appeared by no means to be in that desperate extremity that would have justified the step in military judgment; and it was thought by a considerable portion of the public, not without apparent reason, that the evacuation, at the time it was undertaken, was ill-advised, hasty, and the result of panic or selfish clamors in the community.

The evacuation was begun on the 24th of April. At this time the river forts had not fallen; but two of the enemy's gunboats actually threatened the city; and the works at Chalmette—five 32-pounders on one side of the river, and nine on the other—were still intact. But it is known that there were reasons other than those which were apparent to the public, which decided Gen. Lovell to evacuate the city, and which were kept carefully to himself for obvious reasons. Gen. Lovell was fully aware that a single frigate anchored at Kenner's plantation, ten miles above the city, where the swamp and the river approached within less than a mile of each other, and through which narrow neck the railroad passes, would have effectually obstructed an exit of troops or stores from the city by land.

This was doubtless the real or most powerful reason for the evacuation of the city.*

On the morning of the next day, the Federal ships appeared off the Chalmette batteries, which exchanged a few shots with them, but without effect. Passing the lower batteries, the ships came up the river under full headway, the Hartford leading, then the Brooklyn, the Richmond, the Pensacola, and six gunboats. On and on they came, until they had extended their line a distance of about five miles, taking positions at intervals of about 900 yards apart. The scene on the water and in the city was alike extraordinary. The Confederate troops were still busy in the work of evacuation, and the streets were thronged with carts, drays, vehicles of all descriptions, laden with the multifarious articles constituting the paraphernalia and implements of warfare. Officers on horseback were galloping hither and thither, receiving and executing orders. The streets were

---

* The water at Kenner's was so high that a ship's guns could have had a clear sweep from the river to the swamp, and there would have been no necessity of any bombardment; the people and the army of New Orleans would have been cut off and starved into a surrender in a short time. The failure of the enemy to occupy Kenner's, for which it is impossible to account, enabled Gen. Lovell to bring out of the city nearly all the portable government property necessary for war purposes, as well as a large part of the State property.

crowded with persons rushing about with parcels of sugar, buckets of molasses, and packages of provisions plundered from the public stores. Others were busying themselves with patriotic zeal to destroy property of value to the enemy, and huge loads of cotton went rumbling along on the way to the levee.

No sooner had the Federal fleet turned the point and come within sight of the city, than the work of destruction of property commenced. Vast columns of smoke ascended to the sky, darkening the face of heaven, and obscuring the noon-day sun; for five miles along the levee fierce flames darted through the lurid atmosphere, their baleful glare struggling in rivalry with the sunlight; great ships and steamers, wrapped in fire, floated down the river, threatening the Federal vessels with destruction by their fiery contact. In front of the various presses, and at other points along the levee, the cotton had been piled up and submitted to the torch. It was burned by order of the governor of Louisiana and of the military commander of the Confederate States. Fifteen thousand bales were consumed, the value of which would have been about a million and a half of dollars. The tobacco stored in the city, being all held by foreign residents on foreign account, was not destroyed. The specie of the banks, to the amount of twelve or fifteen millions, was removed from the city and placed in a secure place; so were nearly all the stores and movable property of the Confederate States. But other materials were embraced in the awful conflagration. About a dozen large river steamboats, twelve or fifteen ships, some of them laden with cotton, a great floating battery, several unfinished gunboats, the immense ram, the Mississippi, and the docks on the other side of the river, were all embraced in the fiery sacrifice. The Mississippi was an iron-clad frigate, a superior vessel of her class, and accounted to be by far the most important naval structure the Confederate government had yet undertaken.

On evacuating the city, Gen. Lovell had left it under the exclusive jurisdiction of Mayor Monroe. That officer, although he had appealed to Gen. Lovell to evacuate the city, so as to avoid such exasperation or conflict as might put the city in peril of bombardment, was not willing to surrender it to the enemy; but was content, after due protestations of patriotic fervor, that the enemy should perform, without interruption, the ceremony of surrender for himself in taking down the flags flying over all the public buildings of the city. A correspondence ensued between the mayor and the flag-officer of the enemy's fleet. The correspondence was certainly of very unnecessary length on the part of the mayor, and was travestied in the Northern newspapers as a controversy between "*Farrago and Farragut.*" But the sentiments of the mayor, although tedious and full of vain repetitions, were just and honorable. He declared, with explanations that were not necessary to be given to the enemy, and at a length that showed rather too much the vanity of literary style, that the citizens of New Orleans yielded to physical force alone, and that they maintained their allegiance to the government of the Confederate States.

On the morning of the 26th of April, a force landed from the sloop-of-war Pensacola, lying opposite Esplanade-street and hoisted a United States flag upon the mint. It had not remained there long before some young men, belonging to the Pinckney battalion, mounted to the dome of the mint, tore it down and dragged it through the streets.

Whether Flag-officer Farragut was exasperated or not by this circumstance, is not known; but he seemed to have determined to spare no mortification to the city, which its civil officers had already assured him was unprepared to resist him, and to hesitate at no misrepresentation in order to vilify its citizens. In one of his letters to the mayor, he had sought to publish the fact to the world, that helpless men, women, and children had been fired upon by the citizens of New Orleans "for giving expression to their pleasure at witnessing the old flag;" when the fact was, that the cheering on the levee referred to had been, in defiance of the enemy, for "the Southern Confederacy," and the only firing in the crowd was that of incautious and exasperated citizens at the Federal fleet.

The *State* flag of Louisiana still floated from the City Hall. It was an emblem of nothing more than State sovereignty, and yet it too was required to be lowered at the unreasonable and harsh demand of the invader. A memorial, praying the common council to protect at least the emblem of State sovereignty from insult, was signed by a large number of the noble women of New Orleans, including many of the wealthiest, fairest, and highest in social position in the city. The reply of the council was feeble and embarrassed. They passed a resolution declaring that "no resistance would be made to the forces of the United States;" approving, at the same time, the "sentiments" expressed by the mayor, and requesting him "to act in the spirit manifested by them."

On the 28th of April, Flag-officer Farragut addressed his ultimatum to the mayor, complaining of the continued display of the flag of Louisiana on the City Hall, and concluding with a threat of bombardment of the city by notifying him to remove the women and children from its limits within forty-eight hours. The mayor replied with new spirit, that the satisfaction which was asked at the hands of a vanquished people, that they should lower with their own hands their State flag, and perform an act against which their natures rebelled, would not, under any circumstances, be given; that there was no possible exit from the city for its immense population of the women and children, and that if the enemy chose to murder them on a question of etiquette, he might do his pleasure.

In the delay of the enemy's actual occupation of the city while the correspondence referred to between the mayor and the enemy was in progress, the confidence of the people of New Orleans had, in a measure, been rallied. There were yet some glimmers of hope. They thought that, with the forts still holding out, and the enemy's transports unable to get up the river, the city might be saved. The fleet had no forces with which to occupy it, and there was no access for an army except by way of the lakes. They had determined to cut the levee below should Gen Butler, in command of the land forces, attempt an approach from Lake Borgne, and above the city, should he make the effort from Lake Pontchartrain. In the last resort, they were determined to man the lines around the city, armed with such weapons as they could procure, and fight the Federal land forces whenever they might make their appearance.

These hopes were suddenly dispelled by the unexpected news of the fall of Forts Jackson and St. Philip. Fort Jackson had been very little damaged in the bombardment. It yielded because of a mutiny of three or four hundred of the garrison who refused to obey the commands of its brave officer, Gen. Duncan. He had no alternative but to give up the place. At the first signs of the mutinous disposition, he threatened to turn his guns on his own men, but found a large number of them spiked. He surrendered, in fact, to his own garrison. The post could, probably, have been held, if the men had stood to their guns. He stated this in an address on the levee to the people, and, while stating it, cried like a child.

The news of the surrender of the river forts effected a sudden change in the views of Flag-officer Farragut. He was evidently anxious lest Gen. Butler, to whose transports a way had now been opened to the city, should arrive before he could consummate the objects of his expedition. He had already involved himself in a maze of incongruities and contradictions. First, he demanded peremptorily that the flag should be taken down; then he insisted that it should be removed before 12 M. on Saturday, the 28th; on Monday, he repeated the demand, under a threat of bombardment, giving forty-eight hours for the removal of the women and children. On Tuesday morning, he reiterated his peremptory demand, but, within an hour, he agreed to waive every thing he had claimed, and reluctantly consented to send his own forces to take down the flag.

About noon, a Federal force, consisting of about two hundred armed marines and a number of sailors, dragging two brass howitzers, appeared in front of the City Hall, and the officer in command, mounting to the dome of the building, removed the flag of the State in sight of an immense crowd of the citizens of New Orleans. No interruption was offered to the small party of the Federals, and the idle utterances of curiosity were quelled by the sadness and solemnity of the occasion. Profound silence pervaded the immense crowd. Not even a whisper was heard. The very air was oppressive with stillness. The marines stood statue-like within the square, their bayonets glistening in the sunbeams, and their faces stolid with indifference. Among the vast multitude of citizens, the wet cheeks of women and the compressed lips and darkened brows of men betrayed their consciousness of the great humiliation which had overtaken them. But among them all there was not one spirit to emulate the devotion of the martyr-hero of Virginia, who, alone and unaided, on the steps of the Marshall

House, in Alexandria, had avenged with his life the first insult ever offered by the enemy to the flag of his country.

Thus was the surrender of the city of New Orleans completed. Gen. Butler took possession on the 1st of May, and inaugurated an administration, the despotism and insolence of which might have been expected from one of his vile personal character and infamous antecedents. He was a man who had all the proverbially mean instincts of the Massachusetts Yankee; he had been a disreputable jury lawyer at home; as a member of the old Democratic party, he had been loud in his professions of devotion to the South; but his glorification in this particular had been dampened in the Charleston Convention, where he pocketed an insult from a Southern delegate, and turned pale at the threat of personal chastisement. The war gave him an opportunity of achieving one of those easy reputations in the North which were made by brazen boastfulness, coarse abuse of the South, and aptitude in lying. We shall have future occasion to refer to the brutal and indecent despotism of this vulgar tyrant of New Orleans, who, in inviting his soldiers to treat as prostitutes every lady in the street who dared to show displeasure at their presence, surpassed the atrocities of Haynau, and rivalled the most barbarous and fiendish rule of vengeance ever sought to be wreaked upon a conquered people. If any thing were wanting to make the soldiers of the South devote anew whatever they had of life, and labor, and blood to the cause of the safety and honor of their country, it was the infamous swagger of Butler in New Orleans, his autocratic rule, his arrest of the best citizens, his almost daily robberies, and his "ingenious" war upon the helplessness of men and the virtue of women.

The narrative of the fall of New Orleans furnishes its own comment. Never was there a more miserable story, where accident, improvidence, treachery, vacillation, and embarrassment of purpose, each, perhaps, not of great importance in itself, combined under an evil star to produce the astounding result of the fall, after an engagement, the casualties of which might be counted by hundreds, of a city which was the commercial capital of the South, which contained a population of one hundred and seventy thousand souls, and which was the largest *exporting* city in the world.

The extent of the disaster is not to be disguised. It was a heavy blow to the Confederacy. It annihilated us in Louisiana; separated us from Texas and Arkansas; diminished our resources and supplies by the loss of one of the greatest grain and cattle countries within the limits of the Confederacy; gave to the enemy the Mississippi river, with all its means of navigation, for a base of operations; and finally led, by plain and irresistible conclusion, to our virtual abandonment of the great and fruitful Valley of the Mississippi.—It did all this, and yet it was very far from deciding the fate of the war.

CHAPTER XIII.

CONCLUSION.

Prospects of the War.—The Extremity of the South.—Lights and Shadows of the Campaign in Virginia.—Jackson's Campaign in the Valley.—The Policy of Concentration.—Sketch of the Battles around Richmond.—Effect of McClellan's Defeat upon the North.—President Davis's congratulatory Order.—The War as a great Money Job.—*Note:* Gen. Washington's Opinion of the Northern People.—Statement of the Northern Finances.—Yankee Venom.—Gen. Pope's Military Orders.—Summary of the War Legislation of the Northern Congress.—Retaliation on the part of the Confederacy.—The Cartel.—Prospects of European Interference.—English Statesmanship. —Progress of the War in the West.—The Defence of Vicksburg.—Morgan's great Raid.—The Tennessee-Virginia Frontier.—A Glance at the Confederate Congress.— Mr. Foote and the Cabinet.—The Campaign in Virginia again.—Rapid Movements and famous March of the Southern Troops.—*The signal Victory of the Thirtieth of August on the Plains of Manassas.*—Reflections on the War.—Some of its Characteristics.—A Review of its Military Results.—Three Moral Benefits of the War.—Prospects and Promises of the Future.

We have chosen the memorable epoch of the fall of New Orleans, properly dated from the occupation of the enemy on the 1st of May, 1862, as an appropriate period for the conclusion of our historical narrative of the events of the first year of the war. Hereafter, in the future continuation of the narrative, which we promise to ourselves, we shall have to direct the attention of the reader to the important movements, the sorrowful disasters, and the splendid achievements, that more than compensated the inflictions of misfortune, in the famous summer campaign in Virginia. In these we shall find full confirmation of the judgment which we have declared, that the fall of New Orleans, and the consequent loss of the Mississippi Valley, did not decide the fate of the war; and, indeed, we shall see that the abandonment of our plan of frontier defence made the way for the superior and more fortunate policy of the concentration of our forces in the interior.

The fall of New Orleans and consequent loss of our command of the Mississippi river from New Orleans to Memphis, with all its immense advantages of transportation and supply; the retreat of Gen. Johnston's forces from Yorktown; the evacuation of Norfolk, with its splendid navy-yard—an event accomplished by a mere *brutum fulmen*, and without a blow; the stupid and unnecessary destruction of the Virginia, "the iron diadem of the South;"* the perilous condition of Charleston, Savan-

---

* The destruction of the Virginia was a sharp and unexpected blow to the confidence of the people of the South in their government.

How far the government was implicated in this foolish and desperate act, was never openly acknowledged or exactly ascertained; but, despite the pains of official concealment, there are certain well-attested facts which indicate that in the destruction of this great war-ship, the authorities at Richmond were not guiltless. These facts properly belong to the history of one of the most unhappy events that had occurred since the commencement of the war.

The Virginia was destroyed under the immediate orders of her commander, Commodore Tatnall, a little before five o'clock on the morning of the 11th of May, in the vicinity of Craney Island. During the morning of the same day a prominent politician in the streets of Richmond was observed to be very much dejected; he remarked that it was an evil day for the Confederacy.

On being questioned by his intimate friends, he declared to them that the government had determined upon, or assented to, the destruction of the Virginia, and that he had learned this from the highest sources of authority in the capital. At this time the news of the explosion of the Virginia could not have possibly reached Richmond; there was no telegraphic communication between the scene of her destruction and the city, and the evidence appears to be complete, that the government had at least a provision of the destruction of this vessel, or had assented to the general policy of the act, trusting, perhaps, to acquit itself of the responsibility for it on the unworthy plea that it had given no *express* orders in the matter.

Again, it is well known that for at least a week prior to the destruction of the Virginia, the evacuation of Norfolk had been determined upon; that during the time the removal of stores was daily progressing; and that Mr. Mallory, the Secretary of the Navy, had within this period, himself, visited Norfolk to look after the public interests. The evacuation of this port clearly involved the question, what disposition was to be made of the Virginia.

If the government made no decision of a question, which for a week stared it in the face, it certainly was very strangely neglectful of the public interest. If Mr. Mallory visited Norfolk when the evacuation was going on, and never thought of the Virginia, or, thinking of her, kept dumb, never even giving so much as an *official nod* as to what disposition should be made of her, he must have been even more stupid than the people who laughed at him in Richmond, or the members of Congress who nicknamed without mercy, thought him to be.

It is also not a little singular that when a court of inquiry had found that the destruction of the Virginia was unnecessary and improper, Mr. Mallory should have waived the calling of a court-martial, forgotten what was due to the public interest on such a finding as that made by the preliminary court, and expressed himself satisfied to let the matter rest. The fact is indisputable, that the court-martial was called at the demand of Commodore Tatnall himself. It resulted in his acquittal.

nah, and Mobile, and the menace of Richmond by one of the largest armies of the world, awakened the people of the South to a full appreciation of the crisis of the war, and placed their cause in an extremity which nothing could have retrieved but the undiminished and devoted spirit of their brave soldiers in the field.

We shall have, however, to mingle with this story of disasters, the triumphs, not indeed of the government, but of brave and adventurous spirits in the field. We shall tell how it was that the retreat from Yorktown, although undertaken without any settled plan as to the line of defence upon which it was to be reorganized, led to the successful battle of Williamsburg; we shall recount the events of the glorious battle of Seven Pines, the sound of whose guns was heard by the people of Richmond, and was followed by the speedy messages of a splendid victory; and we shall tell how it was that, while the news of the destruction of the Virginia was still the bitterest reminiscence of the people of the South, and while Secretary Mallory was making a drivelling show of alacrity to meet the enemy by advertising for "timber" to construct new naval defences, a powerful flotilla of Yankee gunboats was repulsed by a battery of four guns on the banks of James river, and the scale of war turned by even such a small incident as the action of Drury's Bluff. In this connection, too, we shall have to record the evidences of the heroic spirit that challenged the approaching enemy; the noble resolution of the citizens of Richmond to see their beautiful city consigned to the horrors of a bombardment, rather than to the hands of the enemy; and the brave resolution of the Virginia Legislature, which put the Confederate authorities to shame, and infused the hearts of the people with a new and lively spirit of courage and devotion.*

---

* "*Resolved by the General Assembly:* That the General Assembly hereby express its desire that the capital of the State be defended to the last extremity, if such defence is in accordance with the views of the President of the Confederate States; and that the President be assured that whatever destruction or loss of property of the State or individuals shall thereby result, will be cheerfully submitted to."—*Resolution Va. Legislature, May* 14.

"Some one said to me the other day, that the duty of surrendering the city would devolve either upon the President, the Mayor, or myself. I said to him,

But we shall have occasion to tell of even more brilliant triumphs of Southern spirit, and to explain how, for some time at least, the safety of Richmond was trusted not so much to the fortunes of the forces that immediately protected it, as to the splendid diversion of the heroic Jackson in the Valley of Virginia.

We shall see how this brave general, whom the government had determined to recall to Gen. Johnston's lines, rejected the suggestions of the surrender of the Valley, and his personal ease, and adventured upon a campaign, the most successful and brilliant in the war. We shall trace with particular interest the events of this glorious expedition, and we shall find reason to ascribe its results to the zeal, heroism, and genius of its commander alone. We shall recount the splendid victory over Banks, the recovery of Winchester, the capture of four thousand prisoners, the annihilation of the invading army of the Valley, and the heroic deeds which threw the splendor of sunlight over the long lines of the Confederate host. The reader will have occasion to compare the campaign of General Jackson in the Valley of Virginia, with some of the most famous in modern history. We shall show that, in this brief, but brilliant campaign, a gallant Southern army fought four battles and a number of skirmishes; killed and wounded a considerable number of the enemy, took several thousand prisoners, secured millions of dollars of stores, destroyed many millions of dollars' worth for the enemy, and chased the Federal army, commanded by General Banks, out of Virginia and across the Potomac; and that all these events were accomplished within the period of three weeks, and with a loss scarcely exceeding one hundred in killed and wounded.

In this story of disaster, mingled with triumph, we shall be

---

if the demand is made upon me, with the alternative to surrender or be shelled, I shall reply, BOMBARD AND BE DAMNED."—*Speech of Gov. Letcher, May* 16.

"I say now, and will abide by it, when the citizens of Richmond demand of me to surrender the capital of Virginia and of the Confederacy to the enemy, they must find some other man to fill my place. I will resign the mayoralty. And when that other man elected in my stead shall deliver up the city, I hope I have physical courage and strength enough left to shoulder a musket and go into the ranks."—*Speech of Mayor Mayo, May* 16.

disappointed if we do not discover the substantial prospect of brighter fortunes and final triumph for the South.

Indeed, the fact will be shown to be, that events, although mixed and uncertain to the views taken of them at the time of their occurrence, were preparing the way for a great victory and a sudden illumination of the fortunes of the South.

The disasters on the Mississippi frontier and in other directions had constrained the government to adopt the policy of concentrating its forces in the interior of Virginia. The object of all war is to reach a decisive point of the campaign, and this object was realized by a policy which it is true the government had not adopted at the instance of reason, but which had been imposed upon it by the force of disaster. There were childish complaints that certain districts and points on the frontier had been abandoned by the Confederates for the purpose of a concentration of troops in Virginia. These complaints were alike selfish and senseless, and, in some cases, nothing more than the utterance of a demagogical, shortsighted, and selfish spirit, which would have preferred the apparent security of its own particular State or section to the fortunes of the whole Confederacy. The fact was, that there was cause of intelligent congratulation even in those districts from which the Confederate troops had been withdrawn to make a decisive battle, that we had at last reached a crisis, the decision of which might reverse all our past misfortunes, and achieve results in which every State of the Confederacy would have a share.

On the Richmond lines, two of the greatest and most splendid armies that had ever been arrayed on a single field confronted each other; every accession that could be procured from the most distant quarters to their numbers, and every thing that could be drawn from the resources of the respective countries of each, had been made to contribute to the strength and splendor of the opposing hosts.

Since the commencement of the war, the North had taxed its resources for the capture of Richmond; nothing was omitted for the accomplishment of this event; the way had to be opened to the capital by tedious and elaborate operations on the frontier of Virginia: this accomplished, the city of Richmond was surrounded by an army whose numbers was all that could be desired; composed of picked forces; having every advantage that science and art could bestow in fortifications and every appliance of war; assisted by gunboat flotillas in two rivers, and endowed with every thing that could assure success.

The Northern journals were unreserved in the statement that the commands of Fremont, Banks, and McDowell, had been consolidated into one army, under Major-general Pope, with a view of bringing all the Federal forces in Virginia, to co-operate with McClellan on the Richmond lines. A portion of this army must have reached McClellan, probably at an early stage of the engagements in the vicinity of Richmond. There is little doubt but that, in the memorable contest for the safety of Richmond, we engaged an army whose superiority in numbers to us was largely increased by timely reinforcements, and with regard to the operations of which the Northern government had omitted no conditions of success.

Of this contest, unparalleled in its duration; rich in dramatic incident and display; remarkable for a series of battles, any one of which might rank with the most celebrated in history; and distinguished by an obstinacy, on the part of the sullen and insolent enemy, that was broken only by the most tremendous exertions ever made by Southern troops, we shall have to treat in a future continuation of this work, with the utmost care as to the authenticity of our narrative, and with matured views as to the merits and importance of what is now supposed to be a great and decisive event.

For the present, merely for the purpose of extending the general record of events in this chapter to the present stand-point of intelligent reflection on the future of the war, we must content the reader with a very brief and summary sketch of the battles around Richmond. Such a sketch is necessarily imperfect, written amid the confusion of current events, and is limited to the design of acquainting the reader with the general situation at this writing, without venturing, to a great degree, upon statements of particular facts.

SKETCH OF THE BATTLES AROUND RICHMOND.

Upon taking command of the Confederate army in the field, after Gen. Johnston had been wounded in the battle of Seven Pines, Gen Lee did not hesitate to adopt the spirit of that commander, which had already been displayed in attacking the enemy, and which indicated the determination on his part that the operations before Richmond should not degenerate into a siege.

The course of the Chickahominy around Richmond affords an idea of the enemy's position at the commencement of the action. This stream meanders through the tide-water district of Virginia—its course approaching that of the arc of a circle in the neighborhood of Richmond—until it reaches the lower end of Charles City county, where it abruptly turns to the south and empties into the James. A portion of the enemy's forces had crossed to the south side of the Chickahominy, and were fortified on the Williamsburg road. On the north bank of the stream the enemy was strongly posted for many miles; the heights on that side of the stream having been fortified with great energy and skill from Meadow Bridge, on a line nearly due north from the city, to a point below Bottom's Bridge, which is due east. This line of the enemy extended for about twenty miles.

Reviewing the situation of the two armies at the commencement of the action, the advantage was entirely our own. McClellan had divided his army on the two sides of the Chickahominy, and operating apparently with the design of half circumvallating Richmond, had spread out his forces to an extent that impaired the faculty of concentration, and had made a weak and dangerous extension of his lines.

On Thursday, the 26th of June, at three o'clock, Major-general Jackson—fresh from the exploits of his magnificent campaign in the Valley—took up his line of march from Ashland, and proceeded down the country between the Chickahominy and Pamunkey rivers. The enemy collected on the north bank of the Chickahominy, at the point where it is crossed by the Brooke turnpike, were driven off, and Brigadier-general Branch, crossing the stream, directed his movements for a junction with the column of Gen. A. P. Hill, which had crossed at Meadow Bridge. General Jackson having borne away from the Chickahominy, so as to gain ground towards the Pamunkey, marched to the left of Mechanicsville, while Gen. Hill, keeping well to the Chickahominy, approached that village and engaged the enemy there.

With about fourteen thousand men (Gen. Branch did not arrive till nightfall), Gen. Hill engaged the forces of the enemy until night put an end to the contest. While he did not succeed, in that limited time, in routing the enemy, his forces stubbornly maintained the possession of Mechanicsville and the ground taken by them on the other side of the Chickahominy. Driven from the immediate locality of Mechanicsville, the enemy retreated during the night down the river to Powhite swamp, and night closed the operations of Thursday.

The road having been cleared at Mechanicsville, Gen. Longstreet's *corps d'armée*, consisting of his veteran division of the Old Guard of the Army of the Potomac, and Gen. D. H. Hill's division, debouched from the woods on the south side of the Chickahominy, and crossed that river. Friday morning the general advance upon the enemy began; Gen. A. P. Hill in the centre, and bearing towards Coal Harbor, while Gen. Longstreet and Gen. D. H. Hill came down the Chickahominy to New Bridge. Gen. Jackson still maintained his position in advance, far to the left, and gradually converging to the Chickahominy again.

The position of the enemy was now a singular one. One portion of his army was on the south side of the Chickahominy, fronting Richmond, and confronted by Gen. Magruder. The other portion, on the north side, had fallen back to a new line of defences, where McClellan proposed to make a decisive battle.

As soon as Jackson's arrival at Coal Harbor was announced, Gen. Lee and Gen. Longstreet, accompanied by their respective staffs, rode by Gaines's Mill, and halted at New Coal Harbor, where they joined General A. P. Hill. Soon the welcome sound of Jackson's guns announced that he was at work.

The action was now to become general for the first time on the Richmond lines; and a collision of numbers was about to take place equal to any that had yet occurred in the history of the war.

From four o'clock until eight the battle raged with a display of the utmost daring and intrepidity on the part of the Confederate army. The enemy's lines were finally broken, and his strong positions all carried, and night covered the retreat of McClellan's broken and routed columns to the south side of the Chickahominy.

The assault on the enemy's works near Gaines's Mills is a memorable part of the engagement of Friday, and the display of fortitude, as well as quick and dashing gallantry of our troops on that occasion, takes its place by the side of the most glorious exploits of the war. Gen. A. P. Hill had made the first assault upon the lines of the enemy's intrenchments near Gaines's Mills. A fierce struggle had ensued between his division and the garrison of the line of defence. Repeated charges were made by Hill's troops, but the formidable character of the works, and murderous volleys of grape and canister from the artillery covering them, kept our troops in check. It was past four o'clock when Pickett's brigade, from Longstreet's division, came to Hill's support. Pickett's regiments fought with the most determined valor. At last Whiting's division, composed of the "Old Third" and Texan brigades, advanced at a "double quick," charged the batteries, and drove the enemy from his strong line of defence. The works carried by these noble troops would have been invincible to the bayonet had they been garrisoned by men less dastardly than the Yankees.

To keep the track of the battle, which had swept around Richmond, we must have reference to some of the principal points of locality in the enemy's lines. It will be recollected that it was on Thursday evening when the attack was commenced upon the enemy near Meadow Bridge. This locality is about six miles distant from the city, on a line almost due north. This position was the enemy's extreme right. His lines extended from here across the Chickahominy, near the Powhite Creek, two or three miles above the crossing of the York River railroad. From Meadow Bridge to this railroad, the distance along the Chickahominy on the north side is about ten miles. The different stages between the points indicated, along which the enemy were driven, are Mechanicsville, about a mile north of the Chickahominy; further on, Beaver Dam Creek, emptying into the Chickahominy; then the New Bridge road, on which Coal Harbor is located; and then Powhite Creek, where the enemy had made his last stand, and been repulsed from the field.

The York River railroad runs in an easterly direction, intersecting the Chickahominy about ten miles from the city. South of the railroad is the Williamsburg road, connecting with the Nine Mile road at Seven Pines. The former road connects with the New Bridge road, which turns off and crosses the Chickahominy. From Seven Pines, where the Nine Mile road joins the upper one, the road is known as the old Williamsburg road, and crosses the Chickahominy at Bottom's Bridge.

With the bearing of these localities in his mind, the reader will readily understand how it was that the enemy was driven from his original strongholds on the north side of the Chickahominy, and how, at the time of Friday's battle, he had been compelled to surrender the possession of the Fredericksburg and Central railroads, and had been pressed to a position where he was cut off from the principal avenues of supply and escape. The disposition of our forces was such as to cut off all communication between McClellan's army and the White House, on the Pamunkey river; he had been driven completely from his northern line of defences; and it was supposed that he would be unable to extricate himself from his position without a victory or a capitulation. In front of him being the Chickahominy, which he had crossed—in his rear, were the divisions of Generals Longstreet, Magruder, and Huger, and, in the situation as it existed Saturday night, all hopes of his escape were thought to be impossible.

On Sunday morning, it appears that our pickets, on the Nine Mile road, having engaged some small detachments of the enemy, and driven them beyond their fortifications, found them deserted. In a short while, it became known to our generals that McClellan, having massed his entire force on this side of the Chickahominy, was retreating towards James river.

The intrenchments which the enemy had deserted, were found to be formidable and elaborate. That immediately across the railroad, at the six-mile post, which had been supposed to be light earth-work, designed to sweep the railroad, turned out to be an immense embrasured fortification, extending for hundreds of yards on either side of the track. Within this work were found great quantities of fixed ammunition, which had apparently been prepared for removal, and then deserted. All the cannon, as at other intrenchments, had been carried off. A dense cloud of smoke was seen issuing from the woods two miles in advance of the battery, and half a mile to the right of the railroad. The smoke was found to proceed from a perfect mountain of the enemy's commissary stores, consisting of sugar, coffee, and bacon, prepared meats, vegetables, &c., which he had fired. The fields and woods around this spot were covered with every description of clothing and camp equipage. No indication was wanting that the enemy had left this encampment in haste and disorder.

The enemy had been imperfectly watched at a conjuncture the most critical in the contest, and through some omission of our guard—the facts of which have as yet been but imperfectly developed—McClellan had succeeded in massing his entire force, and taking up a line of retreat, by which he hoped to reach the cover of his gunboats on the James. But the most unfortunate circumstance to us was, that since the enemy had escaped from us in his fortified camp, his retreat was favored by a country, the characteristics of which are unbroken forests and wide swamps, where it was impossible to pursue him with rapidity, and extremely difficult to reconnoitre his position so as to bring him to decisive battle.

On Sunday morning, the divisions of Generals Hill and Longstreet crossed the Chickahominy, and were, during the whole of the day, moving in the hunt for the enemy. The disposition which was made of our forces brought General Longstreet on the enemy's front, immediately supported by General Hill's division consisting of six brigades. The forces commanded by General Longstreet were his old division, consisting of six brigades.

The position of the enemy was about five miles northeast of Darbytown, on the New Market road. The immediate scene of the battle was a plain of sedge pines, in the cover of which the enemy's forces were skilfully disposed—the locality being known as Frazier's farm. In advancing upon the enemy, batteries of sixteen heavy guns were opened upon the advance columns of Gen. Hill. Our troops, pressing heroically forward, had no sooner got within musket range than the enemy, form ing several lines of battle, poured upon them from his heavy masses a devouring fire of musketry. The conflict became terrible, the air being filled with missiles of death, every moment having its peculiar sound of terror, and every spot its sight of ghastly destruction and horror. It is impossible that in any of the series of engagements which had taken place within the past few days, and had tracked the lines of Richmond with fire and destruction, there could have been more desperate fighting on the part of our troops. Never was a more glorious victory plucked from more desperate and threatening circumstances. While exposed to the double fire of the enemy's batteries and his musketry, we were unable to contend with him with artillery. But although thus unmatched, our brave troops pressed on with unquailing vigor and a resistless courage, driving the enemy before them. This was accomplished without artillery, there being but one battery in Gen. Hill's command on the spot, and that belonged to Longstreet's division, and could not be got into position. Thus the fight continued with an ardor and devotion that few battle-fields have ever illustrated. Step by step the enemy were driven back, his guns taken, and the ground he abandoned strewn with his dead. By half-past eight o'clock we had taken all his cannon, and, continuing to advance, had driven him a mile and a half from his ground of battle.

Our forces were still advancing upon the retreating lines of the enemy. It was now about half-past nine o'clock, and very dark. Suddenly, as if it had burst from the heavens, a sheet of fire enveloped the front of our advance. The enemy had made another stand to receive us, and, from the black masses of his forces, it was evident that he had been heavily reinforced, and that another whole *corps d'armée* had been brought up to contest the fortunes of the night. Line after line of battle was formed. It was evident that his heaviest columns were now being thrown against our small command, and it might have been supposed that he would only be satisfied with its annihilation. The loss here on our side was terrible.

The situation being evidently hopeless for any further pursuit of the fugitive enemy, who had now brought up such overwhelming forces, our troops retired slowly.

At this moment, seeing their adversary retire, the most vociferous cheers arose along the whole Yankee line. They were taken up in the distance by the masses which for miles and miles beyond were supporting McClellan's front. It was a moment when the heart of the stoutest commander might have been appalled. The situation of our forces was now as desperate as it well could be, and required a courage and presence of mind to retrieve it, which the circumstances which surrounded them were not well calculated to inspire. They had fought for five or six hours without reinforcements. All our reserves had been brought up in the action. Wilcox's brigade, which had been almost annihilated, was re-forming in the rear.

Riding rapidly to the position of this brigade, Gen. Hill brought them, by great exertions, up to the front, to check the advance of the now confident, cheering enemy. Catching the spirit of their commander, the brave, but jaded men, moved up to the front, replying to the enemy's cheers with shouts and yells. At this demonstration, which the enemy, no doubt, supposed signified heavy reinforcements, he stopped his advance. It was now about half-past ten o'clock in the night. The enemy had been arrested; and the fight—one of the most remarkable, long-contested, and gallant ones that had yet occurred on our lines—was concluded with the achievement of a field under the most trying circumstances, which the enemy, with the most overpowering numbers brought up to reinforce him, had not succeeded in reclaiming.

Gen. Magruder's division did not come up until 11 o'clock at night, after the fight had been concluded. By orders from Gen. Lee, Magruder moved upon and occupied the battleground; Gen. Hill's command being in such a condition of prostration from their long and toilsome fight, and suffering in killed and wounded, that it was proper they should be relieved by the occupation of the battle-ground by a fresh *corps d'armée*.

Early on Tuesday morning the enemy, from the position to which he had been driven the night before, continued his retreat in a southeasterly direction towards his gunboats on James river. At eight o'clock Magruder recommenced the pursuit, advancing cautiously, but steadily, and shelling the forests and swamps in front as he progressed. This method of advance was kept up throughout the morning and until four o'clock, P. M., without coming up with the enemy. But between four and five o'clock our troops reached a large open field, a mile long and three-quarters in width, on the farm of Dr. Carter. The enemy were discovered strongly intrenched in a dense forest on the other side of this field. Their artillery, numbering fifty pieces, could be plainly seen bristling over their freshly constructed earth-works. At ten minutes before five o'clock, P. M., Gen. Magruder ordered his men to charge across the field and drive the enemy from their position. Gallantly they sprang to the encounter, rushing into the field at a full run. Instantly, from the line of the enemy's breastworks, a murderous storm of grape and canister was hurled into their ranks, with the most terrible effect. Officers and men went down by hundreds; but yet, undaunted and unwavering, our line dashed on, until two-thirds of the distance across the field was accomplished. Here the carnage from the withering fire of the enemy's combined artillery and musketry was dreadful. Our line wavered a moment, and fell back to the cover of the woods. Twice again the effort to carry the position was renewed, but each time with the same result. Night, at length, rendered a further attempt injudicious, and the fight, until ten o'clock, was kept up by the artillery of both sides. To add to the horrors, if not to the dangers, of this battle, the enemy's gunboats, from their position at Curl's Neck, two and a half miles distant, poured on the field continuous broadsides from their immense rifle-guns. Though it is questionable whether any serious loss was inflicted on us by the gunboats, the horrors of the fight were aggravated by the monster shells, which tore shrieking through the forests, and exploded with a concussion which seemed to shake the solid earth itself.

The battle of Tuesday, properly known as that of Malvern Hill, was perhaps the most sanguinary of the series of bloody conflicts which had taken place on the lines about Richmond. It was made memorable by its melancholy monument of carnage. But it had given the enemy no advantage, except in the unfruitful sacrifice of the lives of our troops, and the line of his retreat was again taken up, his forces toiling towards the river through mud, swamp, and forest.

The skill and spirit with which McClellan had managed to retreat was, indeed, remarkable, and afforded no mean proofs of his generalship. At every stage of his retreat he had confronted our forces with a strong rear-guard, and had encountered us with well-organized lines of battle, and regular dispositions of infantry, cavalry, and artillery. His heavy rifled cannon had been used against us constantly on his retreat. A portion of his forces had now effected communication with the river at points below City Point. The plan of cutting off his communication with the river, which was to have been executed by a movement of Holmes' division between him and the river, was frustrated by the severe fire of the gunboats, and since then the situation of the enemy appeared to be that of a division or dispersion of his forces, one portion resting on the river, and the other, to some extent, involved by our lines.

It had been stated to the public of Richmond, with great precision of detail, that on the evening of Saturday, the 28th of June, we had brought the enemy to bay on the south side of the Chickahominy, and that it only remained to finish him in a single battle. Such, in fact, appeared to have been the situation then. The next morning, however, it was perceived that our supposed resources of generalship had given us too much confidence; that the enemy had managed to extricate himself from the critical position, and, having massed his forces, had succeeded, under cover of the night, in opening a way to the James river.*

---

* A great deal was claimed for "generalship" in the battles around Richmond; and results achieved by the hardy valor of our troops were busily ascribed by hollow-hearted flatterers to the genius of the strategist. Without going into any thing like military criticism, it may be said that it is difficult to appreciate the ascription of a victory to generalship, in the face of the exposure and terrible slaughter of our troops in attacking, *in front*, the formidable breastworks of the enemy. The benefit of "generalship" in such circumstances is unappreciable: when troops are thus confronted, the honors of victory belong rather to the spirit of the victors than the genius of the commander.

With reference to McClellan's escape from White Oak Swamp to the river, letters of Yankee officers, published in the Northern journals, stated that when McClellan on Saturday evening sent his scouts down the road to Turkey Island Bridge, he was astonished and delighted to find that our forces had not occupied that road, and immediately started his wagon and artillery trains, which were quietly passing down that road all night to the James river, while our forces were quietly sleeping within four miles of the very road they should have occupied, and should have captured every one of the enemy's one thousand wagons, and four hundred cannon.

Upon this untoward event, the operations of our army on the Richmond side of the Chickahominy were to follow the fugitive enemy through a country where he had admirable opportunities of concealment, and through the swamps and forests of which he had retreated with the most remarkable judgment, dexterity, and spirit of fortitude.

The glory and fruits of our victory may have been seriously diminished by the grave mishap or fault by which the enemy was permitted to leave his camp on the south side of the Chickahominy, in an open country, and to plunge into the dense cover of wood and swamp, where the best portion of a whole week was consumed in hunting him, and finding out his new position only in time to attack him under the uncertainty and disadvantage of the darkness of night.

But the successes achieved in the series of engagements which had already occurred were not to be lightly esteemed, or to be depreciated, because of errors which, if they had not occurred, would have made our victory more glorious and more complete. The siege of Richmond had been raised: an army of one hundred and twenty thousand men had been pushed from their strongholds and fortifications, and put to flight; we had enjoyed the *eclat* of an almost daily succession of victories; we had gathered an immense spoil in stores, provisions, and artillery; and we had demoralized and dispersed, if we had not succeeded in annihilating, an army which had every resource that could be summoned to its assistance, every possible addition of numbers within the reach of the Yankee government, and every material condition of success to insure for it the great prize of the capital of the Confederacy, which is now, as far as human judgment can determine, irretrievably lost to them, and secure in the protection of a victorious army.

The Northern papers claimed that the movements of McClellan from the Chickahominy river were purely strategic, and that he had obtained a position, where he would establish a new

---

It is further stated in these letters, that if we had blocked up that only passage of escape, their entire army must have surrendered or been starved out in twenty-four hours. These are the Yankees' own accounts of how much they were indebted to blunders on our part for the success of McClellan's retreat—a kind of admission not popular with a vain and self-adulatory enemy.

base of operations against Richmond. Up to the first decisive stage in the series of engagements—Coal Harbor—there were certainly plain strategic designs in his backward movement. His retirement from Mechanicsville was probably voluntary, and intended to concentrate his troops lower down, where he might fight with the advantages of numbers and his own selection of position. Continuing his retreat, he fixed the decisive field at Coal Harbor. Again having been pushed from his strongholds north of the Chickahominy, the enemy made a strong attempt to retrieve his disasters by renewing a concentration of his troops at Frazier's farm.

From the time of these two principal battles, all pretensions of the enemy's retreat to strategy must cease. His retreat was now unmistakable; it was no longer a falling back to concentrate troops for action; it is, in fact, impossible to disguise that it was the retreat of an enemy who was discomfited and whipped, although not routed. He had abandoned the railroads; he had given up the strongholds which he had provided to secure him in case of a check; he had destroyed from eight to ten millions dollars' worth of stores; he had deserted his hospitals, his sick and wounded, and he had left in our hands thousands of prisoners, and innumerable stragglers.

Regarding all that had been accomplished in these battles; the displays of the valor and devotion of our troops; the expenditure of blood; and the helpless and fugitive condition to which the enemy had at last been reduced, there was cause for the keenest regrets that an enemy in this condition was permitted to secure his retreat. It is undoubtedly true, that in failing to cut off McClellan's retreat to the river, we failed to accomplish the most important condition for the completion of our victory. But although the result of the conflict had fallen below public expectation, it was sufficiently fortunate to excite popular joy, and grave enough to engage the most serious speculation as to the future.

The effect of the defeat of McClellan before Richmond was received at the North with ill-concealed mortification and anxiety. Beneath the bluster of the newspapers and the affectations of public confidence, disappointment, embarrassment, and alarm were perceptible. The people of the North had been so assured of the capture of Richmond, that it was difficult to reanimate them on the heels of McClellan's retreat. The prospects held out to them so long, of ending the war in "sixty days," "crushing out the rebellion," and eating victorious dinners in Richmond, had been bitterly disappointed and were not to be easily renewed. The government at Washington showed its appreciation of the disaster its arms had sustained by making a call for three hundred thousand additional troops; and the people of the North were urged by every variety of appeal, including large bounties of money, to respond to the stirring call of President Lincoln.

There is no doubt but that the North was seriously discouraged by the events that had taken place before Richmond. But it was a remarkable circumstance, uniformly illustrated in the war, that the North, though easily intoxicated by triumph, was not in the same proportion depressed by defeat. There is an obvious explanation for this peculiarity of temper. As long as the North was conducting the war upon the soil of the South, a defeat there involved more money expenditure and more calls for troops; it involved scarcely any thing else; it had no other horrors, it did not imperil their homes; it might easily be repaired by time. Indeed, there was some sense in the exhortations of some of the Northern orators, to the effect that defeat made their people stronger than ever, because, while it required them to put forth their energies anew, it enabled them to take advantage of experience, to multiply their means of success, and to essay new plans of campaign. No one can doubt but that the celebrated Manassas defeat really strengthened the North; and doubtless the South would have realized the same consequence of the second repulse of the enemy's movements on Richmond, if it had been attended by the same conditions on our part of inaction and repose.

In his congratulatory address to the army on their victory before Richmond, President Davis referred to the prospect of carrying the war into the North. His friends declared that the President had at last been converted from his darling military formulas of the defensive policy; that he was sensible that the only way to bring the war to a decisive point was to invade the North. But it was urged that our army was too feeble to undertake at present an aggressive policy; although the facts were that, counting in our immense forces under Gen. Bragg in the West, which for months had been idly lying in Mississippi, we had probably quite as many troops in the field as the North had; that delay could accomplish but little addition to our forces, while it would multiply those of the North, its resources of conscription and draft being intact; that if our army was small, it was due to the neglect of the executive in enforcing the Conscription Law, which should have furnished three quarters of a million of men; and that if reduced and demoralized by desertion and straggling, it was because of the weak sentimentalism of our military authorities, which hesitated to enforce the death penalty in our armies, or to maintain military discipline by a system much harsher than that of moral suasion. Judgment must be taken subject to these facts as to how far the government was responsible for lingering in a policy which, though of its own choosing at first, it at last confessed to be wrong, and from which, when discovered to be an error and a failure, it professed to be unable to extricate itself on account of a weakness of which itself was sole cause and author. Happily, however, the valor and devotion of our troops came to the rescue of the government, and opened a way in which it had so long hesitated, and found paltry excuses for its tame and unadventurous temper. But to this we shall refer hereafter.

It is curious to observe how completely the ordinary aspects of war were changed and its horrors diminished, with reference to the North, by the false policy of the South, in keeping the theatre of active hostilities within her own borders. Defeat did not dispirit the North, because it was not brought to her doors. Where it did not immediately imperil the safety of the country and homes of the Yankees, where it gave time for the recovery and reorganization of the attacking party, and where it required for the prosecution of the war nothing but more money jobs in Congress and a new raking up of the scum of the cities, the effects of defeat upon the North might well be calculated to be the exasperation of its passions, the inflammation of its cupidity, and the multiplication of its exertions to break and overcome the misapplied power of our armies.

Indeed, the realization of the war in the North was, in many respects, nothing more than that of an immense money job. The large money expenditure at Washington supplied a vast fund of corruption; it enriched the commercial centres of the North, and by artificial stimulation preserved such cities as New York from decay; it interested vast numbers of politicians, contractors, and dissolute public men in continuing the war and enlarging the scale of its operations; and, indeed, the disposition to make money out of the war accounts for much of that zeal in the North, which was mistaken for political ardor or the temper of patriotic devotion.*

---

* The following is an extract from an unpublished letter from Gen. Washington to Richard Henry Lee, and, as an exposition of the character of the Northern people from a pen sacred to posterity, is deeply interesting. There can be no doubt of the authenticity of the letter. It has been preserved in the Lee family, who, though applied to by Bancroft, Irving, and others for a copy for publication, have hitherto refused it, on the ground that it would be improper to give to the world a private letter from the Father of his Country reflecting upon any portion of it while the old Union endured. But now, that "these people" have trampled the Constitution under foot, destroyed the government of our fathers, and invaded and desolated Washington's own county in Virginia, there can be no impropriety in showing his private opinion of the Massachusetts Yankees:

[Copy.]

CAMP AT CAMBRIDGE, Aug. 29, 1775.

Dear Sir: * * *

As we have now nearly completed our lines of defence, we have nothing more, in my opinion, to fear from the enemy, provided we can keep our men to their duty, and make them watchful and vigilant; but it is among the most difficult tasks I ever undertook in my life to induce these people to believe that there is or can be danger, till the bayonet is pushed at their breasts; not that it proceeds from any uncommon prowess, but rather from an unaccountable kind of stupidity in the lower class of these people, which, believe me, prevails but too generally among the officers of the Massachusetts part of the army, who are nearly of the same kidney with the privates, and adds not a little to my difficulties, as there is no such thing as getting officers of this stamp to exert themselves in carrying orders into execution. To curry favor with the men (by whom they were chosen, and on whose smiles possibly they may think they may again rely) seems to be one of the principal objects of their attention. I submit it, therefore, to your consideration, whether there is, or is not, a propriety in that resolution of the Congress which leaves the ultimate appointment of all officers below the rank of general to the governments where the regiments originated, now the army is become Continental? To me, it appears improper in two points of view—first, it is giving that power and weight to an individual Colony which ought of right to belong to the whole. Then it damps the spirit and ardor of volunteers from all but the four New England Governments, as none but their people have the least chance of getting into office. Would it not be better, therefore, to have the warrants, which the Commander-in-Chief is authorized to give *pro tempore*,

But while politicians plundered the government at Washington and contractors grew rich in a single day, and a fictitious prosperity dazzled the eyes of the observer in the cities of the North, the public finances of the Yankee government had long ago become desperate. It is interesting at this point to make a brief summary of the financial condition of the North by a comparison of its public debt with the assets of the government.

The debt of the present United States, audited and floating, calculated from data up to June 30, 1862, was at least $1,300,000,000. The daily expenses, as admitted by the chairman of the Committee on Ways and Means, was between three and four millions of dollars; the debt, in one year from this time, could not be less than two thousand five hundred millions of dollars.

Under the census of 1860, all the property of every kind in all the States was estimated at less than $12,500,000,000. Since

---

approved or disapproved by the Continental Congress, or a committee of their body, which I should suppose in any long recess must always sit? In this case, every gentleman will stand an equal chance of being promoted, according to his merit: in the other, all offices will be confined to the inhabitants of the four New England Governments, which, in my opinion, is impolitic to a degree. I have made a pretty good slam among such kind of officers as the Massachusetts Government abounds in since I came to this camp, having broken one colonel and two captains for cowardly behavior in the action on Bunker's Hill, two captains for drawing more provisions and pay than they had men in their company, and one for being absent from his post when the enemy appeared there and burnt a house just by it. Besides these, I have at this time one colonel, one major, one captain, and two subalterns under arrest for trial. In short, I spare none, and yet fear it will not all do, as these people seem to be too inattentive to every thing but their *interest*.

* * * * * * *

There have been so many great and capital errors and abuses to rectify—so many examples to make, and so little inclination in the officers of inferior rank to contribute their aid to accomplish this work, that my life has been nothing else (since I came here) but one continual round of vexation and fatigue. In short, no pecuniary recompense could induce me to undergo what I have; especially, as I expect, by showing so little countenance to irregularities and public abuses as to render myself very obnoxious to a great part of these people. But as I have already greatly exceeded the bounds of a letter I will not trouble you with matters relative to my feelings.

Your affectionate friend and obedient servant,
(Signed) GEO. WASHINGTON

Richard Henry Lee, Esq.

the war commenced, the depreciation has been at least one-fourth, $3,175,000,000. From $9,375,000,000 deduct the property in the seceded States, at least one-third—$3,125,000,000; leaving in the present United States, $6,250,000,000.

It will thus be seen, that the present debt of the North is one-fifth of all the property of every kind it possesses; and in one year more it will be more than one-third. No people on earth has ever been plunged in so large a debt in so short a time. No government in existence has so large a debt in proportion to the amount of property held by its people.

In continuing the narrative of the campaign in Virginia, we shall have to observe the remarkable exasperation with which the North re-entered upon this campaign, and to notice many deeds of blackness which illustrated the temper in which she determined to prosecute the desperate fortunes of the war. The military authorities of the North seemed to suppose that better success would attend a savage war, in which no quarter was to be given and no age or sex spared, than had hitherto been secured to such hostilities as are alone recognized to be lawful by civilized men in modern times. It is not necessary to comment at length upon this fallacy. Brutality in war was mistaken for vigor. War is not emasculated by the observances of civilization; its vigor and success consist in the resources of generalship, the courage of troops, the moral ardors of its cause. To attempt to make up for deficiency in these great and noble elements of vigor by mere brutal severities—such as pillage, assassination, &c., is absurd; it reduces the idea of war to the standard of the brigand; it offends the moral sentiment of the world, and it excites its enemy to the last stretch of determined and desperate exertion.

The North had placed a second army of occupation of Virginia under command of Gen. Pope, who boasted that he was fresh from a campaign in the West, where he had "seen only the backs of rebels."* This brutal braggart threatened that fire,

---

* This notorious Yankee commander, Major-general John Pope, was a man nearly forty years of age, a native of Kentucky, but a citizen of Illinois. He was born of respectable parents. He was graduated at West Point in 1842, and served in the Mexican war, where he was brevetted a captain.

In 1849, he conducted the Minnesota exploring expedition, and afterwards acted as topographical engineer of New Mexico, until 1853, when he was as

famine, and slaughter should be the portions of the conquered. He declared that he would not place any guard over any private property, and invited the soldiers to pillage and murder. He issued a general order, directing the murder of peaceful inhabitants of Virginia as spies if found quietly tilling their farms in his rear, even outside of his lines; and one of his brigadier-generals, Steinwehr, seized upon innocent and peaceful inhabitants to be held as hostages, to the end that they might be murdered in cold blood, if any of his soldiers were killed by some unknown persons, whom he designated as "bushwackers."

---

signed to the command of one of the expeditions to survey the route of the Pacific railroad. He distinguished himself on the overland route to the Pacific by "sinking" artesian wells and government money to the amount of a million of dollars. One well was finally abandoned incomplete, and afterwards a perennial spring was found by other parties in the immediate vicinity. In a letter to Jefferson Davis, then Secretary of War, urging this route to the Pacific and the boring these wells, Pope made himself the *especial champion of the South*.

On the breaking out of the war, Pope was made a brigadier-general of volunteers. He held a command in Missouri for some time before he became particularly noted. When General Halleck took charge of the disorganized department, Pope was placed in command of the District of Central Missouri. He was afterwards sent to southeastern Missouri. The cruel disposition of the man, of which his rude manners and a vulgar bearded face, with coarse skin, gave indications, found an abundant field for gratification in this unhappy State. His proceedings in Missouri will challenge a comparison with the most infernal record ever bequeathed by the licensed murderer to the abhorrence of mankind. And yet it was his first step in blood, the first opportunity he had ever had to feast his eyes upon slaughter and regale his ears with the cries of human agony.

Having been promoted to the rank of major-general, Pope was next appointed to act at the head of a corps to co-operate with Halleck in the reduction of Corinth. After the evacuation of Corinth by General Beauregard, Pope was sent by Halleck to annoy the rear of the Confederate army, but Beauregard turned upon and repulsed his pursuit. The report of Pope to Halleck, that he had captured 10,000 of Beauregard's army, and 15,000 stand of arms, when he had not taken a man or a musket, stands alone in the history of lying. It left him without a rival in that respectable art.

Such was the man who took command of the enemy's forces in northern Virginia. His bluster was as excessive as his accomplishments in falsehood. He was described in a Southern newspaper as "a Yankee compound of Bobadil and Munchausen." His proclamation, that he had seen nothing of his enemies "but their backs," revived an ugly story in his private life, and gave occasion to the witty interrogatory, if the gentleman who cowhided him for offering an indignity to a lady, was standing with his back to him when he in

The people of the North were delighted with the brigandish pronunciamentos of Pope in Virginia. The government at Washington was not slow to gratify the popular passion; it hastened to change the character of the war into a campaign of indiscriminate robbery and murder. A general order was issued by the Secretary of War, directing the military commanders of the North to take private property for the convenience and use of their armies, without compensation. The public and official expressions of the spirit of the North in the war were even more violent than the clamors of the mob. The abolitionists had at last succeeded in usurping complete control of the government at Washington, and in imparting to the war the unholy zeal of their fanaticism. Nine-tenths of the legislation of the Yankee Congress had been occupied in some form or other with the question of slavery. Universal emancipation in the South, and the utter overthrow of all property, was now the declared policy of the desperate and demented leaders of the war. The Confiscation Bill, enacted at the close of the session of Congress, confiscated all the slaves belonging to those who were loyal to the South, constituting nine-tenths at least of the slaves in the Confederate States. In the Border States occupied by the North, slavery was plainly doomed under a plan of emancipation proposed by Mr. Lincoln with the flimsy and ridiculous pretence of compensation to slaveholders.* Other violent acts of legislation were passed

---

flicted the chastisement. The fact was, that Pope had won his baton of marshal by bragging to the Yankee fill. He was another instance, besides that of Butler, of the manufacture of military reputation in the North by cowardly bluster and acts of coarse cruelty to the defenceless.

* According to the census of 1860—

Kentucky had	225,490	slaves.
Maryland	87,188	"
Virginia	490,887	"
Delaware	1,798	"
Missouri	114,965	"
Tennessee	275,784	"
Making in the whole	1,196,112	
At the proposed rate of valuation, these would amount to	$358,833,600	
Add for deportation and colonization $100 each,	119,244,533	
And we have the enormous sum of	$478,078,133	

with the intention to envenom the war, to insult and torture the South, to suppress the freedom of public opinion in the North, and to keep the government in the hands of the fanatics and crusaders of Abolitionism. Disaffection was threatened with a long list of Draconian penalties. The political scaffold was to be erected in the North, while the insatiate and unbridled fury of its army was to sweep over the South. "Rebellion" was to be punished by a warfare of savages, and the devilish, skulking revenge, that pillages, burns, and assassinates, was to follow in the bloody footsteps of the invading armies.

To this enormous mass of brutality and lawlessness, the Confederate States government made but a feeble response. It proposed a plan of retaliation, the execution of which was limited to the *commissioned officers* of the army of Gen. Pope; which, by declaring impunity to private soldiers, encouraged their excesses; and which, in omitting any application to the army of Butler in New Orleans, who had laughed at female virtue in the conquered districts of the South, and murdered a citizen of the South for disrespect to the Yankee bunting,* was lamentably weak and imperfect. The fact was, that the gov-

---

It is scarcely to be supposed that a proposition could be made in good faith, or that in any event the proposition could be otherwise than worthless, to add this vast amount to the public debt of the North at a moment when the treasury was reeling under the enormous expenditures of the war.

* The act for which William B. Mumford was executed by Butler, was taking down the Yankee ensign from the Mint in that city on the 24th of April. This act of Mumford was committed *before* the city of New Orleans had surrendered. Indeed, the flag was hoisted in the city while negotiations were being conducted between the commander of the Yankee fleet and the authorities; and under these circumstances the raising of the enemy's flag was a plain violation of the rules and amenities of war, and an outrage on the authorities and people of the city. Taking the harshest rule of construction, the act of Mumford, having been committed before the city of New Orleans had surrendered, was nothing more than an *act of war*, for which he was no more responsible than as a prisoner of war.

The unhappy man was hung in the open day by order of the Federal tyrant of New Orleans. The brutal sentence of death on the gallows was carried into effect in the presence of thousands of spectators. The crowd looked on, scarcely believing their senses, unwilling to think that even such a tyrant as Butler could really have the heart for such a wanton murder of a citizen of the Confederate States, and hoping every moment for a reprieve or a pardon; but none came, and the soul of the martyr was ushered by violent hands into the presence of its God.

ernment of President Davis had been weakly swindled in its military negotiation with the North. It was persuaded to sign a cartel for the exchange of prisoners, in which it made a present to its enemy of a surplus of about six thousand prisoners; and its weak generosity was immediately rewarded, not only by the barbarous orders of Pope, which were issued just at the time the cartel was signed, but by the practical proclamation in all the invaded districts of the South of the policy of the seizure and imprisonment of unarmed inhabitants. Our government had left out of the recent cartel any provisions for private citizens kidnapped by the enemy; it had left the North in the undisturbed enjoyment, in many places, of the privilege it claimed of capturing in our country as many political prisoners as it pleased; and it had, to a considerable extent, practically abandoned the protection of its own citizens.

Before the eyes of Europe the mask of civilization had been taken from the Yankee war; it degenerated into unbridled butchery and robbery. But the nations of Europe, which boasted themselves as humane and civilized, had yet no interference to offer in a war which shocked the senses and appealed to the common offices of humanity. It is to be observed, that during the entire continuance of the war up to this time, the British government had acted with reference to it in a spirit of selfish and inhuman calculation; and there is, indeed, but little doubt that an early recognition of the Confederacy by France was thwarted by the interference of that cold and sinister government, that ever pursues its ends by indirection, and perfects its hypocrisy under the specious cloak of extreme conscientiousness. No greater delusion could have possessed the people of the South than that the *government* of England was friendly to them. That government, which prided itself on its cold and ingenious selfishness, seemed to have discovered a much larger source of profit in the continuation of the American war, than it could possibly derive from a pacification of the contest. It was willing to see its operatives starving, and to endure the distress of a "cotton famine,"* that it might have

---

* Great pains were taken alike by the Yankee and the English press to conceal the distress caused in the manufacturing districts of Europe by the withholding of Southern cotton; and the specious fallacy was being con-

the ultimate satisfaction, which it anticipated, of seeing both parties in the American war brought to the point of exhaustion, and its own greatness enlarged on the ruins of a hated commercial rival. The calculation was far-reaching; it was characteristic of a government that secretly laughed at all sentiment, made an exact science of selfishness, and scorned the weakness that would sacrifice for any present good the larger fruits of the future.

In the regular continuation of our historical narrative, in which much that has been said here by way of general reflection will be replaced by the record of particular facts, and special comments upon them, we shall have occasion before

---

stantly put forward that the cotton product in the colonial dominions of Great Britain and elsewhere was being rapidly stimulated and enlarged; that it would go far towards relieving the necessities of Europe; and that one effect of the American war would be to free England from her long and galling dependence on the Slave States of the South for the chief article of her manufacturing industry.

The proofs in reply to the latter fallacy and falsehood are striking and unanswerable. The shipments of cotton from the British colonies, Egypt, Brazil, &c., are actually falling off, and were much less this last summer than for a corresponding period of the year before. The evidence of this fact is furnished in the cotton circulars of Manchester.

India seems to have been cleared out by the large shipments of last year, and the shipments to Europe, from the first of January to the last week in May, showed a decrease of 100,000 bales; the figures being 251,000 bales against 351,000 last year. From the large proportional consumption of Surat cotton, the stock at Liverpool of this description, which, on the 1st of January last, stood at 295,000 bales against 130,000 last year, was, about the close of May, reduced to 170,000 against 133,000 last year; while in the quantity afloat the figures were still more unfavorable, viz.: 184,000 bales against 258,000.

The downward progress of the stock of American cotton is illustrated roughly by the following quarterly table prepared from the Manchester circulars:

	March, 1861.	June.
In American ports	750,000	100,000
Afloat and at Liverpool	918,000	971,000
	1,668,000	1,071,000

	March, 1862.	May.
In American ports	30,000	20,000
Afloat and at Liverpool	160,000	108,000
	193,000	128,000

tracing the active prosecution of the campaign in Virginia, to direct the attention of the reader to the progress of events in the West.

We shall find many remarkable events to record in this direction. We shall see how it was that the evacuation of Corinth was determined upon; that the retreat was conducted with great order and precision; and that, despite the boasts of the North to the contrary, we lost no more prisoners than the enemy did himself, and abandoned to him in stores not more than would amount to one day's expense of our army.

We shall find in the defence of Vicksburg a splendid lesson of magnanimity and disinterested patriotism. We shall see how for several weeks this city resisted successfully the attack of the enemy's gunboats, mortar fleets, and heavy siege-guns; how it was threatened by powerful fleets above and below, and with what unexampled spirit the Queen City of the Bluffs sustained the iron storm that was rained upon her for weeks with continued fury.

New Orleans, Baton Rouge, Natchez, and Memphis were in the hands of the Yankees, and their possession by the enemy might have furnished to Vicksburg, in its exposed and desperate situation, the usual excuses of timidity and selfishness for its surrender. But the brave city resisted these vile and unmanly excuses, and gave to the world one of the proudest and most brilliant illustrations of the earnestness and devotion of the people of the South that had yet adorned the war.

The fact that but little hopes could be entertained of the eventual success of the defence of Vicksburg against the powerful concentration of the enemy's navy, heightened the nobility of the resistance she made. The resistance of an enemy in circumstances which afford but a feeble and uncertain prospect of victory, requires a great spirit; but it is more invaluable to us than a hundred easy victories; it teaches the enemy that we are invincible, and overcomes him with despair; it exhibits to the world the inspirations and moral grandeur of our cause; and it educates our people in chivalry and warlike virtues by the force of illustrious examples of self-devotion.

We shall have, however, the satisfaction of recording an unexpected issue of victory in the siege of Vicksburg, and have occasion to point to another lesson that the history of all wars indicates, that the practical test of resistance affords the only sure determination whether a place is defensible or not. With a feeling of inexpressible pride did Vicksburg behold two immense fleets, each of which had been heretofore invincible, brought to bay, and, unable to cope with her, kept at a respectable distance, and compelled to essay the extraordinary task of digging a new channel for the Mississippi.

In following the track of detachments of our forces in the West, we shall refer to the brilliant movements across the Mississippi that drove the enemy from Arkansas, and harassed him on the Missouri border with ceaseless activity, and to the dashing expedition of the celebrated John Morgan into Kentucky. We shall see that the expedition of this cavalier was one of the most brilliant, rapid, and successful raids recorded in history. He left Tennessee with a thousand men, only a portion of whom were armed; penetrated two hundred and fifty miles into a country in full possession of the Yankees; captured a dozen towns and cities; met, fought, and captured a Yankee force superior to his own in numbers; captured three thousand stand of arms at Lebanon; and, from first to last, destroyed during his raid, military stores, railroad bridges, and other property to the value of eight or ten millions of dollars. He accomplished all this, besides putting the people of Cincinnati into a condition, described by one of their newspapers, as "bordering on frenzy," and returned to Tennessee with a loss in all his engagements of fifteen men killed, and forty wounded.

While some activity was shown in extreme portions of the West, we shall see that our military operations from Greenbrier county, Virginia, all the way down to Chattanooga, Tennessee, were conducted with but little vigor. On the boundaries of East Tennessee, southwestern Virginia, and Kentucky, we had a force in the aggregate of thirty thousand men, confronted by probably not half their number of Yankee troops; yet the southwestern counties of Virginia, and the valley of the Clinch, in Tennessee, were entered and mercilessly plundered by the enemy in the face of our troops.

Turning for a moment from the military events of this period, we shall notice the reassembling of the Confederate Congress on the 18th of August, 1862. We shall then find occasion to review the conduct of this branch of the government, and to observe how it fell below the spirit and virtue of the people; what servility to the Executive it displayed, and what a singular destitution of talents and ability was remarkable in this body. Not a single speech that has yet been made in it will live. It is true, that the regular Congress elected by the people was an improvement upon the ignorant and unsavory body known as the Provisional Congress, which was the creature of conventions, and which was disgraced in the character of some of its members; among whom were conspicuous, corrupt and senile politicians from Virginia, who had done all they could to sacrifice and disgrace their State, who had toadied in "society," as well as in politics, to notabilities of New England, and who had taken a prominent part in emasculating, and, in fact, annulling the Sequestration Law, in order to save the property of relatives who had sided with the North against the land that had borne them and honored their fathers.

But the regular Congress, although it had no taint of disloyalty or Yankee toadyism in it, was a weak, sycophantic, and trifling body. It has made no mark in the history of the government; it was utterly destitute of originality. Its measures were those which were recommended by the Executive or suggested by the newspapers. It produced no great financial measure; it made not one stroke of statesmanship; it uttered not a single fiery appeal to the popular heart, such as is customary in revolutions. The most of the little ability it had was eaten up by servility to the Executive; and the ignorance of the majority was illustrated by a trifling and undignified style of legislation, in which whole days were consumed with paltry questions, and the greatest measures—such as the Conscript Law*—embarrassed by demagogical speeches made for home effect.

---

* The execution of the Conscript Law was resisted by Governor Brown, of Georgia. The correspondence between him and the President on this subject, which was printed and hawked in pamphlet-form through the country, is a curiosity. What will posterity think of a correspondence between such dignitaries, taking place at a time when the destinies of the country trembled in the balance, composed of about equal parts of hair-splitting and demagogueism, and illustrated copiously by Mr. Brown with citations from the Virginia and Kentucky Resolutions of 1798, and exhumed opinions of members of the

It is difficult, indeed, for a legislative body to preserve its independence, and to resist the tendency of the Executive to absorb power in a time of war, and this fact was well illustrated by the Confederate Congress. One of the greatest political scholars of America, Mr. Madison, noticed this danger in the political constitution of the country. He said:— "War is in fact the true nurse of Executive aggrandizement. In war a physical force is to be created, and it is the Executive will which is to direct it. In war the public treasures are to be unlocked, and it is the Executive hand which is to dispense them. In war the honors and emoluments of office are to be multiplied, and it is the Executive patronage under which they are to be enjoyed. It is in war, finally, that laurels are to be gathered, and it is the Executive brow they are to encircle."

There was but little opposition in Congress to President Davis; but there was some which took a direction to his Cabinet, and this opposition was represented by Mr. Foote of Tennessee—a man of acknowledged ability and many virtues of character, who had re-entered upon the political stage after a public life, which, however it lacked in the cheap merit of partisan consistency, had been adorned by displays of wonderful intellect and great political genius. Mr. Foote was not a man to be deterred from speaking the truth; his quickness to resentment and his chivalry, which, though somewhat Quixotic, was founded in the most noble and delicate sense of honor, made those who would have bullied or silenced a weaker person, stand in awe of him. A man of such temper was not likely to stint words in assailing an opponent; and his sharp declamations in Congress, his searching comments, and his great powers of sarcasm, used upon such men as Mallory, Benjamin, and Huger, were the only relief of the dulness of the Congress, and the only historical features of its debates.

---

old Federal Convention of 1787? The display was characteristic of Southern *politicians;* in the most vital periods of the country's destiny they had an eye to making political capital for themselves, and in the fierce tumults of a revolution, refreshed the country with exhumations from the politicians of 1787, and the usual amount of clap-trap about our "forefathers," and the old political system that had rotted over our heads.

Returning to the history of the campaign in Virginia, we shall have occasion to enumerate another brilliant victory of our arms, achieved on that fortunate theatre of the war. We refer to the battle of Cedar Mountain. We shall find other topics to record in the events which, at the time of this writing, are developing themselves, and reaching to the most important consequences, both in Virginia and Tennessee. We shall see how the great army which McClellan had brought for the reduction of Richmond, and in sight of the church steeples of that city, was compelled to retire towards the Potomac, with its proud columns shattered, humiliated, and demoralized; how Pope, who had entered Virginia with a splendid army and the most insolent boasts, was ignominiously whipped on more than one occasion, and with what agony of cowardice he sought safety for his retreat; how considerable portions of Virginia and Tennessee were surrendered to the jurisdiction of the Confederacy; how the enemy in various quarters was pushed back to his old lines; and how intelligent men in the South saw for the first time certain and unmistakable indications of demoralization in the armies of the North, brought on by the remarkable train of victories in Virginia, extending from early June to September.

In these events we shall find bright and flattering prospects renewed to the South. Much of these we shall find already realized in the events in the midst of which we write this imperfect sketch. We shall trace the painful steps by which our worn troops advanced to meet another invading army in Virginia, reinforced not only by the defeated army of McClellan, but by the fresh corps of Generals Burnside and Hunter. We shall tell what hardships were endured by our troops, and what exploits of valor were performed by them on this celebrated expedition; how they were compelled to toil their way with inadequate transportation; how they crossed streams swollen to unusual height, and bore all the fatigues and distresses of forced marches; how their spirit and endurance were tested by repeated combats with the enemy; how at last they succeeded in turning his position; and how, having formed a junction of their columns in the face of greatly superior forces on the historic and blood-stained plains of Manassas, they achieved there the ever-memorable victory of the thirteenth of August,

1862, the crowning triumph of their toil and valor. A nation's gratitude is evoked to repay all that is due to the valor of our troops and the providence of Almighty God.*

We do not trust ourselves to predict the consequences of current events; and the brilliant story of Manassas, grouped with contemporary victories in the West, must be left to the decisions of the future—trusting as we do that we may have occasion to record in another volume the consequences as well as the details of these events, and to find in the future the fulfilment of the promises of to-day.

* * * * A few general reflections on the material and moral phenomena of the war will appropriately conclude our work for the present.

It is a censurable practice to flatter the people. It is equally

---

* The vulgar and unintelligent mind worships success. The extraordinary and happy train of victories in Virginia seems to have had no other significance or interest to a number of grovelling minds in the South, than as a contribution to the personal fame of General Lee, who by no fault of his own (for no one had more modesty, more Christian dignity of behavior, and a purer conversation), was followed by toadies, flatterers, and newspaper sneaks in epaulets, who made him ridiculous by their servile obeisances and excess of praise. The author does not worship success. He trusts, however, that he has intelligence enough to perceive merit, without being prompted by the vulgar cry; he is sure that he has honesty and independence enough to acknowledge it where he believes it to exist. The estimation of General Lee, made in some preceding pages, was with reference to his unfortunate campaign in Western Virginia; it was founded on the events of that campaign, in which there is no doubt Gen. Lee blundered and showed an absurd misconception of mountain warfare; and so far as these events furnished evidence for the historian, the author believes that he was right, unprejudiced, and just in ascribing the failure of that campaign to the misdirection of the commanding general. If, however, it can be shown, as now seems to be likely from incomplete events, that on wider, clearer, and more imposing fields Gen. Lee has shown qualities which the campaign in the mountains of Virginia had not illustrated, the friends of this commander may be assured that the author will be honest and cordial in acknowledging the fact, and that in a future continuation of these annals, justice will be done to the recent extraordinary events in Virginia, fraught with so many critical issues of the war, and associated with so many reputations dear to the people of the South. In writing the facts of this war, the author takes no counsel of popular cries, and notions fashionable in the newspapers; he is neither the panegyrist nor the antagonist of any clique; he is more pleased to praise than to censure, but his aim is truth, and he is resolved to pursue it, no matter what popular prejudice or affection he is compelled to crush in its attainment.

censurable to withhold from them the plain recognition of their accomplishments. The present war will win the respect of the world for the masses of the people of the Confederate States. With inferior numbers, with resources hampered on all sides, we are yet winning the issue of the great struggle in which we are involved. No one claims that this is owing to the wisdom of our government. No one ascribes it to the ability of our military chieftains; for blunders in our military management have been as common as in our civil administration. But there is a huge, unlettered power that wages the war on our side, overcoming everywhere the power of the enemy and the incumbrances of our own machinery. It is the determined, settled will of the people to be free, and to fight themselves free, that has constituted our strength and our safety.

The existing war has, doubtless, disappointed the world in its meagre phenomena of personal greatness, and, to some extent, has disappointed its own people in the bigotry of its policy and the official restraint put upon its spirit. It may be said with singular truth, that it has produced or exhibited but few great men—that it has not raised up to public admiration in the South a statesman, an orator, a poet, or a financier, all which are generally considered as much the natural products of war as military genius itself. For this disappointment, however, we may find an explanation in some degree satisfactory. It is, that the very circumstance of the almost universal uprising of the people of the South, and the equal measures of devotion shown by all classes and intellects, have given but little room for overshadowing names, and presented but little opportunity for marked personal distinctions of greatness.

After all, it is the spirit of the people that is most sure to achieve the victorious results of revolutions; and on this firm reliance, and not on the personal fortunes of master-spirits, or on adventitious aid, or on the calculations of any merely external events, do we rest, under Providence, the hopes of the Southern Confederacy. The verdict of the history of the world is, that no powerful nation has ever been lost except by its own cowardice. All nations that have fought for an independent existence, have had to sustain terrible defeats, live through deep, though temporary distress; and endure hours of profound discouragement. But no nation was ever subdued that really determined to fight while there was an inch of ground or a solitary soldier left to defend it.

As far as the war has been fought, its results, in a military point of view, are deeply humiliating to the North. The war was commenced by the North with the most intense expressions of contempt for its adversary; the idea of the contest being extended beyond a few months, was derided and spit upon; in that short time it was believed that the flag of the Union would float over the cities and towns of the South, and the bodies of "traitors" dangle from the battlements of Washington.

This was not affectation. It was calculated by many people, in a spirit of candor, that a contest so unequal in the material elements of strength as that between the North and the South would be speedily determined. The North had more than twenty millions of people to break the power of eight millions; it had a militia force about three times as strong as that of the South; it had the regular army; it had an immense advantage over the South in a navy, the value of which may be appreciated when it is known that its achievements in the war have been greater than those of the land forces, and that its strength, with proposed additions to its active war vessels, is estimated to-day in the North as equivalent to an army of half a million men.

Nor did the superiority of the North end here. While the South was cut off from the world by the restrictions of the blockade, without commerce, with but scanty manufactures and few supplies on hand, the North had all the ports of the world open to its ships; it had furnaces, foundries, and workshops; its manufacturing resources compared with those of the South were as five hundred to one; the great marts of Europe were open to it for supplies of arms and stores; there was nothing of material resource, nothing of the apparatus of conquest that was not within its reach.

These immense elements of superiority on the part of the North have not remained idle in her hands. They have been exercised with tremendous energy. Within the last fifteen months the government at Washington has put forth all its power to subjugate the South; it has contracted a debt six or seven times more than that of the South; it has called out more than half a million soldiers: it has put Europe under contribution to furnish it not only arms, but soldiers to use them; it has left no resource untried and omitted no condition of success.

The result of all this immense and boasted superiority on the part of the North, coupled with the most immense exertions is, that the South remains unconquered. The result is humiliating enough to the warlike reputation of the North. It has not been separated from its feeble adversary by seas or mountains, but only by a geographical line; nature has not interfered to protect the weak from the strong; three "Grand Armies" have advanced in the Confederate territory; and yet to-day, the Yankees hold in Virginia and Tennessee only the ground they stand upon, and the South, in spirit, is more invincible than ever.

Nor has the war, so far as it has been waged, been without great moral benefits to the South. We may indicate at least three important and inestimable blessings which it has conferred upon our people.

It has made impossible the theory of the "reconstruction" of the old Union, which was no doubt indulged in the early formation of the Confederate government. It has carried a revolution, which, if no war had taken place, would probably have ended in "reconstruction," on the basis of concessions from the Northern States, which would in no way have impaired the advantages of the old Union to them, to a point where the demand for our independence admits of no alternative or compromise. It has revealed to us the true characteristics of the people of the North; it has repulsed us from a people whose vices and black hearts we formerly knew but imperfectly; and it has produced that antagonism and alienation which were necessary to exclude the possibility a reunion with them.

Again: the war has shown the system of negro slavery in the South to the world in some new and striking aspects, and has removed much of that cloud of prejudice, defamation, falsehood, romance, and perverse sentimentalism through which our peculiar institution was formerly known to Europe. It has given a better vindication of our system of slavery than all the books that could be written in a generation. Hereafter there can be no dispute between facts plainly exhibited and the pictures of romance; and intelligent men of all countries will obtain their ideas of slavery from certain leading and indisputable facts in the history of this war, rather than from partisan sources of information and the literary inventions of the North. The war has shown that slavery has been an element of strength with us; that it has assisted us in the war; that no servile insurrections have taken place in the South, in spite of the allurements of our enemy; that the slave has tilled the soil while his master has fought; that in large districts unprotected by our troops, and with a white population consisting almost exclusively of women and children, the slave has continued at his work, quiet, cheerful, and faithful;* and that, as

---

* The following is taken from the letter of an English nobleman, who visited the South while the war was in its active stages, and the result of whose observations there, at the time war was racking the country and many of our own whites were houseless and starving, was, that the condition of the negro slaves in the South was "better than that of any laboring population in the world."

* * * * * * *

"Among the dangers which we had heard at New York threatened the South, a revolt of the slave population was said to be the most imminent. Let us take, then, a peep at the cotton-field, and see what likelihood there is of such a contingency. On the bank of the Alabama river, which winds its yellow course through woods of oak, ash, maple, and pine, thickened with tangled copse of varied evergreens, lie some of the most fertile plantations of the State. One of these we had the advantage of visiting. Its owner received us with all that hospitality and unaffected *bonhomie* which invariably distinguish a Southern gentleman. Having mounted a couple of hacks, we started off through a large pine wood, and soon arrived at the "clearing" of about two hundred acres in extent, on most of which was growing an average cotton crop. This was a fair sample of the rest of the plantation, which consisted altogether of 7000 acres. Riding into the middle of the field, we found ourselves surrounded by about forty slaves—men, women, and children—engaged in "picking." They were all well dressed, and seemed happy and cheerful. Wishing to know what time of day it was, I asked Mr. —— the hour, whereupon one of the darkies by my side took out a watch and informed me.

"'Do your laborers wear watches, sir?' I inquired.

"'A great many of them have. Why, sir, my negroes all have their cotton-plats and gardens, and most of them have little orchards.'

"We found from their own testimony that they are fed well, chiefly upon pork, corn, potatoes, and rice, carefully attended to when sick, and on Sundays dress better than their masters. We next visited the 'station,' a street of cottages in a pine wood, where Mr. ——'s slaves reside. These we found clean and comfortable. Two of the men were sick, and had been visited that

a conservative element in our social system, the institution of slavery has withstood the shocks of war and been a faithful ally of our arms, although instigated to revolution by every art of the enemy, and prompted to the work of assassination and pillage by the most brutal examples of the Yankee soldiery.

Finally, the war has given to the States composing the Confederacy a new bond of union. This was necessary. Commerce and intercourse had been far more intimate between the Slave States on the Lower Mississippi and those on the Upper Mississippi and its tributaries, than between any portions of the Confederate States. The war has broken this natural affinity; it has supplanted sympathy by alienation, interest by hate, between the people of Indiana, Illinois, and Ohio, and those of Tennessee, Louisiana, and Mississippi; and by the principle of repulsion as well as union, by the tie of a common bloodshed, and the memory of a common labor and glory, the stability of our Confederacy has been strengthened and secured.

Such are the inestimable blessings which, although draped in sorrow and suffering, the war has conferred upon the people of the South.

The resolution of the South to achieve its independence has been greatly encouraged as the war has advanced. It is alike prompted by the spirit of her people, and strengthened by motives which address the judgment. These motives are explained in the plain consequences of subjugation. The spirit of the North in the existing war has already been developed far enough to indicate the certain condition of the South, if her enemy should succeed in establishing his dominion over her people. That condition may be described in confiscation, brutality, military domination, insult, universal poverty, the beggary of millions, the triumph of the vilest individuals in these communities, the abasement of the honest and industrious, the outlawry of the slaves, the destruction of agriculture and commerce, the emigration of all thriving citizens, farewell to the hopes of future wealth, and the scorn of the world. The

---

morning by a doctor; in the mean time they were looked after by the nurses of the establishment, of whom there were three to take care of the children and invalids."

resistance of such a destiny, properly conceived, will restore the worst fortunes of war, pluck victory from despair, and deserve the blessing of Providence, which "can save by many or by few," and which has never yet failed to reward a just and earnest endeavor for independence.

RICHMOND, *September*, 1862.

APPENDIX.

The attention of the author was directed to some particulars of his work, which required some correction or explanation, at the time when it was passing through the press. It was then too late to modify the passages referred to, unless in the form of a postscript or appendix. The author congratulates himself that he has found *real* occasion for so few corrections or explanations.

Page 36.—The date of Anderson's evacuation of Fort Moultrie should be the 26th of December instead of the 20th; the error occurred through a mistake of the digit 6 for 0 in the rough notes of the author.

Page 177.—In noticing the expedition of our cavalry to Guyandotte, we should have associated with this bold enterprise the name of Col. Clarkson, who originated it and was intrusted with its execution by Gen. Floyd. The services of Col. Clarkson on this and other enterprises, and his intrepidity on some of the most critical occasions in the western Virginia campaign, deserve mention, and we regret that we can give it no further within the limits of this postscript, than to supply the omission of credit justly due him in connection with the famous expedition of our cavalry to the Ohio.

Page 247.—The circumstances in which Governor Harris left Nashville were imperfectly known at the time; and there is no doubt but that some injustice was done to one of the most ardent and courageous patriots of the South, in attributing his conduct on this occasion to panic or embarrassment. The circumstances in which he acted have been ascertained from unquestionable sources of testimony, and may be briefly narrated here: On the morning of Sunday, the 16th of February, at ten minutes after 4 o'clock, a messenger arrived at Gen. Johnston's head-quarters at Edgefield, opposite Nashville, with a dispatch announcing the fall of Donelson. Orders were at once issued to push the army forward across the river as soon as possible. The city papers or extras of that morning published dispatches announcing a "glorious victory." The city was wild with joy. About the time the people were assembling at the churches, it was announced by later extras that "Donelson had fallen." The revulsion was great. Governor Harris, however, had been informed of the fact early in the morning, and had proceeded to Gen. Johnston's head-quarters to advise with him as to the best course to adopt under the altered circumstances. The action of the State authorities would, of course, be greatly influenced by the course Gen. Johnston intended to adopt with the army. The general told the governor that Nashville was utterly indefensible; that the army would pass right through the city; that any attempt to defend it with the means at his command would result in disaster to the army and the destruction of the city; that the first and highest duty of the governor was to the public trusts in his hands, and he thought, to discharge them properly, he should at once remove the archives and public records to some safer place, and call the Legislature together elsewhere than at Nashville. Governor Harris did all this quietly, energetically, and patriotically. Just as soon as he had deposited these papers, he returned to Nashville. The confusion at Nashville did not reach its height until a humane attempt was made to distribute among the poor a portion of the public stores which could not be removed. The lowest passions seemed to have been aroused in a large mass of men and women, and the city appeared as if it was in the hands of a mob. The military authority, however (Gen. Floyd having been put in command by Gen. Johnston), asserted its supremacy, and comparative order was restored. During these excitements it became publicly known, for the first time, that Governor Harris was out of the city, but few really knowing that he had quietly gone away in the discharge of a public duty. His absence was wholly misunderstood, and, of course, misrepresented. There is no doubt but that, in the course of these misrepresentations in the newspapers, injustice was done to a man who illustrated his devotion to the South by distinguished courage on the battle-field, and who, from the moment that he first rebuffed the Washington government in his famous defiance to Lincoln's call for troops, down to recent periods in the history of the revolution, had given the most constant and honorable proofs of his attachment to the liberties and fortunes of the South.

CONSTITUTION

OF THE

CONFEDERATE STATES OF AMERICA.

We, the people of the Confederate States, each State acting in its sovereign and independent character, in order to form a permanent federal government, establish justice, insure domestic tranquillity, and secure the blessings of liberty to ourselves and our posterity—invoking the favor and guidance of Almighty God—do ordain and establish this Constitution for the Confederate States of America.

ARTICLE I.

Section 1.

All legislative powers herein delegated shall be vested in a Congress of the Confederate States, which shall consist of a Senate and House of Representatives.

Section 2.

1. The House of Representatives shall be composed of members chosen every second year by the people of the several States; and the electors in each State shall be citizens of the Confederate States, and have the qualifications requisite for electors of the most numerous branch of the State Legislature; but no person of foreign birth, not a citizen of the Confederate States, shall be allowed to vote for any officer, civil or political, State or Federal.

2. No person shall be a Representative who shall not have attained the age of twenty-five years, and be a citizen of the Confederate States, and who shall not, when elected, be an inhabitant of that State in which he shall be chosen.

3. Representatives and direct taxes shall be apportioned among the several States which may be included within this Confederacy, according to their respective numbers, which shall be determined by adding to the whole number of free persons, including those bound to service for a term of years, and excluding Indians not taxed, three-fifths of all slaves. The actual enumeration shall be made within three years after the first meeting of the Congress of the Confederate States, and within every subsequent term of ten years, in such manner as they shall by law direct. The number of Representatives shall not exceed one for every fifty thousand; but each State shall have at least one Representative; and until such enumeration shall be made, the State of South Carolina shall be entitled to choose six; the State of Georgia ten; the State of Alabama nine; the State of Florida two; the State of Mississippi seven; the State of Louisiana six; and the State of Texas six.

4. When vacancies happen in the representation from any State, the Executive authority thereof shall issue writs of election to fill such vacancies.

5. The House of Representatives shall choose their Speaker and other officers; and shall have the sole power of impeachment; except that any judicial or other federal officer resident and acting solely within the limits of any State, may be impeached by a vote of two-thirds of both branches of the Legislature thereof.

SECTION 3.

1. The Senate of the Confederate States shall be composed of two Senators from each State, chosen for six years by the Legislature thereof, at the regular session next immediately preceding the commencement of the term of service; and each Senator shall have one vote.

2. Immediately after they shall be assembled, in consequence of the first election, they shall be divided as equally as may be into three classes. The seats of the Senators of the first class shall be vacated at the expiration of the second year; of the second class, at the expiration of the fourth year, and of the third class, at the expiration of the sixth year; so that one-third may be chosen every second year; and if vacancies happen, by resignation or otherwise, during the recess of the Legislature of any State, the Executive thereof may make temporory appointments until the next meeting of the Legislature, which shall then fill such vacancies.

3. No person shall be a Senator who shall not have attained the age of thirty years, and be a citizen of the Confederate States; and

who shall not, when elected, be an inhabitant of the State for which he shall be chosen.

4. The Vice-president of the Confederate States shall be President of the Senate, but shall have no vote unless they be equally divided.

5. The Senate shall choose their other officers, and also a President pro tempore, in the absence of the Vice-president, or when he shall exercise the office of President of the Confederate States.

6. The Senate shall have the sole power to try all impeachments. When sitting for that purpose they shall be on oath or affirmation. When the President of the Confederate States is tried, the Chief-justice shall preside; and no person shall be convicted without the concurrence of two-thirds of the members present.

7. Judgment in cases of impeachment shall not extend further than removal from office, and disqualification to hold and enjoy any office of honor, trust, or profit under the Confederate States; but the party convicted shall, nevertheless, be liable and subject to indictment, trial, judgment, and punishment, according to law.

Section 4.

1. The times, places, and manner of holding elections for Senators and Representatives, shall be prescribed in each State by the Legislature thereof, subject to the provisions of this Constitution; but the Congress may, at any time, by law, make or alter such regulations, except as to the times and places of choosing Senators.

2. The Congress shall assemble at least once in every year; and such meeting shall be on the first Monday in December, unless they shall, by law, appoint a different day.

Section 5.

1. Each House shall be the judge of the elections, returns, and qualifications of its own members, and a majority of each shall constitute a quorum to do business; but a smaller number may adjourn from day to day, and may be authorized to compel the attendance of absent members, in such manner and under such penalties as each House may provide.

2. Each House may determine the rules of its proceedings, punish its members for disorderly behavior, and, with the concurrence of two-thirds of the whole number, expel a member.

3. Each House shall keep a journal of its proceedings, and, from time to time, publish the same, excepting such parts as may in its judgment require secrecy, and the ayes and nays of the members of

either House, on any question, shall, at the desire of one-fifth of those present, be entered on the journal.

4. Neither House, during the session of Congress, shall, without the consent of the other, adjourn for more than three days, nor to any other place than that in which the two Houses shall be sitting.

Section 6.

1. The Senators and Representatives shall receive a compensation for their services, to be ascertained by law, and paid out of the Treasury of the Confederate States. They shall, in all cases except treason and breach of the peace, be privileged from arrest during their attendance at the session of their respective Houses, and in going to and returning from the same; and for any speech or debate in either House, they shall not be questioned in any other place.

2. No Senator or Representative shall, during the time for which he was elected, be appointed to any civil office under the authority of the Confederate States, which shall have been created, or the emoluments whereof shall have been increased during such time; and no person holding any office under the Confederate States shall be a member of either House during his continuance in office. But Congress may, by law, grant to the principal officer in each of the Executive Departments a seat upon the floor of either House, with the privilege of discussing any measure appertaining to his department.

Section 7.

1. All bills for raising revenue shall originate in the House of Representatives; but the Senate may propose or concur with amendments as on other bills.

2. Every bill which shall have passed both Houses, shall, before it becomes a law, be presented to the President of the Confederate States; if he approve, he shall sign it; but if not, he shall return it with his objections to that House in which it shall have originated, who shall enter the objections at large on their journal, and proceed to reconsider it. If, after such reconsideration, two-thirds of that House shall agree to pass the bill, it shall be sent, together with the objections, to the other House, by which it shall likewise be reconsidered, and if approved by two-thirds of that House, it shall become a law. But in all such cases, the votes of both Houses shall be determined by yeas and nays, and the names of the persons voting for and against the bill shall be entered on the journal of each House respectively. If any bill shall not be returned by the President within ten days (Sundays excepted) after it shall have been pre-

sented to him, the same shall be a law in like manner as if he had signed it, unless the Congress, by their adjournment, prevent its return; in which case it shall not be a law. The President may approve any appropriation and disapprove any other appropriation in the same bill. In such case he shall, in signing the bill, designate the appropriations disapproved; and shall return a copy of such appropriations, with his objections, to the House in which the bill shall have originated; and the same proceedings shall then be had as in case of other bills disapproved by the President.

3. Every order, resolution, or vote, to which the concurrence of both Houses may be necessary (except on questions of adjournment) shall be presented to the President of the Confederate States; and before the same shall take effect shall be approved by him; or being disapproved by him, may be repassed by two-thirds of both Houses, according to the rules and limitations prescribed in case of a bill.

SECTION 8.

The Congress shall have power—

1. To lay and collect taxes, duties, imposts, and excises, for revenue necessary to pay the debts, provide for the common defence, and carry on the Government of the Confederate States; but no bounties shall be granted from the Treasury; nor shall any duties or taxes on importations from foreign nations be laid to promote or foster any branch of industry; and all duties, imposts, and excises shall be uniform throughout the Confederate States.

2. To borrow money on the credit of the Confederate States.

3. To regulate commerce with foreign nations, and among the several States, and with the Indian tribes; but neither this, nor any other clause contained in the Constitution, shall be construed to delegate the power to Congress to appropriate money for any internal improvement intended to facilitate commerce; except for the purpose of furnishing lights, beacons, and buoys, and other aids to navigation upon the coasts, and the improvement of harbors, and the removing of obstructions in river navigation, in all which cases such duties shall be laid on the navigation facilitated thereby as may be necessary to pay the costs and expenses thereof.

4. To establish uniform laws of naturalization, and uniform laws on the subject of bankruptcies throughout the Confederate States, but no law of Congress shall discharge any debt contracted before the passage of the same.

5. To coin money, regulate the value thereof, and of foreign coin, and fix the standard of weights and measures.

6. To provide for the punishment of counterfeiting the securities and current coin of the Confederate States.

7. To establish post-offices and post-routes; but the expenses of the Post-office Department, after the first day of March, in the year of our Lord eighteen hundred and sixty-three, shall be paid out of its own revenues.

8. To promote the progress of science and useful arts, by securing, for limited times, to authors and inventors, the exclusive right to their respective writings and discoveries.

9. To constitute tribunals inferior to the Supreme Court.

10. To define and punish piracies and felonies committed on the high seas, and offences against the law of nations.

11. To declare war, grant letters of marque and reprisal, and make rules concerning captures on land and water.

12. To raise and support armies; but no appropriation of money to that use shall be for a longer term than two years.

13. To provide and maintain a navy.

14. To make rules for the government and regulation of the land and naval forces.

15. To provide for calling forth the militia to execute the laws of the Confederate States, suppress insurrections, and repel invasions.

16. To provide for organizing, arming, and disciplining the militia, and for governing such part of them as may be employed in the service of the Confederate States, reserving to the States respectively the appointment of the officers, and the authority of training the militia according to the discipline prescribed by Congress.

17. To exercise exclusive legislation, in all cases whatsoever, over such district (not exceeding ten miles square) as may, by cession of one or more States, and the acceptance of Congress, become the seat of the Government of the Confederate States; and to exercise like authority over all places purchased by the consent of the legislature of the State in which the same shall be, for the erection of forts, magazines, arsenals, dock-yards, and other needful buildings; and

18. To make all laws which shall be necessary and proper for carrying into execution the foregoing powers, and all other powers vested, by this Constitution, in the Government of the Confederate States, or in any department or officer thereof.

Section. 9

1. The importation of negroes of the African race, from any foreign country, other than the slaveholding States or Territories of

the United States of America, is hereby forbidden, and Congress is required to pass such laws as shall effectually prevent the same.

2. Congress shall also have power to prohibit the introduction of slaves from any State not a member of, or Territory not belonging to, this Confederacy.

3. The privilege of the writ of habeas corpus shall not be suspended, unless when, in cases of rebellion or invasion, the public safety may require it.

4. No bill of attainder, or ex post facto law, or law denying or impairing the right of property in negro slaves, shall be passed.

5. No capitation or other direct tax shall be laid, unless in proportion to the census or enumeration hereinbefore directed to be taken.

6. No tax or duty shall be laid on articles exported from any State, except by a vote of two-thirds of both Houses.

7. No preference shall be given, by any regulation of commerce or revenue, to the ports of one State over those of another.

8. No money shall be drawn from the Treasury but in consequence of appropriations made by law; and a regular statement and account of the receipts and expenditures of all public money shall be published from time to time.

9. Congress shall appropriate no money from the treasury except by a vote of two-thirds of both Houses, taken by yeas and nays, unless it be asked and estimated for by some one of the heads of departments, and submitted to Congress by the President; or for the purpose of paying its own expenses and contingencies; or for the payment of claims against the Confederate States, the justice of which shall have been judicially declared by a tribunal for the investigation of claims against the government, which it is hereby made the duty of Congress to establish.

10. All bills appropriating money shall specify in federal currency the exact amount of each appropriation, and the purposes for which it is made; and Congress shall grant no extra compensation to any public contractor, officer, agent, or servant, after such contract shall have been made or such service rendered.

11. No title of nobility shall be granted by the Confederate States; and no person holding any office of profit or trust under them shall, without the consent of the Congress, accept of any present, emolument, office, or title of any kind whatever, from any king, prince, or foreign state.

12. Congress shall make no law respecting an establishment of religion, or prohibiting the free exercise thereof; or abridging the

freedom of speech or of the press; or the right of the people peaceably to assemble and petition the Government for a redress of grievances.

13. A well-regulated militia being necessary to the security of a free State, the right of the people to keep and bear arms shall not be infringed.

14. No soldier shall, in time of peace, be quartered in any house without the consent of the owner; nor in time of war, but in a manner prescribed by law.

15. The right of the people to be secure in their persons, houses, papers, and effects against unreasonable searches and seizures, shall not be violated; and no warrant shall issue but upon probable cause, supported by oath or affirmation, and particularly describing the place to be searched, and the person or things to be seized.

16. No person shall be held to answer for a capital or otherwise infamous crime, unless on a presentment or indictment of a grand jury, except in cases arising in the land or naval forces, or in the militia, when in actual service, in time of war, or public danger; nor shall any person be subject for the same offence to be twice put in jeopardy of life or limb; nor be compelled in any criminal case to be a witness against himself; nor be deprived of life, liberty, or property, without due process of law; nor shall private property be taken for public use without just compensation.

17. In all criminal prosecutions the accused shall enjoy the right to a speedy and public trial, by an impartial jury of the State and district wherein the crime shall have been committed, which district shall have been previously ascertained by law, and to be informed of the nature and cause of the accusation; to be confronted with the witnesses against him; to have compulsory process for obtaining witnesses in his favor; and to have the assistance of counsel for his defence.

18. In suits at common law, where the value in controversy shall exceed twenty dollars, the right of trial by jury shall be preserved; and no fact so tried by a jury shall be otherwise re-examined in any court of the Confederacy than according to the rules of the common law.

19. Excessive bail shall not be required, nor excessive fines imposed, nor cruel or unusual punishments inflicted.

20. Every law, or resolution having the force of law, shall relate to but one subject, and that shall be expressed in the title.

Section 10.

1. No State shall enter into any treaty, alliance, or confederation; grant letters of marque and reprisal; coin money; make any thing but gold and silver coin a tender in payment of debts; pass any bill of attainder, or ex post facto law, or law impairing the obligation of contracts; or grant any title of nobility.

2. No State shall, without the consent of Congress, lay any imposts or duties on imports or exports, except what may be absolutely necessary for executing its inspection laws; and the net produce of all duties and imposts laid by any State on imports or exports, shall be for the use of the Treasury of the Confederate States; and all such laws shall be subject to the revision and control of Congress.

3. No State shall, without the consent of Congress, lay any duty of tonnage, except on sea-going vessels, for the improvement of its rivers and harbors navigated by the said vessels; but such duties shall not conflict with any treaties of the Confederate States with foreign nations; and any surplus of revenue thus derived, shall, after making such improvement, be paid into the common treasury; nor shall any State keep troops or ships of war in time of peace, enter into any agreement or compact with another State, or with a foreign power, or engage in war, unless actually invaded, or in such imminent danger as will not admit of delay. But when any river divides or flows through two or more States, they may enter into compacts with each other to improve the navigation thereof.

ARTICLE II.

Section 1.

1. The Executive power shall be vested in a President of the Confederate States of America. He and the Vice-president shall hold their offices for the term of six years; but the President shall not be re-eligible. The President and Vice-president shall be elected as follows:

2. Each State shall appoint, in such manner as the Legislature thereof may direct, a number of electors equal to the whole number of Senators and Representatives to which the State may be entitled in Congress; but no Senator or Representative, or person holding an office of trust or profit under the Confederate States, shall be appointed an elector.

3. The electors shall meet in their respective States and vote by ballot for President and Vice-president, one of whom, at least, shall

not be an inhabitant of the same State with themselves; they shall name in their ballots the person voted for as President, and in distinct ballots the person voted for as Vice-president, and they shall make distinct lists of all persons voted for as President, and of all persons voted for as Vice-president, and of the number of votes for each; which list they shall sign, and certify, and transmit, sealed, to the Government of the Confederate States, directed to the President of the Senate. The President of the Senate shall, in the presence of the Senate and House of Representatives, open all the certificates, and the votes shall then be counted; the person having the greatest number of votes for President shall be the President, if such number be a majority of the whole number of electors appointed; and if no person have such majority, then, from the persons having the highest numbers, not exceeding three, on the list of those voted for as President, the House of Representatives shall choose immediately, by ballot, the President. But, in choosing the President, the votes shall be taken by States, the representation from each State having one vote; a quorum for this purpose shall consist of a member or members from two-thirds of the States, and a majority of all the States shall be necessary to a choice. And if the House of Representatives shall not choose a President, whenever the right of choice shall devolve upon them, before the fourth day of March next following, then the Vice-president shall act as President, as in case of the death or other constitutional disability of the President.

4. The person having the greatest number of votes as Vice-president shall be the Vice-president, if such number be a majority of the whole number of electors appointed; and if no person have a majority, then, from the two highest numbers on the list, the Senate shall choose the Vice-president; a quorum for the purpose shall consist of two-thirds of the whole number of Senators, and a majority of the whole number shall be necessary for a choice.

5. But no person constitutionally ineligible to the office of President shall be eligible to that of Vice-president of the Confederate States.

6. The Congress may determine the time of choosing the electors, and the day on which they shall give their votes; which day shall be the same throughout the Confederate States.

7. No person except a natural born citizen of the Confederate States, or a citizen thereof at the time of the adoption of this Constitution, or a citizen thereof born in the United States prior to the 20th December, 1860, shall be eligible to the office of President;

neither shall any person be eligible to that office who shall not have attained the age of thirty-five years, and been fourteen years a resident within the limits of the Confederate States, as they may exist at the time of his election.

8. In case of the removal of the President from office, or of his death, resignation, or inability to discharge the powers and duties of the said office, the same shall devolve on the Vice-president; and the Congress may, by law, provide for the case of the removal, death, resignation, or inability, both of the President and Vice-president, declaring what officer shall then act as President, and such officer shall act accordingly until the disability be removed, or a President shall be elected.

9. The President shall, at stated times, receive for his services a compensation, which shall neither be increased nor diminished during the period for which he shall have been elected; and he shall not receive within that period any other emolument from the Confederate States, or any of them.

10. Before he enters on the execution of the duties of his office, he shall take the following oath or affirmation:

"I do solemnly swear (or affirm) that I will faithfully execute the office of President of the Confederate States, and will, to the best of my ability, preserve, protect, and defend the Constitution thereof."

Section 2.

1. The President shall be commander-in-chief of the army and navy of the Confederate States, and of the militia of the several States, when called into the actual service of the Confederate States; he may require the opinion, in writing, of the principal officer in each of the Executive Departments, upon any subject relating to the duties of their respecting offices; and he shall have power to grant reprieves and pardons for offences against the Confederate States, except in cases of impeachment.

2. He shall have power, by and with the advice and consent of the Senate, to make treaties, provided two-thirds of the Senators present concur; and he shall nominate, and, by and with the advice and consent of the Senate, shall appoint ambassadors, other public ministers, and consuls, judges of the Supreme Court, and all other officers of the Confederate States, whose appointments are not herein otherwise provided for, and which shall be established by law; but the Congress may by law vest the appointment of such inferior officers, as they think proper, in the President alone, in the courts of law, or in the heads of departments.

3. The principal officer in each of the Executive Departments, and all persons connected with the diplomatic service, may be removed from office at the pleasure of the President. All other civil officers of the Executive Department may be removed at any time by the President, or other appointing power, when their services are unnecessary, or for dishonesty, incapacity, inefficiency, misconduct, or neglect of duty; and when so removed, the removal shall be reported to the Senate, together with the reasons therefor.

4. The President shall have power to fill all vacancies that may happen during the recess of the Senate, by granting commissions which shall expire at the end of their next session; but no person rejected by the Senate shall be reappointed to the same office during their ensuing recess.

Section 3.

The President shall, from time to time, give to the Congress information of the state of the Confederacy, and recommend to their consideration such measures as he shall judge necessary and expedient; he may, on extraordinary occasions, convene both Houses, or either of them; and, in case of disagreement between them, with respect to the time of adjournment, he may adjourn them to such time as he shall think proper; he shall receive ambassadors and other public ministers; he shall take care that the laws be faithfully executed, and shall commission all the officers of the Confederate States.

Section 4.

The President, Vice-president, and all civil officers of the Confederate States, shall be removed from office on impeachment for, and conviction of, treason, bribery, or other high crimes and misdemeanors.

ARTICLE III.

Section 1.

The judicial power of the Confederate States shall be vested in one Superior Court, and in such inferior courts as the Congress may from time to time ordain and establish. The judges, both of the Supreme and inferior courts, shall hold their offices during good behavior, and shall, at stated times, receive for their services a compensation, which shall not be diminished during their continuance in office.

Section 2.

1. The judicial power shall extend to all cases arising under this Constitution, the laws of the Confederate States, and treaties made or which shall be made under their authority; to all cases affecting ambassadors, other public ministers, and consuls; to all cases of admirality and maritime jurisdiction; to controversies to which the Confederate States shall be a party; to controversies between two or more States; between a State and citizens of another State, where the State is plaintiff; between citizens claiming lands under grants of different States, and between a State or the citizens thereof, and foreign States, citizens, or subjects; but no State shall be sued by a citizen or subject of any foreign State.

2. In all cases affecting ambassadors, other public ministers, and consuls, and those in which a State shall be a party, the Supreme Court shall have original jurisdiction. In all the other cases before mentioned, the Supreme Court shall have appellate jurisdiction, both as to law and fact, with such exceptions and under such regulations as the Congress shall make.

3. The trial of all crimes, except in cases of impeachment, shall be by jury, and such trial shall be held in the State where the said crimes shall have been committed; but when not committed within any State, the trial shall be at such place or places as the Congress may by law have directed.

Section 3.

1. Treason against the Confederate States shall consist only in levying war against them, or in adhering to their enemies, giving them aid and comfort. No person shall be convicted of treason unless on the testimony of two witnesses to the same overt act, or on confession in open court.

2. The Congress shall have power to declare the punishment of treason, but no attainder of treason shall work corruption of blood, or forfeiture, except during the life of the person attainted.

ARTICLE IV.
Section 1.

Full faith and credit shall be given in each State to the public acts, records, and judicial proceedings of every other State. And the Congress may, by general laws, prescribe the manner in which such acts, records, and proceedings shall be proved, and the effect thereof.

Section 2.

1. The citizens of each State shall be entitled to all the privileges and immunities of citizens of the several States, and shall have the right of transit and sojourn in any State of this confederacy, with their slaves and other property; and the right of property in said slaves shall not be thereby impaired.

2. A person charged in any State with treason, felony, or other crime against the laws of such State, who shall flee from justice, and be found in another State, shall, on demand of the Executive authority of the State from which he fled, be delivered up to be removed to the State having jurisdiction of the crime.

3. No slave or other person held to service or labor in any State or Territory of the Confederate States, under the laws thereof, escaping or unlawfully carried into another, shall, in consequence of any law or regulation therein, be discharged from such service or labor; but shall be delivered up on claim of the party to whom such slave belongs, or to whom such service or labor may be due.

Section 3.

1. Other States may be admitted into this Confederacy by a vote of two-thirds of the whole House of Representatives, and two-thirds of the Senate, the Senate voting by States; but no new State shall be formed or erected within the jurisdiction of any other State; nor any State be formed by the junction of two or more States, or parts of States, without the consent of the Legislatures of the States concerned as well as of the Congress.

2. The Congress shall have power to dispose of and make all needful rules and regulations concerning the property of the Confederate States, including the lands thereof.

3. The Confederate States may acquire new territory; and Congress shall have power to legislate and provide governments for the inhabitants of all territory belonging to the Confederate States, lying without the limits of the several States, and may permit them, at such times, and in such manner as it may by law provide, to form States to be admitted into the Confederacy. In all such territory, the institution of negro slavery, as it now exists in the Confederate States, shall be recognized and protected by Congress and by the territorial government; and the inhabitants of the several Confederate States and Territories shall have the right to take to such territory any slaves lawfully held by them in any of the States or Territories of the Confederate States.

4. The Confederate States shall guarantee to every State that now is or hereafter may become a member of this Confederacy, a republican form of government, and shall protect each of them against invasion; and on application of the Legislature (or of the Executive when the Legislature is not in session,) against domestic violence.

ARTICLE V.

Section 1.

Upon the demand of any three States, legally assembled in their several Conventions, the Congress shall summon a Convention of all the States, to take into consideration such amendments to the Constitution as the said States shall concur in suggesting at the time when the said demand is made; and should any of the proposed amendments to the Constitution be agreed on by the said Convention—voting by States—and the same be ratified by the Legislatures of two-thirds of the several States, or by Conventions in two-thirds thereof—as the one or the other mode of ratification may be proposed by the general Convention—they shall thenceforward form a part of this Constitution. But no State shall, without its consent, be deprived of its equal representation in the Senate.

ARTICLE VI.

Section 1.

1. The Government established by this Constitution is the successor of the Provisional Government of the Confederate States of America, and all the laws passed by the latter shall continue in force until the same shall be repealed or modified; and all the officers appointed by the same shall remain in office until their successors are appointed and qualified, or the offices abolished.

2. All debts contracted and engagements entered into before the adoption of this Constitution, shall be as valid against the Confederate States under this Constitution as under the Provisional Government.

3. This Constitution, and the laws of the Confederate States made in pursuance thereof, and all treaties made, or which shall be made under the authority of the Confederate States, shall be the supreme law of the land, and the judges in every State shall be bound thereby, any thing in the Constitution or laws of any State to the contrary notwithstanding.

4. The Senators and Representatives before mentioned, and the members of the several State Legislatures, and all executive and judicial officers, both of the Confederate States and of the several States, shall be bound, by oath or affirmation, to support this Constitution ; but no religious test shall ever be required as a qualification to any office of public trust under the Confederate States.

5. The enumeration, in the Constitution, of certain rights, shall not be construed to deny or disparage others retained by the people of the several States.

6. The powers not delegated to the Confederate States by the Constitution, nor prohibited by it to the States, are reserved to the States respectively, or to the people thereof.

ARTICLE VII.

Section 1.

1. The ratification of the Conventions of five States shall be sufficient for the establishment of this Constitution between the States so ratifying the same.

When five States shall have ratified this Constitution in the manner before specified, the Congress, under the provisional Constitution, shall prescribe the time for holding the election of President and Vice-president, and for the meeting of the electoral college, and for counting the votes and inaugurating the President. They shall also prescribe the time for holding the first election of members of Congress under this Constitution, and the time for assembling the same. Until the assembling of such Congress, the Congress under the provisional Constitution shall continue to exercise the legislative powers granted them; not extending beyond the time limited by the Constitution of the Provisional Government.

Adopted unanimously, March 11, 1861,

At Montgomery, Alabama.

CHRONOLOGY OF THE WAR.

1860.

Apr. 23.—Democratic Convention met at Charleston, South Carolina, and after an ineffectual effort to unite on a candidate, adjourned to meet in Baltimore.

May 9.—Constitutional Union Convention at Baltimore nominated John Bell, of Tennessee, for President, and Edward Everett, of Massachusetts, for Vice President.

" 19.—The Republican Convention at Chicago nominated, for President, Abraham Lincoln, of Illinois, and for Vice President, Hannibal Hamlin, of Maine.

June 11.—The Southern delegates, withdrawing from the Baltimore Convention, nominate John C. Breckenridge, of Kentucky, for President, and Joseph Lane, of Oregon, for Vice President.

" 18.—The adjourned Convention at Baltimore nominated, for President, Stephen A. Douglas, of Illinois, and for Vice President, Benjamin Fitzpatrick, of Alabama. The latter declining the nomination, Herschel V. Johnson, of Georgia, was selected as the candidate.

Nov. 6.—The Abraham Lincoln ticket obtains the highest number of votes, although the majority of the popular vote is against it.

" 10.—The Legislature of South Carolina calls a convention.

Dec. 20.—South Carolina in Convention passes an ordinance of Secession.

Major Anderson retires to Fort Sumter.

" 27-30.—Custom House, Post Office, and U. S. Arsenal at Charleston seized by State authorities.

1861.

Jan. 2.—Fort Macon seized by the State authorities of North Carolina.

Jan. 3.—Fort Pulaski seized by the Georgia State authorities.
" 4.—Fort Morgan and Mobile Arsenal seized by Alabama.
" 9.—Mississippi seceded from the Union.
" 11.—Alabama and Florida seceded from the United States.
" 12.—Fort Barrancas and Navy Yard, Pensacola, seized by Florida.
" 19.—The Legislature of Virginia advises a National Peace Convention.
" 20.—Georgia seceded from the Union.
" 26.—Louisiana seceded.
Feb. 1.—Texas seceded.
" 4.—Convention of six seceding States met at Montgomery; Howell Cobb, Pres., J. F. Hooper, Sec.
" 5.—National Peace Conference met at Washington, John Tyler, President, J. C. Wright, Secretary.
" 8.—Constitution adopted for the Confederate States by the Convention at Montgomery.
" 9.—Confederate Congress elect Jefferson Davis, of Mississippi, President, and Alexander H. Stephens, of Georgia, Vice President.
" 13.—Election of Abraham Lincoln and Hannibal Hamlin formally declared in the Senate by John C. Breckenridge.
" 18.—Jefferson Davis inaugurated.
Mar. 4.—Texas secedes from the Union.
" 6.—Fort Brown, Texas, taken by State troops.
April 1.—Confederate Post Office begins operations.
" 4.—Abraham Lincoln inaugurated President at Washington.
" 11.—Formal demand for the evacuation of Fort Sumter made to Major Anderson by Gen. Beauregard.
" 12.—Fort Sumter bombarded by the Confederate forces.
" 13.—Capitulation of Fort Sumter.
" 15.—President Lincoln issues a proclamation calling for 75,000 men to suppress insurrection, and calling an extra session of Congress.
" 17.—Virginia, by an ordinance passed in secret session, secedes from the Union.
" 19.—Arsenal at Harper's Ferry abandoned and fired by the U. S. troops on the approach of Virginia troops.
" 19.—The Sixth Massachusetts regiment attacked in the streets of Baltimore while on its way to Washington.
" 20.—President Lincoln declares the blockade of the Ports of

South Carolina, Georgia, Alabama, Florida, Mississippi, Louisiana, and Texas.

Apr. 20.—Railroad bridges in Maryland destroyed by the authorities.

" 21.—Destruction of the Navy Yard at Gosport, Va., and of vessels there, by U. S. naval officers.

" 21.—General Robert E. Lee appointed commander of the military and naval forces of Virginia.

" 24.—Cairo, Illinois, occupied by U. S. troops.

" 25.—450 United States troops captured at Salurea by Van Dorn.

" 25.—Fort Smith, Arkansas, seized by the State troops.

" 27.—All officers in the U. S. Service required to take the oath of allegiance.

" 27.—Blockade extended to Virginia and North Carolina.

May 4.—President Lincoln calls for Volunteers for army and navy.

" 4.—George B. McClellan appointed to command Department of Ohio.

" 6.—Tennessee seceded from the Union.
Arkansas seceded from the Union.
Virginia admitted into the Southern Confederacy.

" 7.—Military league formed between Tennessee and the Confederate States.

" 10.—General Lee invested with control of the Confederate forces.
Camp Jackson, St. Louis, seized by Capt. Nathaniel Lyon, U. S. A.

" 11.—Riot at St. Louis.
Blockade of Charleston begun by the Niagara.

" 15.—The Ocean Eagle, of Rockland, Maine, captured by the Calhoun, Privateer.

" 18.—Arkansas admitted into the Southern Confederacy.

" 19.—Attack on the Confederate battery at Sewell's Point, Va., by the Freeborn and Star.

" 20.—Seat of Government of the Confederate States transferred from Montgomery to Richmond.

" 21.—The North Carolina convention passes an ordinance of secession.
General Harney and General Price, commanding the Missouri State troops, enter into a treaty.

" 23.—General Joseph E. Johnston takes command at Harper's Ferry.

May 24.—Alexandria, Va., occupied by 8000 Federal troops; Col Elsworth, of the N.Y. Fire Zouaves, killed by Jackson, of the Marshall House.
" 27.—Brig. Gen. Irvin McDowell takes command of the U. S. forces in Virginia.
General Butler declares slaves contraband.
" 30.—Grafton, Va., occupied by Col. Kelley.
" 31.—Action off Acquia Creek.
June 1.—Second attack on Acquia Creek batteries by the Potomac Flotilla.
" 3.—Stephen A. Douglas died at Chicago.
Colonel Porterfield, C. S. A., surprised at Philippi by Col. Kelley, 1st. Va. Volunteers, and Col. Lander.
" 5.—Harriet Lane attacks Confederate batteries at Big Point.
" 10.—General Pierce with 4000 men defeated at Bethel, Va., by Col. J. Bankhead Magruder.
" 11.—President Davis, through the Maryland Legislature, declares himself willing that hostilities shall cease.
Colonel Lew. Wallace, of Indiana, surprises Confederate troops at Romney.
" 16.—General Patterson, of Pennsylvania, crosses into Virginia.
" 17.—Western Virginia declared independent by a Convention at Wheeling.
Skirmish at Vienna, Va.
Skirmish at Edward's Ferry.
Second collision between troops and people in St. Louis.
Battle of Booneville, Mo., between Gen. Lyon and the Confederate troops under Col. Marmaduke.
" 19.—Colonel O'Kane defeats Home Guard at Cole Camp, Mo., killing 206.
" 20.—Frank H. Pierpont elected Governor of Western Virginia.
" 24.—Attack on Matthias Point battery by U. S. steamer Pawnee.
" 29.—The Sumter privateer escapes from New Orleans.
Steamer St. Nicholas seized by Col. Thomas.
July 1.—Fight at Buckhannon, Va.
" 2.—General Patterson crosses the Potomac a second time, but is severely hauled by Jackson.
Western Virginia Legislature organize.
" 4.—Extra session of U. S. Congress.

July 5.—Battle of Carthage, Mo., between Col. Sigel and Governor Jackson.
" 10.—Col. Pegram, C. S. A., defeated at Laurel Hill, Va.
" 11.—Col. Pegram again defeated at Rich Mountain.
" 12.—Col. Pegram surrenders.
Skirmish at Barboursville, Va.
" 13.—General Garnett, C. S. A., defeated and killed at Carrock's Ford.
" 15.—General Patterson at Bunker Hill.
" 17.—Captain Patton repulses U. S. forces at Scarrey Creek, Va., taking many officers.
" 18.—Battle of Blackburn's Ford, Va., between General Tyler, U. S. Army, and General Longstreet, C. S. A.
" 20.—Confederate Congress at Richmond.
" 21.—Battle of Bull Run or Manassas; General McDowell totally defeated by Generals Beauregard and Johnston; Confederate loss, 369 killed, 1483 wounded; U. S. loss, 479 killed, 1011 wounded, 1500 prisoners.
" 22.—General G. B. McClellan put in command of U. S. forces in Virginia.
" 24.—Fort Fillmore, New Mexico, surrendered by Major Lynde, U. S. A., to the Confederate troops.
" 25.—R. M. T. Hunter made Secretary of State of the Confederate States.
" 31.—H. R. Gamble elected Provisional Governor of Missouri.
Aug. 2.—Battle of Dug Spring, Mo.
War Bill passes U. S. Congress.
" 3.—Skirmish at Mesilla, N. M.
" 7.—Hampton, Va., destroyed.
" 10.—Battle of Oak Hill, or Wilson's Creek; General Lyon defeated and killed.
" 16.—Gen. Jefferson Thompson checks Federals at Fredericktown, Mo.
President Lincoln proclaims non-intercourse with Southern States.
" 19.—Fight at Charlestown, Mo.
" 20.—Western Virginia State Convention erects State of Kanawha.
" 26.—General Floyd defeats Col. Tyler at Cross Lanes, Va.
" 29.—Forts Hatteras and Clark, N. C., commanded by Com. Barron, C. S. N., N. C., taken by Com. Stringham and Gen. Butler.

Sept. 2.—Action near Fort Scott, between Gen. Rains and Colonel Montgomery.
" 4.—Naval engagement off Hickman.
  General Polk, C. S. A., occupies Columbus, Ky.
  Martin Green drives Col. Williams out of Shelbina.
" 7.—Gen. Price, C. S. A., defeats J. H. Lane at Drywood.
" 10.—Battle at Carnifax Ferry, between Gen. Floyd and Gen. Rosencrans.
" 11.—U. S. troops defeated at Tony's Creek, by Col. J. L. Davis.
" 12.—Battle of Cheat Mountain, Va.
" 14.—Cumberland Gap seized by Gen. Zollicoffer, C. S. A.
" 17.—Gen. D. K. Atchison defeats Lane and Montgomery at Blue Mills, Mo.
" 19.—Federal troops at Barbourville, Ky., dispersed by Zollicoffer.
" 20.—Col. Mulligan surrenders Lexington, Mo., after three days' fight. Confederate loss, 25 killed, 72 wounded. U. S. loss, 3500 prisoners.
" 25.—Col. J. W. Davis defeated at Chapmansville, Va., by Col. Pratt.
" 27.—General Price retreats from Lexington.
  Missouri Legislature at Neosho passed an ordinance of secession, and elect delegates to the Congress of the Southern Confederacy.
Oct. 1.—Propeller Fanny taken by Confederates at Chicamacomico, N. C.
" 3.—Battle of Green Briar, Va.; Federal forces repulsed by Gen. H. R. Jackson, of Georgia.
" 4.—Col. Bartow attacks 20th Indiana near Hatteras.
" 8.—Wilson's Camp, Santa Rosa Island, attacked by Confederates from Pensacola. U. S. loss, 13 killed, 21 wounded.
" 12.—Blockading fleet in S. W. pass mouth of the Mississippi attacked by Confederate rams.
" 16.—Battle of Ironton, Mo.
" 21.—Col. Baker defeated and killed in the battle of Leesburg, or Balls Bluff, by General Evans. Confederate loss, 153 killed; U. S. loss, immense.
  Jefferson Thompson defeated, and Col. Lowe killed at Fredericktown, Mo.
" 20. Colonel Taylor attacked at Springfield, Mo., by Colonel Zagonyi, with Fremont's Body Guard.

Oct. 31. Close of the trial of the Savannah privateers for piracy at New York. Jury do not agree.

Agreement entered into between Missouri and the Confederate States.

Nov. 1.—General Scott resigns.
" 2.—Missouri Legislature at Neosho ratifies agreement.

General Fremont, superseded in command of the Department of Missouri, turns over forces to General Hunter.
" 7.—Forts Walker and Beauregard, Port Royal, S. C., bombarded and taken by U. S. fleet under Commodore Dupont.
" 7.—General Grant attacks Col. Tappan's Confederate camp at Belmont, Mo., but is driven to his boats with loss by Gen. Pillow and Gen. Cheatham, from Columbus. Confederate loss, 632.
" 8.—Col. Williams driven from Piketon, Ky., by Gen. Nelson, U. S. A., retires to Pound Gap.
" 9.—Guyandotte taken by Col. Jenkins' cavalry.
" 18.—Secession convention meets at Russellville, Ky.
" 20.—Secession ordinance passed by Kentucky convention, and George W. Johnson chosen Governor.

Dec. 8.—Mason and Slidell taken from the English mail steamer Trent.
" 13.—Col. Edward Johnson, C. S. A., attacked in Camp Alleghany by General Milroy. Confederate loss, 20 killed, 96 wounded. U. S. loss, 21 killed, 107 wounded.
" 17.—Battle of Woodsonville, Ky. Federal forces defeated by Brig.-gen. Hindman. U. S. loss 50 killed.
" 18.—Confederate camp near Martinsburg surprised by General Pope.
" 22.—General Stuart with 2500 men defeated at Dranesville by Gen. McCall. Confederate loss 200 killed and wounded.

1862.

Jan. 1.—Battle on Port Royal Island.
Fort Pickens opens fire.
" 2.—Messrs. Mason and Slidell released.
" 4.—Gen. Jackson attacks and defeats the 5th Connecticut near Bath, Va.
" 10.—Battle of Middle Creek, Ky., between Humphrey Marshall and Col. Garfield.

Jan. 19.—Battle of Mill Springs, or Somerset, Ky. Major-general George B. Crittenden, C. S. A., defeated by Generals Thomas and Schoepf. Gen. Zollicoffer killed. Confederate loss 300 killed and wounded, 50 prisoners, 100 wagons, 1200 horses, 500 to 1000 muskets, and boxes of arms.

" 26.—Burnside's expedition enters Hatteras Inlet.

Feb. 4.—Fort Henry, Tenn., attacked by Flag Officer Foote with seven gunboats, and surrendered by Gen. Lloyd Tilghman.

" 8.—Battle of Roanoke Island. Confederate forces under Col. Shaw defeated and taken by Gen. Burnside. Confederate loss, 23 killed, 58 wounded, 62 missing, 2527 prisoners. U. S. loss, 50 killed, 222 wounded.

" 11.—Elizabeth City taken by Commodore Rowan.

" 12.—General Price retreats from Springfield.
Fort Donelson invested by Gen. U. S. Grant, U. S. A.

" 13-14.—Attack on the Fort.

" 15.—Outer work carried by Grant.

" 16.—Surrender of Fort Donelson, by Gen. S. B. Buckner; Floyd and Pillow escaping. Confederate loss, 231 killed, 1007 wounded, 13,829 prisoners; U. S. loss, 446 killed, 1735 wounded, 150 prisoners.

" 18.—First regular Congress of the Confederate States convened.

" 19.—The vote for President counted by Confederate Congress. Jefferson Davis and Alexander H. Stevens elected for six years by unanimous vote of 109.

" 21.—Col. Canby, U. S. A., defeated by Gen. Sibley at Valverde, near Fort Craig, N. M. Confederate loss, 38 killed, 120 wounded; Federal loss, 300 killed, 400 or 500 wounded, 2000 missing.

" 22.—Inauguration of Jefferson Davis.

" 23.—Gen. Nelson, U. S. A., enters Nashville.

Mar. 3.—Columbus evacuated by the Confederate forces.

" 4.—Andrew Johnson appointed by Pres. Lincoln provisional Governor of Tennessee.

" 6-8.—Battle of Elk Horn or Pea Ridge, Ark., between the U. S. forces under Gen. Samuel R. Curtis, and the Confederate troops, under Gen. Earl Van Dorn. Confederate loss, 600 killed and wounded; U. S. loss, 700 killed. Gen. Ben McCulloch, C. S. A., mortally wounded.

Mar. 7.—St. Mary's, Fernandina, and Fort Clinch, Florida, taken by U. S. naval forces.
" 8.—The Confederate iron clad ram Virginia, formed out of the U. S. steamer Merrimac, sinks the Cumberland, sloop of war, in Hampton Roads, and compels the U. S. frigate Congress to surrender. She then engaged the U. S. steam frigate Minnesota, and gunboats Dragon and Whitehall, disabling the Dragon, and setting the Whitehall on fire. Loss, on the Cumberland, 100 killed, 50 wounded; Congress, 94 killed, 29 wounded; Minnesota, 6 killed, 25 wounded; Dragon, 4 wounded; Whitehall, 1 killed. Total, 201 killed, 108 wounded.
" 9.—Battle between the Virginia and Ericsson's battery Monitor, in which the Virginia was damaged, and was towed off. Confederate loss in the two days, 7 killed, 17 wounded.
" 10.—Manassas Junction evacuated by the Confederate forces. General Sibley, C. S. A., takes Santa Fe, N. M.
" 11.—Confederate troops evacuate Winchester.
St. Augustine, Florida, taken by Com. Dupont.
" 12.—Brig.-gen. Campbell, C. S. A., defeated and captured at Lebanon, Mo.
" 13.—Confederate troops evacuate New Madrid, Mo.
" 14.—Battle of Newberne, N. C. The confederate forces under L. O. B. Branch defeated and driven out by Gen. Burnside. Confederate loss, 64 killed, 101 wounded, 413 prisoners or missing; U. S., 91 killed, 466 wounded.
" 16.—Attack begun on Island No. 10 in the Mississippi river.
Severe skirmish at Salem, Ark.
Gen. Garfield attacks the Confederate forces at Pound Gap, in the Cumberland Mountains.
" 22.—Skirmish at Winchester, Va.
" 23.—Battle of Kernstown, or Winchester Heights. Gen. Jackson, C. S. A., defeated by General Shields. U. S. loss, 103 killed, 440 wounded, 24 missing; Confederate loss, 270 killed.
" 26.—Quantrill attacks Warrensburg, Mo.
" 28.—Colonel Slough defeats Confederate forces at Apache Cañon, N. M.
" 31.—Col. N. B. Buford disperses Confederate force at Union City, Tenn.
Apr. 5.—U. S. Troops, under McClellan, attack Yorktown, Va.

Apr. 6.—Gen. Beauregard defeats U. S. Grant at Shiloh, or Pittsburgh Landing, Tenn., capturing 2500 prisoners. Gen A. S. Johnston, C. S. A., killed.
" 7.—Gen. Beauregard defeated by Grant and Buell. Gen. W H. L. Wallace, U. S. A., killed. Confederate loss on the two days' fight, 1728 killed, 8012 wounded, 959 missing; U. S. loss, 1614 killed, 7721 wounded, 3963 missing.
" 8. Surrender of Island No. 10 by the Confederate forces to Com. Foote and Gen. Pope.
" 10–12.—Fort Pulaski, Ga., bombarded and taken by General Hunter, with loss of 1 man.
" 11.—Huntsville, Ala., taken by Gen. O. M. Mitchell, U. S. A.
" 14.—Fort Wright attacked by Com. Foote.
" 16.—Engagement on Warwick river, near Yorktown, Va.
" 18.—Com. Farragut attacks Forts Jackson and St. Philip.
" 19.—Battle of Camden, N. C.
" 22.—Action at Lee's Mill's, Va.
" 24.—Flag Officer Farragut passes the forts, and appears before New Orleans.
" 24.—Fort Macon, N. C., bombarded and taken by Gen. Burnside.
" 26. Part of the Confederate works at Yorktown carried by 1st Massachusetts.
   Battle at Neosho, Mo.
" 28. New Orleans and Forts St. Philip and Jackson surrender.
" 29.—Gen. O. M. Mitchell defeats Gen. E. Kirby Smith at Bridgeport, Ala.
May 3.—Confederates evacuate Yorktown.
" 5.—Battle of Williamsburg, Va.
" 7.—Battle of West Point, Va., between Gen. Franklin, U. S. A., and Gen. Lee, C. S. A.
" 9.—Battle of Farmington, Miss.
" 10.—General Wool, U. S. A., takes Norfolk.
   Naval action above Fort Wright, on the Mississippi.
" 12.—Natchez surrendered.
" 17.—U. S. gunboats repulsed at Fort Darling, Drury's Bluff, on James River, Va.
" 22–23.—Engagement on the Chickahominy.
" 22.—Col. Kenly defeated at Front Royal, by Gen. Ewell.
" 23.—Col. Crook repulses Gen. Heath at Lewisburg, Va.
" 25.—Gen. Banks retreats from Winchester to Williamsport, Md.

May 29.—Battle of Hanover Court House. Confederate forces defeated by Gen. Fitz John Porter.
" 31.—Battle of Chickahominy, or Fair Oaks. Gen. Casey and Couch driven from their camps by Gen. Johnston, C. S. A., and U. S. forces saved by arrival of Gen. Sumner.
June 1.—Confederate forces driven back. U. S. loss in two days, 890 killed, 3627 wounded, and 1217 missing.
" 4.—General Benham repulsed in an attack on Confederate works on James Island.
" 5.—Fort Wright evacuated by Confederate forces.
" 6.—Confederate naval force entirely defeated and destroyed before Memphis, by Flag Officer Davis and Col. Ellet.
" 7.—William B. Mumford hung in New Orleans.
" 8.—General Fremont defeats Jackson at Cross Keys. Gen. Ashby, C. S. A., killed.
" 13.—Fort St. Charles, White River, taken by U. S. land and naval forces. The U. S. steamer Mound City blew up.
" 14.—Stuart's raid on the Pamunky.
" 25.—Battle of Oak Grove, Va. Gen. Hooker commanding U. S. forces.
Armies of Fremont, Banks, and McDowell united under Gen. Pope.
" 26.—Battle of Mechanicsville, Va.
" 27.—Battle of Gaines Mill; Fitz John Porter defeated and driven across the Chickahominy.
" 29.—Battles of Peach Orchard and Savage's Station.
" 31.—Battle of White Oak Swamp, or Glendale.
July 1.—Battle of Malvern Hills.